Grades 4–6

Everyday Mathematics®

Teacher's Reference Manual

**The University of Chicago
School Mathematics Project**

A Division of The McGraw·Hill Companies

Columbus, Ohio
Chicago, Illinois

UCSMP Elementary Materials Component

Max Bell, Director

Authors

Max Bell
Jean Bell
John Bretzlauf*
Amy Dillard*
Robert Hartfield
Andy Isaacs*
James McBride, Director
Kathleen Pitvorec*
Peter Saecker

Technical Art

Diana Barrie*

Second Edition only

Photo Credits

Phil Martin/Photography
Jack Demuth/Photography
Cover: Bill Burlingham/Photography
Photo Collage: Herman Adler Design
p. 189 (Center Bottom) Decorative Palace Wall: Adam Woodfitt/CORBIS
p. 189 (Left Bottom) Engaged column and tiled wall: Adam Woodfitt/CORBIS
p. 189 (Right Bottom) Colorful geometric inlay: John Heseltine/CORBIS
p. 218 Fractal, A Birth of Lightning: Gregory Sams/Science Photo Library
p. 219 Fractal, a detail from the Mandelbrot Set: Dr. Fred Espenak/Science Photo Library
p. 235 United States, Department of the Interior, Geological Survey

Contributors

James Flanders, Deborah Arron Leslie

www.sra4kids.com

SRA/McGraw-Hill

A Division of The McGraw-Hill Companies

Send all inquiries to:
SRA/McGraw-Hill
P.O. Box 812960
Chicago, IL 60681

Printed in the United States of America.

ISBN 1-57039-961-1

2 3 4 5 6 7 8 9 QW 05 04 03 02 01

Contents

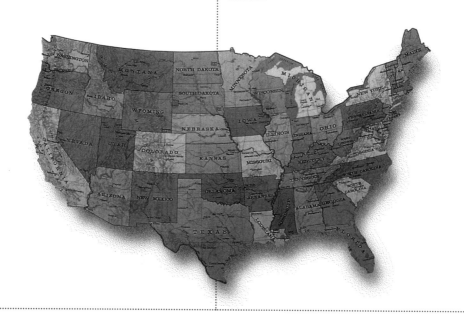

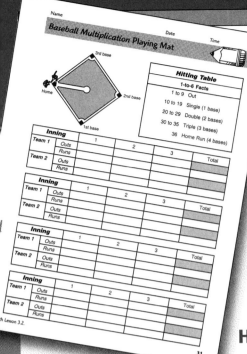

Introduction

How to Use This Book

This *Teacher's Reference Manual* has three main parts: a Management Guide, a collection of ten Mathematical Topics essays, and a Glossary. The Management Guide includes suggestions about how to implement the *Everyday Mathematics* program; ideas for organizing the curriculum, your students, and program materials; and descriptions of some features of *Everyday Mathematics*. The Mathematical Topics essays are a good source of reliable information on the mathematics in the *4–6 Everyday Mathematics* curriculum. The essays are followed by a detailed glossary of mathematical and special terms used in *Everyday Mathematics*. Many glossary entries include references to related portions of the Mathematical Topics essays.

You may want to read through the Management Guide section of this book before you begin teaching with *Everyday Mathematics* in order to familiarize yourself with the program's features and routines and to help you decide on some organizational strategies for your classroom. As the school year progresses, you may want to refer to some sections again in order to gain further insights.

The Mathematical Topics section of this book provides the essays as background. The essays do not have to be read in their entirety or in any particular order. At the beginning of each essay, you will find a table of contents that outlines the presented material. You can skim an essay, consult its table of contents for a specific topic, or read the essay straight through.

Alternatively, you can look up a term in the glossary and then follow the reference to a related essay or section. For example, the glossary defines *fact power* as "the ability to recall basic number facts automatically without having to figure them out." Included is a reference to Section 8.3 of the Estimation, Mental Arithmetic, and Fact Power essay. This section is an extended discussion of how *Everyday Mathematics* approaches the basic facts, why they are so important, and how the program works to ensure that all students achieve fact power. You may elect to read Section 8.3 or perhaps the entire essay.

Every effort has been made to make this manual easy to use. We hope you find it worthwhile. Please send us any suggestions on how we can improve it.

A brief introduction to *Everyday Mathematics* follows. The Management Guide begins on page 7, the Mathematical Topics essays on page 57, and the Glossary on page 297.

The *Everyday Mathematics* Program

Everyday Mathematics is a complete K–6 mathematics curriculum embracing many of the traditional goals of school mathematics as well as two ambitious new goals:

- To substantially raise expectations with respect to the amount and range of mathematics that students can learn
- To provide materials for students and support for teachers that enable them to meet these higher expectations

Philosophy

The students of the twenty-first century need a mathematics curriculum that is both rigorous and balanced:

- a curriculum that emphasizes conceptual understanding while building a mastery of basic skills
- a curriculum that explores the full mathematics spectrum, not just basic arithmetic
- a curriculum based on how students learn, what they're interested in, and the future for which they must be prepared

We must change both the mathematics we teach and how we teach it if our students are to measure up to the ever-increasing demand for mathematics competence and problem-solving ability. *Everyday Mathematics* makes these changes by introducing students to all the major mathematical content domains—number sense, algebra, measurement, geometry, data analysis, and probability—beginning in Kindergarten. The program helps teachers move beyond basic arithmetic and nurture higher-order and critical-thinking skills in their students, using everyday, real-world problems and situations—while also building and maintaining basic skills, including automatic fact recall.

Everyday Mathematics differs from textbook-centered instruction in a number of ways. The program has been created so that it is consistent with the ways students actually learn mathematics, building understanding over a period of time, first through informal exposure and then through more formal and directed instruction.

Since learning proceeds from the known to the unknown, new learning needs to be connected to and built upon an existing knowledge base.

Students using *Everyday Mathematics* are expected to master a variety of mathematical skills and concepts, but not the first time they are encountered. Mathematical content is taught in a repeated fashion, beginning with concrete experiences. It is a mistake to proceed too quickly from the concrete to the abstract or to isolate concepts and skills from one another or from problem contexts. Students also need to "double back," revisiting topics, concepts, and skills, and then relating them to each other in new and different ways.

Pacing is important. Students learn best when new topics are presented briskly and in an interesting way. Most students will not master a new topic the first time it is presented, so *Everyday Mathematics* allows students to revisit content in varied contexts, integrating new learning with previous knowledge and experiences. If newly learned concepts and skills are not periodically reviewed, practiced, and applied in a wide variety of contexts, they will not be retained.

It is important to note how the differences between *Everyday Mathematics* and other programs may affect your day-to-day planning and teaching. Daily routines and games are a necessary part of the program, not optional extensions. Routines and games are designed to build conceptual understanding and ensure mastery of basic skills in authentic and interesting contexts. Another way in which *Everyday Mathematics* differs from other programs is that it is designed for the teacher, rather than being centered on a student textbook, offering materials that provide students with a rich variety of experiences across mathematical content strands.

Because language, communication, social interaction, tools, and manipulatives all play important roles in helping students acquire skills, *Everyday Mathematics* employs cooperative learning activities, explorations, and projects. The classroom needs to be set up to accommodate group work, and students must be able to work together without direct supervision. To facilitate this learning process, the authors have provided a section about Cooperative Grouping on page 23 of the Management Guide section of this book.

In *Everyday Mathematics*, assessment is closely linked with instruction. While some formal assessment is necessary, a balanced approach including less formal, ongoing methods will provide a more complete picture of each student's progress. A number of assessment tools are built into the *Everyday Mathematics* program to help you create an assessment program that will give you feedback about your students' instructional needs and information you can use to assign grades. For more information, see the section on Assessment in the Management Guide, as well as the *Assessment Handbook*.

Everyday Mathematics assumes that virtually all students are capable of a much greater understanding of and proficiency in mathematics than has been traditionally expected. The program establishes high expectations for all students and gives teachers the tools they need to help students meet, and often exceed, these expectations. *Everyday Mathematics* is committed to establishing world-class mathematics standards for our nation's schools.

Program Highlights

Key features of the *Everyday Mathematics* program include:

- *Problem solving for everyday situations.* Research and experience show that students who are unable to solve problems in purely symbolic form often have little trouble with these problems when they are presented in everyday contexts.

- *Developing concepts through hands-on activities.* *Everyday Mathematics* offers many suggestions for activities with manipulative materials. These activities pave the way for the introduction of new mathematical ideas.

- *Establishing links between past experiences and explorations of new concepts.* Ideas that have been explored with concrete materials or pictorial representations are revisited through oral descriptions and symbolic representations. Students learn to shift comfortably among various representations and to select models that are most appropriate for given situations.

- *Sharing ideas through discussion.* Students gain important insights about mathematics by building on one another's discoveries; one idea leads to another or to refinements of a student's own understanding. Discussion promotes good listening habits and fosters a receptive attitude to the ideas of classmates. Because verbalization often clarifies concepts, talking about mathematics is an important part of thinking about mathematics.

- *Cooperative learning through partner and small-group activities.* Students discover that working together is usually more enjoyable and stimulating than working independently. Moreover, as students learn to work as a team, cooperation replaces competition, and the less skilled benefit by drawing support from the more skilled.

- *Practice through games.* Frequent practice is imperative for a student to attain mastery of a skill. Unfortunately, drills tend to become monotonous and gradually lose effectiveness over time. Games, however, (1) relieve the tedium of rote repetition, (2) reduce the use of worksheets, and (3) offer an almost unlimited source of problem material, because, in most cases, numbers are generated randomly.

- *Ongoing review throughout the year.* It is rare that students master something new the first time they encounter it. For this reason, repeated exposures to key ideas presented in slightly different contexts are built into the *Everyday Mathematics* program. In addition, Math Boxes pages in each lesson provide opportunities for cumulative review or assessment.

- *Daily routines.* The program provides routines that students perform on a regular basis—for example, answering Math Message questions and solving Mental Math and Reflexes problems. Other regular classroom tasks help students develop a sense of order, initiative, and responsibility while reinforcing numerous mathematical concepts.

- *Informal assessment.* In addition to independent review exercises and unit assessments, *Everyday Mathematics* provides many suggestions for small-group activities to help you assess students' progress. Through your interactions with small groups of students, you will obtain a clearer understanding of individual strengths and weaknesses.

- *Home-and-school partnership.* Optimal learning involves the student, the teacher, and the home. The *Home Connection Handbook* (included in the program) offers many suggestions for this. Family Letters help inform parents and guardians about each unit's topics and terms, offering ideas for home-based mathematics activities that supplement classroom work. Also, parents or others at home are invited to participate in their student's mathematics experiences through the Study Links included in most lessons.

Mathematical Content

Everyday Mathematics Grades 4–6 is organized into the following content strands:

- Data and Chance

- Geometry

- Measurement and Reference Frames

- Numeration

- Operations and Computation

- Patterns, Functions, and Algebra

Woven throughout the content strands are several key mathematical themes:

- Algorithmic and Procedural Thinking

- Estimation Skills and Number Sense

- Mental Arithmetic Skills and Reflexes

- Problem Solving

Special emphasis is placed on:

- Establishing links from past experiences, activities with concrete materials, pictures, oral statements, and symbolic arithmetic statements. For example, students might act out a problem or talk about it to get a feel for what is happening. Or they could draw pictures or diagrams or do some mental arithmetic, which would eventually lead them to write a number model.

- Discussing and sharing ideas. (*Can you tell us how you do that? Why do you think so? Does everyone agree?*)

- Using and comparing equivalent expressions. (*What other ways can we say or write this?*)

- Expressing quantities and measurements in context by including labels or units. (*Five what?*)

- Learning about reversibility: put in, take out; add, subtract; put together, take apart; multiply, divide; expand, shrink; get money, spend money; positive, negative; and so on.

- Using calculators as a tool for displaying numbers, developing concepts and skills, doing numerous or complicated calculations, and solving problems—especially real-life problems.

By becoming a part of everyday work and play, the lessons, activities, and exercises in *Everyday Mathematics* will gradually shape students' ways of thinking about mathematics and foster the development of students' mathematical intuition and understanding.

Management Guide

This Management Guide explains the program's features and materials and presents ideas for organizing students, using routines and displays, and reaching all students. It also highlights the program's approach regarding mathematical tools, student assessment, home-and-school communication, and problem solving.

outline

Managing the Curriculum

Perhaps the single greatest difference between *Everyday Mathematics* and other programs is that *Everyday Mathematics* is written for the teacher rather than focused on a student textbook. Student materials are designed as supplements to facilitate the teacher's use of the program. This section discusses program features and describes materials that support the program design.

Daily Routines

Students learn a great deal of mathematics through the daily routines they perform both independently and as a class. Most of the routines in *Everyday Mathematics* should be introduced in the first unit and then maintained throughout the year. Although these routines require special attention and extra time at the beginning of the year, you will find that investing this time will make teaching easier in the long run. Once routines have been established, they become self-sustaining, as much by the students' energy as by the teacher's effort. Learning becomes much more efficient and effective. For more information on routines, see the Organizing Routines and Displays section on page 31 of this Management Guide.

Games

Many parents and educators make a sharp distinction between work and play. They tend to allow play only during prescribed times. However, students naturally carry their playfulness into all of their activities. This is why *Everyday Mathematics* sees games as enjoyable ways to practice number skills, especially those that help students develop fact power. For more on using games to develop fact power, see Section 8.3 in the Estimation, Mental Arithmetic, and Fact Power essay.

Games can be played frequently without the same mathematical problems repeating because the numbers in most games are generated randomly. The game format eliminates the tedium typical of most drills. However, not all games offer sufficient practice for a concept. For those concepts, you may want to employ traditional drill problems. In some instances, you may also wish to use timed drills. Always strive for balance in your approach to drills and practice. Too much monotonous, rote pencil pushing has helped produce generations of people who dislike mathematics.

Games are an integral part of the *Everyday Mathematics* program, rather than an optional extra as they are traditionally used in many classrooms. Make sure that all students have time to play games, especially those who work at a slower pace or encounter more difficulty than their classmates. If students play the games only after finishing other work, many of the students who need these experiences most will get fewer opportunities to have them.

You may want to set up a Games Corner using some of your students' favorite games. That way, students can get additional practice while playing games of their own choosing during free time. Rotate games often to keep the Games Corner fresh and interesting. Game masters can be found in the *Math Masters* book. In addition, rules for some of the most popular games from Grades 4–6 are included in the *Student Reference Books*. Game rules and masters can be copied for use in a Games Corner and for students to borrow so they can play at home.

Competition

One issue frequently raised concerning the inclusion of games in the curriculum is competition. Many teachers do not want young students to compete against each other. As one teacher writes, "I prefer to have students work in cooperative groupings, staying away from win-or-lose games. I can't think of a quicker way to turn a child off to the concept one is trying to teach than to inject the emotional disaster of 'I've lost!' into the experience."

It is true that many of the games in the *Everyday Mathematics* program are competitive. Fair and friendly competition can generate many good things: excitement, determination, independence, and challenge. Game rules may also be changed to fit the players' needs for fairness, harmony, and equality. It is possible to modify most of the games so that students practice the same number skills while working cooperatively. The challenge and excitement will come from working together, making joint decisions, doing one's best, and having fun.

We will use *Multiplication Top-It* to demonstrate how a competitive game can be modified to make it non-competitive. In *Multiplication Top-It*, students use a deck of 1–10 number cards, consisting of four cards of each number, for a total of 40 cards. Each student turns over two cards and calls out the product. The player with the highest product takes all the cards played in that turn. The player with the most cards at the end of the game wins.

Suppose, however, that two or three students are asked to play the same game but are given a group objective: "Play until all 40 cards are used, putting all the used cards into a single discard pile. Time the game. Play again until all 40 cards are used. Try to beat your best time to play the whole deck."

This modified game allows practice of the same multiplication skills but does not declare "winners" and "losers." Instead, the focus is on the group objective of achieving a faster time.

Many of the games, as they are, identify the winner as the player with the highest total after a certain number of turns. Here are some strategies for converting these games to relatively non-competitive games:

- Have the students take turns (as usual), but ask them to record their results for each round on the same sheet of paper. Each game total will then represent the combined efforts of all group members.
- Redefine the game objective. For example, ask groups to play a sequence of games and "report the highest and lowest single game totals." This modification may inspire some measure of healthy competition among groups, but the one-on-one competitive nature of the standard game will be reduced.

These are only examples. The best ideas for modifying games will probably come from your own classroom experiences. Involve your students in the revisions. If they realize that their input will result in improved games, they will become more eager players—and learners.

The Everything Math Deck

The Everything Math Deck is a deck of 54 number cards used for a variety of Everyday Mathematics games and activities. The deck can be purchased through the publisher. It contains four of each card for the numbers 0 to 10, and one of each card for the numbers 11 to 20. On the reverse of the 0–10 cards are fractions represented in a variety of ways.

You can transform an ordinary deck of 54 playing cards to function like an Everything Math Deck (whole number side), as follows:
- Change the four queens to 0s.
- Remove the four jacks, four kings, and two jokers. Label each of these ten cards with one of the numbers from 11 to 20.
- Change the four aces to 1s.
- All number cards represent their face value.

Math Boxes

 Math Boxes, originally developed by *Everyday Mathematics* teacher Ellen Dairyko, are an excellent way to review material on a regular basis.

In *Everyday Mathematics,* Math Boxes are one of the main components of review and skills maintenance. Once this routine has been introduced, almost every lesson includes a Math Boxes page in the *Math Journal* as part of the Ongoing Learning & Practice section.

Math Boxes problems are not intended to reinforce the content of the lesson in which they appear. Rather, they provide continuous distributed practice of all skills and concepts in the program. Math Boxes pages come in pairs or, sometimes, sets of three. The problems in each set are the same except for the numbers. The first Math Boxes page in each set includes pointers to relevant pages in the *Student Reference Book.* The first problem on most Math Boxes pages involves a prerequisite skill or concept for an upcoming unit.

Math Boxes are designed as independent activities. The Math Boxes page does not need to be completed on the same day as the lesson, but it should not be skipped. Expect that your guidance will be needed, especially at the beginning of the school year when some problems review skills from prior years. If students struggle with a problem set, it is not necessary to create a lesson to develop these skills. You can modify or skip problems that you know are not review for your students. Lesson activities revisit skills throughout the year. Math Boxes also provide useful assessment information on review skills.

NOTE: Although Math Boxes are designed primarily as independent activities, at times it may be useful to have students work with partners or work through some problems as a class.

Math Messages

A Math Message is provided at the beginning of each lesson. The Math Message usually leads into the lesson for the day; sometimes 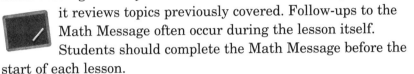 it reviews topics previously covered. Follow-ups to the Math Message often occur during the lesson itself. Students should complete the Math Message before the start of each lesson.

You can display Math Messages in a number of ways. You may want to write them on the board, the Class Data Pad, overhead transparencies, post them on the bulletin board, or duplicate them ahead of time on quarter-sheets as handouts.

Many teachers find it useful to have students record their answers to the Math Message. In some classrooms, students keep a daily Math Journal where they enter Math Message questions and answers. In other classrooms, students record their answers on quarter- or half-sheets, which teachers collect from time to time.

Although the *Teacher's Lesson Guide* contains many suggestions for Math Messages, you are encouraged to create your own, designed around the needs of your students and on the activities that take place in your classroom. You may also want to provide a Suggestion Box into which students can put their own Math Message ideas as well as number stories.

Mental Math and Reflexes

The term *Mental Math and Reflexes* refers to exercises, usually oral, designed to strengthen students' number sense and to review and advance essential basic skills. Mental Math and Reflexes sessions should be brief, lasting no more than five minutes. Numerous short interactions are far more effective than fewer prolonged sessions.

There are several kinds of Mental Math suggestions provided in the *Teacher's Lesson Guide*. Some involve a choral drill; many are basic-skills practice with counts, operations, or measures; and some are problem-solving exercises.

For Mental Math and Reflexes exercises that require students to record their answers on slates, see the section on Slates on page 21 of this guide for one possible procedure as well as suggestions for alternatives if you do not have slates.

The *Teacher's Lesson Guide* suggests Mental Math and Reflexes exercises for almost every lesson. (In the first unit of *Fifth Grade Everyday Mathematics,* they are replaced by a Multiplication Facts Routine.) You are encouraged to use these exercises based on your students' needs and your classroom activities. If the suggested exercises do not meet the needs of your class, feel free to provide an alternate set.

Museums

Everyday Mathematics encourages the development of classroom museums—using a bulletin board or table where related items can be collected, categorized, and labeled. These museums could include the following:

- *Rates Museum* Students collect examples of rates, such as speeds, prices per pound, and so on.
- *Grams and Ounces Museum* Students collect objects of different weights measured in grams and in ounces.
- *Graphs Museum* Students collect graphs and other data displays from newspapers and magazines.
- *Tessellations Museum* Students collect pictures of tessellations, such as floor and ceiling tiles, brick work, wallpaper patterns, and so on.

Everyday Mathematics museums are sometimes supplemented with posters of 2-dimensional representations of items. Along with helping to connect concepts between solid objects and 2-D pictures, the posters help summarize categories of objects that students are likely to have identified in their concrete manipulations.

If you take your class to a museum in your community, encourage the students to look for the uses of mathematics that abound there. Examples include statistics about objects in exhibits and different ways of categorizing those objects—ways that often have some underlying frame of reference, such as size or time.

Name-Collection Boxes

A name-collection box is a diagram of an open-top box with a label attached to it. It is used to structure work with equivalent names for numbers. The name on the label identifies the number whose names are collected in the box. For example, the box shown in the margin is a 16-box, a name-collection box for the number 16. For more information on name-collection boxes, see Section 1.9.2 of the Numeration and Order essay.

Number Grids

A number grid is a matrix that consists of rows of boxes, ten to each row, containing a set of consecutive whole numbers. Students use number grids to explore number patterns, reinforce place-value concepts, and calculate sums and differences.

16
4^2
$\sqrt{256}$
$(4 + 6) * 6 - 4 * 11$
XVI

16-box

									0
1	2	3	4	5	6	7	8	9	10
11	12	13	14	15	16	17	18	19	20
21	22	23	24	25	26	27	28	29	30
31	32	33	34	35	36	37	38	39	40
41	42	43	44	45	46	47	48	49	50
51	52	53	54	55	56	57	58	59	60
61	62	63	64	65	66	67	68	69	70
71	72	73	74	75	76	77	78	79	80
81	82	83	84	85	86	87	88	89	90
91	92	93	94	95	96	97	98	99	100
101	102	103	104	105	106	107	108	109	110

For more on number grids, see Section 7.3.1 of the Reference Frames essay.

Number Lines

A number line is a line on which points correspond to numbers. There is one point for every number and one number for every point. Students use number lines when counting and skip counting, performing measuring activities, and adding and subtracting. Number lines are also used as the axes in coordinate graphing systems. The Real Number Line poster used in sixth grade summarizes and orders the kinds of numbers students have worked with since Kindergarten and gives a preview of other numbers that they will work with in later grades.

For more on number lines, see Section 7.3.1 of the Reference Frames essay.

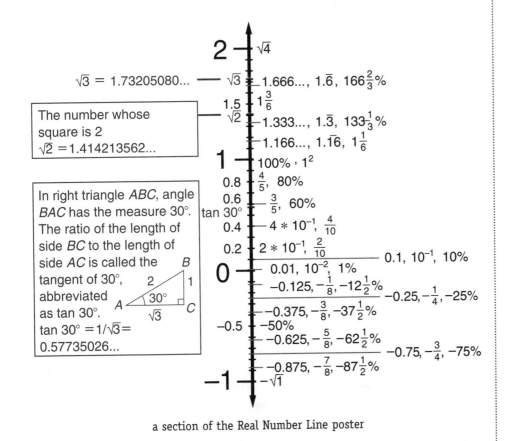

$\sqrt{3} = 1.73205080...$

The number whose square is 2
$\sqrt{2} = 1.414213562...$

In right triangle ABC, angle BAC has the measure $30°$. The ratio of the length of side BC to the length of side AC is called the tangent of $30°$, abbreviated as tan $30°$.
$\tan 30° = 1/\sqrt{3} = 0.57735026...$

2 — $\sqrt{4}$
$\sqrt{3}$ — $1.666..., 1.\overline{6}, 166\frac{2}{3}\%$
1.5 — $1\frac{3}{6}$
$\sqrt{2}$ — $1.333..., 1.\overline{3}, 133\frac{1}{3}\%$
— $1.166..., 1.\overline{16}, 1\frac{1}{6}$
1 — $100\% , 1^2$
0.8 — $\frac{4}{5}, 80\%$
0.6 — $\frac{3}{5}, 60\%$
tan $30°$ — $4 * 10^{-1}, \frac{4}{10}$
0.4 —
0.2 — $2 * 10^{-1}, \frac{2}{10}$ — $0.1, 10^{-1}, 10\%$
0 — $0.01, 10^{-2}, 1\%$
— $-0.125, -\frac{1}{8}, -12\frac{1}{2}\%$ — $-0.25, -\frac{1}{4}, -25\%$
— $-0.375, -\frac{3}{8}, -37\frac{1}{2}\%$
-0.5 — -50%
— $-0.625, -\frac{5}{8}, -62\frac{1}{2}\%$ — $-0.75, -\frac{3}{4}, -75\%$
— $-0.875, -\frac{7}{8}, -87\frac{1}{2}\%$
-1 — $-\sqrt{1}$

a section of the Real Number Line poster

Projects

The Projects suggested in *Everyday Mathematics* cover a wide array of mathematics activities and concepts and are created around themes that interest students. Project ideas are found in the Projects Appendix of the *Teacher's Lesson Guide* for each grade. Project Masters are found in the Project Masters section of the *Math Masters* book.

Projects are cross-curricular in nature and often include the following processes:

- Observing
- Communicating
- Reading for mathematical content
- Identifying
- Collecting, organizing, and graphing data
- Using numbers
- Measuring
- Determining patterns and relationships

You can consider many Projects and other activities suggested in the *Everyday Mathematics* program to be a part of other areas in your curriculum: for example, science, social studies, and art. And, of course, reading and language arts skills are always involved.

Projects may take a day or more to complete. They are an important part of the curriculum and memorable to students, so please take the time needed to carry them out. While projects are linked to topics in the units, we strongly encourage you to extend them with your own materials and link them to other areas in your curriculum.

Projects especially appropriate at particular points during the school year are suggested in various Unit Organizers in each *Teacher's Lesson Guide*. Since many ideas have been included in the Projects—more than can usually be used—choose those that interest your students and feel free to add your own.

In addition to the projects described in the Projects Appendix of the *Teacher's Lesson Guide,* there are also projects that appear in the *Student Reference Book* for each grade. In Grades 4 and 5, these are special year-long projects that focus on a particular topic. In fourth grade, students go on a World Tour, which is easily linked to geography and other social studies and language arts topics. In fifth grade, the year-long project is the American Tour, a series of activities that examine the history, demographics, politics, and environment of the United States. *Sixth Grade Everyday Mathematics* includes a set of projects that explore uses of mathematics in art and design. Materials for each of these special projects are found in a separate section in the *Student Reference Book* for each grade level. Lessons pertaining to these projects are interspersed in the *Teacher's Lesson Guide* throughout the year.

Reading Mathematics

The authors of *Everyday Mathematics* have attempted to balance the presentation of material to students according to the problem representation model shown below. In early grades, this means giving much more attention to verbal and concrete representations than in the traditional mathematics curriculum and less focus on symbolic aspects. Students in Grades 4–6 are expected to spend more time reading and writing mathematics, for several reasons.

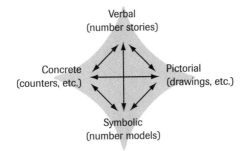

- The language of algebra, which students begin to learn in earnest in fourth grade, was invented so that people can communicate symbolically in an efficient way. It is also a core part of all computer languages.
- Being able to read mathematics, and about mathematics, allows students more independence. In particular, it allows them to have an opinion other than that of the teacher.
- Secondary school mathematics, including the reform curricula developed in recent years, usually requires students to be able to read mathematical text and symbols. *Everyday Mathematics* has a responsibility to help prepare students for such experiences.

Throughout the program, you are given hints on how to help students read and write numbers, number models, and sentences containing variables. This section is intended to give you additional suggestions on how to help your students read mathematics text.

There are three main levels of comprehension of mathematical texts, each of which brings its own kind of challenges.

Literal Comprehension

Unless symbols are recognized and defined, a reader has no hope of understanding a passage. The first task in achieving a literal comprehension of text is **decoding,** or the simple recognition of symbols. For example, the square root symbol is introduced to students of *Fourth Grade Everyday Mathematics*. While the symbol itself is not too difficult to learn, its unfamiliarity and peculiar look will probably mean that students need time to become comfortable with it to use it properly.

A potential obstacle to literal comprehension of mathematics is the habit of reading English text from left to right. This is not always strictly the case when reading mathematics text. For example, reading a simple sum of fractions from left to right can easily lead to adding numerators and adding denominators. Note that reading such a sum not only involves left-to-right eye movement but down-and-up movement as shown below. Reading graphs, as you can imagine, is even more unpredictable.

$$\left\downarrow \frac{1}{2} \nearrow + \nwarrow \right\downarrow \frac{1}{3} \nearrow =$$

How can you help students at this literal decoding level? The key word is patience—although such tasks may seem trivial to us, it is only because of our extensive practice rather than some innate understanding. Typically, a little time spent having students pronounce equations, describe graphs, or name symbols can have a big payoff down the line both in terms of student success and a steady class pace.

Once a symbol has been decoded, it must have an **attached meaning.** Here the potential for misunderstanding is great. Richard Earle compiled a list of 437 words that appeared most frequently in eight series of elementary (Grades 1–3) math texts. Of the 437 words, 71 (or 16 percent) were words like *function, difference,* or *solution,* which have distinctly different meanings in a mathematical context than in other contexts.

How do you help students assign meanings to mathematical symbols and words? Mostly, make yourself aware of as many possible misinterpretations or different interpretations as you can. It is surprising how many of us assume that the meaning we have for a word is "the" meaning, when actually we haven't thought about alternatives at all. Some general categories of questions that can be used to encourage accurate literal comprehension of mathematics are listed below. These may be presented verbally, as homework, or in quizzes.

Questioning students for literal comprehension of mathematical text

Ask students:

- Whether a given symbol is the same as or different from one in the text;
- To rewrite or redraw a given symbol on their slates;
- To pronounce a given symbol;
- Whether alternative forms of a given symbol are acceptable replacements;
- To define a given symbol;
- To interpret between variations of symbol meaning;
- To describe characteristics of a symbol;
- To identify examples or instances of use of a symbol; or
- To make representations of a symbol.

As basic as many of these activities may seem, they are well worth the time it takes to do them—especially when symbols and words are first introduced. Keep in mind that a student having any trouble understanding words or symbols at this level of comprehension is unlikely to be successful drawing inferences or solving problems using them.

Inferential Comprehension

A reader has inferential comprehension of text if he or she understands the "signals" in the text. Signals include:

- Catching relational structures (e.g., "first . . . ," "second . . . ," "third, . . . ");
- Dealing with premature abstractions of a concept (e.g., "The main ideas of this lesson are . . . ");
- Understanding summary statements (e.g., "In short, . . . "); and
- Awareness of "pointer" words or phrases (e.g., "more importantly," or "unfortunately").

Basically, inferential comprehension is finding meaning in the way that literal symbols and words are connected. In the sentence "My dog has fleas," a reader can know the meaning of *dog* and *fleas,* but not the ownership of the dog; the fact that the bugs are here now, not in the past; and that the fleas are somehow in contact with the dog. These are all meanings that are inferred from the sentence.

Questions for inferential comprehension should focus on relationships. Some general categories of questions that can be used to improve inferential comprehension of mathematics are listed below. These were developed in part by Steven Kulick.

Questioning students for inferential comprehension of mathematical text

Ask students:

- To complete a sentence;
- To verify relationships of symbols in a sentence;
- To give their opinion about the meaning of relationships of symbols;
- To determine the cause and/or effect of relationships in and between sentences;
- To use an algorithm;
- To order mixed-up steps of algorithms; or
- To fill in missing steps in an algorithm.

Analytic Comprehension

If readers of text can be motivated to do something relevant to the subject being written about, then they have achieved an analytic comprehension of it. (The "relevant" aspect is important because they could just throw down their books in frustration if they didn't comprehend a word.) There are two general types of analytic comprehension: one that allows readers to *apply* their literal and inferential understanding of text; the other that allows them to *critique* what they have read.

Applying the reading

Solving written mathematical problems requires the literal and inferential comprehension described in the previous sections and then the realization that certain mathematical skills and models will help. The difficulty that most people have in decoding and interpreting mathematical text and symbols is a major reason *Everyday Mathematics* is based on a concrete, informal experience with mathematical ideas well before the ideas are expressed formally and symbolically.

How can you help students achieve greater analytic comprehension in reading mathematical applications (number stories)? Once again, the answer is to give them time—time to develop the building blocks they need to apply mathematics in symbolic situations, and time to read progressively more challenging text. Have all students read material that is rich in ideas, full of connections (i.e., words like *then, but, unless,* etc.), and is relatively dense (i.e., much information is packed into a small space) both in and outside of mathematics class time. Researchers have found that removing connectives and rewriting text in short sentences actually made comprehension more difficult rather than easier. Note that patience is especially needed for older students who may be transferring into your school and classroom. Take the time to find out their background in talking about mathematics before assuming they may have the same expertise as students with an *Everyday Mathematics* background.

Critical reading

Understanding text well enough to judge its value is arguably the highest level of comprehension—as long as the criticism is backed with reasonable evidence.

Critical readers ask themselves good questions; the challenge to the teacher is to help students ask good questions. If the quality of the questions asked is weak, then much of the benefit of motivating students to learn mathematics through applications is lost. On the other hand, if the questions being asked require hard, critical thinking, then the jobs of both reader and teacher are likely to be much easier. Often, unraveling the context of an honest, everyday problem (which must necessarily come before solving it) makes the necessary mathematics comparatively trivial to the reader.

How can you help students become more critical readers? Try to ask the following types of questions.

Questioning students for analytic comprehension of mathematical text

Ask students:

- To make generalizations from specific instances;
- To find exceptions to a rule;
- To complete and make analogies;
- To identify missing information in text;

- To identify irrelevant information in text;
- To tell whether an algorithm is appropriate in a given problem situation;
- To generate logical consequences from stated facts;
- To simplify details to grasp global meanings;
- To guess and check; and
- To make mathematical models.

Reading Strategies

Beginning in *Fourth Grade Everyday Mathematics*, students are asked to do more reading than in previous grades. In particular, they are expected to read essays in their journals and in the *Student Reference Book.*

Group Reading Strategies

For a class to read an essay together, consider the ideas that follow.

Round Robin Choose a student to read a portion of the text aloud while the rest of the class listens. At a convenient stopping point, the teacher or the reader chooses another student to read aloud.

Choral Reading One student begins reading aloud. At some point another student "jumps in" and "picks up" the reading. Continue in this way until the essay is complete.

Independent Read Students first read a paragraph to themselves. It is then read aloud to the class by the teacher or another student. Continue in this way until the essay is complete.

Partner Read Students read the essay in partnerships or small groups. When all students have completed the reading, the class discusses the essay as a whole group. You might have the small groups or partnerships write one question about the text and one comment before the class meets. In this way each small group is responsible for interacting with the text.

Independent Reading Strategies

To help students become independent readers, consider these strategies.

The Three-Minute Pause When reading text aloud during class or when students are reading silently to themselves, stop several times for about 3 minutes each time and have students turn to partners and summarize what they have read or heard so far, ask questions about something that is still confusing, or relate what they have read to something in their own lives.

The K-W-L Strategy Before reading text, ask students to write anything that they think they know about the topic being presented (K). Also have them write anything they would like to know about the topic (W). After reading the text, students identify what they have learned (L).

Advance Organizer Questions Prior to reading the text, provide students with questions about the key points of the text. In this way, their reading can focus on what you consider most important. Also, identify key vocabulary in the reading and discuss it beforehand. Create a "word wall" of key vocabulary.

Graphic Organizers To help students sort information:

- Provide time for students to outline, to "web," or to create a flowchart of a procedure or other information in the text.
- Provide Venn diagrams or other visual devices for sorting information.

Note-Taking Strategies Suggest the following ideas for note-taking.

- Draw pictures in the margin of the page to represent the text.
- Highlight key information or the answers to advance organizer questions.
- Put a check mark in the margin next to paragraphs that make sense and a question mark next to paragraphs in which the information is unclear.

Interact with the Text Better readers do things to relate information to their lives and to clarify questions they may have about the material. For example:

- Write questions in the margin as you read.
- Picture in your mind what is being described in the text.
- Think about how the information relates to something you already know.
- Summarize the main points of the text.
- Write three questions that are answered by the text.

Situation Diagrams

In *Everyday Mathematics,* various diagrams are used to help students organize information in simple one-step problem-solving situations. Parts-and-total diagrams, comparison diagrams, change diagrams, and rate diagrams (also called multiplication diagrams and multiplication/division diagrams) are some examples:

For more on situation diagrams, see Section 2.1.1. of the Arithmetic Operations essay.

Quantity	
12	

Quantity	Difference
8	?

Quantity
12

Quantity
8

?
difference

comparison diagrams

Start	Change	End
35	−6	?

change diagram

children	cards per child	cards
4	?	24

rate diagram

Slates

Most students and teachers genuinely enjoy using slates. They afford an excellent opportunity for everyone to quietly answer a question at the same time, and they help you to see at a glance which students may need extra help. They also save paper. Two kinds of slates are particularly easy to use:

Plastic Write-on/Wipe-off Slates Students write on these small, white slates with dry-erase markers. They can store both the markers and the slates in their tool kits or stack them on a counter or shelf for easy distribution when needed.

Chalkboard Slates Chalk may be kept in old socks that can also be used as erasers. Small rug scraps or pieces of cloth also make good erasers. One teacher recommends small, cosmetic, cotton-quilt pads.

There are, of course, alternatives to slates. Students can fold a piece of paper into fourths, which will give them eight cells in which to write answers. Another alternative is to use laminated tagboard and dry-erase markers.

Establish a routine for using slates. You might want to use one-word cues, such as *Listen, Think, Write, Show, Erase.* The following procedure, if used consistently, helps prevent confusion:

- Explain each exercise aloud. Tell students to *Listen.* If students find the problems too challenging, you may want to write them on the board or overhead.

- Have students work the problems mentally. Be sure to give them time to *Think.*

- Instruct students to *Write* their answers on their slates and keep them covered.

- When most students have written their answers, tell them to *Show* their slates at the same time by holding them up facing you. Afterward, when appropriate, take a few minutes to have the students share their strategies.

- Have students *Erase* their slates.

Instead of doing oral and slate assessments with the whole class, another strategy would be to work with small groups of students, one group at a time, over several days. While you do this, the rest of the class can work on Assessment Masters. When using slates, it is not necessary to record every student's performance on every problem. Instead, you need to keep a record of only those students who are struggling. You can go back later and enter positive comments for students you know are doing well.

Student Reference Book

Each student in Grades 3 through 6 receives a *Student Reference Book* for his or her grade level. The *Student Reference Book* is a resource in which students can look up and review information related to the topics covered in *Everyday Mathematics*. It consists of brief summaries of the major mathematical topics introduced in each grade (including many worked examples), a section on calculator usage, rules of the most popular games from Grades 4–6, a glossary of mathematical terms, descriptions of projects, and reference material such as tables of measures, fraction-decimal-percent conversion tables, and place-value charts. Although it is written for students, teachers and parents may also find the *Student Reference Book* to be a useful resource.

Study Links

For more information on Study Links, see "Providing for Home-and-School Communication" on page 52 in this Management Guide.

Study Links are the *4–6 Everyday Mathematics* version of homework assignments. Each lesson has a Study Link, which can be found in the *Math Masters* book. The next lesson has a follow-up to the previous Study Link. Study Links consist of active projects, extensions of lessons, and ongoing review problems. They show parents and guardians what the students are doing in mathematics. The Study Link for the last lesson in each unit is a Family Letter outlining the next unit. A blank Study Link form has also been provided for you to create your own.

Unit Boxes

A unit box is a rectangular box displayed next to a problem or a set of problems. Unit boxes contain the labels or units of measure used in the corresponding problem(s). Unit boxes help students to think symbolically by encouraging them to see numbers as quantities or measurements of real objects.

unit box

"What's My Rule?"

"What's My Rule?" is an activity in which students analyze a set of number pairs to determine the rule that relates the numbers in each pair. The data are often presented in the form of a function table generated by a function machine. "What's My Rule?" problems appear from time to time in Mental Math and Reflexes, lesson activities, and Math Boxes.

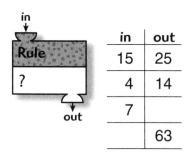

in	out
15	25
4	14
7	
	63

For more on "What's My Rule?" see Section 9.1.3 of the Patterns, Sequences, Functions, and Algebra essay.

Organizing Students

The previous sections contain suggestions for managing features of the *Everyday Mathematics* program. The following sections outline hints for managing your classroom as you do mathematics.

Cooperative Groupings

Cooperative learning improves attitudes toward learning and academic achievement, improves social skills and time on task, and helps develop speaking, listening, and writing skills. Cooperative learning also creates an atmosphere in which students can share ideas and ways of thinking as they solve problems. One benefit is that students are exposed to strategies they may not have discovered on their own. Cooperative learning also prepares students for real-life situations. On the job, people share responsibilities with others, cooperate, and work together toward common goals.

Since students will be working together much of the time, it is important that they understand your expectations with respect to working in partnerships and small groups.

Consider making and displaying a poster of Partnership Principles, listing rules for working with a partner.

Groups and Partnerships

For simplicity, the word *group* is used to refer both to partners and small groups. In group activities, learning becomes a dynamic process in which interactions among group members encourage an inquisitive spirit and introduce new avenues for exploration, while instilling a spirit of teamwork.

Because *Everyday Mathematics* is filled with group activities, both teacher-directed and independent, you may want to plan seating arrangements accordingly. That way, students can make the transition from whole-class work to group work with minimal disruption.

To maximize success, thought and planning must be given to setting up groups. The best lessons can fail if groups are not properly formed. Having students work with their best friends does not always create an ideal learning environment. And if teams are formed at random, students with the lowest or highest skill levels could end up in one group. Along with your personal knowledge of each student's respective skill level, the following strategies suggested by teachers may be helpful:

- Groups should be heterogeneous in terms of skill, gender, and race or ethnicity. The mixed achievement levels within groups allow for peer tutoring. Random groups or special-interest groups can be formed to vary the learning experience, but heterogeneous groupings usually work best. (During games for skill and practice, you may sometimes want to group students by ability to facilitate practice at an appropriate level for each student.)

- To arrange the class into groups, list your students from high to low according to skill or achievement level. Take one student from the top of the list, one from the bottom, and two from the middle to form each group. When it is necessary to break a team into partners, match high-medium and medium-low.

Partnership Principles
1. Guide
2. Check
3. Praise

management guide

- A good size for small groups is four students, which also allows for pairs working together within the group. If the class does not divide by four equally, place one or two remaining students in a group that will best fit their needs. If there are three remaining, form another group.

- Keep groups together for several weeks. If situations develop that impede a group's progress, make changes as necessary.

Team Building and Group Etiquette

For students to work cooperatively in groups, there often needs to be a team-building process that establishes the team's identity, spirit, and responsibility to one another. If students don't know one another, "getting to know you" activities will help. For example, have students make lists of likes and dislikes and then have them look for differences and common interests.

Even though students have worked in groups before, it is important that you take time during the first few weeks of school to review partner and small-group etiquette. The value of group study is diminished if social interaction replaces purposeful learning.

Post the three basic principles of constructive partner and group interaction: Guide, Check, and Praise. Then, during the first few days of the year, have students share what they think these terms mean. Guide the discussion to cover the following points:

Guide

- Help and demonstrate what to do without telling or doing everything yourself.
- Take turns.
- Only one student should get help from the teacher if the group needs it.

Check

- Pay attention and listen to others.
- If someone makes a mistake, respond positively and in a helpful way. (Make a list of helpful phrases such as "Try again," "Good try," "Close," and so on.)
- Help fellow group members find correct responses.

Praise

- Let others know they are doing a good job.
- Praise others. (Help students compile a list of appropriate praise words and phrases.)

To establish a positive learning environment, it is also worthwhile to have students brainstorm with you about a good set of general rules. You then might post these rules on the bulletin board so that students can refer to them as needed. Such rules might include the following:

- Do not let others do all of the work.
- Use quiet voices.

- Move quietly.
- Share materials.
- Talk about problems, but don't argue.
- Be polite to one another.

Duties of Group Members

Each group member may be assigned a specific role that changes daily or weekly. Some roles can be eliminated or modified depending on the activity and grade level.

Recorder Writes group answers and strategies used; can also act as the reporter for the group.

Reader Reads problems, text selections, directions, and so on.

Facilitator Makes sure everyone is on task and encourages participation from each group member. Uses positive phrases such as the following:

- "We need to work on problem three."
- "Which step is next?"

Gatekeeper Makes sure one person does not monopolize the activity and ensures equal participation. Uses positive phrases, such as the following:

- "Denise, how would you do this?"
- "Do you agree, Eric?"
- "What do you think, Shawna?"

Materials/Supply Handler Gathers and returns all materials needed for group activities.

Summarizer Sums up group solutions, opinions, or findings.

Duties of the Teacher

- Explains the activity.
- Monitors groups to make sure they are working in the right direction, and that behavior is appropriate.
- Answers group questions and provides assistance as necessary.
- Assesses group/individual skills.
- Provides closure for each lesson or activity.

Group Structures

The following group structures are recommended by Spencer Kagan and other cooperative-learning experts:

Numbered Heads Together This is a simple structure for reviewing basic facts and general information.

- Students in each group are numbered 1 to 4.
- The teacher asks a question.
- Students put their heads together and discuss possible solutions.
- The teacher calls a number at random. The student in each group with that number reports his or her group's findings.

Pairs-Check This structure works well for learning a new skill.

- Groups of four students break into pairs.
- One student in each pair works a problem while the other coaches as necessary.
- The coach checks the solution. If a pair does not agree on an answer, they may ask the other pair in their group. If the whole group does not agree, the teacher then helps the group.
- Students continue in this manner, changing roles after each problem.

Inside-Outside Circle Students make two circles, one inside the other. Students in the inside circle face the students in the outside circle so each student on the inside has a partner on the outside.

The teacher asks a question and partners discuss a solution. If they can't find an answer, they may confer with students on either side of them. The teacher calls for a response from either the inside or outside circle of students.

Inside-Outside Circle: Variations with Flash Cards Students have flash cards with questions on one side and answers on the other. They rotate in their circles so they practice with a new partner for each rotation.

Think-Pair-Share The teacher asks a question. Students are given a specified amount of time to think about the answer. Once the time has elapsed, students share their ideas, opinions, and answers with teammates or partners. The teacher then asks for volunteers to share their solutions with the class.

Expert Jigsaw The jigsaw strategy for cooperative grouping is different because it involves the initial use of rather large groups (8-to-10 students). Suppose you want the class to learn computation tricks. The class is divided into three large groups. Each group learns and practices a different computation trick. Each member of the group must be able to perform and explain the trick. The three large groups then "jigsaw" to form new groups. Each of the new groups consists of three students, each an expert on one of the tricks. Each student performs and explains his or her trick to the other two students.

For many students, working with so many others at one time may be a new experience. However, an important part of the jigsaw strategy is that the students are responsible for finding ways to work together. You might expect one or all of the following things to happen.

- Students decide to work together as a large group with one or two students acting as the group leader(s).
- Students decide to initially work individually, in partnerships, or in smaller groups. Then they come together in the larger group to compare their work.

- Students are unable to decide what to do in such a large unstructured situation. They are unable to organize the group and therefore are not able to complete their assignment.

If the last situation occurs, you will need to provide some guidance. After allowing the students some time to try to organize themselves, you might assist them by asking the following questions:

- What is the task that you are trying to accomplish?
- What are the difficulties that you are having now?
- Can you think of any other ways that you could organize your group to complete the task?
- What are some of the ways that the other groups have organized themselves to complete the task?

Group-Related Resources

Adrini, Beth and Spencer Kagan. *Cooperative Learning and Mathematics.* San Juan Capistrano, California: Kagan Cooperative Learning, 1992.

Johnson, David W. and Roger T. Johnson. *Learning Mathematics and Cooperative Learning.* Edina, Minnesota: Interaction Book Company, 1991.

Johnson, David W., Roger T. Johnson, and Edythe Johnson Holubec. *The Nuts and Bolts of Cooperative Learning.* Edina, Minnesota: Interaction Book Company, 1994.

Kagan, Spencer. *Cooperative Learning.* San Juan Capistrano, California: Kagan Cooperative Learning, 1992.

Group Responses

Group-response activities allow all students to participate at their own levels without being put on the spot. More skilled students will have the opportunity to lead while others hear them and are thereby strengthened in the concepts in which they are weak.

Establish a lively rhythm, with responses given simultaneously and clearly. Keep group-response activities brief. If you have students work in small groups or sit around tables, you can focus on one group at a time, even if the whole class is responding. This will help you identify students who may need extra help.

Ideas for "Built-in" Mathematics

The following suggestions were contributed by teachers who piloted the *Everyday Mathematics* program:

- When disputes between two students arise that could be settled in either one's favor, have each disputant choose a number between 1 and 100. Pick a number yourself and tell it to a third party or write it down secretly. Explain that the one who guesses closer to your number will be the "winner." After settling the issue, ask questions such as, "Is this fair? What makes it fair?" You can extend or limit the range of numbers as appropriate for the situation or the grade level.

- Whenever the opportunity to choose an option presents itself, have the students vote. Tell them to vote for what they want, and tell them that they can vote only once. Be sure they understand that the option receiving the most votes is the one by which they all must abide. Students can then tally, count, and compare totals. In case of ties, ask the students to suggest a fair way to proceed.

- Whenever possible, have students line up according to specified categories, such as "everyone wearing something red" or "everyone wearing brown shoes." Extend the routine by using logical operators like *or, and, not,* and so on: "Everyone wearing a belt or shorts and not wearing brown shoes."

- Alternatively, have students line up without revealing the category to them. For this version of "What's My Rule?" determine a category and then call out the names of students who fit the category. Then ask the class to explain why you chose those particular students. (*"What's My Rule?"*) Don't insist on your rule if students see one that is equally valid. ("What I had in mind was . . . , but yours works, too," or "I didn't think of yours.")

- Dice and spinners are good random-number generators. You can make nonstandard dice by putting stick-on number labels on standard dice or on wooden cubes. Vary the numbers to make new games.

- When minor decisions need to be made or when you can't quite think of a way to perform a particular task, take a few minutes to have students think about the problem. Discuss their ideas— sometimes they can be great! This also gives students a chance to solve real problems.

- If you have a Math Center, don't let it get too cluttered. Introduce new items and remove old ones to maintain students' interest.

- Assign an "identification number" to each student at the beginning of the year, possibly using large numbers (e.g., 10,001) with older students. Once you have assigned students their numbers, you can then use those numbers to number non-consumable items such as books, calculators, rulers, and other tools the students may borrow during the year. This will help you match a misplaced item with its user. You can also use the numbers in various games and activities such as the following:
  - Tell students, "Prime numbers stand up," or "Multiples of 5 line up in order (or count off in order)."
  - Write the identification cards on small slips of paper and put them in a container. Draw a number at random when you need to pick someone for an activity or task. Most students will readily recognize the fairness of this method of selection.

Students with Special Needs

Everyday Mathematics is a hands-on curriculum that builds on students' interests and experiences, reinforcing content over time.

These and other key features make it an accessible and effective program for all students, even a class with a wide range of special needs.

Pacing is important in the overall schematic of the *Everyday Mathematics* curriculum. Since the program is designed to continually build on students' prior experiences, topics and concepts are revisited in a number of ways throughout the year and in the years that follow. Do not dwell on one skill area or concept, even if some have yet to master it. *Everyday Mathematics* provides many opportunities for students to master the content. Staying too long with a topic may help some students attain temporary mastery, but for maximum long-term retention, it is best to follow the basic structure of the curriculum as it is written.

When changes to lesson content or instruction do need to be made in order to accommodate specific students, the authors recommend an approach of modification, rather than supplementation. Modify lessons only when there is a mismatch between the learner and the type of instruction or materials, or within the task assigned. Focus on the simplest change possible and be sensitive to the social aspects of modification.

The lessons in the *Teacher's Lesson Guide* include specific information about modifying content and/or instruction to meet the needs of particular students. The "Options for Individualizing" component, which can be found at the end of almost every lesson, suggests optional activities for extra practice, reteaching, and enrichment to reinforce, extend, or fine-tune the main content of that lesson. Additionally, "Adjusting the Activity" suggestions provide ideas for making particular activities more or less challenging.

Be sure that all students have a chance to participate in learning games. Modify the games to best meet students' needs, if necessary, or model game strategies prior to playing games. Many important concepts and skills are reinforced through games in *Everyday Mathematics*. Students at all levels can participate and gain from these experiences.

As you assess students' progress, examine and analyze individual responses through a variety of activities, varying the types of cues given and responses required (visual, auditory, tactile, verbal, written, drawing a diagram, and so on). Ask the following questions to determine what types of modification may be needed:

- Is the task developmentally too difficult?
- Is there a mismatch between instructional and learning styles or between required and preferred response modes?
- Is the task too lengthy?
- Is there a pattern to the errors?
- Are there environmental barriers to learning such as distractions, inappropriate seating, and so on?
- What are this student's strengths?

If students are involved in gifted or special education programs, network with other teachers, counselors, or program leaders. Share information, objectives, and strategies within the Individual Education Plan (IEP) to best meet the needs of each student. Monitor the IEP objectives to determine whether they need to be modified when tasks, assessments, or assignments are changed.

Involve the students in helping themselves and one another. Promote student accountability by involving students in setting goals, monitoring progress toward their goals, planning practice activities, and seeking and receiving help from peers, staff members, or parents. Explain to students what they should do when they get stuck on a task. *For example:*

- Think about the problem or task carefully.
- Use a predetermined signal to indicate the need for assistance from a peer or an adult.
- Work on another activity or task until help is available.

Provide opportunities for peer tutoring as well as cross-age peer tutoring. Use math buddies from upper grades to practice math strategies or play math games.

When sending Study Links home, provide completed examples, definitions, or further explanations to help students have a successful experience at home. At times it may be helpful for students to have their *Student Reference Books* at hand when they work on Study Links. Read and discuss the directions with students prior to sending the Study Links home. Also send home games for students to play with parents. Use parent volunteers in the classroom who can play math games and assist during guided practice. Utilize other available adults in the building during math time by arranging opportunities for students to play math games with the principal, custodians, cooks, specialists, and so on.

Language Diversity

Good instruction in mathematics and ESL education share many teaching strategies. *Everyday Mathematics* supports an effective learning environment in mathematics for the ESL student by incorporating group work into daily lessons, teaching English through content that is relevant to students' experiences, and developing mathematical language proficiency through the use of manipulatives, models, and demonstrations. The *Teacher's Lesson Guide* also includes occasional Adjusting the Activity notes and Options for Individualizing activities that focus on language diversity.

Daily group work is strongly encouraged. *Everyday Mathematics* provides opportunities for students to use and hear language through games and activities in student journals. In small groups, students have more opportunities to express ideas, ask questions, and clarify their thinking. Procedures for working in groups ought to be established early in the year. Group work is complemented by whole-class instruction, in which the teacher models and uses mathematical language to reinforce skills and concepts addressed during group work.

English, as with any foreign language, is learned through content and contact that are relevant to the students. With *Everyday Mathematics* there are opportunities for students to experience mathematics in many contexts. Attention is paid to teaching vocabulary in contexts relevant to the students. Concrete examples, visual aids, and diagrams from students' experiences and backgrounds are all provided. Involving students physically in the activity—asking all students to show their responses by raising fingers or making other hand motions, for example—is often effective.

Developing mathematical language proficiency in *Everyday Mathematics* is accomplished through written and oral activities within a problem-solving context. Conceptual development is enhanced through the use of concrete aids, models, and discussion.

Students have many opportunities to explain their reasoning in their journals, on slates, and orally. They may represent their thinking in multiple ways. If they lack the skills to explain their thinking in writing, their text can be supplemented with drawings, diagrams, or models.

Substitute Teachers

The *Everyday Mathematics* approach may be unfamiliar to some substitute teachers, so you may want to provide additional materials for those times when you must be absent. Many lessons can be handled by substitutes, especially if they let the students think things through for themselves. Here are some suggestions:

- Reserve the Math Boxes from several lessons or create extra Math Boxes of your own. Routines like "What's My Rule?" problems can also be included.

- Set aside several engaging games for students to play. Game days are always a favorite, and yet it can sometimes be difficult to find time for them.

- Prepare suggestions for practice with Fact Triangles. Students can sort the facts by strategy or into facts that they know and those they still need to practice. Partners can take turns quizzing each other. Known facts can be recorded in the *Math Journal*.

- Make an "emergency box" with activities to be done on days when your absence is unexpected. As you teach, identify activities from *Everyday Mathematics* that could be included.

Organizing Routines and Displays

Daily Routines

In *K–3 Everyday Mathematics,* students took an active role in daily routines such as taking attendance, keeping track of the date, counting the days in school, observing and recording weather conditions, and managing the daily schedule and classroom job assignments. These routines provided numerous opportunities to encounter mathematics in everyday contexts and to develop and practice skills in all mathematical strands. While fourth, fifth, and sixth graders are probably too advanced to benefit from spending a great deal of time on these routines, you may want to consider continuing and extending one or two of them in your classroom. The following sections contain some suggestions. Feel free to add your own and to look for the mathematics potential in routines that are already in place in your classroom.

- If you collect and save daily attendance information, students can use the data later in the school year. For example, they might make graphs to investigate trends, such as whether certain weekdays or certain months have substantially more absences than others. This may lead to interesting discussions about possible reasons.

- Use a number line to establish a school year timeline. The time line can be the basis of one of the rotating class jobs, that of class historian, whose responsibilities would include writing about something memorable from each school day and attaching it to the timeline. The number line can also serve as a frame of reference for counting and numeration activities throughout the year.

- Collect daily temperature and/or weather data. For temperature, use both Fahrenheit and Celsius scales so students have practice comparing and converting between them. Make graphs or other displays to look for trends in the data. In previous grades, students made bar graphs of temperature data by color-coding sections of a thermometer scale. Older students could make line graphs of temperature data for each day or of average temperatures for each week or month.

- You might also want to use a weather map from a local or national daily newspaper on a monthly basis so that students can observe that temperatures change greatly in some parts of the country and remain fairly constant in others. If possible, mount each map as it is used or keep the maps on the Class Data Pad (see below) so that the entire nine-month school period can eventually be seen and the data compared. These weather maps also help students become familiar with the United States map in a meaningful way.

Class Data Pad

Throughout the year, you and the students will have opportunities to collect information that will greatly enrich the content of the program. Such information might include data collected in and outside the classroom to be analyzed and graphed as well as interesting facts and information to be used in making up number stories.

Much of this information can be used several times over the course of the year. For example, students might find the middle number for a collection of data; graph the data set at some other time; and compare it with a related set of data at still another time. In order to save this information for repeated use, we suggest that you record it on a Class Data Pad—a large pad of newsprint. Although you could set aside a portion of a bulletin board or the chalkboard to record data, this might be inconvenient, because both have limited surface area. With the Class Data Pad you can save sheets on the pad for later use. If you label large, stick-on notes and position them so that they extend over the edges of pages, you can easily index and retrieve stored data when students write their own number stories or when you need information for problems.

Semipermanent Chalk—A Useful Display Tool

There will be times when you will want to write or draw things on the board that cannot be erased with a standard board eraser. You can do this by using "semipermanent" chalk. For example, you might want to draw a picture of a geoboard by making an array of dots using the semipermanent chalk—and then use regular chalk to draw a figure on the geoboard. If you then want to draw a new figure, you can erase the old figure with a board eraser, while leaving the geoboard dots intact. The semipermanent drawing can be washed off later using a damp cloth or sponge.

Here are two ways to make "semipermanent" chalk:

- Dissolve sugar in some hot water until the water can no longer absorb any additional sugar. Drop a piece of porous chalk into the sugar solution and let it stand overnight. The chalk will soak up the sugar solution and become resistant to erasure. When not in use, keep the chalk in a sealed container so that it will not dry up completely. When you make a mark on the board with this chalk, the mark may not be visible at first. It will become visible once the chalk mark has dried. Once dried, the marks cannot be erased with a board eraser, but can be easily erased with a wet cloth or sponge.
- To make a semipermanent drawing on the chalkboard, thoroughly wet the area where you want it. Draw with regular chalk while the board is wet. Wait for it to dry completely. Now you will be able to write on the base drawing and erase a number of times without losing the base drawing. To remove the base drawing, simply wash it off with water.

Tools

Tools are extremely important in the *Everyday Mathematics* program. The authors define tools broadly, to include anything that can be used to facilitate mathematical thinking and problem solving. Calculators, rulers, and manipulatives (such as pattern blocks or geoboards) can be employed as tools, as can paper and pencil, slates, and reference books, to name a few. *Everyday Mathematics* strives to develop students' skills in effectively using a variety of tools and in choosing the proper tool for each particular problem.

By emphasizing the power of tools and helping students learn how to employ them intelligently, *Everyday Mathematics* is working to make the mathematics in school resemble mathematics of the real world. Without this type of approach, school math risks becoming abstract and disconnected from everyday life—a complaint that many adults make about their own mathematics education!

The following sections focus on tools that are often used in *Everyday Mathematics*. Although we have classified these tools by type and/or primary function, keep in mind that many of the tools described below can be used for a variety of purposes. More information about these and other mathematical tools can be found in some of the Mathematical Topics essays, which include discussions of specific tools that are useful for the teaching, learning, and application of particular topics.

Electronic tools

Electronic tools for mathematics education include calculators, computers, and computer peripherals such as probes, videodiscs, and CDs. Access to electronic tools is varied, and *Everyday Mathematics* is quite conservative in its assumptions about which tools are available to every student. In fact, students are expected to have access only to four-function calculators in Grades K–3 and to scientific calculators in Grades 4–6.

Calculators

In the quarter-century since electronic calculators have become widely available, many researchers have studied their effects on how students learn. The preponderance of evidence from these studies suggests that the proper use of calculators can enhance students' understanding and mastery of arithmetic, promote good number sense, and improve problem-solving skills.

Two summaries of this research are "Research on Calculators in Mathematics Education," by Ray Hembree and Donald J. Dessart, and "A Meta-analysis of Outcomes from the Use of Calculators in Mathematics Education," by Brian A. Smith. (For details on these and other calculator studies, see the sources cited at the end of this section.) Smith's study also concludes that calculator usage does not hinder the development of paper-and-pencil skills. Moreover, both teacher experience and educational research show that most students develop good judgment about when to use and when not to use calculators. Students need to learn how to decide when it is appropriate to solve an arithmetic problem by estimating or calculating mentally, by using paper and pencil, or by using a calculator. The evidence indicates that students who use calculators are able to choose appropriately.

Everyday Mathematics encourages students to think about developing algorithms as they solve problems. To foster this habit, students need to study particular algorithms, but once the algorithms are understood, repeated use will become tedious.

One reason that calculators are so helpful in the mathematics curriculum is that they free both students and teachers from having to spend so much time on dull, repetitive, and unproductive tasks. Calculators also allow students to solve interesting, everyday problems requiring computations that might otherwise be too difficult for them to perform, including problems that arise outside of mathematics class. There is no evidence to suggest that this will cause students to become dependent on calculators or make them unable to solve problems mentally or with paper and pencil.

In fact, the biggest obstacle with calculators is that sometimes the display in the window is nonsense. Reasons for this could be that the calculator wasn't properly cleared, a number or operation was miskeyed, or the analysis of the problem was faulty. For whatever reason, sometimes the calculator's answer just doesn't make sense, and the user must determine whether an answer is reasonable according to the context of the original problem situation. *Everyday Mathematics* stresses this final step of checking to make sure the answer generated by a calculator makes sense. It is important for teachers to emphasize it in class as well.

Before the availability of inexpensive calculators, the elementary school mathematics curriculum was designed primarily so that students would become skilled at carrying out algorithms. Thus, there was little time left for students to learn to think mathematically and solve problems. Calculators enable students to think about the problems themselves, rather than focusing on carrying out algorithms without mistakes.

Sources:

Groves, Susie and Stacey Kaye. "Calculators in Primary Mathematics: Exploring Numbers before Teaching Algorithms." In *The Teaching and Learning of Algorithms in School Mathematics,* edited by Lorna J. Morrow, pp. 120–129. Reston, VA: National Council of Teachers of Mathematics, 1998.

Hembree, Ray and Donald J. Dessart. "Research on Calculators in Mathematics Education." In *Calculators in Mathematics Education: 1992 Yearbook,* edited by James T. Fey and Christian R. Hirsch, pp. 23–32. Reston, VA: National Council of Teachers of Mathematics, 1992.

National Research Council. *Everybody Counts: A Report to the Nation on the Future of Mathematics Education,* pp. 46–48, 61–63. Washington, D.C.: National Academy Press, 1989.

Smith, Brian A. "A Meta-analysis of Outcomes from the Use of Calculators in Mathematics Education." *Dissertation Abstracts International* 58 (1997):787A.

Types of Calculators As with all electronic technology, the types of calculators and features they contain are always changing. There are calculators that print on paper, send infrared beams to computers or other calculators, draw pictures, graphs, and geometric constructions. Who knows what they'll do tomorrow? This section briefly describes five general types of calculators that students in Grades K–6 may encounter in and out of school.

- *Four-function calculators* Four-function calculators originally got their name because all they did was add, subtract, multiply, and divide. Thirty years ago such a calculator could cost hundreds of dollars. Today, however, it is difficult to find a recently manufactured four-function calculator that does only those four operations. Most have at least a percent key and maybe a square root key as well. Even most of the 'credit card' calculators that are given as promotional items with magazine subscriptions and the like have the percent key. So today, four-function calculators usually do more than four functions, but they are still referred to by that name because they fall short of being scientific calculators.

As a teacher, you should be less concerned with the number of available functions than with how the four-function calculator works. Some four-function calculators are programmed to follow the algebraic order of operations; others are not. To find out whether or not a calculator is an algebraic calculator, you can try the following test: Key in the sequence 10 [−] 2 [×] 4 [=] into the calculator. If the result is 2, yours is an algebraic calculator (the most common kind these days). If the result is 32, it is not. The algebraic calculator multiplies the 2 and 4 first and subtracts the result, 8, from 10. The other calculator does the operations in the order in which they were entered: $10 - 2 = 8$ and $8 * 4 = 32$. If a calculator has parentheses keys [(] and [)]), then it is almost certainly algebraic.

- *Scientific calculators* More complicated and capable than four-function calculators are so-called scientific calculators. These calculators use scientific notation to display numbers that have more digits than will fit on the display. Usually, such calculators also have keys, such as [E] or [EE], for entering numbers in scientific notation. For example, to enter $2.345 * 10^8$, you would press 2 [.] 3 4 5 [EE] 8.

Scientific calculators tend to have a great many more functions that four-function calculators. Beside the enter-exponent key used for entering numbers in scientific notation, they usually also have a separate key for exponentiation with bases other than 10, often marked [EXP], [y^x], or [^]. To enter 3^5, for example, you would press 3 [^] 5. Such exponentiation keys can also be used to enter numbers in scientific notation. To enter $2.345 * 10^8$, you would press 2 [.] 3 4 5 [×] 1 0 [^] 8. Scientific calculators may also have keys for the trigonometric functions ([COS], [SIN], [TAN], and their inverses), certain combinatorial functions (permutations and combinations), statistics (including regression and correlation), and logarithms. (These are not topics in *Everyday Mathematics*.)

Scientific calculators also conform to the conventional rules for the order of operations, rather than simply carrying out operations in the order in which they are entered. (Some exotic calculators observe a different order of operations known as reverse Polish, or postfix, notation in which A + B is represented as AB+. Such calculators are usually used by engineers and similar professionals.)

Students in Grades 4–6 of *Everyday Mathematics* are expected to have scientific calculators.

- **Fraction calculators** A fraction calculator allows you to enter and manipulate fractions in fractional form. Such calculators generally allow the user to compute with fractions, simplify fractions, and convert between fractions and decimals. Fraction calculators differ in their procedures for handling fractions, so you will need to check the owner's manual for details. Fraction calculators often have a special key for integer division. This key, usually [INT ÷], can be used to carry out whole-number division with quotient and remainder. For example, pressing 2 3 [÷] 5 [ENTER =] will yield 4.6, but pressing 2 3 [INT ÷] 5 [ENTER =] will yield 4 R 3.

- **Graphing calculators** Graphing calculators let you enter equations and then graph them on a coordinate plane. As with the other types of calculators, new graphing calculators enter the market with even more bells and whistles than the previous versions; nowadays, many are programmable, do statistics, and make tables of values; one such calculator even contains dynamic geometry software. Students do not need a graphing calculator for *Everyday Mathematics*.

- **Computer calculators** There are an assortment of calculators written to run on computers. Some Macintoshes, for example, currently include a graphing calculator program with the machine. Four-function type calculator programs have been standard features of most computer operating systems since personal computers were invented. If you use computers with your students, you might want to check and see what calculator program is available and use the preceding comments to help determine its type.

Key Sequences As with any tool, proper and effective use of a calculator requires instruction. Research has shown that students using calculators who have had no instruction in their use do not do calculations any better than students not using them. Whenever an operation that may be performed on a calculator is introduced, students should be explicitly instructed about the new key and key sequence (see below). It is recommended that you draw new key(s) on the chalkboard, on an overhead transparency, or use a poster which some manufacturers supply, and then allow students to practice the new skill on their calculators.

The order in which keys need to be pressed to accomplish a calculation is called a **key sequence.** In keystroke sequences in *Everyday Mathematics,* non-numeric keys are written with square brackets or are shown by pictures of the actual keys. Numbers are always written without brackets, with extra space between the digits.

NOTE: *Everyday Mathematics* recommends the use of the TI-15 calculator in Grades 4–6. This is a scientific, fraction calculator. For more information, see "Key Sequences" later in this section, Section 3.4.1 of the Algorithms essay, and the *Student Reference Book.*

management guide

For example, the keystroke sequence for the expression 12 − 3 + 5 may be written as

$$12 \, [-] \, 3 \, [+] \, 5 \, [=]$$

or

$$12 \, \ominus \, 3 \, \oplus \, 5 \, \boxed{\text{Enter}}$$

A key sequence is a form of algorithm. Encouraging students to "discover" an appropriate key sequence is a fine first activity at any grade level and fits well into *Everyday Mathematics'* algorithm invention philosophy.

Using calculators may require learning alternative symbols for operations. Study your calculator manual to become familiar with the symbols for operations on your calculators.

The four basic arithmetic keys [+], [−], [×], and [÷], along with the number keys, decimal-point key, and clear key, are introduced by *Third Grade Everyday Mathematics*. In Grades 4–6, students learn to use a variety of other keys, including those for manipulating fractions, using the calculator's memory, defining a constant operation, and exponentiation. For further information, see Section 3.4.1 of the Algorithms essay and the calculator section of the *Student Reference Book*.

NOTE: Before you begin using calculators, they should be marked in some way. For example, mark students' names on calculators that they supply and identification numbers on those that the school supplies.

When using calculators as a teaching tool in the classroom, everyone in the room ought to have the same calculator. Since there are variations in calculator symbols and key sequences required to perform various tasks, it can be confusing if several different calculators are being used at the same time in your class. *Everyday Mathematics* recommends use of the TI-15 calculator in Grades 4–6. This is a scientific, fraction calculator. If you are using a different calculator with your class and the key sequences in the lessons do not work, look at your calculator's directions to find out the correct key sequence for your particular model.

Computers

Because computer access and availability vary widely across the United States, computer-based activities are currently not integrated into the core curriculum but are occasionally included as optional investigations. Students in Grade 6, for example, work with spreadsheets in optional activities.

Numerous existing software programs can be used with *Everyday Mathematics*. Some of these software programs are designed as instructional tools that can be used by teachers to model, demonstrate, or explain mathematical concepts. Other programs can be used by students for concept development, practice, enrichment, motivation, and exploration. To assist you in choosing appropriate software to meet your instructional needs, Everyday Learning Corporation publishes an *Everyday Mathematics Technology Guide and Software Correlation*. This handbook matches specific units and lessons to existing software programs. Copies may be obtained from the publisher (1 800 382 7670).

Spreadsheets A **spreadsheet** has been a business tool for a long time. It gets its name from a ledger sheet for financial records, similar to the one shown below. Such sheets were often large pages, folded or taped, that were spread out for examination.

	A	B	C
1	Player	Hits	Runs
2	Carl	9	4
3	Amala	5	2
4	Noreen	1	0
5	Doug	11	5
6	David	3	3
7	Annina	2	1
8	Ted	7	3
9	Raoul	12	7
10	Cheryl	3	0
11			
12	Total	53	25

When one or more numbers in a spreadsheet are changed, related numbers on the sheet may need to be recalculated and changed. This is called *updating* or revising a spreadsheet. For example, if Amala got another hit, then the cell B3 in the spreadsheet above would be updated to a 6. The total in cell B12 would also need to be changed to 54.

When done by hand on ledger paper, spreadsheets are a practical way of organizing data, but their usefulness is limited. What if you forget to update the total? When computerized spreadsheets became available, their usefulness exploded, primarily because values in cells in the sheet could be *dynamically linked* to other values by formulas. This means that changing one value, say updating Amala's hits, automatically changes the values of any cells dependent on that value, in this case the total number of hits for the team.

As one of the first practical applications of microcomputers in business, spreadsheet programs were instantly successful. They put the microcomputer revolution into high gear and revolutionized business practice at the same time. Over the years, spreadsheet programs such as Lotus 1-2-3™ and Microsoft Excel™ have become increasingly sophisticated; they can solve complicated financial problems, do a variety of statistical analyses, and create wonderfully informative graphs and charts. Most of your students will probably use some form of computer spreadsheet in their lives.

As optional activities, sixth graders use spreadsheets:

- to calculate and compare mean and median values of data sets;
- to practice using formulas for calculating sums and products dynamically; and
- to examine graphs based on the data and formulas they have entered.

The Internet As the Internet has become more widely available to the public and to schools, *Everyday Mathematics* has incorporated it into the program in a modest way. Fourth through sixth grade teachers are advised of Web sites that seem destined to survive over the years and which supplement activities in a substantive way. At this writing these include the following.

Mathematics Sites:

UCSMP EM Center
http://everydaymath.uchicago.edu/

Everyday Learning Corporation
http://www.everydaylearning.com/em/index.html

Eisenhower National Clearinghouse
http://enc.org

NCTM
http://www.nctm.org/

The Math Forum
http://forum.swarthmore.edu

Shell Centre
http://acorn.educ.nottingham.ac.uk/ShellCent/

For **Fourth Grade Everyday Mathematics:**

The CIA World FactBook
http://www.cia.gov/cia/publications/factbook/index.html

For **Fifth Grade Everyday Mathematics:**

The U.S. Bureau of the Census
http://www.census.gov/

National Weather Service
http://www.nws.noaa.gov

Information about the history of pi
http://www-history.mcs.st-andrews.ac.uk/history/HistTopics/Pi_through_the_ages.html

For **Sixth Grade Everyday Mathematics:**

NASA K–12 Internet Initiative
http://quest.arc.nasa.gov/

NASA Spacelink
http://spacelink.msfc.nasa.gov/

Jet Propulsion Laboratory Planetary Data System
http://stardust.jpl.nasa.gov

NASA Ames Research Center
http://www.arc.nasa.gov

It is likely that as you read this there are new Web sites just as relevant to specific activities in *Everyday Mathematics*. Keep in mind too that often the most important sites for teachers are the search engines.

Internet Search Engines

Alta Vista	http://altavista.com
Lycos	http://www.lycos.com
Yahoo!	http://yahoo.com
Google	http://www.google.com

Tools for Exploring Data and Chance

Along with measurement tools for collecting data, random-number generators play an important role in *Everyday Mathematics,* especially within the context of games.

The Probability Meter is another tool for exploring data and chance that is discussed in this section.

Random-Number Generators

Many games involve generating numbers randomly to inject both an element of chance and a sense of fairness. Several tools for helping students generate random numbers are listed below. Often these devices do not generate perfectly random outcomes, but they are good enough for most purposes.

The Everything Math Deck This deck of cards consists of four sets of number cards 0–10 and one set of number cards 11–20. Fractions are on the reverse side of the 0–10 cards. You can limit the range of numbers to be generated simply by removing some of the cards from the deck. If the whole deck is used, you have a greater chance of drawing a 0–10 card than a 11–20 card. To use the cards, simply shuffle and draw. The better the shuffle, the more unpredictable the draw will be.

Standard Playing Cards Use the 2–9 cards, the aces for 1s, and the queens for 0s. Draw one card to get a 1-in-10 chance of a digit 0–9. Draw two cards to make double-digit numbers, and so on. (If more than one card is drawn, you will need to decide whether to replace it before another card is drawn. If the first card is replaced in the deck and the deck is reshuffled, the probability will remain the same for each draw. If the card is not replaced, the chance of pulling that digit decreases.)

Dice Use a regular die to generate numbers 1 through 6. Use a polyhedral die (with 12 or 20 sides) to extend the range of numbers to be generated. Note that rolling more than one die and adding the resulting number of dots produces a nonuniform distribution of possible outcomes. For example, if you roll two standard dice, there are 36 possible ways for them to land. Only one of the 36 has a sum of 2 (two 1s), but six of the 36 have a sum of 7 ([1,6], [2,5], [3,4], [4,3], [5,2] and [6,1]). (See below.) Therefore, the chance of rolling a 7 is much greater than the chance of rolling a 2.

sums of two dice

Shaking a die in a cup may lead to slightly more random results than throwing the die by hand.

For more on probability tools, see Section 4.2.2 of the Data and Chance essay.

See page 10 for directions on how to transform an ordinary deck of cards into a substitute for the Everything Math Deck.

management guide

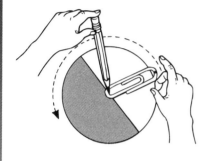

Egg Cartons Label each egg carton cup with a number. For example, you might label the cups 0–11. Place one or more pennies or centimeter cubes inside the carton, close the lid, shake the carton, and then open the carton to see which cups the objects landed in. Randomness depends on how thoroughly the carton is shaken. This is probably the least random of all the methods in this list.

Spinners Spinners are used throughout *Everyday Mathematics,* usually in games. They are extremely useful for helping students visualize chances. There are many commercially available spinners, though it is not necessary to purchase them. Students can use a pencil and paper clip as shown in the margin. Use either a large (2″) or standard (1″) paper clip for the part that spins. The larger size is preferred because it spins more easily. Make a mark, as a pointer, at one end of the paper clip, using a permanent felt-tip pen.

The spinning mat may be drawn on cardstock or paper. Sometimes a mat is supplied as a master or journal page. If you make your own mat, start with a circle or square big enough for the paper clip. Mark the center of the circle, choose the number and size of the divisions, and then measure the appropriate angles. For example, six equal wedges would be 360° divided by 6, or 60° each. Of course the wedges do not have to be the same size, as in the *Money Game* spinner mat shown in the margin. You can make the edge of the mat any shape you wish.

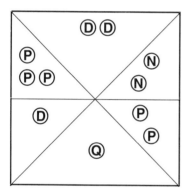

Money Game spinner mat

Before spinning, tape the mat to a level surface. You need only two small pieces of tape, one at the top and one at the bottom. To spin, place the tip of a pen or pencil on the center of the circle and within the paper clip (as shown in the diagram). Flick the paper clip about halfway between the center of the circle and the tip of the paper clip. (Flicking the paper clip near the pointer end will generate less of a spin.)

Calculators Many scientific calculators have a key that generates a random number. Usually it is labeled [RND] or [RAND]. How the key works varies from one brand of calculator to another. Check your calculator's directions.

Calculators that do not have a random-number key can be used to generate random numbers in various ways, including by extracting square roots.

For example, random numbers can be generated on the TI-15 calculator by setting a constant operation to extract square roots. After a seed number is entered, pressing the constant operation key will generate a sequence of decimal numbers. The last digits of these numbers are close to random.

Example:

Key Sequence	Display
(Op1) (∧) 0 (·) 5 (Op1)	Op1 ∧0.5
578 (Op1)	Op1 578∧0.5 24.04163056
(Op1)	Op1 4.903226546
(Op1)	Op1 2.214323045
(Op1)	Op1 1.488060162
(Op1)	Op1 1.219860714

NOTE: Technically, a calculator-generated random number is called a pseudo-random number because the machine has to follow an algorithm to do the job! The algorithm varies, but often consists of a series of operations on an irrational number like π or √2, rounding, and reading some digit or digits in the result. Statistically, it can be shown that the numbers resulting from using the [RAND] key are as unpredictable as we might practically need, and certainly as unpredictable as those generated by any of the other methods discussed in this section.

Probability Meter

Students encounter informal games and activities dealing with probability beginning in first grade. Starting in fourth grade, probability ideas are extended and made more formal. In fifth grade, the concept of probability is extended by means of a Probability Meter. The **Probability Meter** visually represents the likelihood of the occurrence of a given event. Throughout the year, the probabilities of events occurring are recorded on stick-on notes and placed on the meter.

Numerical representations of chance events are presented as fractions, decimals, and/or percents to familiarize students with the different ways probability is expressed. The Probability Meter also serves as an expanded number line for rational numbers between 0 and 1. For some numbers, several notations are shown; for example, the repeating decimal $0.3\overline{3}$ and $\frac{1}{3}$ are shown.

Tools for Geometry

In *Everyday Mathematics,* the study of geometry involves many hands-on experiences, such as manipulating pattern blocks and attribute blocks, tracing shapes from templates, working with geoboards, cutting out shapes, folding shapes, drawing shapes with a straightedge and compass, constructing shapes out of straws, and constructing 3-dimensional figures from 2-dimensional patterns or nets.

Compass and Straightedge

Students use a compass and straightedge for geometry constructions beginning in *Fourth Grade Everyday Mathematics.* Fourth and fifth

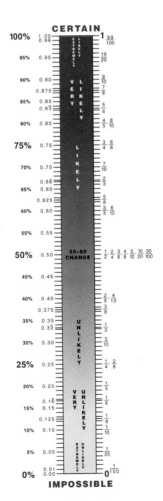

Probability Meter

For more on geometry tools, see Section 5.13.3 of the Geometry essay.

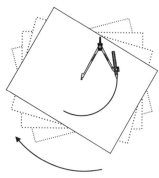

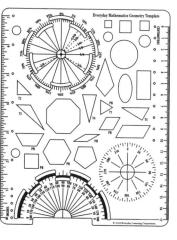

Geometry Template

grade students need plenty of practice in simply drawing a circle with a compass. There are two methods—fix the paper and rotate the compass, or hold the compass still and rotate the paper. Students experiment and select the method they find easier.

To demonstrate constructions at the chalkboard, you will need a board compass and straightedge; or you can use an overhead projector and a compass with a felt-tip pen. Remind students that a straightedge is for drawing straight lines in constructions, not for measuring. The primary difference between a compass-and-straightedge construction and a drawing or sketch of a geometric figure is that measuring is not allowed in constructions.

Pattern-Block and Geometry Templates

Students in Grades K–3 of *Everyday Mathematics* use a Pattern-Block Template for explorations of plane figures. Beginning in fourth grade, students use a Geometry Template (which might better be called a geometry and measurement template). The number and variety of shapes is increased (compared to the Pattern-Block Template) to help students in their more detailed explorations of categories of triangles and quadrangles. The measuring devices include inch and centimeter scales, a Percent Circle useful for making circle graphs, and both a full-circle and a half-circle protractor.

Pattern Blocks and Geometric Solids

In *K–3 Everyday Mathematics,* students use building blocks and pattern blocks to motivate the study of 1- and 2-dimensional geometry. These activities serve as background for a methodical approach, beginning in fourth grade, to making 2-dimensional maps of structures and 3-dimensional models of prisms and pyramids from 2-dimensional patterns. Pattern blocks are also used for fractions work in Grades 2–6.

Straws and Twist-Ties

From first through fourth grades, students construct 2- and 3-dimensional objects with straws and twist-ties, and in Lesson 3.6 in fifth grade, students use straws and twist-ties to learn about congruent triangles. Although such activities do not appear in the program thereafter, they can be very helpful for students who need more concrete representations of geometric objects. This section has several suggestions to help you manage such activities.

It is important to remember that these activities result in representations of geometric shapes and not to lose sight of the true nature of such shapes. Two-dimensional shapes such as polygons and circles are defined as boundaries of flat regions, without the interiors. For example, a polygon is made up of line segments; the region inside a polygon is not part of the polygon. Similarly, 3-dimensional shapes, such as prisms, pyramids, and cylinders, are made up of flat or curved surfaces, not including the interiors. For example, a rectangular prism is best modeled by an empty cereal box, the box without the corn flakes. Polygons constructed with straws are true representations of such shapes—the straws actually show the line segments. On the other hand, 3-dimensional straw constructions only suggest the actual shapes—the straws are the edges of the 2-dimensional shapes that make up the faces of the 3-dimensional object.

Materials and Advance Preparation The *Everyday Mathematics* authors have found that straw constructions work best if plastic straws are used with twist-ties as connectors. Drinking straws are usually about 8 inches long; some coffee-stirrer straws also work well but are shorter, so directions for some exercises may need to be adjusted if they are used. Straws with small diameters work much better than those with larger diameters.

About 1,000 straws and 2,000 twist-ties are ample for a class of 30 students. Eight-inch, small-diameter drinking straws are available (and inexpensive) in bulk boxes of 500 at party, restaurant-supply, or paper-goods stores. Perhaps the supplier for your school lunchroom can help, but the lunchroom straws themselves probably will not be suitable. Avoid large-diameter and individually wrapped straws.

Four-inch twist-ties that are often used as fasteners for plastic bags work well as connectors. Craft pipe cleaners, cut in halves, are also good connectors, but twist-ties work better and cost far less. Bulk packages of the twist-ties may be available through your grocery store, bakery, or produce market, or at the same party or paper-goods stores that have small-diameter straws. Some businesses respond to requests from schools and may be happy to order additional twist-ties for you at their cost.

Both straws and connectors are reusable. Except for figures that you or the students wish to keep, shapes can be dismantled and the straws and connectors returned to their storage containers for use at other times.

Preparation for Activities You or your students can easily cut straws with scissors to different lengths. For cutting many straws at one time, some paper cutters work well. For most exercises specified in the lessons, three sizes suffice: the standard 8" length, 4" length, and 6" length. You might want to prepare an initial supply of straws in these three sizes. Don't worry about small variations in length. For a few exercises, students may cut full-length straws to meet special conditions. For example, students may be told to construct triangles with no two sides the same length (scalene triangles).

Management of Materials Keep straws and twist-ties in small open boxes or bins so that students can pick them up as directed (often in a Math Message). Lessons often call for straws of various lengths. Try to keep straws with the standard equal lengths together, and a special box for straws of assorted lengths. Work out a routine with students so that straws and twist-ties are returned to their proper

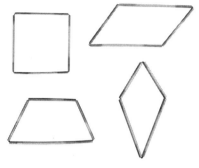

2-D straw constructions

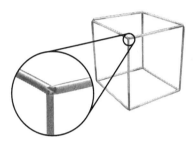

3-D straw constructions

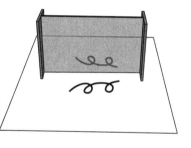

transparent mirror

boxes or bins at the end of a lesson or when shapes are dismantled. Such sorting and clean-up routines have value in and of themselves, in addition to making materials for the next shape-construction exercise easily accessible.

Teaching with Straws and Twist-Ties Teachers have found that most students have little trouble constructing polygons with straws and connectors. The ends of the ties may need to be pinched a little to slide into the straws. If you have to use large-diameter straws, fold back an inch or so of the end of the connector for a tighter joint. (With larger-diameter straws, you may want to try chenille sticks, which are large pipe cleaners available from craft stores.)

To keep the size of polygons with more than five sides within sensible limits, use shorter straws. Except for triangles, polygons are easily twisted so they don't lie "flat." When they are not flat, they are no longer in a plane, thus they are no longer 2-dimensional figures. Have students make polygons on flat surfaces and encourage them to try to keep the polygons flat when picking them up.

For 3-dimensional figures, begin by putting two connectors, or one folded connector, into one end of each straw, so that each can be connected to two other straws. When more than three straws need to be connected, insert additional connectors as needed. Or you could connect pairs of straws and bundle them all together using an additional connector.

Transparent Mirrors

Students in *Fourth Grade Everyday Mathematics* experiment with reflections using transparent mirrors to move and draw reflection images. You are familiar with a regular mirror and the symmetric image you see in it. A transparent mirror also reflects an image, but it has the advantage that you can see through it and trace the mirror image. The drawing in the margin illustrates the reflection of a squiggle as you might see it in a transparent mirror.

As with any new tool, it requires time, practice, and patience to develop skills using a transparent mirror. For accurate placement of images:

- Lean down and look directly through the transparent mirror.
- Use the ends of the mirror to keep it perpendicular to the paper—that is, don't hold the mirror off the desk or table.
- Use the inner part of the recessed edge along the bottom of the mirror to place the mirror on points or lines, or to draw mirror lines.
- Hold the transparent mirror firmly in position with one hand while doing any tracing behind it or drawing lines along its recessed edge.

Transparent mirrors are used by students to study lines of symmetry in figures and to draw reflection images of their own artistic designs. The mirrors are especially useful for drawing reflections in tessellations.

Tools for Measuring

In *Everyday Mathematics,* students begin measuring in Kindergarten. They begin measuring with body parts and other informal tools. As they move through the grades, students learn to use more precise tools in more precise ways. The following section discusses the use of some of the most frequently used measuring tools in *Everyday Mathematics.*

Measuring Sticks and Tapes

Weighing scales, balances, rulers, and tape measures are among the first tools for practical, everyday measurements both in human history and in the lives of students. In the early grades, students learn to give "ballpark" estimates of heights and lengths; then, over the years, they become progressively more sophisticated in their use of measuring instruments to find approximate lengths. Carpenters' rules are important tools for applying the "half" fractions in later grades ($\frac{1}{2}$, $\frac{1}{4}$, $\frac{1}{8}$, and so on—each fraction being half the previous one); metersticks and centimeter rulers are important in teaching about decimals.

If your students are using retractable tape measures, teaching and enforcing the "5-centimeter no-zap rule" (do not "zap" the tape measure until no more than 5 centimeters show) will extend the life of these tools. Just as doctors, carpenters, and others respect and take care of the tools they use, students should learn to respect and care for their tools.

Percent Circles and Protractors

Unlike most of us, who had only one precision tool for measuring angles when we learned geometry, students in *Everyday Mathematics* have three: **percent circles, full-circle protractors,** and **half-circle protractors.**

Percent Circle The authors of *Everyday Mathematics* developed the Percent Circle (found on the Geometry Template) to make measuring and constructing circle graphs easier. The Percent Circle is a full-circle protractor with the circumference marked in percents rather than degrees. (Full-circle protractors are described below.) This allows students to interpret and construct circle graphs before they are ready for the complex calculations needed to construct circle graphs with a protractor.

In *Sixth Grade Everyday Mathematics,* students learn the procedures for constructing circle graphs with a protractor. This involves expressing each piece of data as a fractional part of the whole, calculating the degree measure of each slice of the circle graph by finding the appropriate fraction of 360°, and drawing the computed angle in the circle with a protractor. Their fifth grade experience with Percent Circles prepares students for the more complicated task of constructing circle graphs with a protractor.

For more on measuring tools, see Section 6.3 of the Measurement essay.

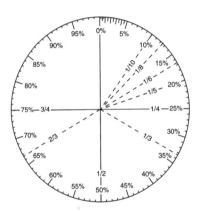

the Percent Circle

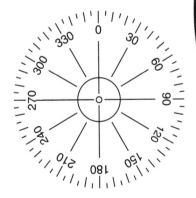

full-circle protractor

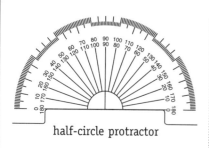

half-circle protractor

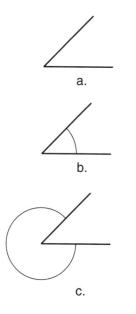

a.

b.

c.

Figure 2

Protractors In *Third Grade Everyday Mathematics,* students explore rotations and angles using straws and measure angles informally, identifying, for example, a right angle as a quarter-turn. Fourth graders review angles with straws, and then use both kinds of protractors to find more precise measures of angles. First, they make a 360° angle measurer from a journal drawing and a straw.

This then leads to their use of a full-circle protractor that they cut out from an activity sheet. To use a full-circle protractor, angles must be measured in a clockwise direction. Finally, students graduate to a half-circle protractor, which is slightly more difficult to use because, unlike a full-circle protractor where angles are measured in a clockwise direction, the half-circle protractor has scales for measuring in either a clockwise or counterclockwise direction.

Take whatever time is necessary to help students interpret various ways of marking angles. Figure 1 below shows a right angle (90°) marked in four different ways. The arcs in angles 1a and 1b have arrows and represent a 1/4-clockwise turn and 1/4-counterclockwise turn, respectively. Using a full-circle protractor, both of these have to be measured in a clockwise direction, but you may want older students to qualify the direction of the measure. Using a half-circle protractor, students could be asked to measure in the direction of the arrow to see if they use the tool properly.

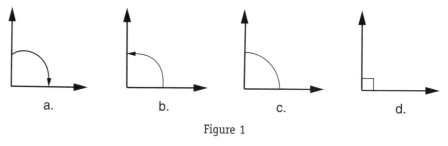

a.   b.   c.   d.

Figure 1

Angle 1c is marked with an arc with no arrows, as is often the case when angles are marked in a polygon. Angle 1d is drawn with the symbol for perpendicular. The important idea for beginning angle measurers is that all four angles measure 90°.

In many cases, an angle may be drawn, but no arc is drawn to indicate the direction of rotation as in Figure 2, angle 2a. Without an arc, this angle could also represent either of angles 2b or 2c. If no arc is shown in an angle, the usual convention is that the smaller of the two angles is to be used. Angle 2c is called a reflex angle.

It is likely that students will find it harder to draw angles of a given measure than to measure existing angles. To practice measuring and drawing angles, you may ask them, frequently, to draw any angle and then measure it, or have someone give a number between 0° and 180° and ask students to draw an angle with that degree measure. The game *Angle Tangle,* introduced in fifth grade, also provides practice estimating and measuring angle size. For more about estimating and measuring angles, see Section 6.8 of the Measurement essay.

management guide

Scales and Balances

A scale is a tool for measuring how heavy something is according to a standard weight. There are three types of scales: balance, mechanical, and electronic. Different scales are used for different purposes, both in the real world and in *Everyday Mathematics*. For more about each type of scale, see Section 6.3.3 of the Measurement essay.

In first grade, pan balances are used to introduce the symbols for relations ($<$, $>$, $=$, and so on). Through third grade, students write number models using these symbols. Beginning in fifth grade, pan balances serve as concrete models for open sentences. One unit of weight may represent a whole (or ONE), and another unit of weight an unknown quantity x. The balance begins with equal total weights on each side, and students endeavor to find how many wholes there are in x. That is, they solve for x. This concrete approach quickly turns into a model—balances are first drawn on paper in journals or on activity sheets, and then replaced with equations and inequalities.

Tools for Numeration and Operations

When teachers hear "manipulatives," they probably think of pattern blocks and what *Everyday Mathematics* calls the tools for numeration and operations: base-10 blocks, counters, number tiles, and a host of other devices. This section contains a few comments about how these numeration tools are used in *Everyday Mathematics*.

Base-10 Blocks

In *Third* and *Fourth Grade Everyday Mathematics,* base-10 blocks help develop decimal exchange concepts. A long (or rod) may represent the ONE, and 1-cm cubes represent tenths. If a flat is assumed to represent the ONE, then 1-cm cubes represent hundredths. This last model is quickly made pictorial as students color or shade hundredths of a 10-by-10 grid to represent decimals. Students work in the other direction as well, writing decimals for partially-shaded grids. In fourth and fifth grades, shaded grids help develop fraction sense and the relationship between fractions, decimals, and percents.

In third grade, students also use base-10 blocks to model the partial-products algorithm for multiplication. First they work out 1-digit by 2-digit problems with arrays of the blocks and, eventually, 2-digit by 2-digit problems.

Sometimes you may want to make a written record of work with base-10 blocks. The system of shorthand shown below works well. This shorthand is handy for drawing quick pictures of base-10 blocks. Such pictures are often more convenient than the actual blocks, especially for the larger blocks, and can be useful for explaining and recording solutions.

NOTE: A variety of names are used for base-10 blocks. The following names are used in *Everyday Mathematics*: *cube* for the smaller 1-cm cube, *long* for the block consisting of 10 cm cubes ($1 \times 1 \times 10$), *flat* for the block consisting of 100 cm cubes ($1 \times 10 \times 10$), and *big cube* for the larger cube consisting of 1,000 1-cm cubes ($10 \times 10 \times 10$). (Giving such names to the blocks helps avoid confusion when, for example, the flat is defined to be the ONE.)

2,045 in "base-ten" shorthand

Name Block Shorthand		
Name	**Block**	**Shorthand**
cm cube	◻	▪
long		|
flat		◻
big cube		◻

Fact Triangles

Fact Triangles help students develop their mental arithmetic reflexes. You might think of them as the *Everyday Mathematics* version of flash cards. Fact Triangles are more effective than flash cards in helping students memorize facts, however, because they emphasize fact families and the relationships between operations. Sample Fact Triangles are shown below, one for an addition/subtraction fact family and one for a multiplication/division fact family.

Fact Triangles can be found in the *Math Masters* book. A more durable, plastic version of these triangles can be purchased from Everyday Learning Corporation.

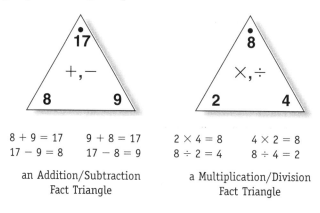

8 + 9 = 17 9 + 8 = 17	2 × 4 = 8 4 × 2 = 8
17 − 9 = 8 17 − 8 = 9	8 ÷ 2 = 4 8 ÷ 4 = 2
an Addition/Subtraction Fact Triangle	a Multiplication/Division Fact Triangle

Fraction-Stick Charts and Fraction Sticks

Students in *Fifth Grade Everyday Mathematics* use the **Fraction-Stick Chart** shown below to find equivalent fractions and to compare fractions. Each row in the chart is a **fraction stick** divided into unit fractions, or pieces, for a particular denominator. Fraction sticks are pictorial representations of fractions, with each stick representing a whole, or one.

To use the Fraction-Stick Chart to find equivalent fractions for $\frac{2}{3}$:

- Use the "thirds" stick to locate the fraction $\frac{2}{3}$. Count the $\frac{1}{3}$ pieces from left to right. The right edge of the second piece is $\frac{2}{3}$.
- Place one edge of a straightedge at $\frac{2}{3}$, that is, along the right edge of the second $\frac{1}{3}$ piece. The straightedge should be parallel to the sides of the Fraction-Stick Chart.
- On the "sixths" stick, the straightedge passes through the end of the fourth piece, which is $\frac{4}{6}$. So $\frac{4}{6} = \frac{2}{3}$.
- On the "ninths" stick, the straightedge passes through the end of the sixth piece, which is $\frac{6}{9}$. So $\frac{6}{9} = \frac{2}{3}$.
- On the "twelfths" stick, the straightedge passes through the end of the eighth piece, which is $\frac{8}{12}$. So $\frac{8}{12} = \frac{2}{3}$.
- On any other stick, the straightedge cuts through one of the pieces, and $\frac{2}{3}$ cannot be written as an equivalent fraction using the pieces on that stick.

To use the chart to find which fraction is greater, $\frac{4}{9}$ or $\frac{3}{8}$:

- Place one edge of a straightedge at $\frac{4}{9}$ (the right side of the fourth piece of the "ninths" stick).
- Locate $\frac{3}{8}$ at the right side of the third piece on the "eighths" stick. Because $\frac{3}{8}$ is to the left of $\frac{4}{9}$, $\frac{3}{8}$ is smaller than $\frac{4}{9}$, that is, $\frac{3}{8} < \frac{4}{9}$.

Fraction sticks can also be used to help visualize the addition of fractions with certain denominators, as the following two examples illustrate.

$$\frac{3}{16} + \frac{9}{16} = \qquad = \frac{12}{16} \text{ or } \frac{3}{4}$$

$$\frac{5}{8} + \frac{1}{4} = \qquad = \frac{7}{8}$$

NOTE: The Fraction-Stick Chart is available as a master in fifth grade and in the *Student Reference Book* for sixth grade.

Assessment

Everyday Mathematics encourages a balanced approach to student assessment, one that tracks the development of a student's mathematical understanding while giving the teacher useful feedback about instructional needs. Assessment also provides documentation for assigning grades.

Many different assessment techniques are built into the program. These include ideas for using lesson activities and components for ongoing assessment, something the authors call "kid-watching"; suggestions for collecting work samples for product or portfolio assessment; and tools for conducting more formal periodic assessment. Assessment suggestions are incorporated into the lesson descriptions, compiled for each unit in the Unit Organizers, and discussed in the *Assessment Handbook*. Feel free to pick and choose from the assessment tools and techniques suggested to design your own balanced assessment plan.

The following simple rubric can be used to categorize progress with any of the assessment activities:

General Rubric

Beginning (B)

Students cannot complete the task independently. They show little understanding of the concept or skill.

Developing (D)

Students show some understanding. However, errors or misunderstandings still occur. Reminders, hints, and suggestions are incorporated with understanding.

Secure (S)

Students can apply the skill or concept correctly and independently.

Other rubrics are suggested in the *Assessment Handbook*.

Providing for Home-and-School Communication

Dialogue and discussion, as well as experimentation and discovery, are at the heart of *Everyday Mathematics*. Parents accustomed to conventional mathematics programs may think that because students are not bringing home daily arithmetic drill sheets, they are not learning or doing mathematics. The Study Links and Family Letters (see below) reassure them that this is not the case. In addition, the *Home Connection Handbook* can help you inform parents about the *Everyday Mathematics* curriculum.

Study Links and Family Letters

Study Link activities serve three main purposes: They (1) promote follow-up, (2) provide enrichment, and (3) involve parents or guardians in their students' mathematics education.

Other reasons for using Study Links throughout the year include the following:

- The assignments encourage students to take initiative and responsibility.
- The activities help reinforce newly learned skills and concepts.
- Many of the assignments relate what is learned in school to the students' lives outside of school, tying mathematics to their everyday world.
- The assignments can serve as informal assessment tools.

Occasionally, Study Links require students to interact with parents, other adults, or older students. Since primary caregivers or those likely to help with homework are not necessarily "parents," Study Links instruct students to complete the activity with someone at home. At the beginning of the year, you might send home the introductory Family Letter. Continue to involve families throughout the year by sending home unit-specific letters that explain the content that will be covered. (The Study Link for the last lesson in each unit is a Family Letter for the next unit.) These letters explain ideas or activities that may be unfamiliar to parents.
All Family Letters and Study Links are included in the *Math Masters* book.

Think of the Study Link suggestions as a beginning. As you and your students become familiar with the program, you may want to send home activities of your own as Study Links. You may also want to use the Study Links format to extend various Projects. Blank Study Links forms have been provided for these purposes in the *Math Masters* book.

Home Connection Handbook

Every teacher receives a *Home Connection Handbook* as part of his or her Teacher Resource Package. This book contains articles, explanatory material about the *Everyday Mathematics* philosophy and program, and suggestions for parents regarding how to become involved in their students' mathematics education. All of the information in the *Home Connection Handbook* can be copied and sent home to parents to help you inform them about and involve them in the *Everyday Mathematics* curriculum.

Information from the *Home Connection Handbook* is also available on Everyday Learning's Web site at www.everydaylearning.com/infofor/parents/elementary.html.

The Importance of Problem Solving

In *Everyday Mathematics,* problem solving is much more than solving word problems. Problem solving is a process of building a mathematical model of a situation and then reasoning with the model to draw conclusions about the situation. The process typically involves some or all of the following steps, not necessarily in the order presented.

- Identifying precisely what the problem is
- Analyzing what is known and seeking out further data as necessary
- Playing with the data to try to discover patterns and meaning
- Identifying mathematical techniques that can help in finding a solution
- Looking back and asking, "Does the solution make sense?"

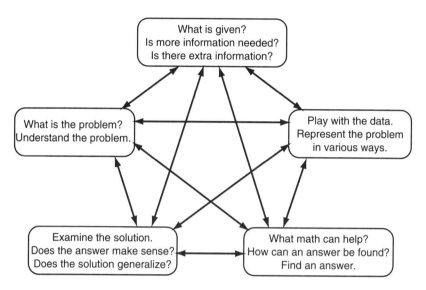

Everyday Mathematics regards problem solving as an approach applied to all topics rather than as a topic unto itself. In every strand in the curriculum, students solve a wide range of problems. Some require students to apply their current mathematical knowledge; others stretch students' skills and understanding. Problems for which students have no method of solution immediately at hand are often the most productive. Students are encouraged to solve all problems in many different ways; sharing and comparing solution methods is a prominent feature of the *Everyday Mathematics* program.

From time to time in *Everyday Mathematics*, students are presented with a problem for which finding an exact answer is difficult, time-consuming, or even impossible. They are challenged to come up with a best estimate and to explain their strategy for arriving at it. For example, students are given a noteworthy location about 40 to 200 miles from their school and asked to imagine getting there in a time when there were no cars, trains, or planes. They have no other transportation and need to walk. Using a map, they are asked to estimate how far away the destination is, how many steps and how much time it might take to get there, and when they might arrive if they left at 7:00 A.M. on a Monday. Students are given ample time to think about the problem, prepare their estimates, and then compare approaches to the problem.

Traditional word problems have a place in *Everyday Mathematics*— such problems have value as exercises—but problem solving permeates the entire curriculum. Each unit organizer in the *Teacher's Lesson Guide* has a section that identifies activities where problem solving is particularly prominent, but many other opportunities for problem solving will present themselves as students grapple with the rich material in the program.

For more about mathematical modeling and the *Everyday Mathematics* approach to problem solving, see Section 10.3 in the Problem Solving essay.

The range of experiences that *Everyday Mathematics* provides is designed to help students develop mathematical sense, which includes both an understanding of the body of knowledge we call mathematics and students' abilities to do mathematics to solve problems. *Mathematical sense* has the following principal components:

• *Number sense* is crucial. Students must have enough experience with numbers of various kinds and sizes to have a feeling for where they come from and what they mean. Which numbers make sense in a given situation? What is a reasonable answer? Number sense helps students check the accuracy of answers regardless of the means by which they were obtained (mentally, with pencil and paper, with a calculator, or by other means).

• *Operations sense* is also essential. What do addition, subtraction, multiplication, and division mean? Why is it, for example, that multiplication of whole numbers gives products greater than one or both factors (unless zero is one of the factors), but multiplication of fractions or decimals can give products less than the factors?

• *Measure sense* tells what measurement means, what kinds of measures and units are appropriate in different situations, and what range of results are reasonable to accept. (Is 20 square feet a sensible measure of the area of the backyard? Might my dog really weigh 800 kilograms?)

• *Data sense* is an appreciation of a collection of numbers as a whole. How reliable are the numbers? How might they be used? What are the "spreads" and "landmarks" of the collections, such as the range and middle values?

• *Spatial sense* comes from extensive experience with 2-dimensional and 3-dimensional geometric objects, and from hands-on constructions that apply geometric principles. (How many grocery bags will fit in the trunk of my car? Can I cover all the walls in my bedroom with a quart of paint?)

• *Function or Pattern sense* comes from looking for visual and number patterns and predicting outcomes from applying a rule. It helps students relate pictorial, symbolic, verbal, and concrete representations of a pattern and so develop multiple perspectives. (Which is better—doubling $2 every year, or adding $50 every year?)

Finally, *Everyday Mathematics* is committed to helping students recognize and develop their own common sense. By *common sense* the authors mean an understanding of one's own basic ideas and how they are useful for judging between reasonable alternatives in everyday situations.

Mathematical Topics

contents

mathematical topics

Numeration and Order

The history of mathematics records the invention of increasingly sophisticated systems of numbers in order to solve problems in daily life. The natural numbers 1, 2, 3, …, enabled people to count and to measure. Later, fractions allowed people to describe parts of objects and to report measurements between whole units. Decimals, which came into use in Europe in the 1500s, greatly simplified computation and provided a unified system of notation. Negative numbers were introduced to represent change relative to a fixed position, as in profit and loss. *Everyday Mathematics* emphasizes the various representations of numbers and the equivalencies between them.

1.1 Counting

In the early grades of *Everyday Mathematics,* the most frequent use of the numbers 1, 2, 3, 4, …, is in counting. *Everyday Mathematics* is committed to having students view numbers in use, and counting involves a counting unit: 4 cars, 8 cats, 101 people, and so on. The numbers 1, 2, 3, 4, …, are often referred to as the **counting numbers** or the **natural numbers.**

Sometimes, 0 is considered to be a natural number. (Computer scientists, for example, often begin counting with 0.) If 0 is included with the set of natural numbers, the result is what most elementary school curricula call the **whole numbers.**

It is more important for students to understand what zero means than it is for them to know the names for various sets of numbers. Zero does not represent "nothing"; rather, it is the number of cats in the room if there are no cats in the room. It is the starting place for measures and for reference frames such as thermometers. The digit 0 "holds places" in place-value numeration and permits the use of efficient procedures for adding, subtracting, multiplying, and dividing numbers.

By Grade 4, *Everyday Mathematics* students are expected to be familiar with numbers to 1,000,000 and beyond, and to have mastered the following counting skills:

- Counting by 1s up and back, to and from, any number through 10,000 and beyond;
- Counting by 2s, 3s, and 5s to and from any multiples of these numbers in the same range;
- Counting by 10s, 100s, and 1,000s to and from any number in the same range;
- Counting by multiples of 4, 6, 7, 8, and 9, up to 100 and beyond; and
- Counting by negative numbers forward and backward from a given number, but especially crossing over 0 into the positive numbers.

1.2 Number Theory

Beginning in Grade 4, students begin to explore topics in the study of the whole numbers, the branch of mathematics known as number theory. Several of these topics—prime and composite numbers, perfect numbers, and abundant and deficient numbers—are described in the following sections.

1.2.1 Prime and Composite Numbers; Divisibility

Probably the most fundamental distinction in number theory is the classification of whole numbers greater than 1 as either prime or composite. A **prime number** has exactly two **divisors** or **factors,** 1 and itself. For example, 2 is a prime number because it is divisible only by 1 and by 2. Any whole number that has more than two divisors is a **composite number.** For example, 6 is a composite number because it is divisible by 2 and 3 as well as 1 and 6. The numbers 0 and 1 are neither composite nor prime.

Beginning in Grade 3, when multiplication becomes a center-stage topic, teachers are advised to find a shorthand notation to record students' solution strategies to problems involving factors. In *Everyday Mathematics,* brackets are used to separate factor pairs. For example, 8 [500s] represents eight 5-hundreds, or 4,000. Students will quickly accept whatever notation is adopted as long as it is used consistently.

Prime and composite numbers show interesting features when modeled by rectangular arrays. A prime number can be modeled by only two arrays. For example, arrays for the prime number 5 have a single column or a single row of five elements. The former can be said to model 5 * 1, the latter to model 1 * 5. The composite number 10, however, can be shown by four arrays. These represent 10 * 1, 1 * 10, 5 * 2, and 2 * 5.

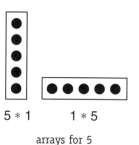

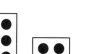

arrays for 5

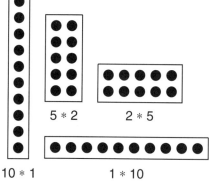

arrays for 10

Students in *Fifth* and *Sixth Grade Everyday Mathematics* experiment to find **divisibility rules** to help identify prime numbers. These rules are extensions to the set of multiplication and division facts. For example:

- All even numbers are divisible by 2. Hence, any number ending in 0, 2, 4, 6, or 8 is divisible by 2.
- A number is divisible by 3 if the sum of its digits is divisible by 3. (The sum of the digits of a number is obtained by adding the number's digits. The sum of the digits of 256, for example, is 2 + 5 + 6, or 13. The sum of the digits of 8,793 is 8 + 7 + 9 + 3, or 27.) For example, 57 is divisible by 3 because 5 + 7 = 12, and 12 is divisible by 3.
- A number is divisible by 4 if the last two digits are divisible by 4. For example, 78,468 is divisible by 4 because 68 is divisible by 4.
- A number ending with 0 or 5 is divisible by 5.
- A number that is divisible by both 2 and 3 is divisible by 6. For example, 12,612 is divisible by 6 since it ends in 2 (and is therefore divisible by 2) and the sum of its digits is 1 + 2 + 6 + 1 + 2 = 12 (which is divisible by 3, which means that 12,612 is divisible by 3).

- A number is divisible by 8 if the last three digits are divisible by 8. For example, 2,456,864 is divisible by 8 because 864 is divisible by 8.
- A number is divisible by 9 if the sum of its digits is divisible by 9. For example, 567 is divisible by 9 because $5 + 6 + 7 = 18$, and 18 is divisible by 9.

A Note on Divisibility by 9

The divisibility rule for 9 given above is a special case of a general rule about sums of digits and division by 9: When a number is divided by 9, the remainder is the same as the remainder when the sum of the number's digits is divided by 9. If the sum of a number's digits is divisible by 9 (the remainder is 0), then the number itself is also evenly divisible by 9.

- The sum of the digits of 256 is $2 + 5 + 6$ or 13, so $256 / 9$ has the same remainder as $13 / 9$. Since $13 / 9$ has remainder 4, the remainder when 256 is divided by 9 is also 4: $256 / 9 \rightarrow 28$ R4.
- The sum of the digits of 8,793 is $8 + 7 + 9 + 3$, or 27. Since 27 is divisible by 9, so is 8,793: $8,793 / 9 = 977$.

The key to the proof of this rule is that numbers such as 999 and 99 are always divisible by 9. Before giving a general argument, it may help to see an example worked out with numbers.

$$256 / 9 = [2 * 100 + 5 * 10 + 6] / 9$$
$$= [2 * (99 + 1) + 5 * (9 + 1) + 6] / 9$$
$$= [2 * 99 + 2 + 5 * 9 + 5 + 6] / 9$$
$$= [2 * 99 + 5 * 9] / 9 + [2 + 5 + 6] / 9$$

Since 9 divides both 99 and 9 evenly, $(2 * 99 + 5 * 9) / 9$ has remainder 0. The remainder for $256 / 9$, therefore, is the same as the remainder when $2 + 5 + 6$ is divided by 9. Since $(2 + 5 + 6) / 9 \rightarrow 1$ R4, the remainder of $256 / 9$ is also 4: $256 / 9 \rightarrow 28$ R4.

A complete proof of this rule is beyond the scope of this manual, but an argument for 3-digit numbers illustrates the main idea. Suppose the digits of a 3-digit number are represented by H (for the hundreds), T (for the tens), and U (for the units or ones digit). Then the number may be written H T U or $H * 100 + T * 10 + U$. Then, as in the example above, we may write:

$$H T U / 9 = (H * 100 + T * 10 + U) / 9$$
$$= ((H * 99 + H) + (T * 9 + T) + U)) / 9$$
$$= (H * 99 + T * 9) / 9 + (H + T + U) / 9$$

Since $H * 99$ and $T * 9$ are both divisible by 9, the remainder for H T U $/ 9$ will come only from $(H + T + U) / 9$. Thus, as the rule states, the remainder when the number is divided by 9 is the same as the remainder when the sum of the number's digits is divided by 9.

Almost exactly the same argument can be used to show that when a number is divided by 3, the remainder is the same as the remainder when the sum of the number's digits is divided by 3. The other divisibility rules above can also be proved by using similar arguments.

Prime Factors and Factorization

Two key topics in number theory are *prime factors* and *factorization*. For elementary school students, these are useful for arithmetic with fractions. The traditional paper-and-pencil algorithms for finding common denominators, simplifying fractions, and adding and subtracting fractions all require students to factor numbers.

A **factorization** of a number is a product of whole numbers that equals the number. Usually 1s do not appear in factorizations, and the order of the factors doesn't matter. For example, 24 has the following factorizations:

$$2 * 12$$
$$3 * 8$$
$$4 * 6$$
$$2 * 2 * 6$$
$$2 * 3 * 4$$
$$2 * 2 * 2 * 3$$

Notice that only the last factorization above contains only prime numbers. The Fundamental Theorem of Arithmetic states that for each whole number greater than 1, there is only one factorization that consists entirely of prime numbers. The unique factorization of a number into primes is called its **prime factorization.**

In *Everyday Mathematics,* students are encouraged to develop their own approaches to finding prime factorizations. One approach is to use **factor strings.** The first step is to determine whether a number is prime or composite through the use of multiplication and division facts, arrays, and divisibility rules. If a number is composite, then look for **factor pairs**—two factors whose product is that number. For example:

$$24 = 1 * 24 = 2 * 12 = 3 * 8 = 4 * 6$$

Then choose a factor pair and repeat the process. That is, look for factor pairs for each factor in the pair. This creates a factor string. For example:

$$24 = 4 * 6$$
$$= 2 * 2 * 2 * 3$$

Since both 2 and 3 are prime numbers, $2 * 2 * 2 * 3$ is the longest factor string that equals 24. The factors are all prime, so this is the prime factorization of 24.

A prime factorization can often be written using the shorthand notation of exponents. For example:

$$2 * 2 * 2 * 3 = 2^3 * 3$$

This notation links to exponential and scientific notations used as shorthand for big numbers, especially in calculators and computers.

Exploration of factors begins in *Third Grade Everyday Mathematics* to reinforce links between multiplication and division. Students are introduced to factor strings early in fourth grade; later in the year, they learn to find prime factorizations by making factor trees.

Factor Trees

Making a **factor tree** is an algorithm for finding the prime factorization of a whole number. The algorithm consists of three steps:

1. Write the number to be factored.

2. Underneath the number, write any two factors whose product is the number.

3. Repeat Step 2 for each factor, and each factor's factors, until all the factors are prime numbers.

For example, three factor trees for the number 36 are shown below.

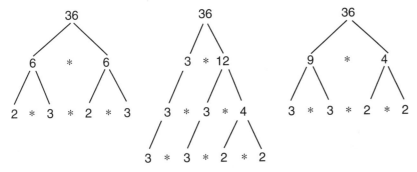

Note that the algorithm gives the same prime factorization regardless of the first pair of factors. (The order of the factors doesn't matter.) The prime factorization of 36 is $2 * 2 * 3 * 3$, or $2^2 * 3^2$.

Students use factor trees to find greatest common factors of two numbers, and, optionally, least common multiples and least common denominators. The latter two activities are optional because the authors of *Everyday Mathematics* believe students have more important, and certainly more interesting, things to do than waste hours writing fractions in an artificially "best" or "simplified" form.

1.2.2 Perfect, Deficient, and Abundant Numbers

The Pythagoreans, a group of philosophers and mathematicians in ancient Greece, were interested in the mystical properties of numbers. Among other things, the Pythagoreans found that certain numbers are equal to the sums of their proper factors. (A **proper factor** of a number is any factor of that number except the number itself.) The first two such numbers are 6 and 28:

$$6 = 1 + 2 + 3 \text{ and } 28 = 1 + 2 + 4 + 7 + 14$$

These numbers are the two smallest **perfect numbers.** The Pythagoreans also found the third and fourth perfect numbers, 496 and 8,128.

St. Augustine (A.D. 354–430) thought perfect numbers had religious significance. He believed that the world could have been created in

NOTE: Factor trees, like probability tree diagrams, are normally drawn upside down, with their "roots" at the top and their "leaves" at the bottom. This is more convenient, since it's usually not known in advance how big a factor tree will be, but it can be confusing since the resulting diagrams do not look much like real trees. Like ordinary trees, however, mathematical trees do have their "branches" in between their roots and their leaves.

one day, but God chose to do it in six days because the number 6 was a symbol of perfection. Other scholars linked the perfect number 28 to the number of days it takes the Moon to revolve around Earth.

The fifth perfect number is 33,550,336 and the sixth is 8,589,869,056. Recently, computers have been used to find perfect numbers. In June 1999, researchers found the thirty-eighth perfect number, which has over 4 million digits. All of the perfect numbers found so far are even and all end with either 6 or 8. An odd perfect number has never been found, but it has not been proven that such a number cannot exist. It is also not yet known whether there are infinitely many perfect numbers.

Perfect numbers provide an historical context in which to practice finding factors. Students can also explore two other types of numbers identified by the Pythagoreans—deficient and abundant numbers.

The sum of the proper factors of a **deficient number** is less than the number. For example, 10 is deficient because the sum of its proper factors is 1 + 2 + 5, or 8, and 8 is less than 10.

The sum of the proper factors of an **abundant number** is greater than the number. For example, 12 is abundant because the sum of its proper factors is 1 + 2 + 3 + 4 + 6, or 16, and 16 is greater than 12.

Students who enjoy playing with these numbers might like to explore **amicable numbers.** Two whole numbers are amicable numbers if each is equal to the sum of the proper factors of the other. For example, the sum of the proper factors of 220 is 1 + 2 + 4 + 5 + 10 + 11 + 20 + 22 + 44 + 55 + 110, or 284, and the sum of the proper factors of 284 is 1 + 2 + 4 + 71 + 142, or 220. So 220 and 284 are amicable (which means friendly).

1.3 Fractions, Decimals, and Rational Numbers

"God created the integers; the rest is the work of man."

–Leopold Kronecker (1823–1891)

Dealing with the world involves much more than counting. **Fractions** arise when items, such as a pizza or a bag of oranges, are shared. Transactions with money are expressed in **decimal** form, sometimes with **negative numbers.** Both fractions and decimals are used to represent measures, since the real world is made up of objects with lengths, weights, and other measures that cannot be expressed by referring only to whole-number marks on rulers, scales, and the like.

Fractions are confusing to many people, perhaps because the procedures for adding, subtracting, multiplying, and dividing them seem arbitrary and unpredictable. For example, it is likely that few people really understand the "invert and multiply" rule for the division of one fraction by another. It may be that these mysterious fraction manipulations, often taught without real-life problems or concrete embodiments to give them meaning, are what have convinced so many adults that mathematics is impossible to understand and that getting "correct" results is more a matter of good luck than good management.

One reason many people experience difficulties with fractions may be that many school programs avoid fractions for several years while students work exclusively with whole numbers. When students are finally introduced to fractions, many find them confusing because the results often run counter to what they expect from having dealt exclusively with whole numbers. For example, fractions, unlike whole numbers, are generally harder to add than to multiply; a product may be smaller than its factors; a quotient may be larger than the number being divided; and "repeated addition" has little meaning in the multiplication of two fractions.

1.3.1 Fraction and Decimal Notation

Much of the content of mathematics programs for the primary grades is concerned with whole numbers, including place-value notation, addition, subtraction, and multiplication. *Everyday Mathematics* extends traditional work with these numbers by introducing negative numbers in Kindergarten (with temperatures, timelines, and number lines); fractions (with measures and "part of" situations) and decimals (mainly with notation) in first grade; and easy percents as alternatives to easy fractions ("one-tenth of ..." and "ten percent of ...") in second grade. This early attention to fractions, decimals, and percents prepares students for learning about operations with numbers in these notations in Grades 4–6.

Fractions, decimals, and percents are readily understood by students as long as the numbers are closely associated with their everyday experiences. For example, even before the authors began to develop *Everyday Mathematics,* they found, through interviews with 5- and 6-year-olds, that young students respond quickly and accurately when asked for "half of" something—probably as a result of sharing things equally with siblings and friends. Building on these observations, the primary grade program includes negative numbers, fractions, decimals, and percents. These are used mainly to convey information, without becoming involved in operations such as addition, subtraction, or division. The authors found, in contrast to addition, subtraction, and division of fractions, that multiplication such as "half of..." or "a tenth of..." is readily accepted by students, especially in contexts that pair "two of..." with "half of..." or "ten of..." with "one-tenth of..."

The importance of alternate notations for numbers is emphasized throughout *Everyday Mathematics.* All three notations for rational numbers—fractions, decimals, and percents—can help students see connections between rational numbers and whole numbers.

NOTE: Fractions may also be difficult for students simply because they are complicated symbols compared to single numbers.

For more information, see the Management Guide, pages 15–20.

Fractions build on ideas of equal sharing and whole-number operations, decimals extend the whole-number place-value system, and percents connect to important ideas of ratio and proportion.[1]

Decimals, fractions, and percents are technically interchangeable, but many common situations use one or the other as "standard notation." For example, although fractions were once standard in stock market reports, today decimals are used in most financial applications. Measures are commonly expressed as fractions in carpentry and other building trades, but decimals are used for virtually all measures in science and industry. Percents are used in interest rates as well as in many advertisements and statistics.

The story of the historical development of fractions is fascinating. Fractions were developed in ancient times, probably in response to the need for more precise measures in situations where whole-number units were insufficient. The ancient Egyptians used unit fractions—fractions with a numerator of 1, such as $\frac{1}{2}$, $\frac{1}{3}$, and $\frac{1}{8}$— almost exclusively. More complicated fractions were then expressed as the sums of unit fractions (for example, $\frac{1}{2} + \frac{1}{4}$ for $\frac{3}{4}$). Even in modern times, unit fractions are sufficient for the everyday needs of many people.

The development of decimal notation for rational numbers, which occurred many centuries after fraction notation was first used, has a similarly rich history. See *The Norton History of the Mathematical Sciences* by Ivor Gratten-Guinness (New York: W. W. Norton, 1997) or *Number Words and Number Symbols: A Cultural History of Numbers* by Karl A. Menninger (New York: Dover, 1992).

1.3.2 Uses of Fraction Notation

One reason fractions are confusing is that they have many different meanings. The fraction $\frac{1}{4}$, for example, can have any of the following meanings:

- a part of a whole: $\frac{1}{4}$ of a pizza
- a part of a collection: $\frac{1}{4}$ of a group of students
- a measurement: $\frac{1}{4}$ mile
- a division: $1 \div 4$
- a rate or ratio: 1 part vinegar to 4 parts oil
- a probability: 1 chance in 4
- a pure number: the number halfway between 0 and $\frac{1}{2}$

The idea of a unit whole is essential in the first two of these meanings. How big $\frac{1}{4}$ of a pizza is, for example, depends on how big the whole pizza is. To know how many students are in $\frac{1}{4}$ of a group, one needs to know how big the whole group is. In order to understand such "part-whole" fractions, students must appreciate

NOTE: The horizontal bar in a fraction is called a **vinculum.**

---

[1]You may sometimes encounter the terms *common fraction* and *decimal fraction*. While these terms emphasize that these are two different notations for the same numbers, we prefer the simpler terms *fraction* and *decimal*.

the role of the unit whole. They should also understand that the denominator tells how many parts are in the whole and that the numerator tells how many parts are included in the fraction. In *Everyday Mathematics* the unit whole is called the ONE. Part-whole fractions are perhaps the easiest to understand, and many primary grade activities in *Everyday Mathematics* involve them.

In fractions in measurements, the unit is also vitally important: $\frac{1}{4}$ mile is quite different from $\frac{1}{4}$ inch. Using fractions makes possible more precise measurements. With a ruler marked only in whole inches, for example, it is possible to measure precisely only to the nearest inch. But if the spaces between the whole-number marks are subdivided into equal intervals, then more precise measurements become possible. Other measuring tools such as graduated cylinders, measuring cups, and kitchen scales also subdivide the spaces between whole numbers of units. A significant part of learning to use such tools is learning to interpret the marks on the scales correctly.

In most other uses of fractions, there is no clear unit whole. In ratios, for example, there is no unit whole. A ratio like $\frac{1}{4}$ (which can also be written 1:4 or "1 to 4") might mean one tablespoon of vinegar to four tablespoons of oil in a salad dressing. There is no unit whole in such fractions, nor is there a unit whole in fractions that indicate division.

Fractions as equal parts and fractions as measures on scales and number lines get a lot of attention in Grades 1–3. These kinds of fractions, along with fractions as representations of division, appear often in applications in Grades 4–6, where fractions representing rates and ratios also become common.

1.3.3 Rates, Ratios, and Proportions

Both in everyday situations and in technical work, perhaps the most common use of fraction notation involves expressing *rates* and *ratios*. Rates, ratios, and what is sometimes called "proportional thinking" are very common in the everyday world, and people with good "number sense" and "measure sense" can handle such number relationships with ease. Unfortunately, for many people, everyday uses of rates seem to be difficult. Much of the poor performance in mathematics reported in the professional literature and the popular press reflects failure with rate or ratio problems on inventory tests, or an inability to do proportional thinking in the workplace.

Rates

The key to understanding rates is repeated exposure to the many uses of rates in everyday life. **Rates** express comparisons of pairs of quantities by division. The counts or measures in the numerator and denominator of a rate have *different* units, resulting in a compound unit for the rate. The rate of travel, or speed, can be expressed in miles per hour. For example, if a car travels 150 miles in 3 hours, its average speed is 150 miles/3 hours or 50 miles per hour (also expressed as 50 mi/hr or 50 mph). Automobile fuel consumption can be expressed in miles per gallon. For example, if a car travels 250 miles and uses 10 gallons of gasoline, its rate of fuel consumption is 250 miles/10 gallons or 25 miles per gallon (also expressed as 25 mi/gal or 25 mpg).

Beginning in *Fourth Grade Everyday Mathematics*, rate tables and rate diagrams are used to aid in problem solving. Rate diagrams are described in Section 10.2 of the Problem Solving essay and Section 2.1 of the Arithmetic Operations essay. Students may recognize rate tables as a special kind of "What's My Rule?" table, and may also notice similarities to the incomplete number-line problems used throughout the program. A **rate table** has two rows or columns, one for each unit of measure in a rate problem, and an associated rate, which is used to fill out the table. Students may be given a table and rate with values already included for one measure as in the following example.

Gasoline mileage: 35 miles per gallon

Miles	35							
Gallons	1	2	3	4	5	6	7	8

Students may also be given a table with some values for each measure included.

There are 8 pints in a gallon.

Pints	8	16			40			
Gallons	1		3					

In Grades 4–6, students work with rates represented as tables, formulas, and graphs. They also learn to find **per-unit** rates. Per-unit rates can be a big help when grocery shopping—do you want the 12-ounce can of juice for $1.57 (about 13¢/oz) or the 16-ounce can for $1.95 (about 12¢/oz)?—but they are also useful for solving rate problems in other situations, especially before more algebraic methods like cross multiplication are introduced in *Sixth Grade Everyday Mathematics.*

Ratios

Whereas rates compare quantities that have different units, **ratios** compare quantities that have the same unit. In effect, the units cancel each other, and the resulting number has no unit. For example, the fraction 2/20 could mean that 2 people out of 20 people in a class got an A on a test, or that 2 pears out of 20 pears are ripe. It may even be a simplified fraction that expresses the fact that 20,000 people out of 200,000 people voted for a certain candidate in an election. One important use of percent is to express ratio comparisons in a standardized form that is easier to understand.

Another frequent use of ratios is to indicate relative size or **scale.** For example, a picture of an object in a dictionary, drawn to $\frac{1}{10}$

NOTE: Rate tables need not be horizontal, as in the example below from *Fifth Grade Everyday Mathematics.* In this problem, students are looking at three representations of a rate: table, formula, and graph. Each has its advantages, and an important goal of the program is to help students easily shift from one representation to another.

Frank types an average of 45 words a minute.

Rule: Words typed = 45 ∗ number of minutes

Time (min) (*t*)	Words (45 ∗ *t*)
1	
2	
3	
	225
6	

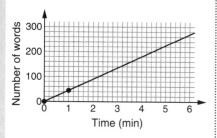

scale, means that every length in the picture is $\frac{1}{10}$ the corresponding length in the actual object. In the language of transformations, the picture in the dictionary is a size-change image of the object by a factor of $\frac{1}{10}$. Such ratios can also be found on maps and scale drawings.

Students begin making ratio comparisons informally in *Second Grade Everyday Mathematics,* when they look at weather data and investigate questions such as "What city has about twice as much rain as Vancouver?" By Grade 4 they are applying ratio comparisons to scale drawings and size changes of geometric figures. In Grade 5, the *American Tour* has students make ratio comparisons of populations and other data using fractions, decimals, and percents. Fifth graders also calculate ratios of circumferences to diameters of circles to explore the value of π. Grade 6 students use ratios to explore similar figures and unit ratios to compare ratios with each other, and they investigate an interesting application of scale known as the Golden Ratio.

The Golden Ratio

A pleasingly shaped figure called the **Golden Rectangle** appears in ancient Greek art and architecture, as well as many other works of art throughout history. Students in *Sixth Grade Everyday Mathematics* read about the Golden Rectangle and construct one of their own using the procedure shown below. *AHGD* is called a Golden Rectangle because the ratio of the lengths of its longer side to its shorter side—*AH/GH*—is the Golden Ratio, approximately 1.618 to 1. The Golden Ratio is often denoted by ϕ, the Greek letter phi.

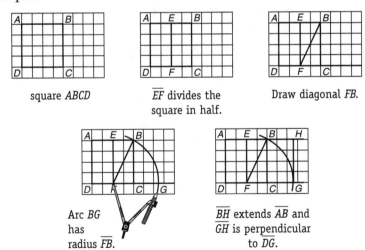

square *ABCD*

$\overline{EF}$ divides the square in half.

Draw diagonal *FB*.

Arc *BG* has radius $\overline{FB}$.

$\overline{BH}$ extends $\overline{AB}$ and $\overline{GH}$ is perpendicular to $\overline{DG}$.

Although students are not expected to know where the approximation $\phi \approx 1.618$ came from, other than by verifying it for several instances, the derivation is shown below. The calculation uses a little algebra and the Pythagorean theorem (see "The Pythagorean Theorem" in Section 5.4 of the Geometry essay).

First, to make things simpler, let's suppose that the length of a side of square *ABCD* is 1 inch. So the shorter legs of the right triangles

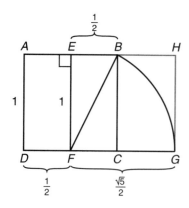

in the figure in the margin have length $\frac{1}{2}$ inch, and the longer legs have length 1 inch.

By the Pythagorean theorem, the length of the hypotenuse *FB*, in inches, is

$$\sqrt{1^2 + (\tfrac{1}{2})^2} = \sqrt{1 + \tfrac{1}{4}} = \sqrt{\tfrac{5}{4}} = \frac{\sqrt{5}}{2}$$

This length is also the length of $\overline{FG}$, because that segment is the image of the hypotenuse $\overline{FB}$ under a rotation.

So the length, in inches, of the longer side of the Golden Rectangle is

$$\frac{1}{2} + \frac{\sqrt{5}}{2}, \text{ or } \frac{1}{2}(1 + \sqrt{5})$$

The length of the shorter side is simply 1 inch. The Golden Ratio is

$$\phi = \frac{\frac{1}{2}(1 + \sqrt{5}) \text{ in.}}{1 \text{ in}} = \frac{1 + \sqrt{5}}{2}$$

Note that the unit, inches, in the numerator and denominator of the fraction above are the same, so the inches "cancel" and the final answer, the Golden Ratio, has no units. To ten digits, this number is 1.618033989, which rounds to 1.618, the approximate value of the Golden Ratio used in *Sixth Grade Everyday Mathematics*.

The Fibonacci Sequence

The Golden Ratio occurs in a fascinating way in a sequence of numbers called the **Fibonacci sequence.** The Fibonacci sequence starts with two 1s, after which the rule for the sequence is that the next number is the sum of the previous two numbers. The Fibonacci numbers are

$$1, 1, 2, 3, 5, 8, 13, 21, \ldots$$

If you take the ratios of successive terms in the Fibonnaci sequence, you get a new sequence

$$\frac{1}{1}, \frac{2}{1}, \frac{3}{2}, \frac{5}{3}, \frac{8}{5}, \frac{13}{8}, \ldots$$

This sequence, expressed in decimal form, is

$$1, 2, 1.5, 1.\overline{6}, 1.6, 1.625, \ldots$$

Mathematicians have proved that these numbers, the ratios of successive terms in the Fibonacci sequence, approach closer and closer in value to the Golden Ratio.

The Golden Ratio has many fascinating properties. For example, if you subtract 1 from the Golden Ratio, then you get its reciprocal. That is

$$\phi * (\phi - 1) = 1$$

The Fibonacci numbers were extensively studied over 800 years ago by Leonardo of Pisa (1170–1250), the greatest mathematician of medieval Europe, who was known as Fibonacci. The Fibonacci numbers often appear in natural settings such as the arrangement of leaves on certain plants and the shape of the spirals of the shells of certain shellfish. The Fibonacci sequence, the Golden Ratio, and related topics continue to be investigated today by both pure and

For more about Fibonacci, see, for example, the mathematics history site maintained by the School of Mathematics and Statistics at the University of St. Andrews, Scotland (http://www-groups.dcs.st-and.ac.uk/~history/Mathematicians/Fibonacci.html).

applied mathematicians. There is even a journal, the *Fibonacci Quarterly,* devoted to the Fibonacci numbers.

A Note on Rate *versus* Ratio

In many mathematics books and in many dictionaries, *rate* and *ratio* are synonymous. But there is a growing tendency among technicians and scientists to use *rate* when the quantities have different units, resulting in a quantity with a compound unit, and *ratio* when the quantities have the same unit, resulting in a number that has no unit (often called a *scalar*).

The authors of *Everyday Mathematics* think this distinction is useful and have maintained it in the program. However, the use of *rate* and *ratio* as synonyms is so entrenched in school mathematics and in daily life that the student materials do not make an issue of it. The rate and ratio issues are entangled with the larger concern of how to handle *units* and *units analysis* in calculations with counts and measures. Keeping track of units is easy for sums and differences (only counts or measures with exactly the same unit can be added or subtracted) but become more complicated with products, quotients, squares, cubes, and square roots, all of which are important in Grades 4–6 of *Everyday Mathematics.*

Proportions

A **proportion** is a number sentence that asserts the equality of two fractions.

Examples:

$$\frac{1}{2} = \frac{50}{100}$$

$$\frac{2}{3} = \frac{60}{90}$$

$$\frac{2}{5} = \frac{30}{75}$$

Proportions can be used to model many rate and ratio situations. For example, a car traveling at a constant rate of 50 miles per hour can travel 300 miles in 6 hours. This situation can be modeled by the proportion

$$\frac{50 \text{ mi}}{1 \text{ hr}} = \frac{300 \text{ mi}}{6 \text{ hr}}$$

If any three numbers in a proportion are known, then the fourth number can be found. Since the information in many rate and ratio problems can be organized in a proportion with one missing number, using proportions is a powerful problem-solving technique.

Example: A gray whale's heart beats 24 times in 3 minutes. At this rate, how many times does it beat in 2 minutes?

A simple rate table can help with writing a correct proportion.

Beats	24	x
Minutes	3	2

This table leads to the following proportion:

$$\frac{24 \text{ beats}}{3 \text{ minutes}} = \frac{x \text{ beats}}{2 \text{ minutes}}$$

This proportion can be solved in several ways. One way is to use a unit rate:

$$\frac{24 \text{ beats}}{3 \text{ minutes}} = \frac{8 \text{ beats}}{1 \text{ minute}}$$

So, in 2 minutes the whale's heart would beat 16 times.

Another approach is to use cross multiplication:

$$24 * 2 = 3x$$
$$48 = 3x$$
$$16 = x$$

Solving proportions is discussed further in Essay 9, Patterns, Sequences, Functions, and Algebra.

1.3.4 Rational Numbers and Decimals

A **rational number** is any number that can be expressed as a quotient of the form a/b or $\frac{a}{b}$, where a is an integer and b is a non-zero integer. A rational number can be positive, negative, or 0.

Any rational number can be written as either a *terminating decimal* or a *repeating decimal*. That is, the decimal for a rational number may terminate, as in

For more on fraction notation, see Section 1.3.1.

$$\frac{1}{8} = 0.125$$

or it may repeat the same pattern without terminating, as in

$$\frac{2}{3} = 0.666... = 0.\overline{6}$$
$$\frac{1}{7} = 0.142857142857... = 0.\overline{142857}$$

To find a fraction for a non-terminating, repeating decimal such as 0.123123..., multiply by an appropriate power of 10 and subtract the original number.

The bar is used to indicate the digit or group of digits that repeats.

$$
\begin{aligned}
1{,}000n &= 123.123123... \\
- \quad 1n &= 0.123123... \\
\hline
999n &= 123 \\
n &= \frac{123}{999}
\end{aligned}
$$

Not all decimals represent rational numbers. For example, there is a pattern in 0.101001000100001..., but it is not a repeating pattern. This decimal represents an irrational number. To write an irrational number as a decimal is actually impossible because an infinitely long decimal would be required. Although computer scientists have calculated over 200 billion digits of the irrational number π, for example, there are still infinitely many more digits to be calculated.

For more on irrational numbers, see Section 1.6.

1.3.5 Percents

Landowner Jones has $\frac{3}{4}$ of an acre and landowner Smith has $\frac{4}{5}$ of an acre. Who owns more land?

Answering this question may be difficult because the denominators are not the same: One represents fourths of an acre, and the other, fifths of an acre. Several methods could be used to rewrite the data in comparable terms, or to **standardize** the data. Three forms of standardization are shown below.

- **Draw pictures.**

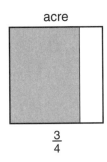 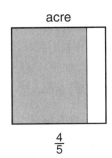

- **Rewrite the fractions with the same denominators.**

$$\frac{3}{4} = \frac{15}{20} \qquad \frac{4}{5} = \frac{16}{20}$$

- **Rewrite the fractions as decimals or percents.**

$$\frac{3}{4} = \frac{75}{100} = 0.75 = 75\% \qquad \frac{4}{5} = \frac{80}{100} = 0.80 = 80\%$$

Each of these standardization methods shows that Smith owns more land than Jones.

One of the oldest standardization methods is percent. This is because of its convenience (it would be hard to draw a diagram for every situation as in the first method above) and its efficiency (finding common denominators is not always as simple as in the second method above). A **percent** is a ratio comparison based on 100ths. The word *percent* comes from the Latin *per centum,* meaning "for each 100."

The percent symbol (%) has three equivalent meanings:

times 0.01	$5\% = 5 * 0.01 = 0.05$
times $\frac{1}{100}$	$5\% = 5 * \frac{1}{100} = \frac{5}{100}$
divided by 100	$5\% = 5/100 = 0.05$

Before calculators became a standard tool in classrooms, the elementary school mathematics curriculum usually treated topics in the following order.

1. Operations with whole numbers

2. Operations with fractions

3. Operations with decimals

4. Operations with percents

> **NOTE:** Most calculators with a [%] key apply the first meaning of percent. For example, keying in 25 [%] multiplies 25 by 0.01 and displays 0.25.

"Easy" Fractions	Decimals	Percents
$\frac{1}{2}$	0.50	50%
$\frac{1}{3}$	$0.\overline{3}$	$33\frac{1}{3}\%$
$\frac{2}{3}$	$0.\overline{6}$	$66\frac{2}{3}\%$
$\frac{1}{4}$	0.25	25%
$\frac{3}{4}$	0.75	75%
$\frac{1}{5}$	0.20	20%
$\frac{2}{5}$	0.40	40%
$\frac{3}{5}$	0.60	60%
$\frac{4}{5}$	0.80	80%
$\frac{1}{8}$	0.125	$12\frac{1}{2}\%$
$\frac{3}{8}$	0.375	$37\frac{1}{2}\%$
$\frac{5}{8}$	0.625	$62\frac{1}{2}\%$
$\frac{7}{8}$	0.875	$87\frac{1}{2}\%$
$\frac{1}{10}$	0.10	10%
$\frac{3}{10}$	0.30	30%
$\frac{7}{10}$	0.70	70%
$\frac{9}{10}$	0.90	90%

The tedious process of rewriting fractions as decimals required long division and was a key to the old ordering. Calculators make the division step much easier and give students access to more interesting applications much sooner. Thus, students see many kinds of numbers in appropriate contexts in every year. The exception is percent, which is first introduced in third grade.

The payoff for many early, informal experiences with whole numbers, fractions, and decimals comes later in the program. By seeing relationships among numbers, students use mental computation and estimation with sophistication. For example:

- "How many are 25% of 28 peaches?" Knowing that 25% is equal to $\frac{1}{4}$ makes this easy to do mentally by taking $\frac{1}{4}$ of 28. Taking $\frac{1}{4}$ of, or dividing by 4, is much simpler than multiplying 28 by 0.25 to get 7 peaches.
- "Last year 315 seniors out of 435 in the graduating class went on to college. About what percent went to college?" By rounding to 300 out of 400, or $\frac{3}{4}$, it is easy to see that about 75% of seniors went to college. If a more accurate percent is required, then this estimation helps check a calculator or pencil-and-paper result of about 72.4%.
- "Thirty fifth graders, or 20% of all the fifth graders in the school, are going to the museum. How many fifth graders are in the school?" Knowing that 20% is $\frac{1}{5}$ of all the fifth graders means there are 5 * 30, or 150 fifth graders in all.

A goal of *Everyday Mathematics* is for students completing sixth grade to instantly recognize decimal and percent equivalents for many common fractions. These include halves, thirds, fourths, eighths, fifths, and tenths. In fourth grade, students explore strategies for finding equivalencies. In fifth grade, students practice recognizing different forms by playing a *Frac-Tac-Toe* game. Throughout Grades 4–6, students use real-world contexts to practice operations with rational numbers in these several notations.

Everyday Mathematics students should be prepared to handle everyday percents much more successfully than Dilbert's boss.

DILBERT reprinted by permission of United Feature Syndicate Inc.

1.4 Positive and Negative Numbers

The invention of negative numbers was prompted by both practical and mathematical considerations. From the mathematical point of view, negative numbers are needed:

- To make subtraction closed. When negative numbers are allowed, there is an answer to every subtraction problem (including problems such as $3 - 10$).
- To complete the number line. With negative numbers, the number line can extend below 0.
- So every number has an additive inverse. The sum of a number and its additive inverse is 0. The additive inverse of a positive number is negative.

In the everyday world, negative numbers answer the need for specifying locations in reference frames in relation to a starting point (the zero point) and for naming measures that extend in both directions from the zero point. Examples include temperatures above and below a zero temperature, elevations above and below sea level, and profits and losses in business.

Beginning in Kindergarten, students use positive and negative numbers to locate points in reference to a zero point (e.g., on a temperature scale) and to represent the result of a change situation (e.g., a loss of 3 pounds is -3 pounds). Other situations in which positive and negative numbers are used include the following:

Situation	Negative	Zero	Positive
bank account	withdrawal	no change	deposit
time	before	now	after
games	behind	tied	ahead
business	loss	break even	profit
elevation	below sea level	sea level	above sea level

Such situations are useful in helping students understand that negatives are opposites of positives. Positives and negatives come in pairs, and familiarity with negatives can be improved by comparing them with their positive opposites.

One way to represent negative numbers and their relationships to positive numbers is on a number line. If the number line is on paper, the opposite relationship can be illustrated by folding on zero and comparing where points coincide. This demonstration also shows that points on the negative side of zero are reflections of points on the positive side, and vice versa. Students should be encouraged to draw number lines in their journals, on their slates, and on the chalkboard—anywhere that may help them visualize the relative locations of positive and negative numbers while they solve problems.

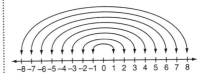

Negative numbers are opposites of positive numbers. 0 is its own opposite.

1.4.1 Possibly Confusing Notation with Negative Numbers

Reading and writing expressions with positive and negative numbers has always been a difficult topic for mathematics teachers and students. Notations with several distinct meanings can be confusing. This is certainly true of the symbol "−".

- The symbol "−" immediately preceding a numeral, as in −3 or −0.5 or −37, is read "negative" and is used in naming numbers on the number line (negative 3, negative five-tenths, negative 37).

- The symbol "−" as in −(+3) or −(−17) is read "opposite of." The opposite of a negative number is a positive number; the opposite of a positive number is a negative number. For example, the "opposite of positive 3" is negative 3, and the "opposite of negative 17" is positive 17. The number 0 is the only number that is its own opposite: −(0) = 0.

- The symbol "−" in 17 − 3 = 14 is read "minus" or "subtract" or "take away" and indicates the operation of subtraction.

The meaning of the symbol "−" can get tangled in number sentences such as the following:

−17 − 3 = −20 or "negative 17 minus 3 is equal to negative 20"

12 − −(−4) = 8 or "12 minus the opposite of negative 4 is equal to 8"

Some mathematics programs try to reduce confusion by using "−" only for subtraction. Positive and negative numbers are represented with small raised symbols (for example, ⁻3, ⁻17, ⁺17), and the opposite may be indicated by "OPP" or "op." But everyday usage and nearly all algebra books continue to use traditional notation, so students eventually have to reconcile the two notations.

The distinction between operation and sign may be clarified with a calculator on which there is an *opposite* or *change-sign* key. A variety of labels are used for this key. The change-sign key can be used to change a number to its opposite.

Other calculators have a (−) key for entering the opposite of a number. This key looks like the key for subtraction, but it is not an operation symbol, as the last line in the table below shows.

Keystrokes	Display
(−) 8 Enter	−8
(−) (−) 8 Enter	8
(−) (−) (−) 8 Enter	−8
12 − 8 Enter	4
12 − (−) 8 Enter	20
12 (−) 8 Enter	ERROR

On some calculators, the opposite key is pressed before the number. On others, it is pressed after entering the number. To enter −5 on the latter type, for example, first press 5, then press the opposite key. The negative sign may appear in the margin of the display rather than next to the 5. Other than that, expressions are entered left to right as always.

Everyday Mathematics uses the traditional notation for "negative" and "minus," although occasionally "OPP" appears in Grade 6. We urge you to help students sort out the meanings of these symbols by reading "+" as "plus" or "positive" and "−" as "minus," "negative," or "opposite," as required by the context. Eventually, students should do likewise when they read mathematical expressions.

1.4.2 Positive and Negative Rational Numbers

In *Everyday Mathematics,* **negative rational numbers** are presented to students as a natural extension of fractions, or positive rational numbers, in much the same way that negative integers are presented as an extension of whole numbers. Both the idea of negative numbers and the symbols for recording them probably originated in India and were used there in a systematic way by about A.D. 650.

A major use of negative numbers is to express quantities with reference to a zero point. For example, a temperature of 10 degrees below zero can be written as $-10°$ and a depth of 2,356 feet below sea level as $-2,356$ feet. Positive and negative numbers are also used to express changes in quantities. For example, a weight gain of $4\frac{1}{2}$ pounds can be recorded as $+4\frac{1}{2}$ pounds, and a decrease in income of 1,000 dollars as $-\$1,000$.

Positive and negative rational numbers can be shown on a number line that extends in both directions from zero. Each negative number is shown by a point that is a mirror image of a point for a positive number.

The Integers

An important subset of the rational numbers is the set of **integers,** which include the natural numbers, their negatives, and 0. In practice, students of *Everyday Mathematics* investigate negative integers more than negative rational numbers; the latter appear occasionally as answers in fraction subtraction problems in Grade 6.

There are few everyday uses of negative fractions and decimals, except in finance. Temperatures below zero and elevations below sea level are usually rounded to the nearest integer.

The authors have generally avoided using the term *integer,* choosing instead to call numbers simply positive or negative when a distinction is necessary. The goal is to have students of *Everyday Mathematics* become comfortable with positive and negative numbers in general and not to have undue concern if a problem contains a negative non-integer. They are most likely to encounter non-integer negative numbers in pre-algebra and algebra classes, and these are most likely to be negative rational numbers.

1.5 Properties of Rational Numbers

By the time students complete *Sixth Grade Everyday Mathematics,* they will have investigated all of the basic properties of the rational number system, almost all of them in the context of everyday problems. These properties are summarized for sixth graders in their *Student Reference Book* (pages 102–104), and they are included in the Reference Pages section at the end of this book for the information of teachers in Grades 4 and 5.

For more about quantities in reference frames, see Essay 7.

1.6 Irrational Numbers

If a decimal neither terminates nor has a digit or block of digits that repeats endlessly, then it represents an **irrational number.** An irrational number cannot be rewritten as a fraction, or ratio, $\frac{a}{b}$ where a and b are integers and $b \neq 0$. Examples of irrational numbers include 0.101001000100001..., $\sqrt{2}$ (1.41421356...), and π (3.14159265...). Since a decimal for an irrational number has no repeating pattern, an infinitely long decimal would be required to write it in standard notation. In practice, this means that special symbols such as " $\sqrt{}$ " and "..." must be used in representing irrational numbers.

The ancient Babylonians and Egyptians (c. 3000 B.C.) were able to solve what we now call algebra problems, and in so doing they came upon irrational numbers. For example, $\sqrt{2}$ is the answer to "What is the length of the diagonal of a square with sides each 1 unit long?" This problem is solved in the margin using the Pythagorean Theorem. A definition of $\sqrt{2}$, in fact, could be "the number that makes the equation $2 = n^2$ true."

The Babylonians and Egyptians did not understand the "irrational" nature of $\sqrt{2}$. They gave fractional approximations of $\sqrt{2}$ as though they were the exact answer. Since most calculations were done in the context of a concrete problem in engineering, architecture, or surveying, a rational approximation was appropriate, as it still is today in practical situations.

In the fifth or sixth century B.C., Greek mathematicians and philosophers known as the Pythagoreans realized that numbers such as $\sqrt{2}$ are *not* rational, because they do not coincide with points on the rational number line.

The Greeks knew that the whole numbers—negative numbers were unknown at the time—could be represented on a number line by multiples of a unit length. Fractions could be represented by splitting the unit into smaller and smaller pieces—halves, thirds, fourths, fifths, 99ths, 120,000ths, and so on. By subdividing and adding unit lengths, the Greeks were able, in theory, to generate infinitely many numbers, all those that today we call the rational numbers. Howard Eves writes in *Great Moments in Mathematics (Before 1650):*

> To the early mathematicians it seemed evident, as indeed it seems to anyone today who has not been initiated into the deeper mysteries of the number line, that all the points on the line are ... used up; ordinary common sense seems to indicate this to us.

> It must have been a genuine mental shock for man to learn that there are points on the number line not corresponding to any rational number. This discovery was certainly one of the greatest achievements of the early Greeks, and it seems to have occurred some time in the fifth or sixth century B.C. among the ranks of the Pythagorean brotherhood. A truly GREAT MOMENT IN

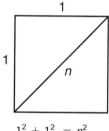

$$1^2 + 1^2 = n^2$$
$$1 + 1 = n^2$$
$$2 = n^2$$
$$\sqrt{2} = n$$

MATHEMATICS had arisen. (pp. 43–44)

[Eves, Howard. *Great Moments in Mathematics (Before 1650)*.
The Mathematical Association of America, 1983.]

This was a "great moment" because, according to the Pythagorean philosophy, all of mathematics was based on whole numbers and their relationships under addition, subtraction, multiplication, and division (a view not uncommon to many traditional elementary school mathematics programs). This limited mathematics to rational numbers, those that can be represented by ratios of whole numbers. The discovery of the irrationals, numbers that cannot be represented as ratios of whole numbers, was a revolutionary event. According to Eves:

> So great was the "logical scandal" that ... efforts were made for a while to keep the matter secret, and one legend has it that the Pythagorean Hippasus of Metapontum perished at sea for his impiety in disclosing the secret to outsiders, or (according to another version) was banished from the Pythagorean community and a tomb erected for him as though he were dead. (p. 53)

The crisis was profound. Not only did the rational numbers not account for all the points on the number line, there were infinitely many irrational numbers mixed in with them! Happily, the crisis was overcome—the irrational numbers were accepted—and *Everyday Mathematics* students can ponder the results.

It is actually easy to construct a point on a number line with an irrational coordinate. The number line in the margin shows how to construct a point at $\sqrt{2}$. First draw a unit square with its base along the line. Set a compass to the length of the diagonal, and with center at the zero point, draw an arc so that it intersects the number line at point P. The length of OP is $\sqrt{2}$ units, and it can be proven that this length cannot be a rational number.

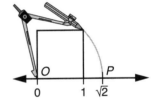

See Section 5.4.2 of the Geometry essay for more about the Pythagorean Theorem.

Students in *Everyday Mathematics* begin exploring the irrational number π in Grade 3 by investigating ratios of circumferences and diameters in circles. Students work with the square-root operation in Grade 5 as a process for "un-squaring" numbers. (When the square root of a whole number does not "come out even," then it is irrational.) Sixth graders review square roots when they use the formula for the area of a circle to find the radius of a circle with known area and when they investigate the Pythagorean Theorem.

1.7 Real Numbers

The **real numbers** are simply all the rational and irrational numbers together. The set of real numbers accounts for all the points on the number line. Between any two points on the real number line, there are infinitely many points, and infinitely many real numbers to go with them. And, just as important, there are no other kinds of numbers on the number line. Every point on the number line can be matched with a real number, and every real number can be matched with a point on the number line.

The illustration of the real number line below is from the *Student Reference Book* for *Sixth Grade Everyday Mathematics.*

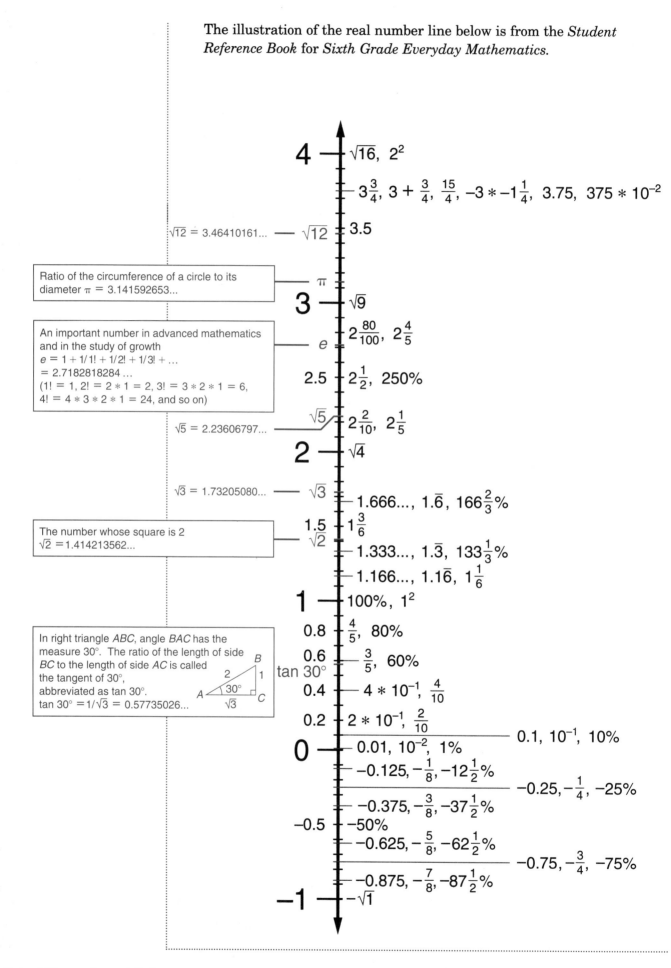

All the numbers in *Everyday Mathematics*—counting numbers; positive rational numbers expressed as fractions, decimals, and percents; irrational numbers like $\sqrt{2}$ and π; negative rational numbers—are real numbers. In the school mathematics curriculum, however, most work with the irrational real numbers is reserved for secondary school mathematics, so most numbers students encounter before high school are rational.

There are infinitely many rational numbers. You could count them, but it would take forever. The number of rational numbers is represented by the symbol $\aleph_0$, which is read "aleph null." There are even more irrational numbers than rational numbers. In the late nineteenth century, the mathematician Georg Cantor proved that counting the real numbers is impossible, even if you could count forever.

1.8 Number Systems

Students in *Everyday Mathematics* explore systems of whole numbers, positive rational numbers, and positive and negative rational numbers. They are introduced to the real number system in Grade 6. As complete as this may sound, it is just the beginning of the journey. The next number system they are likely to see includes *imaginary numbers,* which together with the real numbers form the complex number system. The keystone of the **complex number system** is the number $\sqrt{-1}$, which is defined as the solution to $x^2 = -1$. Students will study these numbers in algebra and pre-calculus courses.

1.9 Numerical Order

Rational counting skills are those by which students assign numbers to the objects in a set. The order of the objects in the set isn't important, just the count. Rote counting (counting on, counting back, and skip counting) is students' first experience with numbers in order. Beginning in Kindergarten, the representations of counts on timelines, number lines, number grids, and scrolls help students experience ordered patterns. These patterns form a foundation for understanding place value, arithmetic operations, and patterns in sequences and functions.

The next two sections are about two basic mathematical concepts used to describe and communicate about numerical order: ordinality and comparison.

1.9.1 Ordinal Numbers

The counting numbers tell how many: 5 apples, 3 books, 2 birds. To tell the order of objects in a sequence, a different kind of number is used: first, second, third, and so on. These are called the **ordinal numbers.**

The ordinal numbers are not as simple as they seem. Suppose, for example, we have an apple, a pear, a peach, a banana, and a plum. Counting these pieces of fruit is easy: There are five of them. But

assigning ordinals is not so easy. The apple is listed first, but it could easily be listed third or fifth instead. Indeed, the apple might be first in alphabetical order and fifth in weight. Also, *5* refers to the entire collection of fruit, but *fifth* refers only to the last piece in some sequential ordering of the five fruits. Fortunately, students can learn to use ordinal numbers without having to bother about these rather abstract issues.

1.9.2 Numerical Relations

In mathematics, a **relation** tells how one thing compares to another. In this section, we discuss numerical relations. The most important numerical relations are equality (=) and inequality (≠, <, and >), but there are others. Geometric relations are discussed in Section 5.7.2, Congruence and Similarity.

Even preschool students have some idea of "more" and "less." They may be deceived by appearances but, under the right conditions, they can judge bigger/smaller, shorter/taller, heavier/lighter, and so on. This capacity for judging more/less is the basis for understanding numerical relations.

As students begin to attach counts and measures to objects, they learn ways to write the relations between those objects symbolically. Table 1 shows the most common symbols for expressing numerical relations.

Beginning in *First Grade Everyday Mathematics,* students write simple number sentences with =, <, and >. In later grades, they add ≤, ≥, and ≠ to their mathematical toolboxes. In Grade 6, students begin combining variables with the symbols for the inequalities to write open sentences that compare sets of numbers rather than just two numbers.

Table 1. Symbols for Numerical Relations		
Symbol	**Meaning**	**Examples**
=	*"is equal to"* *"is the same as"*	$3 = \frac{6}{2}$ 3.0 seconds = 3 seconds $\frac{1}{2} = 50\%$
>	*"is greater than"*	$12 > 4$ $1.23 > 1.2$ $12{,}346 \text{ ft} > -12{,}346 \text{ ft}$
<	*"is less than"*	$8 < 12$ million $0.1 < 1.1$ $\frac{5}{2} < 4$
≥	*"is greater than or equal to"*	The crowd ≥ 250 people. The temperature ≥ 32°F. The area ≥ 2 acres.
≤	*"is less than or equal to"*	The rent ≤ $700. The fee ≤ $25. The time ≤ 2 hours.
≠	*"is not equal to"* *"is not the same as"*	$10 \neq 100$ $\frac{10}{120} \neq \frac{1}{2}$ $85\% \neq 85$

Equality

Although the concept of equality seems straightforward, students who have been through several years of schooling often have difficulty using the "=" symbol. Research studies show that many older students reject number sentences such as $5 = 5$ (they say there is no problem), $4 = 2 + 2$ (they say that the answer is on the wrong side), and $4 + 3 = 5 + 2$ (they say there are two problems, but no answers).

The origin of these errors seems clear. Students in school usually see number sentences written only with a problem on the left-hand side of the equal sign and the answer on the right-hand side: $5 + 7 = 12$. The cure is obvious: Deliberately write $12 = 5 + 7$ as often as $5 + 7 = 12$, and encourage students to say "means the same as" or "looks different, but is really the same as" when the equal symbol appears.

In large part, arithmetic consists of simply replacing numbers or expressions with equivalent (equal) numbers or expressions.[2] We replace $7 + 8$ with 15, or substitute 27 for $\frac{459}{17}$. When it suits us, we use $\frac{1}{2}$ in place of $\frac{1}{3} + \frac{1}{6}$ and vice versa. Number sense and arithmetic skills consist largely of being aware of the many possibilities for equivalent names for numbers and being able to exploit them flexibly.

For most collections of equivalent names, one name is often recognized as the "simplest" and serves to identify the entire collection. But simplest doesn't necessarily mean best: $\frac{50}{100}$ (as in 50 per 100) may convey more information in a given situation than its simpler cousin $\frac{1}{2}$ and also serves as a better bridge to understanding that 50% is equivalent to $\frac{1}{2}$. Unfortunately, much of the traditional mathematics curriculum has made the "simplification" of numbers synonymous with mathematics itself. Students of *Everyday Mathematics* will not have this sterile experience.

Name-Collection Boxes

Beginning in *First Grade Everyday Mathematics,* students use name-collection boxes to help them recognize equivalent names for numbers. These devices offer a simple way for students to experience the notion that the same number can be expressed in many different ways. Names can include sums, differences, products, quotients, the results of combining several operations, words in English or other languages, tally marks, arrays, Roman numerals, numerals in bases other than ten, and so on.

In Kindergarten through third grade, a **name-collection box** diagram is an open-top box with a label attached to it. The name

NOTE: The symbol $\approx$ is introduced in *Fifth Grade Everyday Mathematics* as a convenient shorthand for "is approximately equal to." Although $\approx$ is not well enough defined to qualify as a mathematical relation, it is nevertheless useful in situations involving estimation and approximation.

---

[2]The French mathematician Henri Poincaré (1854–1912) went even further. He once remarked that "Mathematics is the art of giving the same name to different things." For example, mathematicians give the name *polygon* to squares, triangles, pentagons, and many other different things.

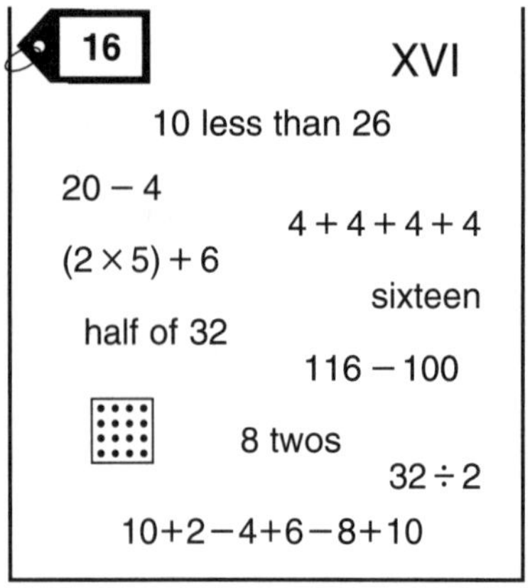

16

XVI

10 less than 26

20 − 4

$4 + 4 + 4 + 4$

$(2 \times 5) + 6$

sixteen

half of 32

$116 - 100$

8 twos

$32 \div 2$

$10+2-4+6-8+10$

12

$6 + 6$

$4 * 3$

$36 \div 3$

12-box

on the label identifies the number whose names are collected in the box. For example, the box shown on the left above is a 16-box, a name-collection box for the number 16. Beginning in fourth grade, students use a more compact name-collection box such as the one shown for 12.

1.10 Number Uses

If you're looking for one phrase to capture the overall philosophy of *Everyday Mathematics,* it might be "Numbers All Around." In Kindergarten, students explore magazines and other media in search of numbers. In Grade 1, students create a "Numbers All Around Museum" and collect numbers about themselves. In Grade 2, students collect numbers about their worlds and curate another Numbers All Around Museum. In Grade 3, students build a "Mathematics All Around" bulletin board and look for mathematics in their world. In Grades 4–6, students find numbers in almanacs, atlases, encyclopedias, the World Tour (Grade 4) and American Tour (Grade 5) sections of the *Student Reference Book*, and many other sources.

The numbers that surround us in today's world are not all the same. Some are measurements, some are counts, and others still are used for identification. The developers of *Everyday Mathematics* have identified five basic categories, or use classes, that cover 90 percent of number uses:

- counts
- measures
- locations
- ratio comparisons
- codes

Counts and measures are straightforward: 6 eggs, 3 pounds, and so on. Locations are a bit trickier: 9:05 A.M. expresses a location in time; 72 °C is a location on a temperature scale; pairs of numbers such as 42 °N, 87 °W mark a location on Earth's surface. A ratio comparison is a number like 3 times as much or $\frac{1}{2}$ as many. Ratio comparisons are less common than counts and measures in primary grade

For more on this use of numbers and how it differs from measurement, see the Reference Frames essay.

mathematics, but become increasingly important in later grades. Codes are numbers used as identification tags, which often also include letters. Codes are used for credit cards, Social Security numbers, phone numbers, and so on. Often a code has several parts. For example, in the ZIP code 60637:

6 refers to Illinois, Missouri, Nebraska, or Kansas

06 refers to Chicago

37 refers to the neighborhood in Chicago that includes the University of Chicago

In Grades 4–6, students begin to encounter numbers used as constants in formulas, such as the number π in the formula for the circumference of a circle, $C = \pi * d$. In this formula, π is a ratio comparison. In other formulas, constants may represent counts, measures, or other use classes.

In organizing *Everyday Mathematics,* the authors have been careful to balance the types of numbers that students are exposed to in lessons, journals, and activity sheets. Although occasionally use classes are made explicit, more often than not they are simply implicit in the context of a problem.

ESSAY

2

Arithmetic Operations

outline

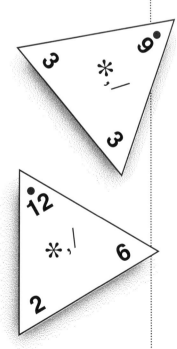

For many adults, elementary school mathematics consisted of little more than learning to add, subtract, multiply, and divide whole numbers, fractions, and decimals. Unfortunately, this is still the experience of many students today. The authors of *Everyday Mathematics* hope that your acquaintance with our texts and your reading of this manual have convinced you that elementary school mathematics must be far more than arithmetic with the four basic operations.

Nevertheless, the importance of arithmetic in mathematics and in everyday life cannot be denied. By combining activities that focus on understanding the basic arithmetic operations with activities that apply arithmetic in geometry, data exploration, measurement, and other contexts, *Everyday Mathematics* ensures both that students receive ample practice with arithmetic skills and also that they will be better able to make use of those skills to solve problems. Furthermore, rather than encountering only addition and subtraction in first and second grades, with multiplication and division delayed until third grade or later, students in *Everyday Mathematics* see many uses of all the operations from the beginning and build upon these uses year after year.

Many adults who equate school mathematics with arithmetic also tend to think that an arithmetic operation is what you "do" to get the answer. To these adults, for example, division is simply carrying out the traditional long-division algorithm. In *Everyday*

Mathematics, how one "does" an operation is referred to as "applying an algorithm" or "carrying out a computation." Although *Everyday Mathematics* recognizes the importance of knowing algorithms and introduces a variety of algorithms for each operation, the program also emphasizes that students need to understand the meanings behind each operation. Choosing the proper algorithm and interpreting the result correctly depend on understanding the operation itself. Both understanding the operations and proficiency at carrying out algorithms are required for successful problem solving.

This essay discusses the meanings of the basic arithmetic operations. Paper-and-pencil algorithms for these operations are discussed in Essay 3; mental arithmetic, estimation, and basic facts are discussed in Essay 8; and arithmetic symbols, number sentences, variables, and algebra are discussed in Essay 9.

2.1 Use Classes and Situation Diagrams

One way to understand something is to examine how it is used. A hammer is used for driving nails. An umbrella is used for keeping dry in the rain. This is how *Everyday Mathematics* approaches the basic operations of arithmetic. At a certain stage, formal definitions are necessary, but in the elementary grades it is better to approach the operations indirectly, by looking at how they are used.

The basic operations of arithmetic—addition, subtraction, multiplication, and division—can be applied in many different situations, but most of those situations can be sorted into just a handful of categories. In *Everyday Mathematics,* the three basic categories for addition and subtraction are called **parts and total, change,** and **comparison.** Depending on what is known and what is unknown, each kind of situation can lead to either addition or subtraction problems. Multiplication and division situations are harder to sort out, but several basic categories can be distinguished: **equal groups, arrays and area, rate and ratio, scaling,** and **Cartesian product.** Again, each kind of situation can lead to either multiplication or division problems depending on what is unknown.

Everyday Mathematics uses special diagrams to help sort out these various kinds of problem situations. These situation diagrams help students organize the information in simple, one-step number stories. (The diagrams in *Everyday Mathematics* are adapted from work done by Karen Fuson at Northwestern University.)

2.1.1 Addition and Subtraction

Most situations that lead to addition and subtraction problems can be categorized as *parts and total, change,* or *comparison.*

Although the examples on the next page are easy and appropriate for students in second and third grades, the principles they illustrate can be applied to more complicated problems for students in Grades 4–6.

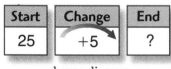

parts-and-total diagram

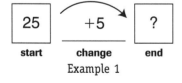

change diagram

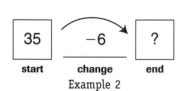

Example 1

Parts-and-Total Diagrams

A parts-and-total diagram is used to represent situations in which two or more quantities (parts) are combined to form a total quantity.

Example: Twelve fourth graders, 8 third graders, and 5 first graders are on a bus. How many students in all are on the bus?

The parts are known. You are looking for the total.

Possible number model: 12 + 8 + 5 = ___

Total		
?		
Part	Part	Part
12	8	5

Total		
?		
Part	Part	Part
12	8	5

If you know the total but don't know all the parts, you could use subtraction instead of addition to find the unknown part.

Example: Thirty-five students are riding on a bus. 20 of them are boys. How many girls are riding on the bus?

One part and the total are known.
You are looking for the other part.

Possible number models:

20 + ___ = 35

35 − 20 = ___

Change Diagrams

Change diagrams are used to represent problems in which a given quantity (start) is increased or decreased.

Example 1: Twenty-five students are riding on a bus. At the next stop, 5 more students get on. How many students are on the bus now?

The number with which you started has been increased.

Possible number model: 25 + 5 = ___

Example 2: A bus leaves school with 35 students. At the first stop, 6 students get off. How many students are left on the bus?

The number with which you started has been decreased.

Possible number model: 35 − 6 = ___

Compare Diagrams

Compare diagrams are used for problems involving two quantities and the difference between them. Compare situations can lead to either addition or subtraction problems, depending on whether one of the compared quantities or the difference between them is unknown.

Example: There are 12 fourth graders and 8 third graders. How many more fourth graders are there than third graders?

You are comparing the number of fourth graders with the number of third graders.

Possible number models:

$12 - 8 = $ ___

$8 + $ ___ $= 12$

Quantity
12

Quantity	Difference
8	?

4th graders
12

3rd graders	
8	?

difference

Teaching with Addition/Subtraction Diagrams

It is important to remember that the diagrams described above are simply devices to help organize problem solving; they are not ends in themselves. Some students do not need to organize their thinking on paper, and to require them to do so would not be constructive.

For those students who do find diagrams useful, *Everyday Mathematics* suggests that they follow these steps, though not necessarily in this order:

- Choose a diagram that fits the problem situation. Sometimes more than one diagram can fit a given situation. One person might think of a situation as parts-and-total while another person might see the same situation as change. Be flexible about which diagram is the most appropriate for a given situation, and remember that many situations are not suitable for any diagram. Multistep problems, for example, do not easily fit into these diagrams.

- Write the known quantities and a question mark for the unknown quantity in the appropriate parts of the diagram.

- Use the diagram to help decide how to solve the problem. Most problems can be solved in more than one way.

- Find the answer.

- Write a number model that fits the problem. Often several number models can fit a single situation. Connecting number models to problem situations can help students understand both the arithmetic operations and the symbols for those operations.

- Write the answer. Be sure to include a measurement unit or other label.

- Check to see if the answer makes sense.

The importance of including the unit in the answer must be emphasized again and again. Numbers make most sense when they are thought of in real-world contexts.

Unit Boxes

Because labeling each number can become tedious, *Everyday Mathematics* suggests that you and your students use unit boxes for addition and subtraction problems. These rectangular boxes can be displayed beside the problem or at the top of a page of problems. Unit boxes contain the labels or units of measure used in the problem(s). Unit boxes help students organize their mathematics while keeping a particular context in mind.

Unit
cents ¢

unit box

You might consider posting a unit box for the day on the chalkboard so that students will think of all abstract numbers used in the day's activities (for example, facts practice) in some context. Or students can supply the context themselves; they can choose topics of current interest or, if they prefer, fanciful or silly labels.

2.1.2 Multiplication and Division

Multiplication and division arise in many different situations, but most of these situations can be sorted into just a few categories. These are equal groups, arrays and area, rate and ratio, scaling, and Cartesian product.

Everyday Mathematics uses diagrams to organize the information in many of these situations. The diagrams have two rows of rectangles. The top row is for the units; the bottom row is for the numbers. As with the diagrams for addition and subtraction situations, these diagrams are meant as problem-solving tools, not as ends in themselves. If using such a diagram is not helpful, try some other approach, such as making a table, drawing a different diagram, or writing a number model. See Essay 10 for a discussion of problem solving, Essay 9 for a discussion of solving proportions and other number sentences, and Essay 7 for a discussion of maps and model scales.

Equal Groups

In an equal-groups situation, there are several groups of objects with the same number of objects in each group. Depending on what is unknown, equal-groups situations can lead to either multiplication or division problems.

If the total is unknown in an equal-groups situation but the number of groups and the number of objects in each group are known, then the problem can be solved by multiplication.

Example: A vase holds 5 flowers with 6 petals on each flower. How many petals are there in all?

Possible number model: $5 * 6 = $ ___

flowers	petals per flower	total petals
5	6	?

If the number of groups and the total number of objects are both known, then the problem is to find the number in each group. In *Everyday Mathematics* these are called **equal-sharing problems.** Equal-sharing is also known as partitive division.

Many students solve equal-sharing problems by "dealing out" the objects to be shared.

NOTE: In the upper grades of *Everyday Mathematics,* the usual symbol for multiplication is $*$. This symbol has several advantages over $\times$. One is that $*$ can be found on a standard keyboard, whereas $\times$ cannot. Another is that $*$ is used to denote multiplication in many computer programming languages. A third is that $*$ avoids possible confusion between $\times$ and the letter $x,$ something that is increasingly important with the introduction of letter variables.

Example: Twenty-eight baseball cards are shared equally by 4 students. How many cards does each child get?

Possible number models:

4 * ___ = 28

28 / 4 = ___

students	baseball cards per student	total number of cards
4	?	28

NOTE: In the upper grades of *Everyday Mathematics,* the usual symbol for division is /. This symbol has several advantages over ÷. One is that / can be found on a standard keyboard, whereas ÷ cannot. Another is that / is used to denote division in many computer programming languages. A third is that using / emphasizes the connection between division and fractions. Outside elementary school mathematics, in fact, the symbol ÷ is almost never seen; division is typically denoted using fraction notation.

If the number in each group and the total number of objects are known, then the problem is to find the number of groups. In *Everyday Mathematics,* these are called **equal-grouping problems.**

Many students solve equal-grouping problems by making as many groups of the correct size as possible and then counting the number of groups.

Example: Twenty-four Girl Scouts are going on a canoe trip. Each canoe can hold 3 scouts. How many canoes are needed?

Possible number models:

3 * ___ = 24

24 / 3 = ___

canoes	scouts per canoe	total number of scouts
?	3	24

Equal-grouping is also called measurement division or quotitive division. The term *measurement division* comes from thinking about using the divisor to "measure" the dividend. For example, consider the problem 26 / 6. The question is, "How many 6s would it take to make 26?" Imagine measuring off 6-unit lengths on a number line:

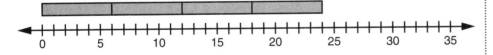

The figure shows that there are four 6-unit lengths in 26, with 2 left over. Thus 26 / 6 is 4 with remainder 2.

Arrays and Area

Arrays are closely related to equal-groups situations. If the equal groups are arranged in rows and columns, then a rectangular array is formed. As with equal-groups situations, arrays can lead to either multiplication or division problems.

Example: There are 6 rows with 15 socks in each row. How many socks are there in all?

Possible number model: 6 * 15 = ___

rows	socks per row	total number of socks
6	15	?

Arrays are closely related to *area*. An array of square centimeter tiles with no gaps between the tiles will have an area in square centimeters equal to the number of tiles. Unlike any of the previous models, the concept of area generalizes to multiplication with fractions, decimals, and mixed numbers.

Example: The area of a rectangle is 48 square cm. The rectangle's length is 8 cm. What is its width?

Possible number models:

8 * ___ = 48

48 / 8 = ___

length (cm)	width (cm)	area (sq cm)
8	?	48

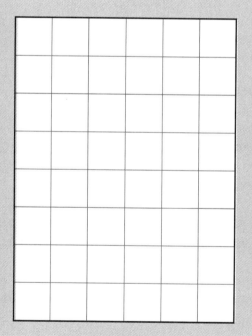

Rate and Ratio

Rate and ratio situations are common in higher mathematics and real-world applications. The basic model for rates and ratios is speed, which is the rate of distance per time, but many other situations can also be thought of as rates or ratios as well. When you buy apples, for example, the total cost depends on the amount you purchase and the price per pound, a rate. See Section 1.3.3 for further discussion of rates and ratios.

Example: The 8 people on the pep squad worked a total of 20 hours preparing for the school assembly. What was the average number of hours per person?

Possible number models:

20 / 8 = ___

8 * ___ = 20

people	hours per person	total person-hours
8	?	20

Scaling

Scaling is another kind of situation that leads to multiplication or division. The **scale factor** tells how much larger or smaller something becomes. When you double a recipe, for example, you are scaling by 2. If the scale factor is less than 1, then the scaling makes the object smaller.

Example 1: Hector weighed 6 lb at birth. At one year, he weighed 3 times his birth weight. What was his weight at one year?

Possible number model: 3 * 6 = ___

scale factor	birth weight	one-year weight
3	6 lb	?

Scale factors, also known as scalars, can also be expressed as fractions or percents. Scaling problems can involve either multiplication or division, depending on what is known and what is to be found.

Example 2: A store has a $\frac{1}{2}$ off (or 50% off) sale. What was the original price of an item that cost $30 on sale?

Possible number models:

$\frac{1}{2}$ * ___ = 30

30 / $\frac{1}{2}$ = ___

scale factor	original price	sale price
$\frac{1}{2}$	?	$30

Cartesian Product

The last kind of multiplication and division situation is called the Cartesian product. Despite the imposing name, the idea is not so

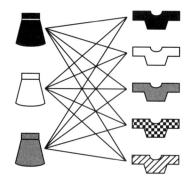

difficult. A Cartesian product is the number of pairs that match one item from each of two sets. For example, suppose someone has 3 skirts (black, white, gray) and 5 blouses (black, white, gray, checked, striped). The Cartesian product, 3 * 5, tells how many outfits that person has: black skirt and black blouse, black skirt and white blouse, and so on. If the two sets are not too big, this can be shown in a diagram.

Teaching with Multiplication/Division Diagrams

See "Teaching with Addition and Subtraction Diagrams" in Section 2.1.1 for suggestions on how students might use these diagrams. Keep in mind that the diagrams are devices to help organize problem solving, not ends in themselves. Some students simply do not need to organize their thinking on paper, and to oblige them to do so is not advisable.

2.2 Powers and Exponents

Addition, subtraction, multiplication, and division are the four basic arithmetic operations, but there are other operations that are important in school mathematics. One of these is raising to powers, or exponentiation.

Positive whole-number exponents were first used by René Descartes in the early seventeenth century to represent the number of factors in a repeated multiplication. For example, in $2 * 2 * 2 * 2 = 2^4$, the **exponent** (4) is the number of times the **base** (2) is used as a **factor.** 2^4 is read "2 to the fourth power" or simply "2 to the fourth." In most books and with paper and pencil, the exponent is written as a superscript, above and slightly to the right of the base. This notation is easy to read and write, but it can be difficult to enter from typewriters or computer keyboards. Hence, in the computer age, other notations have become common.

In most computer programs, 2^4 would be typed as 2^4, where the ^, called a *caret,* represents exponentiation. On a keyboard, ^ is the upper case of the "6" key. In some early computer programs, 2^4 was typed as 2 * * 4, which suggests the connection between multiplication and exponentiation.

Many scientific calculators have a power key, usually labeled [^] or [y^x]. To calculate 2^4 on a scientific calculator, for example, press: 2 [^] 4 [=]. The display will show 16. The [^] key means "raised to the" as in "2 raised to the fourth power." A few calculators use [x^y] or other keys for exponentiation.

When 2 and 3 are used as exponents, they are often read as **squared** and **cubed,** respectively. For example, 4^2 is read "4 to the second power" or "4 squared"; 4^3 is read "4 to the third power" or "4 cubed." These terms reflect the relationship of powering to dimension: the area of a square, which is 2-dimensional, is the length of its side raised to the second power; the volume of a cube, which is 3-dimensional, is the length of an edge raised to the third power.

Any (non-zero) number to the **zero** power is defined to be equal to 1. For example, $4^0 = 1$. This definition may seem peculiar, but it is made to preserve many important patterns with exponents. One such pattern is that every power of a number is the next higher power of the number divided by the number itself. For example, $3^2 = 3^3 / 3 = 27 / 3 = 9$. Extending this pattern to 3^0 yields $3^0 = 3^1 / 3 = 3 / 3 = 1$.

Any number to the **first** power is equal to itself. For example, $4^1 = 4$.

Although exponents are not used in *K–3 Everyday Mathematics*, students in Grade 3 are introduced informally to **square numbers** and **square products** by observing how such numbers can be displayed in square arrays. Beginning in Grade 4, students use **powers of ten**, written in exponential notation, to represent large numbers. Later, beginning in fifth grade, they learn **scientific notation**, a shorthand for writing very large and very small numbers. Students also see how exponential notation can be used in repeated doubling (which involves powers of 2) and in squaring numbers (which involves 2 as a power). Finally, they generalize the use of exponential notation to represent n factors of a base a as a^n, where a is any number and n is any integer. See Section 2.2.2 for further discussion of scientific notation.

2.2.1 Powers of Ten and Negative Exponents

Powers of ten are used for scientific notation. The non-negative powers of ten are easy to remember because the exponent indicates how many zeros appear after the 1 when the number is written in standard notation. (**Standard notation** is ordinary base-ten place-value notation, our familiar system for representing whole numbers and decimals. For example, in standard notation one million is written as 1,000,000.)

Negative exponents, introduced in Grade 5, are used in Grade 6 to represent very small numbers in scientific notation. Powers with negative exponents are read in the same way as powers with positive exponents. For example, 10^{-2} is read "10 to the negative second power" or "10 to the negative 2." The negative two exponent signals that 10^2 is used as a divisor, as shown.

$$10^{-2} = \frac{1}{10^2} = \frac{1}{100}$$

Negative powers of ten can be written in either fraction form or decimal form.

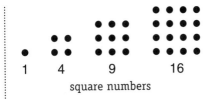

1   4   9   16
square numbers

Doubling:
$2^1 = 2$, $2^2 = 4$, $2^3 = 8$, $2^4 = 16$...

Squaring:
$1^2 = 1$, $2^2 = 4$, $3^2 = 9$, $4^2 = 16$...

Generalization:
$$\underbrace{a * a * a * \ldots * a}_{n \text{ factors}} = a^n$$

$10^1 = 10$
$10^2 = 100$
$10^3 = 1,000$
$10^4 = 10,000$
$10^5 = 100,000$
$10^6 = 1,000,000$

Power of Ten	Fraction	Decimal
10^{-1}	$\frac{1}{10}$	0.1
10^{-2}	$\frac{1}{10^2}$ or $\frac{1}{100}$	0.01
10^{-3}	$\frac{1}{10^3}$ or $\frac{1}{1,000}$	0.001
10^{-4}	$\frac{1}{10^4}$ or $\frac{1}{10,000}$	0.0001
10^{-5}	$\frac{1}{10^5}$ or $\frac{1}{100,000}$	0.00001
10^{-6}	$\frac{1}{10^6}$ or $\frac{1}{1,000,000}$	0.000001

The exponent indicates how many zeros follow the 1 in the denominator when the number is written in fraction form. In the decimal form, the exponent indicates how many digits follow the decimal point.

Powers of ten written with negative exponents are a special case of the general rule $a^{-b} = \frac{1}{a^b}$, where a is any integer except 0 and b is a positive whole number. For example, $2^{-3} = \frac{1}{2^3} = \frac{1}{8}$.

In more advanced mathematics courses, students will be introduced to fractional exponents (for example, $\sqrt{2} = 2^{\frac{1}{2}}$), and then to bases and exponents that are real numbers. These can be demonstrated on a calculator (for example, $\sqrt{2}^{\pi} = 2.97068642\ldots$).

Note on Reciprocals

The product of a number and its **reciprocal,** or **multiplicative inverse,** is 1. For example, 5 and $\frac{1}{5}$ are reciprocals of each other since $5 * \frac{1}{5} = 1$. Every number except 0 has a reciprocal. The reciprocal of any (non-zero) number, a, can be written as a^{-1}. A bit of algebra shows why this is:

$$a * a^{-1} = a * \frac{1}{a} = \frac{a}{a} = 1$$

More generally, a^{-b} is the reciprocal of a^b.

On calculators with an inverse key, the reciprocal is usually labeled $[\frac{1}{x}]$ or $[x^{-1}]$. The two symbols are equivalent. On calculators without an inverse key but with an exponentiation key, the reciprocal of a number can be found by raising the number to the -1 power.

2.2.2 Scientific Notation

It is often cumbersome to read and write very large and very small numbers. At times, it may not even be necessary or appropriate to consider all the digits in a large or small number; a rounded number works fine. For this reason, we often use shorthand forms with large and small numbers.

Consider the area of the Pacific Ocean given in the *World Almanac and Book of Facts 2000:* 64,186,300 square miles. This is about 64,000,000 sq. mi, so one shorthand form is "64 million sq. mi." Such **number-and-word notation** is common in newspapers and magazines. *Everyday Mathematics* students begin using this notation in third grade. In Grades 4 and 5, they are introduced to the exponential notation for powers of ten, described above.

Finally, in Grade 6, students use their knowledge of powers of ten to write large and small numbers in **scientific notation.** A number written in scientific notation is the product of two factors: one factor is a number greater than or equal to 1 and less than 10, and the other factor is a power of ten. Depending on the accuracy needed, the decimal part may be rounded. Estimates of the area of the Pacific Ocean can be written in scientific notation as

$$6.41863 * 10^7 \text{ or } 6.42 * 10^7 \text{ or } 6.4 * 10^7$$

The exponent 7 indicates how many places to the right the decimal point needs to be moved in order to write the number in standard form.

The rounded area of the Pacific Ocean (64,000,000 sq. mi) may also be written as $64 * 10^6$ sq. mi. Strictly speaking, this is not proper scientific notation, since 64 is greater than 10; however, it is very convenient for the purpose of dealing with large numbers at this level.

To express very small numbers, use powers of ten with negative exponents. For example,

$$0.0000075 = 7.5 * 10^{-6}$$

The negative exponent indicates the number of places the decimal point in 7.5 is moved to the left to write the number in standard notation. See Section 2.2.1 for further discussion on powers of ten and negative exponents.

Scientific calculators get their name from their use of scientific notation to display large and small numbers. On scientific calculators, numbers that have more digits than will fit in the display are automatically shown in scientific notation. Some late-model scientific calculators can display numbers using conventional scientific notation, but many older calculators cannot. These older calculators may not even display the 10, but instead use E, EE, or a space to indicate the exponent. Here are some ways $1.3 * 10^7$ may be displayed on such calculators:

$$1.3 \; E7 \qquad 1.3 \; E + 7 \qquad 1.3 \; EE7 \qquad 1.3 \; 07$$

2.3 Operations with Positive and Negative Numbers

Students in Grades K–3 of *Everyday Mathematics* learn to represent addition and subtraction by moving from one point to another on a number line. This informal activity helps prepare them for their first formal experience with operations on positive and negative numbers in Grade 4. Using a business situation of credits and debits, students invent and solve number stories, using integers near zero so problems can be done mentally. It is important in these situations to name both the operation and the numbers: the credit transaction "Add + $3" is read "Add positive 3 dollars" not "Add plus 3 dollars." The debit transaction "Add − $5" is read "Add negative 5 dollars" not "Add minus 5 dollars." This reading distinguishes the addition operation from the numbers involved.

In Grades 4 and 5, students use red and black counters to represent (negative) debits and (positive) credits in transactions. In fifth grade, they use a "slide rule" based on integer number lines to help visualize addition and subtraction of positive and negative numbers.

Another approach to adding and subtracting positive and negative numbers in Grades 4 and 5 is to imagine walking on a number line.

• The first number tells you where to start.

• The operation sign (+ or −) tells you which way to face:
    + means face toward the positive side of the number line.
    − means face toward the negative side of the number line.

• If the second number is negative (has a − sign), then you walk backward. Otherwise, walk forward.

• The second number tells you how many steps to walk.

• The number where you end is the answer.

Example: $4 - (-3)$

Start at 4.

Face toward the negative end of the number line.

Walk 3 steps backward.

You end at 7. So $4 - (-3) = 7$.

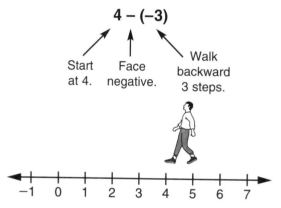

Procedures for addition of integers on a number line tend to be reinforced by real-life situations. Many students quickly move beyond using the number line to add integers and develop their own rules for solving such problems. Having students explain their strategies orally or in writing develops and reinforces their understanding of integers.

Building on skills with mental arithmetic and calculators, students in Grades 5 and 6 extend addition and subtraction from integers to all positive and negative numbers, including decimals and rational numbers. Although multiplying and dividing with negative numbers is not as widely applicable in real-life situations as adding and subtracting, students in sixth grade explore these operations as well. See the Estimation, Mental Arithmetic, and Fact Power essay.

2.3.1 Rules for Subtraction and Multiplication

Because real-life uses of subtraction and multiplication of integers are hard to come by, students may need more guidance in developing rules for these operations. This section describes how counters can be used to encourage rule discovery.

Counters that represent positive and negative numbers can help students discover that subtracting a number is equivalent to adding its opposite. (Use two-color counters, with one color representing positive and the other negative, or small slips of paper labeled + or −.)

- 5 − 3 can be modeled with 5 positive counters, from which 3 are removed, leaving 2 positive counters.
- 5 + (−3) can be modeled with 5 positive and 3 negative counters. Three negative counters are paired with 3 of the 5 positive counters. The sum 3 + (−3) equals 0; the 3 positive and 3 negative counters cancel each other, leaving 2 positive counters. This shows that 5 + (−3) = 2.
- A model for 5 − (−3) starts with 5 positive counters. There are no negative counters to take away. However, 3 positive and 3 negative counters can be added to the model without changing its value, because they represent a sum of 0. Now, when 3 negative counters are taken away, 8 positive counters remain. So 5 − (−3) = 8.

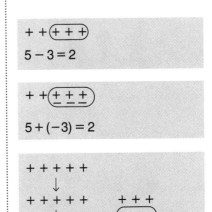

Students will quickly discover that 5 − (−3) has the same answer as 5 + 3. Thus, a subtraction problem can be solved by adding the opposite of the number being subtracted.

Multiplication of a positive integer and a negative number can be related to repeated addition. For example, 3 ∗ (−4) easily translates to (−4) + (−4) + (−4) = −12. Because multiplication is commutative, −4 ∗ 3 also equals −12.

It is not as easy to discover a rule for multiplication of two negative numbers. Consider using the following approaches to solving −3 ∗ (−4), one with patterns, one with properties, and a third with pictures.

Patterns
3 ∗ (−4) = −12
2 ∗ (−4) = −8
1 ∗ (−4) = −4
0 ∗ (−4) = 0
−1 ∗ (−4) = 4
−2 ∗ (−4) = 8
−3 ∗ (−4) = 12

Properties
−3 ∗ 0 = 0
−3 ∗ (4 + (−4)) = 0
(−3 ∗ 4) + (−3 ∗ −4)) = 0
−12 + (−3 ∗ (−4)) = 0
12 + (−12) + (−3 (−4)) = 0 + 12
0 + (−3 ∗ (−4)) = 12
−3 ∗ (−4) = 12

Pictures Imagine using a video camera filming a car going down a street backward (negative) and replaying the film backward (negative). The film will show that the car is going forward (positive).

One benefit of these activities with positive and negative numbers is to show that all four basic operations are possible for all rational numbers.

Algorithms

An algorithm is a well-defined procedure or set of rules used to solve a problem. Having students become comfortable with algorithms is essential to their growth and development as problem solvers.

Section 3.1 of this essay explains how *Everyday Mathematics* approaches computational algorithms, including the role of invented algorithms in developing understanding of operations, place value, and computational procedures.

Section 3.2 describes algorithms for the basic arithmetic operations with whole numbers and decimals. For each operation, one algorithm has been designated as a "focus" algorithm. The focus algorithms are not identical to the computational algorithms that are traditionally taught, but they are similar. In addition to being easier to learn than the traditional algorithms, the focus algorithms reveal more about underlying concepts, such as place value, and are less likely to lead to wrong answers.

Sections 3.3 and 3.4 discuss algorithms for fractions and for calculators. Section 3.5 summarizes the importance of algorithms in mathematics and in the development of students' mathematical thinking.

Other algorithms and procedures are discussed elsewhere in this volume. Geometric algorithms, including compass-and-straightedge constructions, are discussed in the Geometry essay. Procedures for estimation, rounding, and mental arithmetic are discussed in the essay on estimation. Algorithms for averaging are discussed in the essay on data analysis.

3.1 Algorithms and Procedures

As a teacher, you establish many procedures and routines to help your classroom run smoothly. For example, in the beginning of the year, you probably discuss the proper procedures for hanging up coats, lining up, and so on. *Everyday Mathematics* encourages you to establish similar, but more mathematical, routines such as keeping a weather record or solving Estimation Challenges.

An **algorithm** is a well-defined, step-by-step procedure guaranteed to achieve a certain objective, often with several steps that "loop" as many times as necessary. For example, an algorithm for multiplication is a well-defined procedure that will produce the correct product no matter what the factors are. A good algorithm is efficient, unambiguous, and reliable. Though the most familiar algorithms are the traditional elementary school procedures for adding, subtracting, multiplying, and dividing, there are many other algorithms both in mathematics and in real life. A computer program is an algorithm that specifies what a computer is to do at each step. The instructions for operating complicated equipment—fax machines and VCRs, for example—are forms of algorithms.

Everyday Mathematics includes a variety of both standard computational algorithms and students' invented procedures. Inventing procedures is valuable because it promotes conceptual understanding and mental flexibility, both of which are essential for effective problem solving. Inventing computational procedures also helps students learn about our base-ten place-value system of numeration. Finally, inventing procedures involves solving problems that the solver does not already know how to solve. Thus, asking students to devise their own computational methods provides valuable experience in solving non-routine problems. Invented procedures are discussed further in Section 3.1.2.

Using standard algorithms has its advantages, too. Standard algorithms are generally efficient and can also help students understand both our number system and the underlying operations. They also provide a common language that serves as a basis for the further development of mathematical ideas. Many different standard procedures are discussed in Sections 3.2 and 3.3.

3.1.1 Computational Algorithms

Several teachers have asked the *Everyday Mathematics* authors about the role of computational algorithms in elementary school mathematics. Should standard paper-and-pencil algorithms be taught? Should students be expected to use these algorithms to

NOTE: In addition to studying specific algorithms, *Everyday Mathematics* students engage in activities to help them understand algorithms in a more general sense. Mathematics advances in part through the development of efficient procedures that reduce difficult tasks to routine exercises. An effective algorithm will solve an entire class of problems, thus increasing the user's mathematical power. The authors of *Everyday Mathematics* have found that the study of paper-and-pencil computational algorithms can be valuable for developing algorithmic thinking in general.

solve complex computational problems? Should calculators be used in the classroom, and if so, in which circumstances and under what conditions?

Before we attempt to answer these questions, consider the following story told by Professor Zalman Usiskin of the University of Chicago:

Scene 1: An Office. Hal is preparing an end-of-the-month sales report. This involves many calculations, which Hal churns out by hand using paper and pencil. In walks the boss, horrified: "Hal, why aren't you using a calculator? You're wasting valuable time!"

Scene 2: A Fourth Grade Classroom. The class is working on a page of difficult computational problems. Susie gets out her calculator and starts completing the assignment. The teacher walks over to Susie, horrified: "Susie, put that calculator away or you'll get done too quickly!"

These two scenarios highlight the need to rethink the school mathematics curriculum in light of the widespread availability of calculators and computers outside of school. Students certainly still do need to know the meanings and uses of all the arithmetic operations in order to function in the practical world and to succeed in mathematics in high school and beyond. They still do need to know the basic addition and multiplication facts automatically, and they do need to understand and be able to apply paper-and-pencil algorithms for addition, subtraction, multiplication, and division of whole numbers, decimals, and fractions. Mental arithmetic skills are also vitally important in our technological society. But there is no need for students to become skilled at doing difficult paper-and-pencil computations with complicated numbers, since such computations can be performed more quickly and accurately with a calculator. The time saved by reducing attention to complicated paper-and-pencil calculation can be put to better use on such topics as problem solving, estimation, mental arithmetic, geometry, and data analysis.

Some advocates of change assert that standard paper-and-pencil algorithms have no place in the school curriculum. Several strongly argued articles make this case. "It's Time to Abandon Computational Algorithms" by Steven Leinwand (*Education Week,* February 9, 1994) and "Let's Abolish Paper-and-Pencil Arithmetic" by Tony Ralston (*Mathematics Education Dialogues,* May/June 1999) recommend eliminating the teaching of paper-and-pencil algorithms altogether. "Arithmetic: The Last Holdout" by Marilyn Burns (*Phi Delta Kappan,* February 1994) advises teachers to abandon standard paper-and-pencil algorithms in favor of students' own invented algorithms.

Research does show that traditional teaching of the standard algorithms fails with a large number of students. In one study, only 60 percent of U.S. ten-year-olds achieved mastery of subtraction using the standard regrouping ("borrowing") algorithm. A Japanese study found that only 56 percent of third graders and 74 percent of fifth graders achieved mastery of this algorithm. The standard subtraction algorithm can be unreliable because students are plagued by "bugs," such as always taking the smaller digit from the larger, that result from trying to carry out imperfectly understood procedures. There is even evidence that negative attitudes toward mathematics begin to form during the elementary school years when the traditional focus is on rote mastery of standard algorithms for basic arithmetic operations.

Nevertheless, in spite of past failures with traditional paper-and-pencil algorithms, in spite of the fact that calculators make facility with paper-and-pencil computation largely irrelevant in the world outside of school, and in spite of the arguments of people such as Leinwand and Burns, the authors of *Everyday Mathematics* still believe that students should be exposed to paper-and-pencil algorithms. First, if taught properly, with understanding but without demands for "mastery" by all students by some fixed time, paper-and-pencil algorithms can reinforce students' understanding of our number system and of the operations themselves. Second, there are situations in which the most efficient or convenient way to carry out a computation is with paper and pencil. Finally, exploring different algorithms builds estimation skills and number sense and helps students see mathematics as a meaningful and creative subject.

In the debate about algorithms, *Everyday Mathematics* takes a moderate position, combining elements from both the child-centered invented-algorithms approach and the subject-matter-centered standard-algorithms approach. During the early phases of learning an operation, *Everyday Mathematics* encourages students to invent their own procedures. Students are asked to solve problems "from first principles," before they have developed or learned systematic procedures for solving such problems. This helps them understand the operations better, and also gives them valuable experience solving non-routine problems.

Later, when students thoroughly understand the concept of the operation, several alternative standard algorithms are introduced. Some of these algorithms are based on approaches that many students devise on their own. Others are less likely to be discovered by students but have other desirable characteristics. Students are urged to experiment with various algorithms in order to become proficient at using at least one alternative.

Finally, for each operation, one of the several alternative algorithms is designated as the *Everyday Mathematics* focus algorithm. These algorithms are efficient and easy to understand and learn. All students are expected to learn the focus algorithms, though they are not required to use them if they have alternatives they prefer. Focus algorithms provide a common ground for further work and offer reliable alternatives for students who have not developed effective procedures of their own.

NOTE: Kurt Van Lehn had this to say about using the standard subtraction algorithm in some of his research:

[O]rdinary multidigit subtraction . . . is a virtually meaningless procedure [for] most elementary school students . . . . When compared to procedures they use to operate vending machines or play games, subtraction is as dry, formal, and as disconnected from everyday interests as the nonsense syllables used in early psychological investigations were different from real words. This isolation is the bane of teachers but a boon to the psychologist, [allowing] one to study a skill formally. . . .

3.1.2 Algorithm Invention

Because the authors of *Everyday Mathematics* view computational algorithms as more than rote procedures, the program aims to make students active participants in the development of algorithms. Such participation requires a good background in the following three areas:

- ***Our system for number writing.*** In particular, students need to understand place value.
- ***Basic facts.*** To be successful at carrying out multistep computational procedures, students need to know basic facts automatically.
- ***The meanings of the operations and the relationships among operations.*** To solve $37 - 25$, for example, a student might reason, "What number must I add to 25 to get 37?"

The authors of *Everyday Mathematics* believe students should be encouraged to invent their own procedures. As students devise their own methods, they use their prior mathematical knowledge and their common sense, along with new skills and knowledge. They also learn to manage their resources—*How long will this take? Is there a better way?* Such resource management is important in problem solving. As students devise their own methods, they also develop persistence and confidence in dealing with difficult problems. Students who invent their own methods learn that their intuitive methods are valid and that mathematics makes sense.

Inventing procedures also promotes proficiency with mental arithmetic. Many techniques that students invent are much more effective for mental arithmetic than standard paper-and-pencil algorithms. *Everyday Mathematics* wants all students to develop a broad repertoire of computational methods and the flexibility to choose whichever procedure is the most appropriate in any particular situation.

Learning a single standard algorithm for each operation, especially at an early stage, may actually inhibit the development of students' mathematical understanding, and will certainly cause them to miss out on the rich experiences that come from developing their own methods. Although prematurely teaching standard paper-and-pencil algorithms can foster persistent errors and "buggy" algorithms, the main problem with teaching standard algorithms too early is that students may use the algorithms as substitutes for thinking and common sense.

For example, the authors of *Everyday Mathematics* presented the problem in the margin to a large number of students. Most traditionally-taught second and third graders immediately resorted to the standard algorithm, often failing to get the correct answer. Only a handful of these students interpreted the problem as asking, "What number plus 1 gives 300?" or "What is 1 less than 300?" or "What is the number just before 300?" and answered "299" without performing any computations.

$$\begin{array}{r} 300 \\ -1 \\ \hline \end{array}$$

Many children resort to the algorithm to solve this subtraction problem.

In the modern world, most adults reach for calculators when faced with any moderately complex arithmetic computation. This behavior is sensible and should be an option for students, too. Nevertheless, students do benefit in the following ways from developing their own non-calculator procedures:

- Students are more motivated when they don't have to learn standard paper-and-pencil algorithms by rote. People are more interested in what they can understand, and students generally understand their own methods (as obscure as they may sometimes be to others).

- Students become adept at changing the representations of ideas and problems, translating readily among manipulatives, oral and written words, pictures, and symbols. The ability to represent a problem in more than one way is important in problem solving.

- Students develop the ability to transform any given problem into an equivalent, easier problem. For example, $32 - 17$ can be transformed to the easier $35 - 20$ (adding 3 to both numbers in a subtraction problem does not change the answer).

- In devising creative problem-solving strategies, and in refining those strategies for use on a more permanent basis, students gain experience in non-routine problem solving. They learn to manage their resources efficiently and build on what they already know. They also develop persistence and confidence in dealing with difficult problems.

The sharing of students' methods is an important component of this approach. Through classroom discussion of solution methods, you will gain valuable insight into students' progress, while they become more skilled at communicating mathematics and at understanding and critiquing others' ideas. Such communication skills will be especially important in the collaborative workplaces where your students may find themselves when they enter the workforce.

3.1.3 Alternative Algorithms

After students have had plenty of opportunities to experiment with computational strategies of their own, *Everyday Mathematics* introduces several algorithms for each operation. Some of these algorithms closely resemble methods that students are likely to have devised on their own. Others are traditional algorithms, including both standard algorithms customarily taught in U.S. classrooms and other algorithms that have been standard in other times and places. Still others are simplifications of traditional algorithms or wholly new algorithms that have significant advantages in today's technological world. Many of the algorithms presented are highly efficient, and most are easier to understand and learn than traditional algorithms.

Everyday Mathematics also designates one of the alternative algorithms for each operation as a "focus" algorithm. Focus algorithms are powerful, relatively efficient, and easy to understand

NOTE: Algorithm invention develops best when:

- it is allowed to flourish in an accepting and supportive classroom environment
- time for experimentation is allotted
- computational tasks are embedded in real-life contexts
- students share their solution strategies with you and with one another

and learn. At some point, all students should learn the focus algorithm for each operation. In solving problems, however, students may use either the focus algorithm or any other methods they choose. The aim of this approach is to promote flexibility while ensuring that all students know at least one reliable method for each operation.

The authors of *Everyday Mathematics* believe the focus algorithms are superior alternatives to the traditional U.S. standard paper-and-pencil algorithms. Nevertheless, parents and others often pressure students to master specific computational algorithms. This may also be your own preference. Indeed, many students learn the traditional U.S. standard paper-and-pencil algorithms from siblings or from adults at home. Given a choice, however, many students prefer their own procedures—procedures they "own." In any case, *Everyday Mathematics* hopes you will do what is best suited to your situation. The program's aim is to help teachers, not to impose ideas or demands on them.

Finally, *Everyday Mathematics* encourages you to observe your students' algorithmic and procedural thinking when they are engaged in activities dealing with topics other than computation. For example, one student may have an algorithmic approach to drawing geometric figures or patterns, and another may invent ways to convert metric measures by "moving" decimal points. If a procedure warrants it, have a student share it with the class and point out the use of the "idea of an algorithm." A really good procedure might even be named after the student and entered into a class database of algorithms.

3.2 Algorithms for Whole Numbers and Decimals

Base-ten place-value numeration spread from India to the Middle East and eventually all over the world in part because it makes calculation much easier. In the thousand years or so that Hindu-Arabic numeration has been in use, many algorithms have been devised for each of the fundamental arithmetic operations. All of these algorithms are "standard" in some sense—at some time and in some place a group of people used each of these algorithms. The traditional addition algorithm that many of us learned in school is only one of many alternatives. The same can be said for each of the other arithmetic operations.

In the following sections, the authors present some of the dozens of possible algorithms for adding, subtracting, multiplying, and dividing whole numbers and decimals. Some of these algorithms are easier to understand than the traditional U.S. algorithms, though they may seem more complicated at first because they are unfamiliar. Several of the algorithms presented are well suited for mental arithmetic or for very large numbers. Some are easier to learn, if perhaps a bit less efficient. (If efficiency is the goal, however, note that any paper-and-pencil algorithm will be inferior to a calculator or mental arithmetic in most situations.) Several of these algorithms are based on students' mental arithmetic efforts and search for procedures. All are examples that you may suggest to students who need some help getting started.

Many different algorithms for operations with whole numbers and decimals are described in the following sections. For each operation, several alternative algorithms are described, including the *Everday Mathematics* focus algorithm. Procedures for operations with fractions are discussed in Section 3.3.

3.2.1 Addition Algorithms

Here we discuss several algorithms for addition of whole numbers and decimals: Column Addition, the Opposite-Change Rule, Partial Sums, and the U.S. Traditional Algorithm.

Column Addition

In column addition, vertical lines are drawn to separate ones, tens, hundreds, and so on. Once columns have been created, the usual place-value convention that each place must have only one digit can be broken without confusion. (If you wish, the columns can be labeled "ones," "tens," and so on.) The digits in each column are then added, beginning in any column. Finally, any necessary trades are made, again starting in any column.

		9	6	7
	+	4	9	5
Add each column separately, working in any order. →		13	15	12
If necessary, adjust, working in any order. →		14	5	12
If necessary, adjust, working in any order. →		1,4	6	2

Many students find this algorithm natural and instructive. For some, the process becomes so natural they start at the left and write the answer column by column, adjusting as they go without writing any of the intermediate steps. If asked to explain the problem in the margin, for example, they might say something like this:

"200 plus 400 is 600, but (looking at the next column) I need to adjust that, so I write 7. 60 and 80 is 140, but that needs adjusting, so I write 5. 8 and 3 is 11. With no more to do, I can just write 1."

The column addition algorithm was shown and explained to the *Everyday Mathematics* authors by a first grader. It has become a personal favorite. The algorithm occurs naturally to many students, and it also has the advantage of producing a rough estimate of the sum quickly.

The Opposite-Change Rule

The Opposite-Change Rule for addition states: If you add a number to one addend and subtract the same number from the other addend, the sum remains the same.

NOTE: Working on a grid of small squares—a piece of graph paper, for example— can help many students in organizing the placement of digits as they use paper-and-pencil algorithms. The grid lines help students keep digits with the same place value aligned. Often such a grid is provided in *Everyday Mathematics* when students are expected to calculate using paper and pencil.

$$
\begin{array}{r}
268 \\
+\,483 \\
\hline
751
\end{array}
$$

column addition with adjusting done mentally

Consider, for example:

$$8 + 7 = 15$$

If 2 is added to the 8 and 2 is also subtracted from the 7, we have

$$(8 + 2) + (7 - 2) = 10 + 5 = 15$$

The idea behind this method is to rename the addends so that one ends in zeros. This may take several steps, but eventually the addition becomes trivial.

Example: Rename so the first addend ends in zeros.

$$
\begin{array}{ccccc}
268 & \overset{+2}{\rightarrow} & 270 & \overset{+30}{\rightarrow} & 300 \\
+\ 483 & \overset{-2}{\rightarrow} & +\ 481 & \overset{-30}{\rightarrow} & +\ 451 \\
& & & & \overline{751}
\end{array}
$$

Example: Rename so the second addend ends in zeros.

$$
\begin{array}{ccccc}
268 & \overset{-7}{\rightarrow} & 261 & \overset{-10}{\rightarrow} & 251 \\
+\ 483 & \overset{+7}{\rightarrow} & +\ 490 & \overset{+10}{\rightarrow} & +\ 500 \\
& & & & \overline{751}
\end{array}
$$

This approach is also well suited to mental arithmetic. With a little practice, students can become quite proficient.

Focus Algorithm: Partial Sums

As the name suggests, the partial-sums algorithm calculates partial sums, working one place-value column at a time, and then adds all the partial sums to find the total.

$$
\begin{array}{r}
6{,}802 \\
+\ \ 453 \\
\end{array}
$$

Add the thousands.	$\rightarrow$	$(6{,}000 + 0)$	$\rightarrow$	6,000
Add the hundreds.	$\rightarrow$	$(800 + 400)$	$\rightarrow$	1,200
Add the tens.	$\rightarrow$	$(0 + 50)$	$\rightarrow$	50
Add the ones.	$\rightarrow$	$(2 + 3)$	$\rightarrow$	$+\ \ \ \ 5$
Add the partial sums.	$\rightarrow$	$(6{,}000 + 1{,}200 + 50 + 5)$	$\rightarrow$	**7,255**

The partial sums can be found in any order, but working from left to right is the usual procedure. This order seems more natural since we read from left to right, and it also focuses on the most important digits in the addends first (thousands before hundreds, hundreds before tens, and so on). A variation on this algorithm can be used to estimate sums quickly: The sum is estimated using only the partial sum(s) for the addends' leftmost digits. This is known as leading-digit estimation. The partial-sums algorithm can be readily adapted for mental arithmetic.

Partial-sums addition is similar to addition with base-10 blocks. Finding each partial sum corresponds to combining all of one kind of base-10 block. Adding the partial sums corresponds to combining like blocks and then exchanging blocks as necessary.

The partial-sums algorithm, like all the algorithms discussed here, can be easily adapted to work with decimals.

				27.096
				+ 3.507
Add the tens.	→	(20 + 0)	→	20.000
Add the ones.	→	(7 + 3)	→	10.000
Add the tenths.	→	(0.0 + 0.5)	→	0.500
Add the hundredths.	→	(0.09 + 0.00)	→	0.090
Add the thousandths.	→	(0.006 + 0.007)	→	+ 0.013
Add the partial sums.	→	(20 + 10 + 0.5 + 0.09 + 0.013)	→	30.603

U.S. Traditional Addition Algorithm

The traditional addition algorithm used in the United States has much to recommend it. It is widely known, efficient (though obviously less efficient than a calculator or computer for adding lots of numbers and also less efficient than mental arithmetic for many simpler situations), and fairly easy to learn. Many students learn this algorithm from their parents or siblings: it is almost as much a cultural tradition as a mathematical procedure. It is, therefore, likely to be mentioned when you ask students to explain their solutions to multidigit addition problems.

The U.S. traditional addition algorithm, or short algorithm, is similar to column addition, but it requires the user to proceed column-by-column from right to left and to observe place-value conventions at all times. These requirements make the algorithm more efficient but harder to learn.

The user begins with the rightmost column, mentally finds the sum of all the digits in that column, writes the ones digit of the sum below the line, and "carries" the tens digit of the sum to the top of the next column to the left. The process is repeated for each column to the left. The "carry" digits can be mysterious to students, so be sure to explain them in terms of place value and renaming when you discuss this algorithm.

In whole-number addition, the starting column is the ones place. In decimal addition, the starting column can be the tenths, hundredths, or any other decimal place.

The addition algorithm is probably the best of the traditional U.S. computation algorithms. While *Everyday Mathematics* does not emphasize it, it is a viable alternative. If you do decide to teach this addition algorithm, be sure to treat it as one of several possibilities and, as with any algorithm, be sure that students understand why it works.

	588
	+ 143
Add the ones. (8 ones + 3 ones = 11 ones)	1
Regroup. (11 ones = 1 ten and 1 one)	588
	+ 143
	1
Add the tens. (1 ten + 8 tens + 4 tens = 13 tens)	1 1
Regroup. (13 tens = 1 hundred and 3 tens)	588
	+ 143
	31
Add the hundreds. (1 hundred + 5 hundreds + 1 hundred = 7 hundreds)	1
	588
	+ 143
731 is the total.	731

U.S. traditional addition algorithm

3.2.2 Subtraction Algorithms

There are even more algorithms for subtraction than for addition, probably because subtraction is more difficult. In this section, we discuss six algorithms: Counting-Up, Left-to-Right, the Same-Change Rule, "European," Partial Differences, and Trade-First. Several of these methods work equally well for whole numbers and decimals, although the latter may require some extra careful handling if the numbers don't have the same number of decimal places.

There are many other subtraction algorithms that your students may reinvent, including variations on the methods below. These are merely examples that you may suggest to get some students started—you do not need to present all of them to your whole class.

Counting-Up

This algorithm is similar to what cashiers do when they give change. In both procedures, the user begins at the smaller number and counts up to the larger number. In giving change, the cashier tenders bills or coins to the purchaser. In the counting-up algorithm, the user keeps a running record of the amounts counted up and then adds all of the count-up amounts to find the difference.

The counting-up technique that is the basis for this algorithm is useful in mental computation, although keeping a correct running total of the count-up amounts requires practice. When the procedure is carried out mentally, it usually helps to start with the larger places.

Solve $932 - 356$ by counting up.

```
  356
(+   4)   Count to the nearest 10.
  360
(+  40)   Count to the nearest
  400        100.
(+500)    Count to the largest
  900        possible 100.
(+  32)   Count to the larger
  932        number.
```

Then add the numbers you circled:

```
     4
    40
   500
+   32
   576
```

So $932 - 356 = 576$.

Left-to-Right Subtraction

With the left-to-right algorithm, the user starts at the left and subtracts column by column. For the problem $932 - 356$:

$$
\begin{array}{r}
932 \\
\text{Subtract the 100s.} \rightarrow -300 \\
\hline
632 \\
\text{Subtract the 10s.} \rightarrow -\ 50 \\
\hline
582 \\
\text{Subtract the 1s.} \rightarrow -\ \ 6 \\
\hline
576
\end{array}
$$

Like left-to-right addition, this algorithm can be used to find a quick estimate of the final answer.

The Same-Change Rule

The Same-Change Rule for subtraction states:

- If you add the same number to both numbers in a subtraction problem, the difference remains the same.
- If you subtract the same number from both numbers in a subtraction problem, the difference remains the same.

Consider, for example:

$$15 - 8 = 7$$

If 2 is added to both the 15 and the 8, we have

$$(15 + 2) - (8 + 2) = 17 - 10 = 7$$

If 5 is subtracted from both the 15 and the 8, we have

$$(15 - 5) - (8 - 5) = 10 - 3 = 7$$

The usual strategy for applying this approach to multidigit subtraction is to rename the subtrahend so that it ends in zeros. This may take several steps, but eventually the subtraction becomes trivial.

Example: Add the same number:

$$
\begin{array}{r}
932 \\
-\ 356
\end{array}
\quad
\begin{array}{c} +4 \\ \rightarrow \\ +4 \\ \rightarrow \end{array}
\quad
\begin{array}{r}
936 \\
-\ 360
\end{array}
\quad
\begin{array}{c} +40 \\ \rightarrow \\ +40 \\ \rightarrow \end{array}
\quad
\begin{array}{r}
976 \\
-\ 400 \\
\hline
576
\end{array}
$$

Example: Subtract the same number:

$$
\begin{array}{r}
932 \\
-\ 356
\end{array}
\quad
\begin{array}{c} -6 \\ \rightarrow \\ -6 \\ \rightarrow \end{array}
\quad
\begin{array}{r}
926 \\
-\ 350
\end{array}
\quad
\begin{array}{c} -50 \\ \rightarrow \\ -50 \\ \rightarrow \end{array}
\quad
\begin{array}{r}
876 \\
-\ 300 \\
\hline
576
\end{array}
$$

The Same-Change Rule is well suited to mental arithmetic.

"European" Subtraction

The traditional U.S. subtraction algorithm involves "borrowing" from the next place to the left. That is, in a problem like $623 - 345$, one of the 2 tens in 623 is traded for 10 ones. This is written as:

$$
\begin{array}{r}
6\ \overset{1}{\cancel{2}}\ \overset{13}{\cancel{3}} \\
-\ 3\ 4\ 5 \\
\end{array}
$$

A variation on this procedure involves increasing the bottom number in the next column to the left:

$$
\begin{array}{r}
6\ \overset{1}{\cancel{2}}\ \overset{13}{\cancel{3}} \\
-\ 3_1\ 4\ 5 \\
\hline
8
\end{array}
$$

The small mark next to the 4 in 345 is a ten that compensates for adding 10 to the 3 on top. The next step involves subtracting 50 instead of 40. Since the 2 in 623 is too small to take away 5, we use the same trick again, this time increasing the hundreds digit in the bottom number.

$$
\begin{array}{r}
6\ 2\overset{12\ 13}{\diagup}3 \\
-\ _{1}3_{1}4\ 5 \\
\hline
7\ 8
\end{array}
$$

The mark next to the 3 on the bottom is a hundred that compensates for adding 10 tens to the top. The final step is to subtract $(1 + 3)$ hundreds from 6 hundreds.

$$
\begin{array}{r}
6\ 2\overset{12\ 13}{\diagup}3 \\
-\ _{1}3_{1}4\ 5 \\
\hline
2\ 7\ 8
\end{array}
$$

You may find this algorithm confusing, but it is the standard algorithm used in many countries in the world today. You might want to spend a few minutes thinking about how increasing the number on the bottom has the same effect as decreasing the number on the top. If you want to experience what it might be like for a student to learn the traditional U.S. subtraction algorithm, you might try learning this "European" algorithm.

Partial Differences

Partial-differences subtraction is a fairly unusual method, but one that appeals to many students.

The procedure is fairly simple: Write partial differences for each place, record them, and then add them to find the total difference. The complication is that some of the partial differences may be negative.

$$
\begin{array}{r}
932 \\
-\ 356 \\
\end{array}
$$

Subtract 100s: $900 - 300 \rightarrow$　　　600

Subtract 10s: $30 - 50 \rightarrow$　　　$-\ 20$

Subtract 1s: $2 - 6 \rightarrow$　　　$-\ 4$

Add the partial differences. $\rightarrow$　　　576

Focus Algorithm: Trade-First Subtraction

This algorithm resembles the U.S. traditional algorithm, except that all the trading is done before all the subtraction, allowing the user to concentrate on one thing at a time. The following steps are involved:

1. Examine all columns and trade as necessary so that the top number in each place is as large or larger than the bottom number. The trades can be done in any order. Working left-to-right is perhaps more natural, as with partial-sums addition, but working right-to-left is a bit more efficient.

2. Check that the top number in each place is at least as large as the bottom number. If necessary, make more trades.

3. Subtract column by column in any order.

Trade-first subtraction is highly efficient, similar to the traditional algorithm, and relatively easy to learn. It is an effective algorithm for paper-and-pencil calculation.

Many teachers find that drawing vertical lines between the places is helpful for students first learning this algorithm. The vertical lines allow students to focus on one column at a time. They also help students avoid mistakes if unnecessary trades have been made.

$$\begin{array}{r} 8 \quad 10 \; 5 \; 12 \\ 9{,}0\cancel{6}\cancel{2} \\ -\;4{,}738 \end{array}$$

$$\begin{array}{r} 8 \quad 10 \; 5 \; 12 \\ 9{,}0\cancel{6}\cancel{2} \\ -\;4{,}738 \\ \hline 4{,}324 \end{array}$$

trade-first with columns

trade-first with an unnecessary trade

Adding and Subtracting Decimals

In everyday life, most decimals to be added or subtracted tend to have the same precision, or number of decimal places. A common example is money, where most values are rounded to the nearest cent. In fact, there are very few situations where you might need to combine or subtract values with different precisions, and even if a data set has such disparate measures, you would probably want to round them all to the same precision to avoid exaggerating the precision of the final answer. In such cases, when the decimals involved are all expressed to the same precision, the addition and subtraction algorithms described above generalize easily. Except for the decimal points, the procedures work more or less exactly the same as with whole numbers.

In spite of this, students are likely to face a practical need to add or subtract disparate decimals on local, state, or national achievement tests. For this reason, students in *Fifth* and *Sixth Grade Everyday Mathematics* are shown how to rename addends so that they all have the same number of decimal places—by inserting zeros to "even out" the decimals. Writing the values vertically while aligning the decimal point can make this simpler as is shown in the example in the margin.

$$25 + 1.726 + 0.05 = ?$$

$$\begin{array}{r} 25.000 \\ 1.726 \\ +\;0.050 \end{array}$$

"evening out" the decimals

While students can learn to cope with testing demands in this way, the authors of *Everyday Mathematics* believe they should realize that inserting zeros to even out decimals is artificial. In actual work with measures, students should apply the sensible and realistic rule that all data in a problem should be collected or rounded to about the same level of precision. They should also recognize that in complicated computations, calculators can help improve accuracy.

3.2.3 Multiplication Algorithms

Adults usually reach for calculators when they have to multiply "difficult" numbers. Similarly, calculators should be available to students when they deal with problems that they understand but that involve calculations beyond their current skills. This allows the curriculum to include more realistic, interesting, and instructive problems. Nevertheless, for the reasons discussed in Section 3.1.1, *Everyday Mathematics* includes a significant amount of work with paper-and-pencil multiplication.

As always, *Everyday Mathematics* suggests that students share their strategies and discuss how they created their computational procedures. Inventing procedures for multiplication and division is more difficult than for addition and subtraction, but students who have experience with the latter will be well prepared to attempt the former. When doing mental arithmetic, for example, many students begin to compute partial products: "Ten of these would be . . . , so 30 of them would be . . . , and then we need 5 more, so. . . ." Beginning in *Third Grade Everyday Mathematics,* this approach is formalized as the partial-products algorithm, the focus algorithm for multiplication.

There are many multiplication algorithms besides the partial-products algorithm and traditional right-to-left long multiplication. Former University of Chicago graduate student Dan Hirschhorn, after only a few hours' search of old schoolbooks and mathematics education articles, found more than 40 different multiplication algorithms. About 25 of them were special "tricks" for quick mental multiplication of numbers with special characteristics or procedures you may remember from high school algebra. Some were very efficient but difficult to explain. More than 15 of the 40 were general algorithms for multiplying any two whole numbers. Several of these algorithms are discussed below.

Focus Algorithm: Partial Products

In partial-products multiplication, each factor is considered as a sum of ones, tens, hundreds, and so on. For example, in 67 * 53, 67 is thought of as 60 + 7 and 53 as 50 + 3. Each part of one factor is then multiplied by each part of the other factor, and, finally, all of the resulting partial products are added together.

You don't have to work from left to right; any order will do, as long as all possible partial products are found. Working from left to right, however, does help keep the procedure orderly and, as with left-to-

$$
\begin{array}{r}
67 \\
\times \quad 53 \\
\end{array}
$$

$50 \times 60 \rightarrow$	3000
$50 \times 7 \rightarrow$	350
$3 \times 60 \rightarrow$	180
$3 \times 7 \rightarrow$	+ 21
	3551

partial-products multiplication

right procedures for addition and subtraction, produces a quick initial estimate of the product. In order to use the partial-products algorithm efficiently, students must be adept at multiplying multiples of 10, 100, and 1,000—such as 60 * 50 as in the example in the margin on page 114. These skills will help students in making ballpark estimates of products and quotients.

The partial-products algorithm can be demonstrated visually by using arrays. The diagram in the margin shows how a 23-by-14 array represents all of the partial products in 23 * 14.

$$
\begin{array}{r}
14 \\
\times \quad 23 \\
\hline
\end{array}
$$

$$
\begin{array}{rr}
20 \times 10 \rightarrow & 200 \\
20 \times 4 \rightarrow & 80 \\
3 \times 10 \rightarrow & 30 \\
3 \times 4 \rightarrow & +\quad 12 \\
\hline
& 322
\end{array}
$$

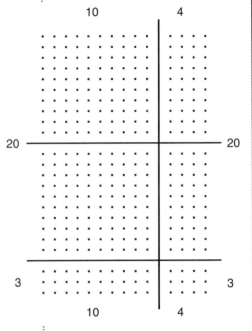

The principles behind this algorithm are taught in the *Multiplication Wrestling* game in *Fourth Grade Everyday Mathematics,* in which every part of one factor "wrestles" every part of the other factor. The partial-products algorithm can get tedious for problems with very large numbers, but we recommend using calculators for those, so this is not a serious drawback.

One value of the partial-products algorithm is that it previews a procedure for multiplication that is taught in high-school algebra, and is related to some algebra in *Sixth Grade Everyday Mathematics*. In multiplying polynomials, expressions like $(x + 5)$ and $(3x^2 - 15)$, every term is multiplied by every other term, and the partial products are added. *For example:*

$$(x + 2) * (x + 3) = (x * x) + (x * 3) + (2 * x) + (2 * 3)$$
$$= x^2 + 5x + 6$$

Lattice Multiplication

Everyday Mathematics initially included lattice multiplication for its recreational value and historical interest, and because it provided practice with multiplication facts and adding strings of single-digit numbers. To our surprise, lattice multiplication has become a favorite of many students.

Why the lattice method works is not immediately obvious, but it is very efficient and powerful. The authors have found that, with practice, it is more efficient than standard long multiplication for problems involving more than two digits in each factor. And problems that are too large for long multiplication or for most calculators can be solved using lattice multiplication. The principal disadvantages of the algorithm are that it is unfamiliar to many adults and making the lattice takes time.

NOTE: The partial-products algorithm uses the distributive property repeatedly. For example, in 23 * 14, both 20 and 3 are distributed over 10 + 4:
  20 * (10 + 4) =
  20 * 10 + 20 * 4,
  and,
  3 * (10 + 4) = 3 * 10 + 3 * 4

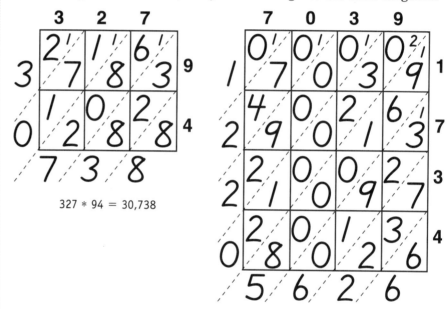

53 * 67 = 3,551

To multiply 67 by 53:

1. Draw a 2-by-2 lattice, including diagonals. (Multiplying larger numbers requires a larger lattice.)

2. Write one factor along the top of the lattice and the other along the right, one digit for each row or column.

3. Multiply each digit in one factor by each digit in the other factor. Write the products in the cells where the corresponding rows and columns meet. Write the tens digit of these products above the diagonal and the ones digit below the diagonal.

4. Add the numbers inside the lattice along each diagonal, beginning with the bottom right diagonal. Write these sums along the bottom and left sides of the lattice. If the sum on a diagonal exceeds 9, carry the tens digit to the next diagonal.

327 * 94 = 30,738

7,039 * 1,734 = 12,205,626

The key to understanding why lattice multiplication works is to note that the diagonals in the lattice correspond to place-value columns. The far right-hand diagonal is the ones place, the next diagonal to the left is the tens place, and so on.

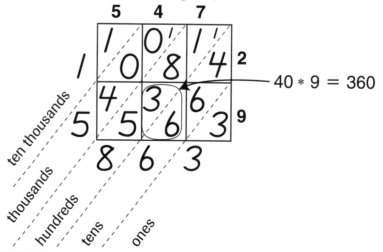

40 * 9 = 360

Modified Repeated Addition

Contrary to what is often taught, multiplication is not merely repeated addition, even for whole numbers and certainly not for decimals and fractions. Moreover, as a computational method for multiplying, repeated addition is inefficient for anything but small numbers. For example, it would be unbearably tedious to add together 53 [67s] in order to compute 67 * 53.

If you think of 10 [67s] as 670, however, you can first add the 670s (there are five of them) and then add the 3 [67s], as shown in the margin. This algorithm is a good Broken Calculator exercise in finding a product without using the [×] key.

Modified Standard U.S. Algorithms

Example A in the margin shows the standard U.S. paper-and-pencil multiplication algorithm for finding 67 * 53. Although this algorithm does indeed work and is moderately efficient, there many people who use it who cannot explain the shifting to the left in successive partial products. Even harder to explain is why the 3 in the 35 from 5 * 7 is written above the 6 in 67. (When asked why the 3 is written in the tens place, many adults say that the 3 stands for 3 tens, which is incorrect. The 3 actually stands for 300 because it comes from 50 * 7 = 350.) Many adults believe they "understand" the algorithm simply because they can carry it out correctly. We believe that real understanding includes both knowing what to do and knowing why it works. By this criterion, many adults' "understanding" of the standard long multiplication algorithm is incomplete.

Example B solves the shift-over-a-place mystery by inserting a zero in the blank. This makes clear that for the second partial product, we are multiplying by 50 (five 10s) and not by 5. The reason for putting the 3 above the 6 is still unresolved—it's actually there for convenience in mentally adding to the product of 5 times 6 (which is really 50 times 60). This version is a bit easier to understand than the traditional form.

Example C uses a left-to-right approach. Though it has its advantages, it is otherwise no different from the standard algorithm with 0s in place of the blanks.

An Egyptian Algorithm

An algorithm for multiplication developed by the Egyptians over 4,000 years ago eliminates the need for all multiplication facts except for the "2s." The idea of doubling, which students find easy and fun, is used repeatedly. This algorithm was used well into the Middle Ages, and a variation, called the Russian Peasant Method, is still used today in Russia, Ethiopia, the Arab world, and the Near East.

Here is how to use the Egyptian method for 13 * 28:

Step 1: In the first column, list the consecutive powers of 2 beginning with 1. Stop with the greatest power of two that is less than or equal to the first factor.

$$
\begin{array}{r}
67 \\
\times\, 53 \\
\hline
670 \\
670 \\
670 \\
670 \\
670 \\
67 \\
67 \\
+\ 67 \\
\hline
3551
\end{array}
$$

670, 670, 670, 670, 670 → 50 [67s] *or* 5 [670s]

67, 67, 67 → 3 [67s]

modified repeated addition

NOTE: The notation 3 [60s] was introduced in third grade. It is read as "3 sixties." When explaining the steps in the partial-products algorithm, encourage students to think and say "3 sixties," and not "3 times 6."

A.	B.	C.
3	3	2
2	2	3
67	67	67
× 53	× 53	× 53
201	201	3350
335	3350	201
3551	3551	3551

modified standard U.S. algorithms

Step 2: In the second column, write the second factor next to the 1, and then double that factor repeatedly, stopping with the last power of 2 in the first column. For example, $112 = 4 * 28$.

Step 3: Check off the powers of 2 whose sum is the first factor. Start at the bottom with the largest powers of 2 and work toward the smaller powers, always taking a power if it would not make the sum too large. $(1 + 4 + 8 = 13)$

Step 4: Cross out the rows that are not checked off.

Step 5: Add the numbers in the second column that are not crossed off. $(28 + 112 + 224 = 364)$

Modern Notation		Egyptian Notation	
1st Column	2nd Column	1st Column	2nd Column
✔ 1	28	✔	
2	56		
✔ 4	112	✔	
✔ 8	224	✔	
13	364		

Source: Nelson, David, George Gheverghese Joseph, and Julian Williams. *Multicultural Mathematics.* Great Britain: Oxford University Press, 1993.

The application of the distributive property shows why this method works.

$$13 * 28 = (1 + 4 + 8) * 28 = (1 * 28) + (4 * 28) + (8 * 28)$$

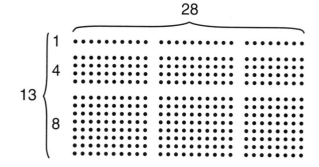

Multiplying Decimals

Everyday Mathematics students are encouraged to find their own algorithms for multiplying decimals in the same way they are asked to find algorithms for operations with whole numbers and fractions. The primary approach suggested in the program is to estimate the product, multiply as though the factors were whole numbers, and use the estimate to place the decimal point in the product.

Example: Find 0.23 * 17.5.

Estimate: 0.23 * 17.5 is about twice as much as 0.1 * 17.5, or 1.75, or about 2. So the product is about 4. Or, using fractions, 0.23 * 17.5 is about $\frac{1}{4}$ of 16 or $\frac{1}{5}$ of 20. Either of these estimates suggests a product of about 4.

Multiply as though the factors were whole numbers, ignoring the decimal points:

$$
\begin{array}{rr}
 & 175 \\
\times & 23 \\
\hline
20 \times 100 \rightarrow & 2000 \\
20 \times 70 \rightarrow & 1400 \\
20 \times 5 \rightarrow & 100 \\
3 \times 100 \rightarrow & 300 \\
3 \times 70 \rightarrow & 210 \\
3 \times 5 \rightarrow & +\quad 15 \\
\hline
 & 4025 \\
\end{array}
$$

Use the estimate to place the decimal point: 4.025.

Several other approaches to multiplying decimals are also included in the program.

- Use a calculator. Verify the size of the answer in the display (perhaps using one of the estimation techniques above) because even experienced calculator users occasionally make mistakes. Also check for accuracy, because the calculator may round the product to fit the display.

- Multiply as if the factors were whole numbers, and use a rule for placing the decimal point in the answer. The usual rule is to count the numbers of decimal places in the factors, add them, and mark off that many decimal places from the ones digit in the whole-number answer.

- Use lattice multiplication adapted for decimals. Simply find the intersection of the decimal points along the horizontal and vertical lines; then slide down its diagonal.

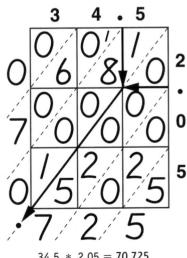

34.5 * 2.05 = 70.725

Because of the way the lattice is arranged, the decimal points meet after the product of the digits in the ones place. In the example above, 4 is in the ones place in 34.5, and 2 is in the ones place in 2.05. The diagonal with 8 (the product of 4 and 2) is the ones diagonal. The decimal point should go just to the right of the ones place.

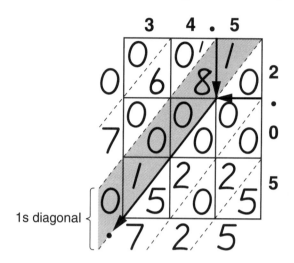

3.2.4 Division Algorithms

The authors of *Everyday Mathematics* do not believe it is worth the time and effort to fully develop highly efficient paper-and-pencil algorithms for all possible whole number, fraction, and decimal division problems. Mastery of the intricacies of such algorithms is a huge undertaking, one that experience tells us is doomed to failure for many students. It is simply counter-productive to invest many hours of precious class time on such algorithms. The mathematical payoff is not worth the cost, particularly because quotients can be found quickly and accurately with a calculator.

This said, the practical needs of students to succeed on standardized tests may require you to teach paper-and-pencil long division algorithms. Moreover, as discussed in Section 3.1.1, there are good reasons for teaching certain paper-and-pencil methods for division. By learning appropriate algorithms, students can acquire useful insights into the operation of division without undue costs in time and effort. Toward these ends, Grades 4–6 of *Everyday Mathematics* contain lessons aimed at helping students develop paper-and-pencil division algorithms that are both easier to learn than traditional long division and more instructive.

Focus Algorithm: Partial Quotients

Equal-grouping division problems ask, "How many of these are in that?" or, more symbolically, a/b asks "How many bs are in a?" One approach to solving such problems is to make a series of "at least, but less than" estimates of how many bs are in a. These interim estimates may be called "partial quotients." At each step, check to see if you have taken as many bs from a as possible. If not, take some more. When you have taken all the bs there are in a, add the partial quotients.

For example, "How many groups of 12 are in 157?" can be solved by finding 157 / 12. You might begin with multiples of 10, because they are simple to work with: There are at least 10 [12s] in 157 (that is, 10 * 12 = 120), but there are fewer than 20 (20 * 12 = 240). Record 10 as your first estimate and subtract 10 [12s] from 157, leaving 37. Next, ask, "How many 12s are in the remaining 37?" You might know the answer right away (12 * 3 = 36), or you might sneak up on it: "More than 1, more than 2, a little more than 3, but not as many as 4 ...." Taking out 3 [12s] leaves 1, which is less than 12, so you can stop estimating. The final result is the sum of your estimates (10 + 3, or 13) plus whatever is left over (the remainder, 1). Of course, you may make a different series of estimates than were made above.

$$
\begin{array}{r|r}
12\overline{)157} & \\
-\quad 120 & 10 \\
\hline
37 & \\
-\quad 36 & 3 \\
\hline
1 & 13 \\
\end{array}
$$

157/12 → 13 R1

This division algorithm, partial quotients, is introduced in *Fourth Grade Everyday Mathematics* and reviewed in Grades 5 and 6. Division with 2-digit divisors, which is introduced in Grade 5 and practiced in Grade 6, can be done by adapting the algorithm as necessary. Making a list of multiples of the divisor can be helpful with multidigit divisors.

NOTE: When we express the result of division in terms of a quotient and remainder, we use an arrow rather than an equals sign. 157/12 = 13 R1, for example, is not a proper number sentence because the right-hand side (13 R1) is not actually a number. To write the solution as a number sentence, express the remainder as a fraction: $157 / 12 = 13\frac{1}{12}$.

Example: Find 758 / 28 = ?

1 * 28 = 28

2 * 28 = 56

3 * 28 = 84

4 * 28 = 112

5 * 28 = 140

8 * 28 = 224

10 * 28 = 280

$$
\begin{array}{r|r}
28\overline{)758} & \\
-\quad 560 & 20 \\
\hline
198 & \\
-\quad 140 & 5 \\
\hline
58 & \\
-\quad 56 & 2 \\
\hline
2 & 27 \\
\end{array}
$$

758 / 28 → 27 R2

Column Division

Column division is a simplification of the traditional long division algorithm, one that is easier to learn and just as powerful, though perhaps a bit less efficient. (Note, however, that if efficiency is an issue, then mental arithmetic or a calculator is usually preferable to paper and pencil.)

In column division, vertical lines separate the digits in the dividend. To understand how the algorithm works, imagine sharing $683 among 5 people. Think about having 6 $100 bills, 8 $10 bills, and 3 $1 bills. Since there are 6 $100 bills, each person can get 1 $100 bill. There will be 1 $100 bill left over.

$$
\begin{array}{r|c|c}
 & 1 & 3 & \\
5\overline{)}\ \ 6 & 8 & 3 \\
-\ 5 & & \\
\hline
1 & & \\
\end{array}
$$

The leftover $100 bill cannot be shared 5 ways, so it gets traded for 10 $10 bills. Since there were 8 $10 bills already, that makes 18 $10 bills. Sharing the 18 $10 bills among 5 people is 3 each and 3 left over.

$$
\begin{array}{r|r|}
 & 1 & 3 \\
5\overline{)} & 6 & \cancel{8} \quad 3 \\
 & -5 & 18 \\
\cancel{1} & & -15 \\ \hline
 & & 3
\end{array}
$$

Trading the 3 leftover $10 bills for 30 $1 bills and adding them to the original 3 $1 bills makes 33 $1 bills. Sharing the 33 $1 bills among five people is 6 each with 3 left over.

$$
\begin{array}{r|r|r}
 & 1 & 3 & 6 \\
5\overline{)} & 6 & \cancel{8} & \cancel{8} \\
 & -5 & 18 & 33 \\
\cancel{1} & & -15 & -30 \\ \hline
 & & \cancel{8} & 3
\end{array}
$$

So, sharing $683 among 5 people works out to be $136 each with $3 left over. So, 683 / 5 → 136 R3.

Column division can also be used with larger numbers. As with partial quotients, it can be helpful to start by making a table of multiples when the divisor has two or more digits. The table of multiples can help with the harder divisions in the columns.

Example: Find 5467 / 28 = ?

$$
\begin{aligned}
1 * 28 &= 28 \\
2 * 28 &= 56 \\
3 * 28 &= 84 \\
4 * 28 &= 112 \\
5 * 28 &= 140 \\
8 * 28 &= 224 \\
10 * 28 &= 280
\end{aligned}
$$

1. Set the problem up.

2. Trade 5 thousands for 50 hundreds.

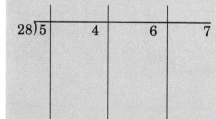

3. Share 54 hundreds 28 ways.

$$28\overline{)5}$$

1	6	7
54 $-\ 28$ 26		

4. Trade 26 hundreds for 260 tens.

$$28\overline{)5}$$

1	8	7
54 $-\ 28$ 26	266	

5. Share the 266 tens 28 ways.

$$28\overline{)5}$$

1	8	7
54 $-\ 28$ 26	266 $-\ 224$ 42 $-\ 28$ 14	

6. Trade the 14 tens for 140 ones.

$$28\overline{)5}$$

1	8	7
54 $-\ 28$ 26	266 $-\ 224$ 42 $-\ 28$ 14	147

7. Share the 147 ones 28 ways.

$$28\overline{)5}$$

1	8	4
54 $-\ 28$ 26	266 $-\ 224$ 42 $-\ 28$ 14	147 $-\ 112$ 35 $-\ 28$ 7

8. Write a number model.

$$5{,}467 / 28 \rightarrow 195 \text{ R7}$$

or

$$5{,}467 / 28 = 195\tfrac{7}{28}$$

Dividing Decimals

As noted earlier, the authors of *Everyday Mathematics* believe that while it is important for students to learn the basic meanings and uses of division, it is not worth spending enormous amount of time mastering the intricacies of division with difficult whole numbers and decimals. The time and effort this would require is better spent on topics in algebra, geometry, and data analysis, among others.

For this reason, the main approach to division with decimals in *Everyday Mathematics* is the same as for multiplication of decimals: Carry out the operation as though the numbers were whole numbers and use an estimate to place the decimal point in the answer. This approach works well for almost all decimal division problems students are likely to encounter in situations where paper-and-pencil calculation is required or desirable. The method also reinforces important estimation skills and can be learned relatively quickly.

Example: 8.25 / 0.3 = ?

Step 1: Divide, ignoring the decimal points.

$$
\begin{array}{r|r}
3\overline{)825} & \\
-\;600 & 200 \\
\hline
225 & \\
-\;210 & 70 \\
\hline
15 & \\
-\;\;15 & 5 \\
\hline
0 & 275
\end{array}
$$

Step 2: Estimate the size of the quotient.

Since 8.25, which is greater than 1, is being divided by 0.3, which is less than 1, the answer must be greater than 8.25. Therefore, the quotient cannot be 2.75.

0.3 is almost $\frac{1}{3}$ and 8.25 is a little more than 8. If each of 8 pieces is divided into thirds, there will be 24 pieces, that is $8 \div \frac{1}{3} = 24$.

Therefore, it makes sense that 8.25 / 0.3 = 27.5.

If there is a remainder, it should be used to round the quotient to the nearest whole number before placing the decimal point.

Example: 3.29 / 0.5

Step 1: Divide, ignoring the decimal points.

$$
\begin{array}{r|r}
5\overline{)329} & \\
-\;300 & 60 \\
\hline
29 & \\
-\;\;25 & 5 \\
\hline
4 & 65
\end{array}
$$

Step 2: Express the remainder as a fraction and round the quotient to the nearest whole number.

The partial-quotients algorithm shows that 329 / 5 = $65\frac{4}{5}$. Rounded to the nearest whole number, this is 66.

Step 3: Estimate the size of the quotient and place the decimal point accordingly.

3.29 / 0.5 is about 3 divided by $\frac{1}{2}$, or 6.

Therefore, correct to one decimal place, 3.29 / 0.5 = 6.6.

As long as the number of decimal places desired is specified at the outset, this method can be used to rename fractions as decimals.

Example: Rename $\frac{5}{8}$ as a 3-place decimal.

    Step 1: Since 3 decimal places are desired, rename 5 as 5.000.

    Step 2: Use partial quotients to find 5000 / 8.

$$
\begin{array}{r|l}
8\overline{)5000} & \\
-\,4000 & 500 \\
\hline
1000 & \\
-\,800 & 100 \\
\hline
200 & \\
-\,200 & 25 \\
\hline
0 & 625
\end{array}
$$

    Step 3: Since $\frac{5}{8}$ is more than 0.5 but less than 1.0, place the decimal point to make a number in the correct range: 0.625.

Column division can also be used to find quotients that have a decimal part. Column division with decimals is an optional algorithm in *Everyday Mathematics,* but one you may want to consider if complex paper-and-pencil divisions with decimals are required by your state or district curriculum guidelines.

The money-sharing metaphor used above in the description of whole-number column division can be extended to decimal column division.

Example: Share $15 among 4 people.

    Step 1: Since 1 $10 bill cannot be shared 4 ways, trade it for 10 $1 bills.

$$
\begin{array}{r|c}
4\overline{)\cancel{1}} & \cancel{5} \\
& 15
\end{array}
$$

    Step 2: Sharing the 15 $1 bills four ways is 3 $1 bills for each person with 3 $1 bills left over.

$$
\begin{array}{r|c}
& 3 \\
4\overline{)\cancel{1}} & \cancel{5} \\
& 15 \\
& -\,12 \\
\hline
& 3
\end{array}
$$

    Step 3: Since the 3 $1 bills cannot be shared 4 ways, they should be traded for 30 dimes. Use decimal points to show that the amounts are now smaller than $1.

$$
\begin{array}{r|c|c|c}
& 3{\,}\centerdot & & \\
4\overline{)\cancel{1}} & \cancel{5}\centerdot & \cancel{0} & 0 \\
& 15 & 30 & \\
& -\,12 & & \\
\hline
& \cancel{3} &
\end{array}
$$

Step 4: Sharing 30 dimes 4 ways is 7 each with 2 left over. The 2 dimes are traded for 20 pennies. 20 pennies shared 4 ways is 5 each.

$$
\begin{array}{r|c|c|c}
 & 3 & 7 & 5 \\
\hline
4)\,\cancel{1} & \cancel{5} & \cancel{0} & \cancel{0} \\
 & 15 & 30 & 20 \\
 & -12 & -28 & -20 \\
\hline
 & \cancel{3} & \cancel{2} & 0
\end{array}
$$

So 15 / 4 = 3.75. This means that \$15 shared 4 ways is \$3.75 each.

Example: 97.24 / 26 = ?

1 * 26 = 26

2 * 26 = 52

3 * 26 = 78

4 * 26 = 104

5 * 26 = 130

8 * 26 = 208

10 * 26 = 260

$$
\begin{array}{r|c|c|c}
 & 3 & 7 & 4 \\
\hline
26)\,\cancel{9} & \cancel{7} & \cancel{2} & \cancel{4} \\
 & {}^{8}\cancel{9}{}^{1}7 & 192 & 104 \\
 & -78 & -182 & -104 \\
\hline
 & \cancel{19} & \cancel{10} & 0
\end{array}
$$

Column division with decimals can be carried out to an arbitrary number of decimal places. This can be used, for example, to show the conversion of a fraction to a repeating decimal.

Example: Rename $\frac{5}{11}$ as a decimal.

$$
\begin{array}{r|c|c|c|c|c|c|c}
 & 4 & 5 & 4 & 5 & 4 & 5 & \ldots \\
\hline
11)\,\cancel{5} & \cancel{0} & \cancel{0} & \cancel{0} & \cancel{0} & \cancel{0} & \cancel{0} & \ldots \\
 & 50 & 60 & 50 & 60 & 50 & 60 & \\
 & -44 & -55 & -44 & -55 & -44 & -55 & \\
\hline
 & \cancel{6} & \cancel{5} & \cancel{6} & \cancel{5} & \cancel{6} & \cancel{5} &
\end{array}
$$

So, $\frac{5}{11} = 0.454545\ldots$

3.3 Algorithms for Fractions

Decimal notation for rational numbers is increasingly important in the United States because of the growing acceptance of the metric system and the rapid spread of digital technology. Nevertheless, rational numbers written as fractions continue to be important both in everyday life and in mathematics beyond elementary school. Being able to add, subtract, multiply, divide, and compare fractions is useful in many practical real-world situations and is also necessary for success in algebra and higher mathematics.

Operations with fractions are treated extensively in the final two years of *Everyday Mathematics*. The overall approach is similar to that for whole numbers. In the beginning, the focus is on building a conceptual basis for understanding fractions. This work starts in *Kindergarten Everyday Mathematics,* considerably earlier than in most other programs, and continues throughout the primary-grade program. Much of this early work is hands-on (using pattern blocks, clock faces, chips, paper strips, and so on) and is closely connected to everyday uses of fractions.

During this period, and increasingly in third and fourth grades, students solve problems using their growing understanding of fractions rather than procedures they have been taught but may not understand. Much of this work continues to be hands-on, using concrete models for fractions, but pictorial and symbolic methods also appear. Often, students solve a problem in several ways, share their solutions, and compare and discuss the various approaches. During these discussions, the teacher may highlight or introduce particularly effective or instructive methods. Important ideas introduced during this stage include the unit whole or ONE in fractions that names a part of a whole, comparing fractions by size, and informal methods for adding and subtracting fractions and mixed numbers.

In fifth and sixth grades, algorithmic work with fractions becomes more systematic. Common-denominator approaches for addition, subtraction, and division are formally introduced—some students will have been using such methods already—and traditional topics such as simplest form and operations with mixed numbers are treated. In keeping with the *Everyday Mathematics* belief in multiple solution methods, students encounter several ways to solve most problems.

In the following sections, we briefly discuss various symbolic methods for operations with fractions.

3.3.1 Common Denominators

Many operations with fractions are more efficient when the fractions share a common denominator. *Everyday Mathematics* includes three main techniques for finding a common denominator.

Example: Rename $\frac{3}{4}$ and $\frac{1}{6}$ with a common denominator.

Method 1: Using Equivalent Fractions

List equivalent fractions for $\frac{3}{4}$ and $\frac{1}{6}$.

$$\frac{3}{4} = \frac{6}{8} = \frac{9}{12} = \frac{12}{16} = \cdots$$

$$\frac{1}{6} = \frac{2}{12} = \frac{3}{18} = \frac{4}{24} = \cdots$$

Both $\frac{3}{4}$ and $\frac{1}{6}$ can be renamed as fractions with the common denominator 12.

$$\frac{3}{4} = \frac{9}{12} \text{ and } \frac{1}{6} = \frac{2}{12}$$

For more information see Sections 1.2 and 1.3 of the Numeration and Order essay.

NOTE: *Everyday Mathematics* does not support the traditional emphasis on finding a least common denominator. The approach is excessively formal and has little meaning for many people. In many cases, the benefits of working with least common denominators are not worth the cost of finding them. In fact, implying that least common denominators are the only permissible denominators is probably harmful to later learning in algebra.

Method 2: Using Multiplication

Multiply the numerator and denominator of each fraction by the denominator of the other fraction.

$$\frac{3 * 6}{4 * 6} = \frac{18}{24} \qquad \frac{1 * 4}{6 * 4} = \frac{4}{24}$$

This method, introduced in fifth grade, gives what *Everyday Mathematics* calls a **quick common denominator.** This approach works even if the denominators are variables, so it is common in algebra.

Method 3: Using the Least Common Multiple

Find the least common multiple of the denominators.

The least common multiple of 4 and 6 is 12.

Rename the fractions so that their denominator is the least common multiple.

$$\frac{3}{4} * \frac{3}{3} = \frac{9}{12} \text{ and } \frac{1}{6} * \frac{2}{2} = \frac{2}{12}$$

This method gives what is known as the **least common denominator.** The least common denominator can be easier to use in complicated calculations.

3.3.2 Fraction Addition and Subtraction

In *Fifth* and *Sixth Grade Everyday Mathematics,* students use "quick common denominators" for adding and subtracting fractions. For example:

$$\frac{1}{3} + \frac{5}{8} = \frac{1 * 8}{3 * 8} + \frac{5 * 3}{8 * 3} = \frac{8}{24} + \frac{15}{24} = \frac{23}{24}$$

$$\frac{2}{3} - \frac{5}{8} = \frac{2 * 8}{3 * 8} - \frac{5 * 3}{8 * 3} = \frac{16}{24} - \frac{15}{24} = \frac{1}{24}$$

This approach may be generalized for sixth graders as formulas, although students should not necessarily be expected to memorize or prove them.

$$\frac{a}{b} + \frac{c}{d} = \frac{(a * d) + (c * b)}{b * d}$$

$$\frac{a}{b} - \frac{c}{d} = \frac{(a * d) - (c * b)}{b * d}$$

3.3.3 Mixed-Number Addition and Subtraction

There are two main approaches to adding and subtracting mixed numbers. One approach is to rename the mixed numbers as improper fractions and then add or subtract them in the same way as any other fractions.

Example: $4\frac{1}{6} + 2\frac{2}{3}$

Rename the mixed numbers as fractions.

$$4\frac{1}{6} = \frac{25}{6}$$

$$2\frac{2}{3} = \frac{8}{3}$$

Add the fractions.

$$\frac{25}{6} + \frac{8}{3} = \frac{25}{6} + \frac{16}{6} = \frac{41}{6}$$

Rename the result as a mixed number.

$$\frac{41}{6} = 6\frac{5}{6}$$

The other main approach to adding and subtracting mixed numbers is to treat the whole number and fraction parts separately, making trades as necessary.

Example: $5\frac{1}{4} - 3\frac{2}{3}$

First, rename the fractions using a common denominator.

$$5\frac{1}{4} \quad \rightarrow \quad 5\frac{3}{12}$$
$$- \quad 3\frac{2}{3} \quad \rightarrow \quad - \quad 3\frac{8}{12}$$

Next, rename the first mixed number so the numerator of the fraction part is large enough to subtract from.

$$5\frac{3}{12} \quad \rightarrow \quad 4\frac{15}{12}$$
$$- \quad 3\frac{8}{12} \quad \rightarrow \quad - \quad 3\frac{8}{12}$$

Finally, subtract.

$$4\frac{15}{12}$$
$$- \quad 3\frac{8}{12}$$
$$\overline{\quad 1\frac{7}{12}}$$

3.3.4 Fraction Multiplication

Even young children can solve problems like, "What is $\frac{1}{2}$ of 6?" This is especially true with problems that arise in real-world fair-sharing situations. Throughout the primary grades, students solve many such "fraction of a number" problems, which helps build a foundation for work with multiplication of fractions in *Fourth* through *Sixth Grade Everyday Mathematics*.

In *Fifth Grade Everyday Mathematics*, students investigate an area model for fraction multiplication that allows them to find products of relatively 'simple' fractions—that is, fractions that have small enough denominators to make drawing a divided rectangle a reasonable task.

For example, to find the product of $\frac{2}{4}$ and $\frac{2}{5}$, you can draw a rectangular region and partition it as shown below.

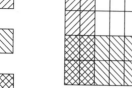

- $\frac{2}{5}$ of the region is shaded this way:
- $\frac{2}{4}$ of the region is shaded this way:
- $\frac{2}{4}$ of $\frac{2}{5}$ of the region is shaded this way:
- That's $\frac{4}{20}$, or $\frac{1}{5}$ of the whole region.

$$\frac{2}{4} \text{ of } \frac{2}{5} = \frac{2}{4} * \frac{2}{5} = \frac{4}{20} = \frac{1}{5}$$

After seeing many problems solved in this way, students should notice a pattern that can be generalized as an **algorithm for multiplying fractions:**

$$\frac{a}{b} * \frac{c}{d} = \frac{a * c}{b * d}$$

Later on in Grade 5, they incorporate this algorithm into one for multiplying fractions and whole numbers, where the first step is to rewrite the whole number as itself over 1. In symbols,

$$a * \frac{b}{c} = \frac{a}{1} * \frac{b}{c} = \frac{a * b}{1 * c} = \frac{a * b}{c}$$

This algorithm is then reviewed and practiced in *Sixth Grade Everyday Mathematics*.

3.3.5 Fraction Division

Situations that involve quotients of rational numbers in decimal form are fairly common in everyday life. However, the same kinds of situations involving quotients of rational numbers in fraction form are rare. Indeed, few adults ever need to divide fractions once they leave school. Therefore, the main goal of division of fractions in *Everyday Mathematics* is not to give students practical skills, but to achieve the following:

- Complete the arithmetic system. Because whole numbers and decimals can be added, subtracted, multiplied, and divided, students should see that all these operations are possible with fractions as well.

- Anticipate future work with rational number expressions in algebra courses.

A "Quick Common Denominator" Fraction-Division Algorithm

The common denominator method for dividing fractions is less mysterious than the traditional "invert-and-multiply" rule described in the next section. Unfortunately, while it may make more sense than the latter rule, it is usually less efficient. The algorithm builds on the "quick common denominator" approach to adding and subtracting fractions. Once a common denominator is found, the quotient of the fractions is simply the quotient of the numerators.

For example:

$$\frac{3}{4} \div \frac{2}{5} = \frac{15}{20} \div \frac{8}{20} = \frac{15/8}{20/20} = \frac{15/8}{1} = \frac{15}{8}, \text{ or } 1\frac{7}{8}$$

You might find it helpful to point out to students that the 20ths behave like units of measure in a ratio—say "15 twentieths divided by 8 twentieths is the ratio 15 to 8."

That the common-denominator method for dividing fractions gives the same result as the more familiar invert-and-multiply method can be shown algebraically:

Step 1: Rewrite the fractions to be divided over a common denominator.

$$\frac{a}{b} \div \frac{c}{d} = \frac{ad}{bd} \div \frac{cb}{db}$$

Step 2: Divide the numerators.

$$= ad \div cb$$

Step 3: Rewrite the division as a fraction.

$$= \frac{ad}{cb}$$

Note that this answer is the same as that obtained by the invert-and-multiply algorithm.

The "Invert-and-Multiply" Fraction-Division Algorithm

Most adults were taught the "invert-and-multiply" rule to divide fractions. A significant advantage of this algorithm is that it is easy to use. A significant disadvantage is that few people understand why it works. Although this is a sixth grade topic, we provide the following for the benefit of fourth- and fifth-grade teachers who have students who are curious about fraction division.

The Division of Fractions Property

To find the quotient of two fractions, multiply the first fraction by the reciprocal of the second fraction.

Examples:

$$\frac{4}{5} \div \frac{2}{3} = \frac{4}{5} * \frac{3}{2} = \frac{12}{10} = 1\frac{2}{10}, \text{ or } 1\frac{1}{5}$$

$$2\frac{3}{4} \div 1\frac{1}{3} = \frac{11}{4} \div \frac{4}{3} = \frac{11}{4} * \frac{3}{4} = \frac{33}{16}, \text{ or } 2\frac{1}{16}$$

The Division of Fractions Property is based on the following rules.

Rule 1: A fraction can have any number in its numerator and any number, except 0, in its denominator.

Examples:

27 / 55 can be written as the fraction $\frac{27}{55}$.

6.3 / π can be written as $\frac{6.3}{\pi}$.

$\frac{2}{3} \div \frac{3}{4}$ can be written as $\frac{\frac{2}{3}}{\frac{3}{4}}$.

Rule 2: $\dfrac{a}{b} * \dfrac{c}{d} = \dfrac{a * c}{b * d}$

where a and c may be any numbers; b and d may be any numbers except 0.

Examples:

$$\frac{5}{8} * \frac{3}{2} = \frac{5 * 3}{8 * 2} = \frac{15}{16}$$

$$\frac{3}{5} * 7 = \frac{3}{5} * \frac{7}{1} = \frac{3 * 7}{5 * 1} = \frac{21}{5} \text{, or } 4\frac{1}{5}$$

Rule 3: If the product of two numbers is 1, then the numbers are called **reciprocals** of each other. If a number is written as a fraction, then its reciprocal is the fraction written "upside down," with numerator and denominator exchanged.

Examples:

5 and $\frac{1}{5}$ are reciprocals of each other because $5 * \frac{1}{5} = 1$.

$\frac{3}{4}$ and $\frac{4}{3}$ are reciprocals of each other because $\frac{3}{4} * \frac{4}{3} = 1$.

$2\frac{3}{5}$ and $\frac{5}{13}$ are reciprocals of each other because

$2\frac{3}{5} = \frac{13}{5}$ and $\frac{13}{5} * \frac{5}{13} = 1$.

Rule 4: If the numerator and denominator of a fraction are multiplied by the same number, then the result is equivalent to the original fraction.

Example:

$$\frac{3}{5} = \frac{3 * 4}{5 * 4} = \frac{12}{20}$$

Rule 5: Any number a, divided by 1, is equal to a.

That is, $a \div 1 = a/1 = a$.

Examples:

$$23 \div 1 = \frac{23}{1} = 23$$

$$46.3 \div 1 = \frac{46.3}{1} = 46.3$$

$$\frac{3}{8} \div 1 = \frac{\frac{3}{8}}{1} = \frac{3}{8}$$

The following example shows why the Division of Fractions Property works.

Example: Divide $\frac{3}{4}$ by $\frac{2}{5}$.

Step 1: Write the problem as a fraction. (Rule 1)

$$\frac{3}{4} \div \frac{2}{5} = \frac{\frac{3}{4}}{\frac{2}{5}}$$

Step 2: Multiply the numerator and denominator of the fraction by the reciprocal of the denominator. (Rules 3 and 4)

$$\frac{\frac{3}{4}}{\frac{2}{5}} = \frac{\frac{3}{4} * \frac{5}{2}}{\frac{2}{5} * \frac{5}{2}}$$

Step 3: Simplify the denominator. (Rule 3)

$$\frac{\frac{3}{4} * \frac{5}{2}}{\frac{2}{5} * \frac{5}{2}} = \frac{\frac{3}{4} * \frac{5}{2}}{1}$$

Step 4: Divide by 1. (Rule 5)

$$\frac{\frac{3}{4} * \frac{5}{2}}{1} = \frac{3}{4} * \frac{5}{2}$$

Step 5: Multiply. (Rule 2)

$$\frac{3}{4} * \frac{5}{2} = \frac{3 * 5}{4 * 2} = \frac{15}{8}, \text{ or } 1\frac{7}{8}$$

You can see from Step 5 that $\frac{3}{4} \div \frac{2}{5} = \frac{3}{4} * \frac{5}{2}$; that is, the first fraction is being multiplied by the reciprocal of the second fraction.

3.4 Calculators

Before the availability of inexpensive calculators, the elementary school mathematics curriculum was designed primarily to make students good at carrying out paper-and-pencil algorithms for whole numbers, decimals, and fractions. There was little time for students to learn to think mathematically and solve problems because it was necessary to prepare them for the sometimes laborious calculations required in life after school. But calculators and computers have greatly reduced the need for paper-and-pencil computation in the world outside of school. This change suggests that the school mathematics curriculum, and especially the place of paper-and-pencil algorithms in that curriculum, should be reexamined. See Section 3.1.1 for a discussion of the role of paper-and-pencil algorithms in school mathematics.

In the quarter-century that electronic calculators have been widely available, a number of researchers have studied the effects of calculators on student learning. The evidence from these studies should reassure parents and others who worry that the use of calculators may undermine students' understanding of basic arithmetic. Research shows that proper use of calculators enhances understanding and mastery of arithmetic, promotes good number sense, and improves problem-solving skills. As a recent review of research put it, "Research has proven that calculators are beneficial to students at every level of education." (Pomerantz & Waits, 1997) See Section 3.4.2 for a short bibliography of calculator research.

One particular concern is that students will become dependent on calculators in situations better suited to mental arithmetic or some other method. The authors of *Everyday Mathematics* believe that besides knowing how to compute mentally, with paper and pencil, and with a calculator, students must also know when to use each of these methods. *Everyday Mathematics* accordingly includes activities, such as the game *Beat the Calculator,* that are specifically designed to help students learn to choose the most appropriate calculation method for a given situation. Research carried out by UCSMP and others indicates that students who use calculators can learn to choose appropriately. This research shows, and teacher experience confirms, that most students do develop good judgment about when to use and when not to use calculators. There is no evidence that proper use will cause students to become dependent on calculators or make them unable to solve problems with paper and pencil or mentally when appropriate.

Calculators are useful teaching tools. Calculators enable students to think about the problems, rather than on carrying out algorithms without mistakes. They make it possible for young children to display numbers before they are skilled at writing. Calculators can be used to count forward or backward by any whole number or decimal—a particularly important activity in the primary grades because counting is so central to number and operations at that level, but also useful for older students who are learning about decimals and fractions. Calculators also allow students to solve interesting, everyday problems requiring computations that might otherwise be too difficult for them to perform, including problems that arise outside of mathematics class. Calculators make it possible for students to do many activities that simply cannot be done on a chalkboard or with paper and pencil.

Everyday Mathematics encourages students to think about developing algorithms as they solve problems. To develop this habit they need to study particular algorithms, but once the algorithms are understood, using them repeatedly may become tedious. Another reason calculators are so helpful in the mathematics curriculum is that they free both students and teachers from having to spend so much time on dull, repetitive, and unproductive tasks.

3.4.1 Calculators for *Everyday Mathematics*

In a sense, using a calculator requires learning new algorithms— namely the key sequences to get an anticipated result. Learning a new key sequence should be a topic of instruction, not something left for students to figure out for themselves. Therefore, when students encounter new keys and key sequences, spend a few minutes talking about the correct procedures for the model of calculator they have. Write the proper key sequences on the board and have students work through several sample problems.

Although the authors recommend the Texas Instruments TI-15 calculator for Grades 4–6, many other calculators are acceptable as well. Much more important than the particular model is that all students have the same model so that the same keystroke sequences work on every student's calculator. It is also strongly recommended that the calculator follow the standard order of operations. If a calculator computes $3 + 4 \times 5$ as 23, then it is following the standard order of operations; if it gives 35 as the answer, it is carrying out the operations in the order they were entered, and is not suitable. Finally, it will also be useful if the calculator can perform operations with fractions.

Keystroke sequences given in the *Teacher's Lesson Guide* or in the student materials are for TI-15s. In most cases, the TI-15 keystroke sequences work with other calculators as well. If you have a different calculator, you should check that the given keystrokes work with your machines. In some cases, you may need to consult the directions that came with your calculators.

The basic operation of the TI-15 is described in the *Student Reference Book*. The TI-15 also has several other features you may find useful. These are discussed briefly below and on several calculator masters for each grade. For further details, consult the instructions that came with your calculators.

Arithmetic Training: Automatic Mode

The TI-15 can be used to practice arithmetic, including basic and extended facts. This feature is invoked by pressing ⊚. In this mode, the calculator displays problems for the user to solve. It tells whether the answer given is correct and gives hints if the answer is wrong. After every five problems, the calculator shows a scorecard. Pressing ⊚ a second time exits the arithmetic training mode.

Example:

Key Sequence	Display
(Clear) ⊚	1 + ? = 5
3 (Enter)	1 + 3 < 5 \n NO
4 (Enter)	1 + 4 = 5 \n YES

Pressing ⊚ and then (Mode) brings up menus for controlling the operation and the level of difficulty. Immediately after (Mode) is pressed, the scorecard appears. Then, after a moment, the scorecard is replaced by a menu that presents a choice between AUTO and MAN. Other menus are reached using ⬇. In each menu, the current choice is underlined. New choices are made by using ⬅ and ➡ to change what is underlined and then pressing (Enter). (If (Enter) is not pressed, then the old menu choice will still be active.)

Key Sequence	Menu	Function
◈ (Mode) (pause)	◆ AUTO MAN	Sets the mode. In AUTO mode, the calculator makes up the problems. In MAN mode, the user makes up the problems. MAN mode is also used for place value.
◈ (Mode) (pause) ⬇	◆ Auto 1 2 3 _ ▪ ■	Sets the level of problem difficulty. Level 1 problems are the easiest.
◈ (Mode) (pause) ⬇ ⬇	◆ Auto + − × ÷ ?	Sets the operation. Choosing ? will cause the calculator to generate problems with missing operations.

Example: Set the calculator for practicing extended multiplication facts.

Key Sequence	Display
◈ (Mode) (pause) ⬇ ⮕ (Enter)	◆ Auto 1 2 3 _ ▪ ■
⬇ ⮕ ⮕ (Enter)	◆ Auto + − × ÷ ?
(Mode)	◆ Auto 9 X ? = 720

Arithmetic Training: Manual Mode

The TI-15's Arithmetic Training: Manual Mode has several features that can be used to practice arithmetic and place value. For example, in manual mode the user can make up practice problems, using ? for a missing number or operation. The calculator tells how many whole-number solutions each problem has and, as with automatic-mode arithmetic training, gives hints and keeps score.

Example:

Key Sequence	Display
◈ (Mode) (pause) ⇨ (Enter)	◆ AUTO <u>MAN</u>
(Mode) 84 ⊖ (?) (Enter) 76 (Enter)	◆ 84 − ? = 76 1 SOL
	◆ 84 − ? = 76
8 (Enter)	◆ 84 − 8 = 76 YES

In manual-mode arithmetic training, one can also use ⟨⟩ to test whether inequalities are true. (Decimals are allowed in inequalities in manual mode.) Pressing ⟨⟩ gives <; pressing ⟨⟩ ⟨⟩ gives >.

Example:

Key Sequence	Display
◈ (Mode) (pause) ⇨ (Enter)	◆ AUTO <u>MAN</u>
(Mode) 1 (·) 75 ⟨⟩ 1 (Enter)	◆ 1.75 < 1 NO

Certain place-value features are also available in manual-mode arithmetic training. These features are invoked by pressing ▆, when the calculator is in manual mode. Then, when a number is entered and one of the red place-value keys (1000.) , (100.) , and so on is pressed, the calculator will tell how many units of that value are in the number. Pressing (Clear) allows the user to enter another number.

Example:

Key Sequence	Display
◈ Mode (pause) ⇨ Enter	◆ AUTO MAN
Mode	◆ ·∎
123 ⊙ 456 ∎	◆∎. 1 2 3 . 4 5 6 ·∎
100.	◆∎. 1 2 3 . 4 5 6 1 … … . … … …
10.	◆∎. 1 2 3 . 4 5 6 1 2 … . … … …
0.1	◆∎. 1 2 3 . 4 5 6 1 2 3 4 . … …

There is one menu for place value. The calculator can be set so that it will tell the place value of a digit in a number or what digit is in a given place in a number.

Key Sequence	Display
◈ Mode (pause) ⇨ Enter	◆ AUTO MAN
⬇ ⇨ Enter	↑ ┊┊ … … ┊ … ∎┊.
Mode	◆ ·∎
123 ⊙ 456 ∎	◆∎. 1 2 3 . 4 5 6 ·∎
10.	◆∎. 1 2 3 . 4 5 6 … 2 … . … … …
0.01	◆∎. 1 2 3 . 4 5 6 … … … . … 5 …
4	◆∎. 1 2 3 . 4 5 6 … … … . 4 … …

	◆■.
	123.456
	4-->0.1

	◆■.
5	123.456
	... ... 5 ...

	◆■.
	123.456
	5-->0.01

To exit from place-value mode, press **Clear**. To exit from arithmetic-training mode, press ⬡.

Memory: ▶M , MR/MC

A calculator's memory is a place where a number can be stored while the calculator is working with other numbers. Later, the number can be recalled from memory. Simple memory functions of the TI-15 are described in the *Student Reference Book* and are not discussed here. The table below, which is included here only for completeness, summarizes the TI-15's more advanced memory features.

Key Sequence	Function
▶M +	Adds the number in the display to the number already in memory.
▶M −	Subtracts the number in the display from the number already in memory.
▶M ×	Multiplies the number in the memory by the number in the display. The product is stored in the memory.
▶M ÷	Divides the number in the memory by the number in the display. The quotient is stored in the memory.
▶M Int÷	Divides the number in the memory by the number in the display. The quotient is stored in the memory and the remainder is discarded.

NOTE: If you press MR/MC more than twice, the TI-15 will append a 0 where the cursor is. For example, pressing 5 MR/MC MR/MC MR/MC MR/MC MR/MC will cause the calculator to display 5000. The reason for this odd behavior is that the odd numbered presses (the first, third, and so on) cause the calculator to "recall" a 0 from memory, while the even numbered presses (the second, fourth, and so on) cause the calculator to "clear" the memory, replacing its contents with 0.

3.4.2 A Short Bibliography of Calculator Research

Campbell, Patricia F., and Elsie L. Stewart. (1993). "Calculators and Computers." In *Early Childhood Mathematics*. Ed. Robert Jensen. NCTM Research Interpretation Project. New York: Macmillan.

Demana, Frank, and Joan Leitzel. (1988). "Establishing Fundamental Concepts Through Numerical Problem Solving." In *The Ideas of Algebra,* K–12. Eds. Arthur F. Coxford and Albert P. Shulte. Reston, VA: NCTM.

Groves, Susie, and Kaye Stacey. (1998). "Calculations in Primary Mathematics: Exploring Number Before Teaching Algorithms." In *The Teaching and Learning of Algorithms in School Mathematics*. Eds. Lorna J. Morrow and Margaret J. Kenney. Reston, VA: NCTM.

Hembree, Ray, and Donald J. Dessart. (1986). "Effects of Hand-Held Calculators in Precollege Mathematics Education: A Meta-Analysis." *Journal for Research in Mathematics Education,* 17, 83–89.

Hembree, Ray, and Donald J. Dessart. (1992). "Research on Calculators in Mathematics Education." In *Calculators in Mathematics Education*. Eds. J. T. Fey and C. R. Hirsch. Reston, VA: NCTM.

National Council of Teachers of Mathematics. (1991). "Position Statement: Calculators and the Education of Youth." Reston, VA: Author. http://www.nctm.org/about/position_statements/position_statement_01.htm

Pomerantz, Heidi, and Bert Waits. (1997). "The Role of Calculators in Math Education." A paper prepared for the Urban Systemic Initiative/Comprehensive Partnership for Mathematics and Science Achievement (USI/CPMSA) Superintendents Forum. Dallas, TX, December 4. [http://www.ti.com/calc/docs/therole.htm]

Smith, Brian A. (1997). *A Meta-analysis of Outcomes from the Use of Calculators in Mathematics Education*. Dissertations Abstracts International.

Suydam, Marilyn, N. (1982). "The Use of Calculators in Pre-College Education: Fifth Annual State-of-the-Art Review." Columbus, OH: Calculator Information Center. (ERIC Document Reproduction Service No. ED 220 273).

Suydam, Marliyn N. (1985). "Research on Instructional Materials for Mathematics." Columbus, OH: ERIC Clearinghouse for Science, Mathematics, and Environmental Education. (ERIC Document Reproduction Service No. 276 569).

Suydam, Marilyn N. (1987). "Research on Instruction in Elementary
    School Mathematics: A Letter to Teachers." Columbus, OH:
    ERIC Clearinghouse for Science, Mathematics, and
    Environmental Education. (ERIC Document Reproduction
    Service No. ED 293 728).

3.5 Algorithmic and Procedural Thinking

Algorithmic and procedural thinking includes:

- understanding specific algorithms or procedures provided by
  other people,

- applying known algorithms to everyday problems,

- adapting known algorithms to fit new situations,

- developing new algorithms and procedures when necessary, and

- recognizing the limitations of algorithms and procedures so they
  are not used inappropriately.

Because a single algorithm can be used to solve an entire class of
problems, knowing algorithms increases students' mathematical
power. In *Everyday Mathematics,* this increase in mathematical
power is achieved at the same time that other important objectives
are being met. The *Everyday Mathematics* approach to algorithms
improves students' mental arithmetic skills and helps them develop
sound number sense, including a good understanding of place value.
The *Everyday Mathematics* emphasis on multiple solutions,
including both inventing new procedures and making sense of
others' inventions, encourages the belief that mathematics is both
creative and understandable.

Everyday Mathematics also includes activities that help students
understand the idea of an algorithm. Many activities in
mathematics are about turning cumbersome, repetitive tasks into
efficient procedures that will work the same way each time—for
example, the creation and use of computer programs. The authors of
Everyday Mathematics have found that paper-and-pencil
computational algorithms are valuable toward gaining an
understanding of algorithmic thinking in general, so explicit
discussions of algorithms occur in lessons devoted to computation.

By studying computational algorithms, students can learn things
that will carry over to other areas of their lives. More and more, we
need to apply algorithmic and procedural thinking in order to
operate technologically advanced devices. Algorithms beyond
arithmetic are increasingly important in theoretical mathematics, in
applications of mathematics, in computer science, and in many
areas outside of mathematics.

Data and Chance

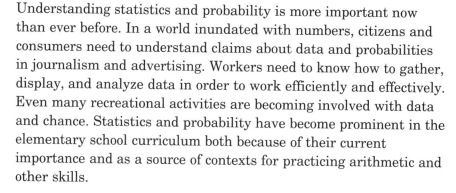

Understanding statistics and probability is more important now than ever before. In a world inundated with numbers, citizens and consumers need to understand claims about data and probabilities in journalism and advertising. Workers need to know how to gather, display, and analyze data in order to work efficiently and effectively. Even many recreational activities are becoming involved with data and chance. Statistics and probability have become prominent in the elementary school curriculum both because of their current importance and as a source of contexts for practicing arithmetic and other skills.

4.1 Data Collection, Organization, and Analysis

Students' initial data explorations should be informal, allowing them to collaborate with you and with one another to decide on methods of collecting, representing, and explaining their data. As students gain experience, they can be introduced to standard methods, such as using bar and line graphs and appropriate statistical landmarks (such as median and mean) to help them answer questions and communicate their findings to others.

In *Everyday Mathematics,* work with data provides a context and motivation for the development of numerical skills that in traditional programs would be developed artificially or in isolation. For example, a number of data lessons are coordinated with the World Tour section in Grade 4 and the American Tour section in Grade 5. Much of the data that students collect and use in these

lessons involve rates and percents—for example, currency exchange rates, cars per 1,000 persons, and percent of urban population. These real-world applications support and enrich other lessons concerned with fractions, decimals, and percents.

In *Everyday Mathematics,* data activities are designed so that students are involved in all aspects of data collection and analysis. For this reason, many data activities span several days and lessons. For example, in fifth grade, students are instructed to investigate whether a card game called *First to 21* is fair. In one lesson, students learn how to play the game and are introduced to the problem of figuring out whether it is fair. In subsequent lessons, they collect data by playing the game numerous times over the course of several days. They record their data individually and collectively on tally charts and on a class bar graph, which is updated daily. In a later lesson, students analyze the data to determine whether the game is fair (it is not) and how it could be made fair. The *First to 21* game and activities also relate to probability, a topic that is discussed later in this essay. Many of the data activities in *Everyday Mathematics* are integrated with other topics in mathematics and other curricular areas in this way. In addition to the many and varied data activities that are included in the lesson guide, many opportunities for working with data will also arise naturally in the course of classroom life.

4.1.1 Formulating a Question

Ordinarily, data are collected and analyzed to describe a situation and/or to make predictions. The process almost always begins with a question. When we want to know something, one way to approach finding an answer is to gather information. Then we look at the information—the data—in various ways in order to determine what we need to know.

There are two important reasons to take time formulating a question for data exploration. The first is motivational. Data-collection activities are usually more meaningful to students if they are connected to a real problem in the class or to the gathering of information students really want to have. *Everyday Mathematics* presents many problem situations that require data collection and analysis, and you are encouraged to add your own and to personalize those suggested.

In one school, an example of such personalization arose when the fifth grade students held a cookie sale for the younger children in the school to raise funds to buy new library books. In order to decide which kinds of cookies to bake and in what amounts, the fifth graders surveyed a sample of younger students (one class per grade level) and asked how many cookies and what type of cookies they were likely to buy at the cookie sale. They tallied and graphed their findings and used them to determine about how many cookies they should bake and which kinds would be most popular. Of course, they could not determine exactly how to stock their sale, but the survey data helped them plan wisely.

A second reason to take time to formulate a question for data exploration is to clarify the essential information that can lead to an answer. In the cookie sale survey, for example, it was important to know which kinds of cookies were preferred, but it was not important to know whether cookies were more popular than ice cream or whether the cookies would be eaten at school or at home. As another example, if students are collecting data to find out who runs the fastest, does hair color matter? Does distance matter? What about footwear or clothing? Even if the questions sometimes seem silly, it is important to ask them to help students develop habits of thinking about the possible effects various factors may have on the data they collect.

4.1.2 Collecting and Recording Data

Everyday Mathematics uses many sources of data and a variety of collection procedures, such as the following:

- Counting and measuring in the classroom
- Observing and measuring at home
- Taking surveys at school (including surveys of other classes)
- Collecting data from such sources as TV, newspapers, magazines, or encyclopedias

Sampling

When collecting and analyzing data, it is important to know a little bit about sampling. A **sample** is a relatively small part of a group chosen to represent the larger group being studied. The larger group is the **population.** The population might be all of the students in a school, all of the people in a state, all adults of voting age in a country, or any other large group that has been designated for study. Often, the collection of data from every member of the population is impossible; therefore, a representative sample of the population is surveyed.

An important aspect of certain samples is that they are random. A **random sample** is taken from a population in a way that gives all members of the population the same chance of being selected. Large samples give more precise estimates of the population characteristics than small samples.

In *K–3 Everyday Mathematics,* the most common data are counts, and the usual goal is to examine the frequency of various occurrences. "How many . . . ?" is the classic beginning to the questions that are formulated by young children. In Grades 4–6, data may involve fractions, decimals, and negative numbers. Students in Grades 4–6 use the World Tour and American Tour sections of the *Student Reference Book,* as well as other pages, as sources of data. Data is recorded on journal pages, on the Class Data Pad, and in bulletin-board displays.

Data analysis begins as the data are collected. If the information is not recorded in an organized table or chart, students will end up with an indecipherable heap of numbers instead of useful data. *Everyday Mathematics* provides various tools to help with the initial collection and organization of data, including journal pages, masters, and suggestions for the Class Data Pad and bulletin-board displays.

4.1.3 Organizing and Displaying Data

The tools in *Everyday Mathematics* provide some built-in organization during data collection, but it is also important for students to design their own ways of recording and displaying data. Organizing data can help you "see the data better"; reorganizing it can help you "see the data differently," in a way that may better suit your needs. Students are encouraged to make and observe a wide variety of data displays.

Two simple methods for organizing data are to arrange the data in order from the smallest value to the largest and to sort the data by one or more characteristics. When the data comes from student characteristics, this can be done very concretely in the classroom. For example, you could order students' age data by having them line up by age. Or you could organize students by gender and then handedness. Direct all boys to move to the north wall of the room and all girls to the south wall; then have all right-handers move to the east wall and all left-handers to the west wall.

Descriptions of several types of data displays follow. Do not insist that all displays be neat and nicely labeled—especially tally plots or line plots. Students should sketch many plots quickly, so that they can "see the data" in several different ways. Once students have analyzed the data, they will often be asked to report on the data in some way. For reports, you should require that any accompanying graphs be neat and nicely labeled.

In *Sixth Grade Everyday Mathematics,* students have the option to use a spreadsheet program that may allow them to draw line plots, bar graphs, and other displays.

Data Tables

Tables are one of the most basic formats for the display of data. Newspapers, reference books, scientific articles, and many other publications contain data tables. Tables have specific uses, such as tally tables, lists, and the input/output tables used in "What's My Rule?" Tables of numbers and arithmetic facts are also used extensively to help students improve their mental-arithmetic skills.

Largest Cities by Population (urban agglomerations)	
City, Country	**Population**
Tokyo, Japan	26,959,000
Mexico City, Mexico	16,562,000
Sao Paulo, Brazil	16,533,000
New York City, U.S.	16,332,000
Bombay (Mumbai), India	15,138,000
Shanghai, China	13,584,000
Los Angeles, U.S.	12,410,000

(Above is from *World Almanac*, 2000.)

National League Standings, 6-9-00				
CENTRAL	**W**	**L**	**Pct**	**GB**
St. Louis	33	26	.559	–
Cincinnati	31	27	.534	1 1/2
Pittsburgh	26	31	.456	6
CUBS	25	35	.416	8 1/2
Milwaukee	23	36	.390	10
Houston	21	38	.356	12
EAST	**W**	**L**	**Pct**	**GB**
Atlanta	37	21	.638	–
New York	33	26	.559	4 1/2
Montreal	31	25	.554	5
Florida	27	33	.450	11
Philadelphia	22	35	.386	14 1/2
WEST	**W**	**L**	**Pct**	**GB**
Arizona	35	24	.593	–
Los Angeles	32	25	.561	2
Colorado	31	25	.553	2 1/2
San Francisco	27	29	.482	6 1/2
San Diego	25	33	.431	9 1/2

(The above was excerpted from the *Chicago Tribune* for Friday, June 9, 2000.)

Line Plots and Bar Graphs

Line plots or sketch graphs are used extensively to organize and display data. A line plot shows the data by using checks, Xs, or stick-on notes to indicate the different data values along a labeled line. A line plot can be thought of as a rough sketch of a bar graph.

Bar graphs are introduced in second grade and are used throughout the rest of the program. Bar graphs are excellent for displaying "how much" or "how many," and can be drawn vertically or horizontally. Students need to be aware of the important parts of a graph, including the title, labels for axes, and the scales for numbering the axes.

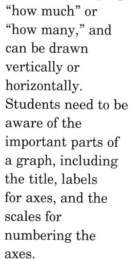

line plot

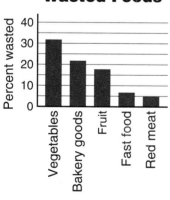

vertical bar graph

Source: *The Garbage Product*

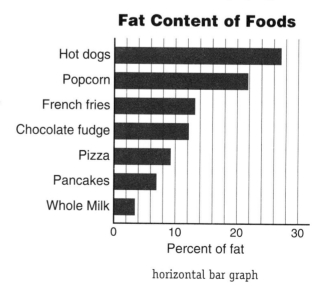

horizontal bar graph

Source: The New York Public Library Desk Reference

If the scale used for numbering an axis is too small or too large, the "look" of the data can be distorted, as in the Favorite Flavors of Ice Cream bar graphs shown.

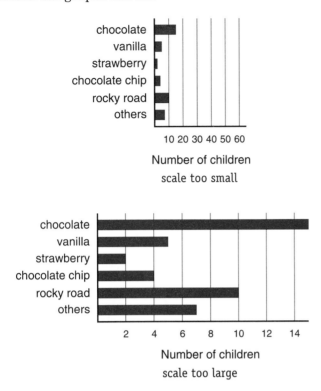

Computer software programs for graphing allow the scale to be set by entering a maximum and minimum for the range and an interval. This is a wonderful way to demonstrate how the change in scale affects the look of a graph.

In *4–6 Everyday Mathematics,* students are introduced to side-by-side and stacked bar graphs. Side-by-side bar graphs display related data in adjacent bars, and stacked bar graphs display related data by subdividing a single bar to represent parts of a total. These graphs are especially good for making comparisons among data because the information is displayed close together, rather than being separated.

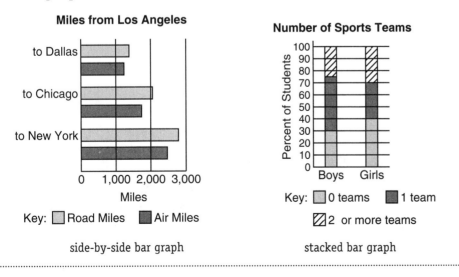

Median Number of Years of School Completed by People, Age 25 or Over, in the United States

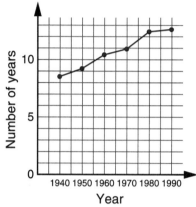

Source: 1995 Digest of Education

Line Graphs

Line graphs are a good application of ordered pairs, which are introduced late in *Third Grade Everyday Mathematics*. Drawing and analyzing line graphs gives students good practice in working with ordered pairs. Line graphs are used often in the World Tour, the American Tour, and in various projects in sixth grade.

Circle Graphs

Circle graphs, also known as pie graphs or pie charts, are used to compare parts of a whole. The circle represents the whole set of data; the circle and its interior are divided into pie-shaped pieces, or sectors, that represent parts of the set of data. The sizes of the sectors are calculated by finding the fraction or percent that each is of the whole.

Areas of the Continents

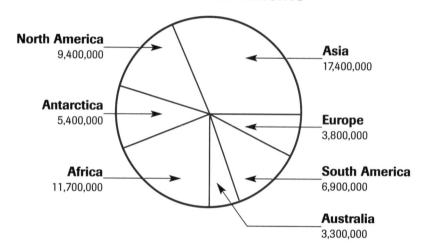

In Grade 5, students use a Percent Circle to construct circle graphs because it eliminates the need to calculate the number of degrees in a sector. In Grade 6, students use protractors to make circle graphs. Although this is a viable alternative to using a Percent Circle, the activity is more an application of a student's skill at taking percents of numbers—in this case, percents of the 360 degrees in a circle.

Tips for Constructing Circle Graphs

Although students in Grades 5 and 6 may develop their own methods for constructing circle graphs, there are steps that need to be taken in order. Following are tips for guiding students in their work.

1. Given data, write a percent for each part of the data to be represented by a sector or slice of the graph. Round to the nearest whole percent. This step can be done quickly with a calculator. As a check, find the total of the percents. It should be 100% but may differ a little because of rounding.

2. If using a protractor to draw the graph: Multiply 360 degrees by each percent in Step 1 to determine the number of degrees in each sector. As a check, the values should total 360 degrees.

Percent Circle

3. Draw a circle and its center on a piece of paper. The Percent Circle on the Geometry Template has an outside radius of about $1\frac{1}{4}$ inch, and the protractor on the template has an outside radius of about $1\frac{5}{8}$ inch, so advise students to center their circle at least 2 inches from the edges of the page. Encourage students to draw the circle big enough so that it is easy to write labels in the sectors.

4. Divide the circle into sectors whose sizes correspond to the percents in Step 1, or degrees in Step 2, depending on the tool used.

   - Make certain the Percent Circle or protractor is centered over the center of the circle.
   - Start with the smallest sector. Mark a point on the paper next to the 0 on the Percent Circle or protractor. Then mark a point at the percent or degree measure of the first sector. Draw a radius from the center of the circle to each of those points.
   - Next, center the Percent Circle or protractor and place the 0% or 0° mark along the second radius drawn for the previous sector. Mark the percent or degree measure for the next-larger sector, and draw the next radius.
   - Continue in this way until all sectors are drawn. (Students will realize that the last sector "graphs itself." Encourage them to measure it to check whether it is the right size.)

5. Label the sectors and title the graph.

Stem-and-Leaf Plots

A stem-and-leaf plot resembles a line plot because it displays the individual pieces of the whole data set. A stem-and-leaf plot differs from a line plot because it shows the data values in order within each "bar" and separates the digits of the numerical data into two columns (stems and leaves). A stem-and-leaf plot is helpful for finding the median of a data set.

The first step in making a stem-and-leaf plot is to find the maximum and minimum values of the data. The table of toaster prices in the margin lists the maximum price as $90 and the minimum as $14. Because the greatest place value is the 10s, the stem values will be the 10s digits in the prices. The stem column is numbered from 1 to 9 (see Figure 1).

The second step is to place the leaves next to the corresponding stems. The leaves in this plot are the digits in the ones place in the prices. The price of the Salton TO-6 is $40. A 0 is placed next to the 4 on the stem (see Figure 1). The remaining leaves are placed to complete the plot (see Figure 2).

Table of toaster prices	
Brand and Model	**Price**
Salton TO-6	$40
Rowenta TO-38A	45
Toastmaster 740	38
Rival Wilde Slot 9150	40
Proctor-Silex T-2830	47
Wide Mouth ET-9	45
Oster 3211-18A	40
Tefal 8443-40	50
Toastmaster 735A	25
Farberware 292	39
Proctor-Silex T33 OW	32
Panasonic NT-131	18
Conair Cuisine CT260	25
Sunbeam 20030	90
Kenmore 4808	18
Black & Decker T215	27
Toastmaster B705A	14
Black & Decker T-235	48

Source: *Consumer Reports,* June 1990.

Stems (10s)	Leaves (1s)
9	
8	
7	
6	
5	
4	0
3	
2	
1	

Figure 1

Stems (10s)	Leaves (1s)
9	0
8	
7	
6	
5	0
4	0507508
3	892
2	557
1	884

Figure 2

Stems (10s)	Leaves (1s)
9	0
8	
7	
6	
5	0
4	0005578
3	289
2	557
1	488

Figure 3

The final step is to arrange the leaves in order, as in Figure 3. Now it is easy to find the mode, $40. The median can be found by counting up from the bottom or down from the top. The middle two prices are $39 and $40, so the median price is (39 + 40) ÷ 2 = $39.50.

As with a line plot, bars can be drawn around the leaves so that the plot looks like a bar graph.

Step Graphs

The step graph, which is introduced in *Sixth Grade Everyday Mathematics,* is used to represent situations in which changes occur in "jumps" rather than gradually. It is a variation of a bar graph that is useful when the variable represented on the *x*-axis is not countable, as in most bar graphs, but a continuous quantity, such as time. The variable displayed on the *y*-axis is discrete, jumping from one value to another (forming the steps). The step graph in Figure A shows how the minimum hourly wage has jumped; the number of years between jumps varies.

At an *x*-value where the step value jumps, the graph should indicate which *y*-value goes with the *x*-value. One way is to place a solid dot at whichever end of the step that belongs with the *x*-value, and no dot at the other end of the step, as is shown in Figure A. To further clarify, an open dot could be placed at the other end of the step value, as shown in Figure B.

Minimum Wage

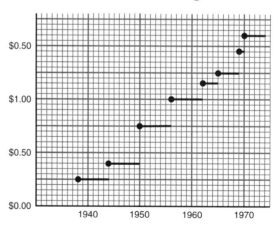

Figure A

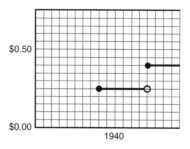

Figure B

Venn Diagrams

Students in *Sixth Grade Everyday Mathematics* use Venn diagrams to analyze events whose descriptions include words such as *not, both, exactly,* and *at least.* The Venn diagram was introduced in 1894 by the English logician John Venn in order to improve on Swiss mathematician Leonhard Euler's use of circles to represent relationships among sets of objects. **Euler's circles,** as they are called, very simply showed relationships such as the following:

Disjoint sets have no common elements. In the example, the sets {1, 2, 3} and {4, 5} are disjoint.

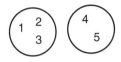
disjoint sets

Overlapping sets share at least one element. In the example, {1, 2, 3} overlaps {2, 4, 5}. They share the value 2.

One set is a **subset** of another if all of its elements are also in the other set. In the example, {2, 3} is a subset of {1, 2, 3}.

overlapping sets

The **intersection** of two or more sets is the set of elements found in *all of* the sets. In the examples above, the intersection of the disjoint sets is empty. The intersection of the overlapping set is the set {2}. For the subset example, the intersection is the same as the subset {2, 3}. An intersection represents the solution to a problem involving the word *and.* For the overlapping sets, the intersection helps answer the question, "What number or numbers are in {1, 2, 3} and in {2, 4, 5}?" (2)

a subset

The **union** of two or more sets is the set of all elements found in any of the sets. For both the disjoint and overlapping sets above, the union is {1, 2, 3, 4, 5}. For the subset example, the union is {1, 2, 3}. A union represents the solution to a problem involving the word *or.* For the overlapping sets, the union helps answer the question, "What numbers are in {1, 2, 3} or in {2, 4, 5}?" (1, 2, 3, 4, 5)

John Venn improved on Euler circles by adding a rectangle around them to represent the **universal set U,** as shown in the margin. The universal set contains all the elements that make sense in a given problem situation, whether or not they are in a set of interest. **Venn diagrams** give the added ability to talk about elements not in any set represented by a circle. If the universal set is the set of all whole numbers, then in the disjoint and overlapping examples in the margin, the region outside both circles, but inside the rectangle, represents all whole numbers greater than 5. In the subset example, the region outside the larger circle and inside the rectangle represents all whole numbers greater than 3.

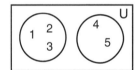
disjoint sets

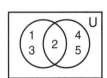
overlapping sets

The set of elements outside a Euler circle and inside the universal rectangle is called the *complement* of the set in the circle. A complement can be used to help answer questions involving the word *not.* For the overlapping sets, the complement helps answer the question, "What numbers are not in {1, 2, 3} or {2, 4, 5}?" *(They are the numbers in the complement of the union of the two sets, or all whole numbers greater than 5.)*

a subset

Along with helping analyze sets of data, Venn diagrams are useful tools in set theory, which students may study in secondary school. Set theory is useful in arithmetic (for example, in comparing the number of whole numbers with the number of rational numbers), algebra (for example, in defining functions), geometry (for example, in considering sets of points or lines), and probability (for example, in counting successful occurrences of an event out of all possible occurrences).

4.1.4 Data Analysis

To many people, data analysis is synonymous with statistics. In *Everyday Mathematics,* however, this is not the case. For our purposes, data analysis means the examination and explanation of data. A good data analysis for a first grader can be summed up in a single well-phrased comment, such as "More than half the class are girls." Statistics may be completely irrelevant in such an analysis. A statistic is simply a number used to describe some characteristic of one or more data sets and may not necessarily shed any particular light on the situation being examined.

One of the most common statistics is the average or mean of a set of data. Finding the mean requires adding a set of numbers and then dividing—tasks too difficult for most young children. Yet a lack of arithmetic skills should not bar students from data analysis of a more general nature. *Everyday Mathematics* provides activities for students to study two general attributes of data at increasingly sophisticated levels. These attributes are the *spread and pattern* of a data set, and useful *landmarks* within it.

Spread and Pattern of Data Sets

Encourage students to talk about the **spread and pattern,** or **distribution,** of the data in tables or graphs. Words such as *clump, hole, bump, way-out number,* and *all-alone number* are fine for describing how data values are arranged in a table or along a number line. Sometimes these characteristics can spark interesting explorations. Data that are clumped too closely together may suggest the need to ask a more discriminating question or to change the scale in a display.

The following are three important measures of spread:

Maximum The *largest* data value observed

Minimum The *smallest* data value observed

Range The *difference* between the maximum and minimum values

Landmarks of Data Sets

Once data have been organized, take every opportunity to have students discuss things they notice about the data. The following terms are commonly used to describe features of ordered data.

mode The "most popular" data value or values; the values observed most often

median The middle data value, or, if there is an even number of values, the number halfway between the two "middle" values

These statistics are called **landmarks** in a data set because they show important features of the data. Students can use landmarks as reference points when they discuss other features of the data, just as cartographers use landmarks as reference points when they discuss the lay of the land on maps.

Note that finding a median may require averaging the two values nearest the middle. This is probably the first use of average students encounter other than as a descriptive term for data found in newspapers, TV, and so on. Students often develop the idea of an average in the context of finding a median. The question "What do we do if there is no middle value?" leads to an important discussion about what is a fair value between two others. One approach to finding that fair value can be to point to a spot on a number line. Another can be to guess and check. Some students may develop the mathematical algorithm of averaging on their own.

In Grades K–3 of *Everyday Mathematics,* students discuss these attributes with "raw" data (data as they are recorded) and with ordered data (data that are numerically ordered, or grouped by categories). Students also discuss their data qualitatively (without using landmarks like median or range), noting where the data bunch together or spread out. Exploring reasons for the "shape of the data" can lead to a better understanding of the data set in question and the data analysis process. Formal treatment of averages and other statistics begins in Grades 4–6. In Grade 6, students learn to play *Landmark Shark,* a game that provides practice in finding the range, mode, median, and mean of data sets.

Remember that the usual reason for analyzing data is to solve a problem, make a prediction, or arrive at a decision. Never finish a data lesson before students have had an opportunity to summarize, discuss, report, or reach some sort of conclusion. Think of data analysis as a process with several stages: gathering the data, displaying the data, analyzing the data, and looking back. In some ways this last step, achieving closure, is the most important one.

4.1.5 Mystery Plots

In *Fifth Grade Everyday Mathematics,* students are introduced to the "mystery plots" routine. In these recurring activities, students match "mystery plots" with the data that could have led to those plots. The plots can be any of the data displays discussed in the preceding "Organizing and Displaying Data" section. The mystery plots routine requires students to act as consumers and critics of data and data displays, rather than as producers. It helps students begin to develop judgment, common sense, and a healthy skepticism regarding the data and claims "based" on data that they encounter daily in our data-filled world.

Although many mystery plot activities are included in the curriculum, you may want to use the idea with data or graphs that you or your students find in newspapers or other sources as well. As with all data activities, mystery plots can be a particularly powerful educational tool if used with data that is highly relevant to the students.

4.2 Probability

Everyday Mathematics believes that most students must be exposed to concepts and skills many times in many different ways, often only briefly, before they are able to master them. The treatment of probability in the curriculum is a good example of this approach. Students play informal games and engage in activities involving the idea of fairness and the use of random-number generators, such as cards, number cubes, and spinners. The first step toward a more formal treatment occurs in the final unit of *Third Grade Everyday Mathematics*. Similar activities are taken up early in *Fourth Grade Everyday Mathematics*, and probability ideas are extended and made more precise throughout the rest of the program. The Probability Meter, a number-line device for recording probabilities, is introduced in Grade 5.

4.2.1 Why Study Probability?

All of us are aware that our world is filled with uncertainties. Of course, there are some things that we can be sure of: The sun will rise tomorrow, for example, or it will be hot this summer in Florida. We also know that there are degrees of uncertainty, and some things are more likely to happen than others. There are also occurrences, which, though uncertain, can be predicted with some accuracy. These qualitative ideas of probability—impossible, possible, likely, certain, and so on—are the basis for the mathematical treatment of probability in *Everyday Mathematics*.

Few people understand how to calculate the chances of something taking place. Yet many decisions in our personal lives, from the trivial (Should I take an umbrella with me?) to the vitally important (Should I undergo surgery?), are based on probabilities. Probability is more useful in daily life than most other branches of mathematics and fully deserves the greater prominence given to it in most contemporary elementary mathematics curricula.

4.2.2 The Language of Chance

Because students should become comfortable talking about chance events as early on as possible, *Everyday Mathematics* begins by focusing on vocabulary development. Many terms are introduced: *sure, certain, probably, 50-50, unlikely, impossible,* and so on. These terms should not be taught formally. Through repeated use, students will gradually make them part of their vocabularies. Many students are familiar with terms like *forecast* and *predict,* but not *probability. Probability* is a difficult word and need not be used at first.

All students have had experience comparing the chances of various outcomes of a random process. They understand everyday statements like, "Rain is more likely than snow today." They may also understand that a seven is more likely than a three when two dice are rolled. Such informal comparisons are a good place to begin, since they provide a context in which the language of chance can be intuitively introduced. Discuss the fact that some things are certain to happen and other things are certain not to happen. The most interesting things are in between, neither certain nor impossible. Point out that if we think hard enough, we can often say which of these uncertain things are more likely to occur than others.

The Probability Meter

The Probability Meter is a tool used in *Everyday Mathematics* to show probabilities expressed as fractions, decimals, and percents. It is part of a number line from 0 to 1 that is divided into 100 equal parts, shown by little black tick marks. Each black tick mark marks off $\frac{1}{100}$ or 0.01 or 1% of the Probability Meter. There are also colored tick marks on the meter that fall between the black marks and indicate other fractions, decimals, or percents. In the middle of the Probability Meter, along its length, are phrases such as "50-50 chance," "unlikely," "impossible," and "extremely likely" that correspond to the numerical figures on the meter.

The Probability Meter is introduced in *Fifth Grade Everyday Mathematics* and is used thereafter to help students develop their understanding of the language of chance by correlating their use of informal phrases with precise locations on the meter. It is used in various lessons to record probabilities and to compare probabilities expressed as fractions, decimals, and percents. The Probability Meter can also be used as a reference for equivalent names for rational numbers.

Randomness

Throughout *Everyday Mathematics,* many activities rely on spinning spinners, drawing from card decks, rolling dice, flipping coins, and so on. All of these are procedures for generating random results, but randomness is not defined until fifth grade. This is because **randomness** is simple to describe with words—such as *haphazard, unpredictable, without pattern,* and *chaotic*—but difficult to define formally and hard to verify in practice. Technically, a **random event** is an event selected from a set of events, all of which have an equal probability of being selected. There are several reasons why randomness is hard to verify in practice.

First, there is the problem of assuring truly equal probabilities. Many variables affect this: position of a spinner, weight distribution in a die, thoroughness of the shuffle of a card deck, and so on. These problems affect classroom activities that rely on randomly generated numbers, but they are essentially beyond control. In *Everyday*

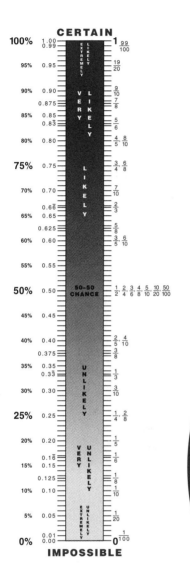

Probability Meter

Mathematics, random-number generators are trusted to provide numbers that are random enough to serve their purpose.

The second problem in verifying random results is an individual's perception of what such results should look like. Imagine a list of 1,000 randomly generated single-digit numbers. Somewhere in the list there are eleven consecutive 3s. Is this a problem? Most people would think so; it is counter to the notion that random means "all shook up." Eleven 3s seems to be a pattern, and therefore the list is suspect. Similarly, if you flip a coin 8 times and get 8 heads, the coin seems suspect.

Results like those described above lead people to believe that previous outcomes can affect the next outcome. "After 8 heads in a row, it seems that I should expect tails on the next flip, because I believe that on average, a fair coin will land tails half the time, and tails are now overdue." The belief that a fair coin will land tails half the time is correct—*on average, in the long run.* However, it is incorrect to think that the previous eight heads affect the ninth toss—for which there is still a 50-50 chance of getting heads (or tails). If you see students acting as though past results affect the probability of future outcomes, you might ask them about their thoughts.

4.2.3 Making Predictions

Most of the probability activities in *Everyday Mathematics* follow a similar pattern: Students make a prediction about the likelihood of a particular outcome of some random process such as rolling a die or flipping a coin. They then check their predictions by performing an experiment that involves collecting, organizing, and interpreting data. Some activities call for students to compare the likelihood of several possible outcomes. Other activities ask students to estimate the chance that something will happen by assigning it a numerical value. For example, when a coin is tossed, the chance of its landing heads-up is 1 out of 2 or $\frac{1}{2}$ because there are two ways the coin could land, one of which is heads-up. When a single die is rolled, the chance of an even number is 3 out of 6 or $\frac{3}{6}$, since out of the six ways the die can land (1, 2, 3, 4, 5, 6), three are even (2, 4, 6).

For some situations, all outcomes are equally likely: tossing a fair coin, rolling a fair die, spinning a spinner that is divided into equal parts, and so on. In other situations, the outcomes are not equally likely. For example, when a twelve-sided die numbered from 1 to 12 is rolled, a 1-digit number is more likely than a 2-digit number. Students may remember activities in earlier grades in which they graphed outcomes of tossing a pair of six-sided dice—the sums 2 and 12 come up much less often than 7. In experiments with

NOTE: For more on random-number generators, see the Management Guide section on Tools for Exploring Data and Chance, page 41.

12-sided die

unequally-divided spinners, most students will probably conclude quickly that the spinner is more likely to land on the larger sectors than on the smaller ones. (Spinners are extremely useful for helping students to visualize chances.)

fair spinner

unfair spinner

Probability of a spin landing in the colored area is $\frac{1}{3}$.

Probability of a spin landing in the colored area is greater than $\frac{1}{3}$.

Many random processes lend themselves to intuitive predictions because their outcomes obey very definite laws of chance. Coin tosses and spinner experiments are good examples of these. Other processes do not lend themselves to such precise analysis. Predicting the weather is much harder than predicting the outcome of a coin toss.

The Law of Large Numbers

In the long run, *Everyday Mathematics* aims to help students understand that the more often they repeat an experiment, the more reliable their predictions will be. For example, if a coin is tossed 10 times, it is possible, but not certain, that it will land heads-up about half the time. (Try it—you may be surprised at how often you obtain a 7–3 or 8–2 split.) But if the coin is tossed 100 times, it is more likely to land heads-up about half the time— heads and tails tend to "even out" with more tosses. If the coin is tossed 1,000 times, it is even more likely that heads will show about half the time.

There are a variety of experiences throughout *Everyday Mathematics* that illustrate this important idea, known to mathematicians as the *Law of Large Numbers*. For example, in *Third Grade Everyday Mathematics*, students participate in a block-drawing experiment. Children are asked to figure out how many blocks of different colors are hidden in a bag by examining the results of repeatedly drawing a block from the bag. The more times they draw a block, the more likely it is that they will make the correct guess. Similarly, in *Fifth Grade Everyday Mathematics*, pairs of students each take small samples from a bowl of multi-colored candy and count how many of each color there are. The class then pools the results from each pair to form one large sample, thereby concluding that a large sample produces a better estimate of the color distribution than the small samples do.

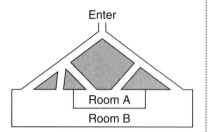

Enter

Room A

Room B

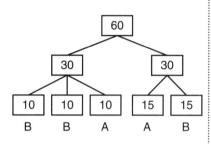

60

30   30

10   10   10   15   15

B   B   A   A   B

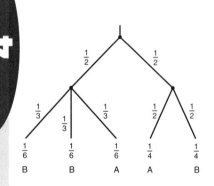

$\frac{1}{2}$ $\frac{1}{2}$

$\frac{1}{3}$ $\frac{1}{3}$ $\frac{1}{3}$ $\frac{1}{2}$ $\frac{1}{2}$

$\frac{1}{6}$ $\frac{1}{6}$ $\frac{1}{6}$ $\frac{1}{4}$ $\frac{1}{4}$

B   B   A   A   B

NOTE: Probability trees were introduced in 1657 in the first published book on probability theory, written by Dutch mathematician Christian Huygens.

Tree Diagrams

In *Sixth Grade Everyday Mathematics,* students investigate situations where there is a sequence of events in which subsequent events depend on the outcomes of previous events. In other words, the events are not independent. **Tree diagrams** are introduced as models to help visualize such situations. For example, the diagram on the left is a maze through which 60 people are going to walk (perhaps a carnival attraction). At each junction in the maze, a person chooses any available path at random. For any one person, the two events in the journey are choosing a path at the first junction, then at the second junction. The problem is to determine how many people are expected to end up in Room A and how many in Room B.

To model this situation, draw a tree diagram like the one shown in the margin. The rectangles represent the junctions in the maze where people make a decision. The number in the rectangle is the number of people expected to be at that point in the maze if decisions are made randomly. All 60 people arrive at the first junction, where half are expected to go to the right and half to the left. This leaves 30 people expected to arrive at the next two junctions, and so on.

The numbers in the last row of boxes represent the number of people expected to have reached Rooms A and B according to each of the possible paths. In all, 25 people are expected to end up in Room A and 35 in Room B.

Tree diagrams of this sort are a first step toward using probability trees. The probability tree in the margin is for the maze problem above.

In a probability tree, the *vertices* represent events. In the example in the margin, the vertices represent choices of paths. Each *branch* between vertices is labeled with the probability of a particular outcome. In the example, the probability of someone taking either path from the first junction is $\frac{1}{2}$.

The probability of taking any one of the five possible paths is given by the last row of fractions in the tree. For example, the probability of someone taking the left-most path is $\frac{1}{6}$. These numbers could have been calculated by using the tree diagram: 10 of 60 people, or $\frac{1}{6}$ of the people, ended up at the end of the leftmost path.

More importantly, the probability tree indicates that $\frac{1}{2}$ of any number of people would take the first left branch, and $\frac{1}{3}$ of that $\frac{1}{2}$ would take the next left branch. So $\frac{1}{3}$ of $\frac{1}{2}$, or $\frac{1}{3} * \frac{1}{2}$, or $\frac{1}{6}$ of the people take the leftmost path. The procedure is the same for each of the paths; the probability of a person taking any one path is the product of the probabilities of taking each of the branches in the path.

The values in the last row of the probability tree let you predict how many people would end up at the end of any path, given any number of people entering the maze. Note that the sum of the probabilities in the last row is 1, meaning all people entering the maze will get to the end of some path.

Students in *Sixth Grade Everyday Mathematics* use probability trees to investigate maze problems, tossing coins, and the probabilities of winning games of chance. They also use trees to help criticize the fairness of games and to design fair games of their own.

4.3 Using Data and Probability

Everyday Mathematics is committed to developing mathematics through applications, and virtually any number drawn from an application is a piece of data. In Grades 4–6, students collect, organize, display, and analyze data, and they explore probability. In Grades 4 and 5, much of the data analysis occurs within the context of the World Tour and the American Tour sections of the *Student Reference Book*. In Grade 6, data analysis and probability are explored in the *Student Reference Book* and within individual lessons.

You probably do not need specific suggestions for data sets as much as you may need suggestions for applications in other topic areas. You know what interests your students, so use your best ideas and theirs. A key goal is to have students understand data exploration as a *sensible process*. Can they ask sensible questions? Can they make sensible graphs? Can they make sense of graphs? If so, then they are intelligent users of data and probability.

NOTE: Factor trees, used to find prime factorizations of numbers, resemble tree diagrams for counting or finding probabilities. For more, See "Factor Trees" in Section 1.2.1 of this manual.

ESSAY
5

Geometry

Geometry, the study of the properties and relationships of objects in space, should be a natural and deeply intuitive part of mathematics for children. From birth, children must make sense of forms and shapes—a mother's face, their own bodies, shapes that move, shapes that don't, curved things, sharp things. Then, with a wealth of informal knowledge about spatial objects, they come to school. The teacher's role is first to acknowledge and value what children already know and then to help them "notice" what they see and to organize their perceptions into a meaningful system.

The word *geometry* derives from Greek words for "earth" and "measure," which gives a clue about the first geometric activity of humans. The earliest records of geometric thinking, from the

Egyptians, Babylonians, and Chinese, confirm that it revolved around solving practical problems—laying out fields, finding areas and volumes, constructing houses and temples, and so on.

The Greeks are credited with formalizing geometry. Most of us encountered the geometry of Euclid with its axioms and theorems in high school. And, for many, this was a mystifying experience. One reason is the inappropriate structure and content of many of these geometry courses—a situation that is slowly changing as new approaches to secondary school geometry instruction are being developed. But, an equally compelling reason is that many students have little or no formal experience with geometry prior to their high school courses. The *Everyday Mathematics* curriculum places significant emphasis on this part of mathematics beginning in Kindergarten.

Students investigate geometry through many hands-on experiences—manipulating pattern blocks; building shapes with straws; tracing, cutting out, and folding shapes; forming figures on geoboards; constructing figures with compasses, straightedges, and protractors; and so on.

—Adapted from *Everyday Teaching for Everyday Mathematics*™ by Sheila Sconiers

In this essay, we first describe common 1-, 2-, and 3-dimensional objects. Next, we discuss some operations on these objects and some relations these objects have with one another. Then we discuss tessellations, topology, and geometric constructions. Finally, we outline the approach used in *Everyday Mathematics* for teaching geometry.

5.1 Dimension

Dimension is a tricky word. One meaning refers to the size of an object, as in the dimensions of a room or of a piece of paper; another meaning, the one implicit in terms like *3-dimensional,* refers to how much information is required to specify an exact location. For example, a checkerboard would be considered 2-dimensional because two pieces of information are needed to specify a particular square: its row and its column. A line is 1-dimensional because to specify a location on a line requires only one number. An opera house is 3-dimensional because to specify a seat requires knowing not only the row and the seat number, but also the level (main floor, mezzanine, first balcony, and so on).

We live in 3-dimensional space, in 3-D. The objects that constitute our physical experience are all 3-dimensional. Objects in other dimensions—lines, triangles, circles—are abstractions that do not physically exist in the way that dogs, cellular telephones, and pencils exist. Even the checkerboard, which we said was 2-dimensional a moment ago, is really 3-dimensional; it has length, width, and depth. The 2-dimensional surface of the checkerboard is an abstraction in our minds.

Many 1- and 2-dimensional abstractions are so useful to us in the 3-dimensional world that we name them and study their properties. We model them with wood or plastic, with drawings, and with special manipulatives. But the models are always 3-dimensional, not the "real" thing. Even a drawing made with ink has thickness, length, and width.

Below we discuss objects in dimensions zero through three and describe how *Everyday Mathematics* engages children in examining them.

5.2 Points

Point is an undefined term in geometry. Since *point* has no mathematical definition, we cannot say what a point is. Nevertheless, we all have some idea what a point is. A point has no extension, no height, no width, and no depth. A point cannot be broken into pieces: it is one indivisible thing. This indivisibility means a point has 0 dimension: since a point has no parts, no information is needed to specify which part of a point is being referred to.

We can model a point by drawing a dot on a piece of paper. If we get a finer pen and draw a smaller dot, then we have a better model of a point. But no matter how small we make our dot, no matter how fine our pen's tip, we still cannot draw a true point. Even the smallest dot of ink has height, width, and depth; therefore it is not a point.

Another way to think about points is as locations: A point is an exact position. On a map, a point marks where something is. There is, for example, a point on a number line that is exactly 3 units from the origin. In fact, there are two such points, one at +3 and one at −3. In *Kindergarten Everyday Mathematics,* children use points on maps when they follow maps and count steps to get from one room in the school to another. Children also locate points on number lines and timelines beginning in Kindergarten. Children must imagine points on objects every time they measure a height, width, or depth: Length is the distance between two points. Points on maps are used to estimate distances and learn about map scale beginning in Grade 3.

Sometimes a location is a point, but in a more abstract way. The vertices (corners) of a polygon, for example, are the points where the edges meet. Unless the polygon is on a coordinate system, the position of a vertex is of little interest. But the fact that it is a vertex is important—often the vertex receives a name and that contributes to a name for the whole polygon. Points are usually named with capital letters: point *A,* point *B,* and so on. Naming geometric figures using the names of points begins in Grade 2 ("triangle *ABC*").

Sometimes, ordered pairs of numbers correspond to points. Graphing ordered pairs begins in third grade. Applications of ordered pairs, such as latitude and longitude, appear in Grades 4–6.

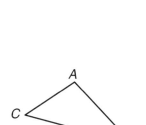

triangle *ABC*

For more on coordinate geometry, see Section 5.9 of this essay and Section 7.3 of the Reference Frames essay.

The idea of a function as a set of ordered pairs can be visualized by plotting the pairs on a coordinate graph.

There are other uses and models of points not discussed here. Our aim is simply to give you some ways to think about points and to help you realize how commonly we use them in our 3-dimensional world.

For more on functions, see Section 9.1.3 of the Patterns, Sequences, Functions, and Algebra essay.

5.3 Lines, Segments, and Rays

Line is another undefined term, but, again, one for which we have good intuition. Lines have length, but not width or depth. We can model a line with pen and ink, by folding a piece of paper, or pulling a piece of string taught. Since one number is enough to specify a position on a line, lines are 1-dimensional.

A line is made up of infinitely many points. Think about "infinite" in two ways here. First of all, "infinite" means the line extends forever in two directions; it never ends. Although it has length, it cannot be measured. If you started marking off unit intervals on a line, you would never finish, no matter how long you kept it up. A drawing of a line has arrowheads on the "ends" to indicate that it does not stop.

Now think about any two points on a line. No matter how close together they are, there are infinitely many points on the line between them. Mathematicians say lines are *dense*, meaning that between any two points on a line there is always another point. The fact that each point on a line can be associated with a number is a key to understanding why our real-number system does not run dry. Just as there is always a point between any two points on a line, there is always a number between any two numbers.

Line segments and rays can be defined in terms of a line. A **line segment** is a part of a line with a beginning point and an ending point. (Mathematicians call both the beginning and ending points *endpoints.*) A segment has a finite length and a measure that you can approximate. A **ray** is a part of a line with a beginning point but no ending point. Rays are sometimes called *half-lines.* A ray, like a line, has no measure. A drawing of a ray usually has an arrowhead at the "end" opposite its endpoint.

Everyday Mathematics is consistent about using arrowheads in drawing lines and rays. Encourage students to use them as well. One place that the arrowheads are not used, however, is in computer geometry packages such as the *Geometer's Sketchpad* and *Cabri Geometry.* It is not practical to draw arrowheads in these packages because you can "grab" lines and rays with a cursor and move them around. What you see, then, are models for rays and lines that extend to the edge of the screen and beyond.

5.4 Planes and Plane Figures

Plane is yet another undefined geometric term for which we have some intuition. A plane is a flat, 2-dimensional object having length and width but no depth. Like a line, a plane does not end; it

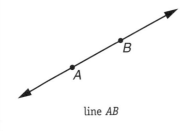
line *AB*

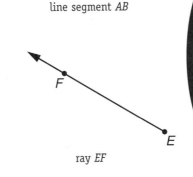
line segment *AB*

ray *EF*

extends forever in every direction. And like a line, a plane cannot be measured. A tabletop, a smooth floor, and the surface of a calm body of water all suggest planes.

Just as 0-dimensional points make up 1-dimensional objects like lines, both 0-dimensional and 1-dimensional objects make up objects in a plane. There are infinitely many points and infinitely many lines in a plane. Objects that are entirely contained in a plane are called *plane figures* or *planar figures*.

5.4.1 Angles and Rotations

In mathematics, an angle consists of two rays that have the same endpoint, called the vertex of the angle. The rays are called the sides of the angle. An angle is usually named with a letter (the name of its vertex), or with three letters (three points on the angle, with the vertex in the middle). When several angles are shown, sometimes they are named with numbers. The symbol ∠ may precede the name, as shown in the margin.

Sometimes it is convenient to think of the sides of an angle as line segments—for example, "the angles of a square"—but strictly speaking, the sides of an angle are rays, each continuing without end. In *Everyday Mathematics,* angles are often modeled by segments because they are introduced in Grade 1 as features of solids and in Grades 2 and 3 as features of polygons. In Grades 4–6, angles are studied as features of polygons and polyhedrons.

It is often useful to think of an angle as being formed by starting with both rays or segments pointing in the same direction and then rotating one ray or segment around the common endpoint. From first grade on, children model angles in this manner by bending a straw in half and rotating one of the halves around the bend.

Angles are measured in degrees. One complete rotation, a full circle, is 360 degrees (360°). If a student begins with both parts of the straw together and then rotates one of the parts one-quarter of the way around the bend, the resulting figure will model an angle of 90 degrees (90°). If the rotation continues another one-quarter of the way around the bend, the straw is straight and models an angle of 180 degrees (180°). A further one-quarter rotation models an angle of 270 degrees (270°). A final one-quarter rotation returns the straw to its starting position—an angle of 360 degrees (360°) (which looks like an angle of 0 degrees).

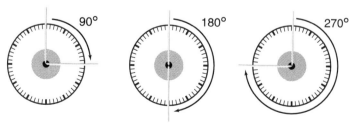

An analog clock also shows angles. At 12 o'clock, the overlapping hands model an angle of 0° (or 360°); at 3 o'clock, the hands model

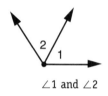

∠A

∠BAC or ∠CAB

∠1 and ∠2

90°

180°

270°

an angle of 90° (or 270°). At 6 o'clock, they model an angle of 180°; at 9 o'clock, 270° (or 90°).

Angles can be categorized according to the orientation of the rays. An angle of exactly 90° is a *right angle.* (A rectangle has four right angles.) An angle of exactly 180° is a *straight angle.* An angle of more than 90° but less than 180° is an *obtuse angle,* an angle of less than 90° is an *acute angle,* and an angle greater than 180° is a *reflex angle.*

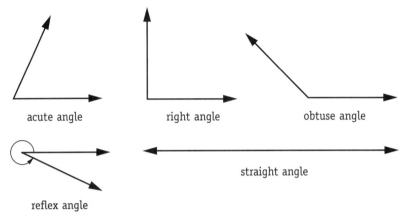

acute angle   right angle   obtuse angle

straight angle

reflex angle

Children in Kindergarten through third grade are not expected to learn the categories of angles, but they have significant experience manipulating angles of each category. Students in Grades 4–6 examine angles more closely—measuring angles with protractors, constructing angles with a compass and straightedge, and learning about categories and relationships of angles.

See Section 5.12 of this essay for more on compass-and-straightedge constructions and Section 5.7.3 for more on relationships among angles.

5.4.2 Polygons

A polygon is a closed, 2-dimensional figure, composed of line segments that do not cross each other. The line segments are the sides of the polygon. The points where the sides meet are called vertices or corners. Exactly two line segments meet at every corner of a polygon. The sides form an angle at each vertex.

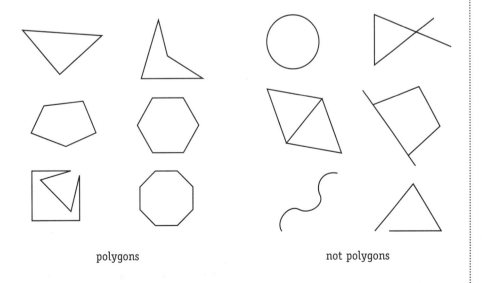

polygons   not polygons

NOTE: The region inside a polygon is not properly part of the polygon. Strictly speaking, the polygon is just the line segments. The term *polygonal region* refers to both the line segments and the region inside. In informal discourse, however, this distinction is often ignored. We say, for example, that a cracker is a square or that a piece of paper is a rectangle. Therefore, do not try to force students to observe the distinction between polygons and polygonal regions.

Number of Angles	Name
3	triangle
4	quadrangle or quadrilateral
5	pentagon
6	hexagon
7	heptagon
8	octagon
9	nonagon
10	decagon
12	dodecagon

See Section 5.6 for more on transformations and Section 5.9 for more on coordinate geometry.

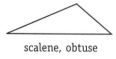
scalene, obtuse

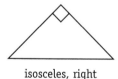
isosceles, right

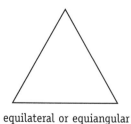
equilateral or equiangular

The term *polygon* comes from the Greek *polu-,* "many," and *-gonon,* "angled." Polygons are named according to the number of angles (or sides or vertices) they have. A polygon with 38 sides is called a 38-gon. In general, a polygon with *n* sides is an *n*-gon.

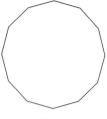
12-gon

Children in Grade 3 classify triangles and quadrilaterals by special features such as parallel sides, right angles, and sides or angles of equal measure. In Grades 4–6 of *Everyday Mathematics,* the exploration of polygons is extended to include transformations of polygons by slides, flips, and turns (translations, reflections, and rotations), and classifications of polygons as regular, concave, and convex. Polygons are also studied in the coordinate plane as part of analytic geometry or coordinate geometry.

Triangles

A three-sided polygon is called a triangle. (Unlike quadrangles, which are also called quadrilaterals, triangles are almost never called trilaterals.) A triangle is usually named for its three vertices, sometimes preceded by the △ symbol , as in △*ABC* for "triangle *ABC*." Triangles may be classified according to side lengths.

• *scalene triangle* A triangle in which no two sides have the same length.

• *isosceles triangle* A triangle with two sides of equal length. This makes two of the angles equal in measure.

• *equilateral triangle* A triangle with three sides of equal length. This makes all the angles equal in measure (60° each), and so an equilateral triangle is also an **equiangular triangle.** Every equilateral triangle is also an isosceles triangle.

scalene triangle

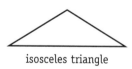
isosceles triangle

equilateral triangle

A triangle may also be classified according to its angles.

• *acute triangle* A triangle with every angle less than 90 degrees.

• *right triangle* A triangle with a right angle.

• *obtuse triangle* A triangle with an angle greater than 90 degrees.

acute triangle

right triangle

obtuse triangle

Any triangle can be given two names, one for its sides and the other for its angles. Some examples are in the margin.

Children in Grades K–3 learn some of the triangle categories, label vertices, write and read names for triangles, and write and read names for their sides. In Grades 4–6, students find areas of triangles, use triangles in tessellations, and represent triangles analytically by graphing them in the coordinate plane. In Grade 6, they learn about one of the most profound discoveries in the history of mathematics—the Pythagorean Theorem.

The Pythagorean Theorem

In a right triangle, the side opposite the right angle is called the *hypotenuse* of the triangle. The other two sides are called legs. In the figure in the margin, a and b represent the lengths of the legs and c the length of the hypotenuse. One of the most useful and celebrated properties of right triangles is the Pythagorean Theorem, which states that, for the figure in the margin, $a^2 + b^2 = c^2$.

The following passage is from the *Sixth Grade Everyday Mathematics Student Reference Book*.

> Nobody knows when this relationship was first discovered. The Babylonians, Egyptians, and Chinese knew of this relationship before the Greeks. But Pythagoras, a Greek philosopher born about 572 B.C., was the first person to prove that the relationship is true for any right triangle. It is called a **theorem** because it is a statement that has been proved.
>
> A Chinese proof of the Pythagorean Theorem (written about A.D. 40) is shown below. Two identical squares, each with sides of length $(a + b)$, are partitioned in different ways.

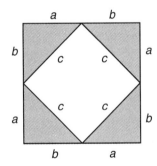

Square 1
Square 1 contains four identical right triangles and one square whose area is $c * c = c^2$.

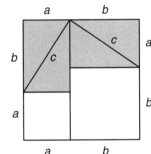

Square 2
Square 2 contains four identical right triangles and two squares whose areas are a^2 and b^2.

The four right triangles inside Square 1 and the four right triangles inside Square 2 all have the same area. Therefore, the area of the large square (c^2) inside Square 1 must be equal to the total area of the two smaller squares $(a^2 + b^2)$ that are inside Square 2. That is, c^2 must equal $a^2 + b^2$.

A slightly different version of Square 2 above was preferred by the famous mathematical problem solver George Polya *(see margin)*. He liked the position of the triangles because it highlighted the squares of the legs of the triangle.

In 1940, E. S. Loomis catalogued 370 different proofs of the Pythagorean Theorem, including one in 1876 by the twentieth President of the United States, James A. Garfield. There may well be more to add to Loomis's list by now.

See Section 5.10 on tessellations, Section 5.9 on coordinate geometry, and Section 6.5 on area in the Measurement essay.

For uses of the Pythagorean Theorem, see Section 7.3.2 of the Reference Frames essay.

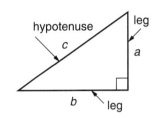

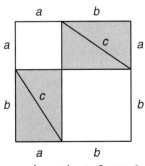

an alternative to Square 2

Quadrangles (Quadrilaterals)

A four-sided polygon is called a *quadrangle* or *quadrilateral*. The line segments that connect opposite vertices of a quadrangle are called *diagonals*. Some quadrilaterals have special features and names.

- **trapezoid** A quadrangle with exactly one pair of parallel sides.[1] If the two non-parallel sides are the same length, the trapezoid is *isosceles*.

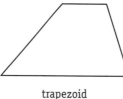

trapezoid

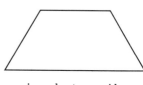

isosceles trapezoid

- **parallelogram** A quadrangle with parallel opposite sides. The opposite sides of a parallelogram are equal in length and the diagonals bisect each other (intersect at their midpoints).

- **rhombus** A parallelogram in which all sides are equal in length. The diagonals of a rhombus bisect each other and are perpendicular. A rhombus with four right angles is a square.

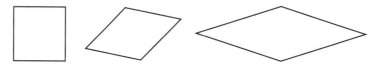

rhombuses

- **rectangle** A parallelogram in which all angles have the same measure (90°). Diagonals of a rectangle are equal in length.

- **square** A rectangle in which all sides are equal in length.

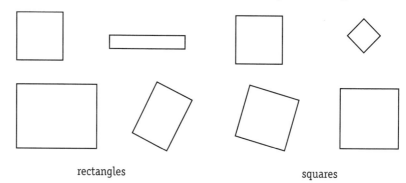

rectangles

squares

- **kite** A quadrilateral with two adjacent sides of one length and two other sides of a different length. Both kites and parallelograms have pairs of equal-length sides, but in kites the equal-length sides are adjacent while in parallelograms the equal-length sides are opposite. The diagonals of a kite are perpendicular.

---

[1]Sometimes the definition of *trapezoid* allows polygons with two pairs of parallel sides. Under such a definition, a parallelogram is a trapezoid. UCSMP prefers the narrower definition.

parallelogram

kite

Some definitions depend on previously defined quadrangles. For example, a rectangle is first a parallelogram, then a parallelogram with equal angles. This means that all the features and properties of parallelograms are also features and properties of rectangles, along with new ones specific to rectangles.

The diagram below shows the hierarchy of quadrangles. You are not expected to use it with your students unless you think they can understand it—many students in Grades 4–6 lack the geometric experience and the logical-thinking skills necessary to understand a hierarchical classification scheme like this one—but you may find it useful yourself. Pick any quadrangle in the hierarchy. It has all the properties of any quadrangle on a path leading to it. For example, a square is a rectangle, a rhombus, a parallelogram, and a quadrangle.

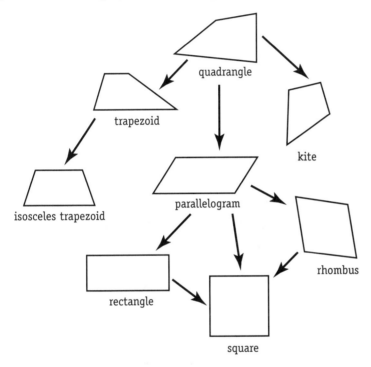

In Grade 3, students find areas of rectangles and squares. In Grades 5 and 6, they learn to formulate clear definitions of quadrangles, find areas of parallelograms, and use quadrilaterals in tessellations and transformations. Features of quadrangles are also important to their investigations into surface area and volume of solids.

For more on area and volume, see Sections 6.5 and 6.6 of the Measurement essay.

Other Features of Polygons

Although children in Grades K–3 explore polygons with the following features, defining them then is not especially helpful. In Grades 4–6, the terminology becomes more useful, especially in compass-and-straightedge constructions and in talking about tessellations.

For more on compass-and-straightedge constructions, see Section 5.12; for more on tessellations, see Section 5.10.

• *regular polygon* A polygon in which all sides are the same length and all angles are equal in measure. If a polygon is regular, then it is possible to draw one circle that passes through all its vertices.

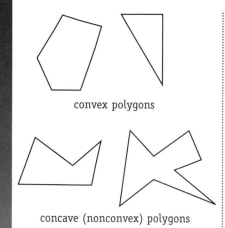

convex polygons

concave (nonconvex) polygons

NOTE: A circle may be distinguished from a circular region, or disk, but this is not something to be emphasized with students.

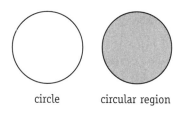

circle   circular region

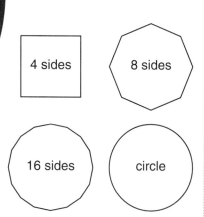

4 sides   8 sides

16 sides   circle

- **convex polygon** A polygon such that every line segment connecting points on two different sides lies completely inside the polygon, except for its endpoints. Each angle of a convex polygon has a measure less than 180 degrees.
- **concave or nonconvex polygon** A polygon that is not convex. At least one line segment connecting points on two different sides contains points that are outside the polygon. At least one angle has a measure greater than 180 degrees.

Most students will have no difficulty distinguishing convex and nonconvex polygons, but they will often give crude explanations—for example, "The hexagon is not convex because these two sides bend in." Try to use more precise definitions yourself, but do not insist that students master them.

5.4.3 Circles and Pi (π)

A *circle* consists of all the points in a plane that are the same distance from a given point in the plane called the *center* of the circle. Many physical objects have circular shapes, although none can be perfectly circular. Features of a circle include the following:

- **radius** A segment connecting the center of a circle and any point on the circle; also, the length of that segment.
- **chord** A segment with endpoints on a circle.
- **diameter** A chord through the center of a circle; also, the length of such a chord. The diameter of a circle is twice its radius.
- **circumference** The distance around, or perimeter of, a circle.

You may want to try to think of a circle as a regular n-gon where n is infinitely large. For example, start with a square. A square is not a very good approximation of a circle, but it's a start. Double the number of sides to obtain a regular octagon. That's closer to a circle. Double the number of sides again to obtain a regular 16-gon. That's closer still. Doubling a few more times would give a figure that could be distinguished from a circle only with a magnifying glass. Double infinitely many times and the result would actually be a circle.

The ratio of the circumference of a circle to its diameter is called *pi*. This ratio, represented by the Greek letter π, is the same for all circles. This fact may be written

$$\frac{c}{d} = \pi$$

or

$$c = \pi d$$

In Grade 3, children begin an inquiry into the relationship between the diameter and the circumference of a circle. They roll food cans to find circumferences, measure across the tops of the cans to find diameters, and display the results in a table. From these results, they discover that the circumference of a circle is consistently about 3 times its diameter. This is a first approximation of π, and a pretty good approximation at that.

Pi is also the ratio of the area of any circle to the square of its radius:

$$\frac{A}{r^2} = \pi$$

or

$$A = \pi r^2$$

Pi is an irrational number; its decimal does not repeat and never ends. Two common approximations for pi are 3.14 and $\frac{22}{7}$.

Mountains of Pi

The earliest known reference to π occurs in an Egyptian papyrus scroll, written around 1650 B.C. by a scribe named Ahmes. He found the area of a circle using a rough approximation of π. Around 200 B.C., Archimedes of Syracuse (in Sicily, then a Greek colony) found that π is between $3\frac{10}{71}$ and $3\frac{1}{7}$: $3\frac{10}{71} < \pi < 3\frac{1}{7}$. Little more was learned about π until the seventeenth century, when new formulas were discovered. Ludolph van Ceulen, a German mathematician, spent most of his life calculating π to thirty-five decimal places. Now most inexpensive calculators display π to 7 or 9 decimal places.

Today, most investigations of π involve powerful computers. Such calculations have been a standard task for each new generation of computers. In 1949, π was calculated to 37,000 places on ENIAC, one of the first computers. Later, π was computed to 100,000 digits on an IBM 7090 computer, and in 1981, to 2 million digits on a NEC supercomputer. In the next few years, these calculations were extended to 17.5 million digits, then 34 million, then past 200 million, and then in 1989 to more than 1 billion digits. As of September 1999, the world record, held by the laboratory of Dr. Yasumasa Kanada of the University of Tokyo, is 206.1 billion digits.

The article "The Mountains of Pi," by Richard Preston (*The New Yorker,* March 2, 1992, pages 36–67), relates the fascinating history of pi and why it has attracted mathematicians for thousands of years. According to the article, "The decimal for pi goes on forever, so the number cannot be written with complete accuracy: 3.14159265358979323846264338327950288 4197... is only an approximation.... No apparent pattern emerges in the succession of digits.... They do not repeat periodically, seeming to pop up by blind chance, lacking any perceivable order, rule, reason, or design...."

"The Mountains of Pi" tells the story of two mathematicians, David and Gregory Chudnovsky, who calculated π to more than two billion digits on a computer of their own design, which they built in

Gregory's apartment using mail-order parts. Calculating π to so many digits not only tests the power of new supercomputers, it also continues the search for patterns in the digits—a search that, so far, has yielded no results. As the article puts it,

> [The Chudnovskys] wonder whether the digits contain a hidden rule, as yet unseen architecture, close to the mind of God.... If we were to explore the digits of π far enough, they might resolve into a breathtaking numerical pattern ... and it might mean something.... On the other hand, the digits of π may ramble forever....

5.5 Space and 3-D Figures

Space is the 3-dimensional world of our experience. Like points, lines, and planes, space cannot be defined mathematically. Spatial objects have length, width, and depth. Like lines and planes, space never ends and it cannot be measured. There are infinitely many points, infinitely many lines, and infinitely many planes in space. Spatial figures are objects in space, and they come in infinitely many shapes, sizes, and orientations.

Having good spatial sense means you can mentally manipulate 1-, 2-, and 3-dimensional objects in space and describe their orientations to one another. Spatial sense is important in constructing 3-dimensional objects, in representing 3-dimensional objects in two dimensions by drawing on paper or on a computer screen, and in interpreting drawings of 3-dimensional objects. Video games often demand a well-developed spatial sense of the latter kind—at least if you want to win.

5.5.1 "Solid" Figures

The items listed below are models for familiar 3-D mathematical shapes known as geometric solids.

empty box with lid	brick
basketball	baseball
empty ice-cream cone	filled ice-cream cone
empty food can	rolling pin

The items in the left column are "hollow." The items in the right column are "filled up" inside.

All the objects listed above are solid in the sense that they can be felt when touched. Virtually all concrete models of 3-dimensional figures are solid in this sense. For example, a cube can be modeled by a construction made of drinking straws, by an empty box, or by a die. All three models are solid, but each highlights a different mathematical aspect of cubes. The drinking-straw model emphasizes a cube's edges, the box emphasizes the surface of a cube, and the die emphasizes a cube and its interior.

For more on volume, see Section 6.6 in the Measurement essay.

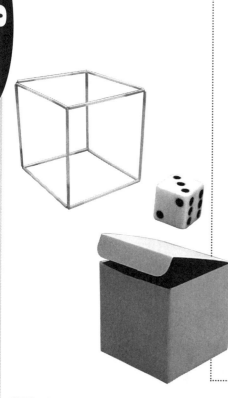

In *Everyday Mathematics,* we define a geometric solid as all the points on the surface of a 3-dimensional figure. According to this definition, a "geometric solid" is actually just the "skin." Thus, despite its name, a geometric solid is "hollow" and does not include the points in its interior. Just the edges and vertices of the figure form what is sometimes called a wire frame, the "skeleton" of the figure. Both a hollow figure and a figure with its interior—for example, a balloon and a baseball—are 3-dimensional.

Common 3-dimensional figures such as cones, pyramids, spheres, cubes, cylinders, and prisms do not include points in their interior. These common solids are only the skins of the figures. That's why the objects in the left column of items at the beginning of this section are better models for a prism, sphere, and cylinder, respectively, than the items in the right column.

However, do not try to keep students from using the names *cone* or *pyramid* when both the figure and its interior are meant. In informal discussions, both the surface and its interior are often meant when terms like *pyramid* or *cone* are used. We do students no favors preaching "right" names. When eventually the distinction becomes mathematically necessary, it can be made and understood easily enough.

5.5.2 Polyhedrons

A **polyhedron** is a closed 3-dimensional figure made up of polygonal regions. (A polygonal region is a polygon together with its interior.) The word *polyhedron* comes from Greek words meaning "many bases" or "many seats." Polyhedrons include cubes, pyramids, prisms, and many other shapes.

The polygonal regions that make up a polyhedron are called *faces.* A face of a polyhedron is sometimes identified by referring to the polygon that encloses it. For example, a face might be called a triangle, although the face is actually a triangular region.

A line segment where two faces come together is called an *edge.* A point where three or more edges come together is called a *vertex* or *corner.*

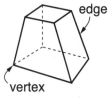

an irregular polyhedron

In a *regular polyhedron,* all the faces are congruent (the same size and shape), and the same number of faces come together at the same angle at every vertex. Although there are infinitely many regular polygons, there are only five regular polyhedrons, which are illustrated below. From left to right they are the *tetrahedron* (4 equilateral triangles), the *cube* (6 squares), the *octahedron* (8 equilateral triangles), the *dodecahedron* (12 regular pentagons), and the *icosahedron* (20 equilateral triangles). The regular polyhedrons are also known as the Platonic solids.

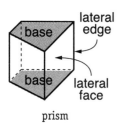

base · lateral edge · base · lateral face

prism

For more on transformations, see Section 5.6.

a crystal

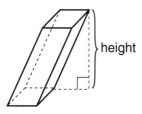

height

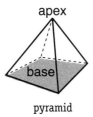

apex · base

pyramid

Prisms

The polyhedron shown in the margin is a prism. The two shaded faces are congruent and parallel polygonal regions. They are called the *bases of the prism.* The other faces are called *lateral faces,* and the edges where the lateral faces intersect are called *lateral edges.*

A **prism** may be defined as a polyhedron with two bases that are congruent and parallel, and whose lateral faces are parallelograms formed by line segments that connect corresponding vertices of the bases.

A prism can also be defined by transformations. Start with a polygonal base in plane P. Translate or "slide" this preimage to a parallel plane Q to get its image (the other base). The line segments that are the sides of the preimage generate lateral faces of the solid as they slide to the image, and the vertices of the preimage generate the lateral edges.

Prisms are named for their bases. If a prism has a triangular base, it is called a triangular prism. If a prism has a pentagonal base, it is called a pentagonal prism. Emerald crystals often take the form of a hexagonal prism.

If a prism's lateral faces are all rectangles, then its lateral edges are perpendicular to the bases and it is called a *right prism;* otherwise, it is called an *oblique* or *slanted prism.*

The height or altitude of a prism is the perpendicular distance between the planes containing the bases.

Pyramids

The polyhedron shown in the margin is a pyramid. The shaded face is the base. The other faces are the *lateral faces.* The lateral faces meet at the lateral edges, and the lateral edges all meet at a point called the *apex.* The lateral faces of a pyramid are all triangles.

A pyramid may be defined as a polyhedron consisting of a polygonal base, a point (apex) not in the plane of the base, and all of the line segments connecting the apex to the edges of the base.

A pyramid can also be defined by transformations. Start with a polygonal base, an apex not in the plane of the base, and a line segment from the apex to a point on the base. Keep one endpoint of the line segment fixed at the apex and slide the other endpoint around the base until it returns to the starting point. As the line segment slides, it generates the other faces of the pyramid.

Like prisms, pyramids are named for their bases. The famous Pyramids at Giza, Egypt, are square pyramids. A triangle base pyramid is also known as a *tetrahedron.*

All prisms and pyramids are polyhedrons, but not all polyhedrons are prisms or pyramids. Three of the five regular polyhedrons, for example, are neither pyramids nor prisms.

5.5.3 Solids with Curved Surfaces

All the surfaces of a polyhedron are flat. Three important geometric solids with curved surfaces are the sphere (entirely curved), the cylinder (two flat surfaces and one curved surface), and the cone (one flat and one curved surface).

A **sphere** consists of all the points in space at an equal distance (the radius) from a given point (the center). A sphere is modeled by a basketball.

A **cylinder** resembles a prism in that it has two flat bases in parallel planes. However, the bases of a cylinder are congruent circles rather than congruent polygons. The curved surface consists of all the line segments that connect points on one circle with points on the other circle and are parallel to the line segment connecting the centers of the two circles. Cylinders are modeled by food cans and mailing tubes.

A cylinder may be defined in terms of transformations. Start with a circular base in plane *P*. Translate or "slide" this preimage to a parallel plane *Q* to get its image (also a base). The circle that encloses the base generates the curved face of the solid as it slides to the image.

If the line segment connecting the centers of the bases of a cylinder is perpendicular to the base, the cylinder is called a *right cylinder;* otherwise it is an *oblique* or *slanted cylinder.* Most cylinders in everyday life are right rather than oblique.

The height or altitude of a cylinder is the perpendicular distance between the planes containing its bases.

A **cone** resembles a pyramid in that it has one flat base and an apex not in the plane of the base. However, the base of a cone is a circle. Line segments from the apex to the circle form the curved surface of the cone. (Alternatively, the curved surface can be generated by a line segment with one endpoint fixed at the apex while the other endpoint slides around the circle that encloses the base.)

If the line segment connecting the apex of a cone to the center of the base is perpendicular to the base, the cone is called a *right cone;* otherwise, the cone is *oblique* or *slanted.*

The height or altitude of a cone is the perpendicular distance from the apex to the plane of its base.

Students of *K–4 Everyday Mathematics* explore geometric solids by manipulating blocks available in most classrooms, paper models constructed from blackline masters, and a variety of real-life materials such as shoe boxes. More formal definitions are introduced in Grades 5 and 6.

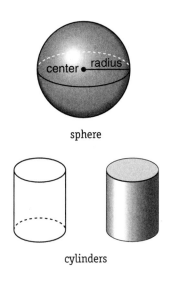

sphere

cylinders

For more on transformations, see Section 5.6.

cones

NOTE: The advent of computer geometry packages is beginning to improve the authors' hopes for more exploration of 2-D and 3-D figures. These packages model the drawing and moving of objects on the surface of the computer monitor. It is hoped that these tools will make it into the hands of children, who will perhaps learn more geometry faster than their high school counterparts.

For more on contour maps, see Section 7.4.2 of the Reference Frames essay.

Cross Sections of a Clay Cone

Form a clay cone. Draw your prediction of the shape of the cross section that will be formed by the first cut shown below. After making the cuts, draw the actual shape and describe (name) the shape. Re-form the cone and repeat these steps for the other cuts.

	Predicted Shape of Cross Section	Actual Shape of CrossSection	Description of Shape
	Answers vary.	○	Answers vary. e.g., circle
		⬭	ellipse
		⌒	half oval
		⬭	ellipse

5.5.4 Connecting 2-D and 3-D

One goal of the geometry strand at all levels of *Everyday Mathematics* is to help students see connections between 2-dimensional figures, such as polygons and curves, and the corresponding polyhedrons and curved surfaces in three dimensions. One way students work toward this goal is to build 3-D models using materials such as straws, twist-ties, paper, and clay. These constructions, which begin in first grade, help children develop good connections between 1-dimensional line segments, 2-dimensional polygons, and 3-dimensional figures having polygonal regions as faces.

In Grade 5, students cut out 2-dimensional patterns of prisms and pyramids to fold and tape together. These models are then used to compare and contrast the properties of vertices, edges, and faces of the solids they represent. Later, patterns for rectangular prisms are constructed to help students make the link between areas of faces and volume.

In Grades 5 and 6, students investigate more sophisticated connections between 2-D and 3-D objects. When a 3-dimensional object is cut by a plane, a **cross-sectional trace** of the intersection is created. **Contour maps** produced by the United States Geological Survey (USGS) display the elevation of the landscape on 2-dimensional maps by drawing curves or **contour lines** representing where horizontal planes at different elevations would cut through terrain. A more generalized contour map shows other features superimposed on a flat map—quantities such as temperature; geographic features such as mountains, plains, wetlands, and so on; and a variety of demographic information such as population intervals and housing costs. Fifth graders examine contour maps as part of the American Tour.

In Grade 6, students investigate **cross sections of geometric solids** made of clay. In a sense, they are creating contour maps of the solids. Quite complicated shapes can be modeled with a series of cross sections—a technique used for decades in the design of automobiles, aircraft, and other industrial products. Computer assisted design (CAD) software has made this technique increasingly accessible to the general public.

One of the sixth grade activities is to cut a cone in several different ways. Some possible 2-dimensional shapes are shown in a journal page (*see margin*). All the different cross sections (including some not shown on the page) are called the *conic sections* and have been a central part of the precalculus curriculum for many years. Students of *Everyday Mathematics* will have a wonderful concrete introduction to this topic that will serve them in later mathematics courses.

5.6 Transformations

A **transformation** is an operation on a figure that produces a new figure. The original figure is called the *preimage;* the figure produced by the transformation is called the *image.* The transformations usually studied in elementary mathematics produce images that have either the same shape as the preimages or both the same size and the same shape as the preimages.

If a preimage and its image are congruent, then the transformation is called an isometry. In *Everyday Mathematics,* students investigate three isometry transformations: reflections (flips), rotations (turns), and translations (slides). They also examine similarity transformations, which change the size but not the shape of figures.

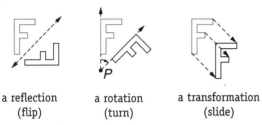

a reflection
(flip)

a rotation
(turn)

a transformation
(slide)

Transformations can be studied using tools such as compasses, straightedges, protractors, and transparent mirrors. This method of study, synthetic geometry, was developed by the Greek geometer Euclid about 300 B.C. Transformations can also be studied using analytic geometry or coordinate geometry. Computer programs enable a user to draw and manipulate figures on a monitor by storing important features of the shapes as coordinate pairs. Transformations are carried out by performing arithmetic on the coordinates.

5.6.1 Slides, Flips, and Turns

In *Everyday Mathematics,* students investigate three isometry transformations: translations, reflections, and rotations. These transformations leave the size and shape of the figure unchanged, so they are known as *isometries,* from the Greek words *isos,* which means equal, and *metron,* which means measure. Under an isometry transformation, the figure remains rigid as it moves; the image and the preimage are congruent.

Translations

In a translation, or slide, every point in a figure moves the same distance in the same direction. A translation or slide is thus defined by a direction and a distance. The direction of the translation may be indicated by a ray.

In coordinate geometry, translations are simple to define. First, define a preimage figure by giving coordinates of important points on the figure. For $\triangle ONM$, for example, the coordinates of the vertices are (0,0), (2,1), and (1,3). To find a translation image of $\triangle ONM$, simply add a value (for example, 5) to each x-coordinate

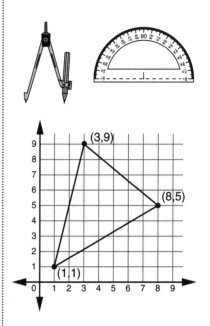

For more on coordinate geometry, see Section 5.9; for more on compass-and-straightedge constructions, see Section 5.12.

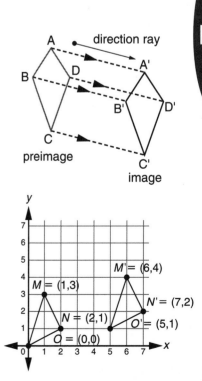

in the preimage. Then add a value (for example, 1) to each *y*-coordinate in the preimage. The coordinates of the vertices of the image, $\triangle O'N'M'$, are (5,1), (7,2), and (6,4). The translation is on a slant, as shown in the diagram. If a number is added to the *x*-coordinates only and the results are plotted, the image is a horizontal translation. If a number is added to the *y*-coordinates only, the result is a vertical translation.

Students of *Everyday Mathematics* are not expected to be able to define a translation. In Grades 4 and 5, they examine translations informally by making frieze patterns and tessellations. Translations are important parts of such artistic designs. In Grade 6, students explore translations in the coordinate plane.

Reflections

Two points are reflection images or flips of each other over a line—sometimes called a mirror—if the line through the points is perpendicular to the line and the line is exactly halfway between the points. If all the points in one figure are reflection images of the points in another figure, the figures are reflection images. The images are congruent, but their orientation is reversed or flipped. Activities with transparent mirrors in *Fourth Grade Everyday Mathematics* help students discover these properties of perpendicularity and equidistance. A good student description of a reflected figure would be "Its image is in the same place on the other side of the mirror, only reversed."

In Grades 4–6, students draw reflection images and find reflection lines for given images. They explore uses of reflections in frieze patterns and quilt designs. In both art forms, designs are repeatedly flipped to produce decorative strips and regions. Students are introduced to the analytic geometry of reflections by reflecting the positive number line over zero. The images are negative numbers—the opposites (reflections) of the positive numbers.

Rotations

To define a rotation, both a center of rotation and an amount of rotation must be specified. Imagine a preimage point *P* on a circle with its center at point *C*. Any other point *P'* on the circle is a rotation image of the preimage point *P* around the center of rotation *C*.

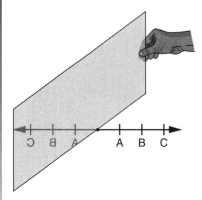

See Section 5.10 for information about tessellations.

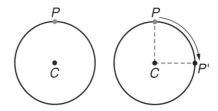

In Grades K–3 of *Everyday Mathematics,* students informally explore rotation transformations when they model angles with drinking straws. Students form angles by bending a straw in half and rotating one half away from the other half. In the language of transformations, the final position of the rotated half is the image of its original position or preimage. So an angle is a preimage ray together with its image after a rotation.

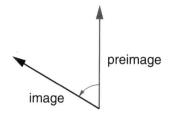

A simple way to draw the image of one point rotated around another is to use a protractor. Place the center of the protractor at the center of rotation (point *C*). Mark a preimage point (*P*) at the 0 mark on the protractor (at the corner where the base and curved part of the protractor meet). A rotation image of *P* is any point *P'* on the curve of the protractor. The magnitude or measure of the rotation is the measure of angle *PCP'*.

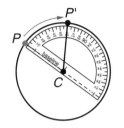

Beginning in *Third Grade Everyday Mathematics,* students explore angles in depth. In fourth through sixth grades, they use half-circle and full-circle protractors to continue this exploration. They take an informal look at rotation symmetry in figures in the contexts of frieze patterns and quilt-making.

In analytic geometry, producing most rotations requires trigonometry, which is beyond the scope of this manual.

5.6.2 Size-Change Transformations

A size-change transformation is defined by a center of similarity and a scale factor. Imagine a ray with its endpoint at point *P,* the center of similarity, passing through point *B,* the preimage. Any other point *B'* on the ray is a size-change image of point *B.* The magnitude of the size-change is equal to *PB'*/*PB,* the ratio of the lengths of segments *PB'* and *PB.* This ratio is called the size-change factor or scale factor. If the scale factor is greater than 1, the size change is called a stretch, enlargement, or expansion. If the scale factor is between 0 and 1, the size change is a shrink, reduction, or contraction. If all the points on a figure are size-change images of corresponding points on a preimage (with the same factor), the figures are size-change images of each other.

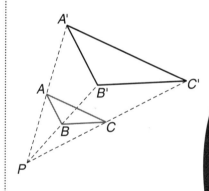

A size-change transformation is sometimes called a **similarity transformation** because the image and preimage are similar to each other.

In analytic or coordinate geometry, a size-change image of a figure is produced by multiplying every coordinate of every point in the figure by the same size-change factor. This is how computer drawing programs zoom in and out on objects. A positive size-change factor zooms in or out. A negative size-change factor zooms in or out and also reflects the object through the origin, producing an image that looks the same as a 180° rotation of the object around the origin.

For more on similarity, see Section 5.7.2.

Students in *Fifth Grade Everyday Mathematics* explore size changes using a copy machine metaphor, but they do not learn any of the terminology discussed above. Grade 6 students learn the terminology as they review reductions and enlargements and then apply size changes to map scales, which they first encountered in Grade 4. Finally, sixth graders tie together their understanding of ratios, scales, and size changes by studying properties of similar polygons.

5.7 Relations

Just as numbers can be related to one another in various ways ($5 > 2$, $\frac{6}{2} = 3$, $5 \neq 3$, and so on), geometric objects can likewise be related to one another in various ways. If two figures are exactly the same size and shape, for example, we say they are congruent. In the following sections, we discuss several of the most important geometric relations.

5.7.1 Parallel and Perpendicular

Two lines in a plane either cross or do not cross. Lines in a plane that never cross are parallel. Parallel lines are always the same distance apart. Many objects in our everyday world suggest parallel lines: window gratings, highway lane markings, and lines on paper. The symbol ∥ means "is parallel to."

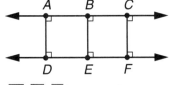

$\overline{AD}$, $\overline{BE}$, $\overline{CF}$ have equal measure.

Two lines that cross each other are said to *intersect*. When two lines intersect, they form several angles. When the angles formed are right angles (90°), the lines are *perpendicular*. The symbol ⌐ is often included in a drawing of perpendicular lines to indicate the right angle. The symbol ⊥ means "is perpendicular to."

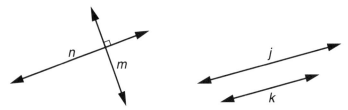

Lines that are neither intersecting nor parallel are called *skew*. An east-west line on the floor of a room and a north-south line on the ceiling, for example, are skew. Only lines that are not in the same plane can be skew.

Skew lines can be modeled with two pencils.

Planes can also be parallel or intersecting. If two planes intersect at right angles, they are perpendicular. The same is true of line segments, squares, and many other geometric objects. Opposite faces of a cube, for example, are parallel; adjacent faces are perpendicular.

parallel faces

adjacent faces

Beginning in first grade, children are introduced to the ideas of parallel and perpendicular through the exploration of solids, their faces and edges. Drawing and naming parallel and perpendicular line segments begins in second grade. You can also point out the vast array of perpendicular and parallel objects throughout your classroom and school.

5.7.2 Congruence and Similarity

Two figures that are exactly the same size and shape are *congruent*. The shapes can be as simple as two line segments or as complicated as two rocket motors. (Of course, no two rocket motors could ever be exactly the same size and shape, since each would have tiny nicks and other marks that the other would lack. Only abstract geometric objects can ever be perfectly congruent. Real objects always differ from one another.) The symbol $\cong$ means "is congruent to" or "is equal in measure to."

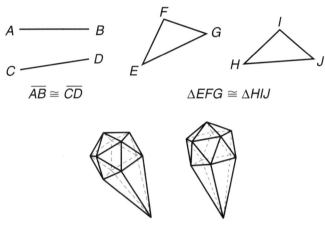

$$\overline{AB} \cong \overline{CD} \qquad \triangle EFG \cong \triangle HIJ$$

congruent polyhedrons

Two figures that are the same shape but not necessarily the same size are *similar*. Any two squares, for example, are similar, as are any two equilateral triangles, or any two copies of Michelangelo's statue of David.

similar polygons

Corresponding angles of similar polygons are equal in measure; corresponding sides are proportional in length. Corresponding sides are often identified in drawings by small slashes called hatch marks, hash marks, or tick marks. In the diagram, $\triangle CAT$ is similar to $\triangle DOG$, with the following relations:

$$\angle C \cong \angle D, \quad \angle A \cong \angle O, \quad \angle T \cong \angle G, \, \overline{CA} \parallel \overline{DO} = \overline{AT} \parallel \overline{OG} = \overline{TC} \parallel \overline{GD}$$

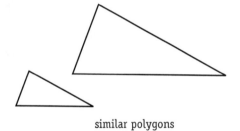

NOTE: It can sometimes be difficult to determine which sides and angles of similar figures correspond. For this reason, the correspondence is always given in *Everyday Mathematics,* except when students construct their own similar figures, in which case the correspondence is usually obvious.

Size-change images are similar to each other, with the size-change factor giving the proportionality of lengths. A size-change factor can also be seen as a ratio comparison of the lengths of the sides of similar figures. If the ratio is equal to 1, then the objects are congruent as well as similar.

For more on size-change transformations, see Section 5.6.2.

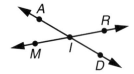

Figure 1

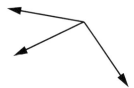

Figure 2

Figure 3

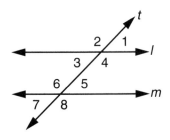

Figure 4

Fifth graders are introduced informally to similarity when they explore how copy machines enlarge and reduce figures and when they measure the effect of these size-change transformations on perimeter and area. Because perimeters are measured in linear units, they are multiplied by the size-change factor. Because areas are measured in square units, they are multiplied by the square of the size-change factor.

As part of their work to link the concepts of ratio, scale, and size change, students in *Sixth Grade Everyday Mathematics* explore similar polygons using drawing and measuring tools. They also solve problems involving similar polygons and other applications of ratio.

5.7.3 Relationships among Angles

Beginning in *Fifth Grade Everyday Mathematics,* students learn names for pairs of angles formed by intersecting lines. Any pair of intersecting lines forms two sets of vertical angles. **Vertical** or **opposite angles** share no sides, only a vertex. (In this context, *vertical* has nothing to do with vertical in relation to the horizon; the word refers to the common vertex.) In Figure 1, ∠*AIM* and ∠*RID* are vertical angles, as are ∠*MID* and ∠*AIR*. Vertical angles are congruent.

Adjacent angles share an endpoint and a side. There are four pairs of adjacent angles in Figure 1: ∠*MID* and ∠*AIM;* ∠*AIM* and ∠*AIR;* ∠*AIR* and ∠*RID;* and ∠*RID* and ∠*MID.* Because the non-common sides of each pair form a line, the sum of the degrees in each pair is 180°. Two angles whose measures add to 180° are called **supplementary angles.** Supplementary angles are introduced in Grade 6.

Adjacent angles do not have to be supplementary, as Figure 2 shows. Figure 3 shows a pair of adjacent angles whose non-common sides form a right angle. This means the sum of the degrees in these angles is 90°. Two angles whose measures add to 90° are called **complementary angles.**

Students in *Sixth Grade Everyday Mathematics* explore the relationships between angles formed when two parallel lines are intersected by a third line called a **transversal.** These relationships are traditionally studied in secondary school geometry, where students prove that certain pairs of angles are congruent or supplementary. Grade 6 students do not prove anything but are encouraged to measure the angles and make conjectures about them.

The following relationships can be proven for any pair of parallel lines cut by a transversal. In Figure 4, lines *l* and *m* are parallel, line *t* is the transversal, and the angles are numbered.

• Pairs of vertical angles—∠1 and ∠3, ∠2 and ∠4, ∠5 and ∠7, ∠6 and ∠8—are congruent.

• Pairs of corresponding angles—∠1 and ∠5, ∠2 and ∠6, ∠3 and ∠7, ∠4 and ∠8—are congruent.

182 Essay 5 Geometry

- Pairs of alternate interior angles—$\angle 3$ and $\angle 5$, $\angle 4$ and $\angle 6$—are congruent.
- Pairs of alternate exterior angles—$\angle 2$ and $\angle 8$, $\angle 1$ and $\angle 7$—are congruent.
- Each of the eight pairs of adjacent angles is supplementary.
- Interior angles on one side of the transversal—$\angle 3$ and $\angle 6$, $\angle 4$ and $\angle 5$—are supplementary.

5.7.4 Other Relationships

Students explore many other relationships between figures in *Everyday Mathematics*. All terms used to describe where one thing is relative to another have geometric ties, such as the following:

Inside/outside

The distinction between inside and outside is obvious to even the youngest children. In precise geometric terms, however, the distinction is a bit complicated: A plane figure has an inside, or interior, if it separates the plane into two parts, one bounded, the other not. The bounded part is the inside; the rest (excluding the figure itself) is the outside. Polygons and circles have insides; lines and angles do not. (Lines and angles do divide the plane into two parts, but neither of the parts is bounded.) A 3-D figure has an inside if it separates space into two parts, one bounded, the other not.

Note that the inside of a plane figure is not part of the figure itself. If you refer to the inside of a 2-D figure, try to call it a *region*. This topic comes up when you want to know how much of a plane is inside a figure—that is, the figure's area.

Consecutive/Opposite

These terms are used to describe how parts of an object relate to each other. If the parts share something such as a side, they are consecutive. If they are "across from each other," they are opposite. This meaning of *opposite* is not the same as the meaning of *antonym*. In hexagon *HEXAGO* in the margin, angles *OHE* and *HEX* are consecutive. Angles *OHE* and *GAX* are opposite. Side *HE* is adjacent to sides *OH* and *EX* and opposite side *GA*.

Note: Along with $\angle GAX$, $\angle OGA$ and $\angle AXE$ are sometimes referred to as angles opposite $\angle OHE$. That is, *opposite* may mean "non-adjacent" in some geometry texts.

For more on area, see Section 6.5 in the Measurement essay.

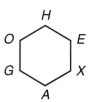

5.8 Symmetry

A figure is symmetric if you can do something to it and it looks the same. For example, a heart is symmetric because you can flip it over and it looks the same. A starfish is symmetric because you can turn it and it looks the same. A strip of wallpaper border is symmetric because you can slide it to a new position and it looks the same.

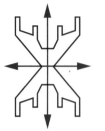
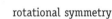

line symmetry   rotational symmetry

translation symmetry

5.8.1 Line Symmetry

The simplest kind of symmetry is *line symmetry*. If there is a line that divides a figure into two halves that match exactly, then the figure has line symmetry. The line is called a **line of symmetry** of the figure. Each point in one of the halves is the same distance from the line of symmetry as the corresponding point in the other half. The two halves look exactly the same but face in opposite directions. A "flip" over the line of symmetry leaves the figure unchanged.

There are easy tests to check a figure for line symmetry. Fold or imagine folding the figure on the line. If the halves match, the fold is a line of symmetry. Figures may also have more than one line of symmetry. An isosceles trapezoid has one line of symmetry. A square has four lines of symmetry. A circle has infinitely many lines of symmetry.

Solid figures can have a form of symmetry very much like line symmetry. Each half of the human face, for example, is the mirror image (more or less) of the other half. Many other living things have this sort of *bilateral symmetry*. The main difference between this sort of symmetry and line symmetry is that the reflection is in a plane instead of a line. (Also, it's not so easy to fold your face in half to show that the two halves match.)

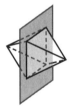
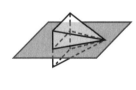

5.8.2 Other Symmetries

Sometimes people think a figure has line symmetry when it doesn't. They may think, for example, that there is a way to fold a parallelogram so the two halves match.

Parallelograms that are not rectangles do not have line symmetry, but they do have **rotational symmetry.** If a parallelogram is given a half-turn, it will look unchanged. The amount of turning required can vary; a pentagon, for example, looks the same after one fifth of a full turn.

For more on slides, flips, and turns, see Section 5.6.1.

line of symmetry

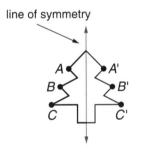

figure with line symmetry

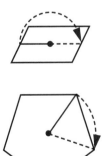

To test for rotational symmetry, turn (or imagine turning) the figure. If it coincides with itself before a full rotation of 360°, then it has rotational symmetry. The number of times a figure coincides with its preimage during one full rotation is called its order of rotational symmetry.

Point symmetry is a special case of rotation symmetry. A figure has point symmetry if it can be rotated 180° around a point to match the original figure exactly. The point is called the **center of symmetry.**

A point-symmetric figure is also a reflection image of itself through the center of symmetry. This means that if you draw a line from any point M on the figure through the center of symmetry C, you will find a reflection image M' on the line where $MC = M'C$. Reflecting any figure through a point in a sense turns the figure inside out.

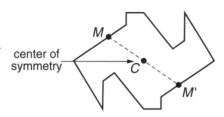
figure with point symmetry

Rotational symmetry, also known as turn symmetry, can be combined with line symmetry. A pentagon, for example, has five lines of symmetry, one through each arm, as well as order-5 turn symmetry.

Line symmetry and rotational symmetry are not the only kinds of symmetry. Many tessellations, or tilings of a plane, involve symmetry based on slides, just as line symmetry is based on flips and rotational symmetry is based on turns.

In *K–3 Everyday Mathematics,* the focus is on line symmetry, but students may notice other symmetries when they are working with pattern blocks or looking for mathematics in their world. Many corporate logos, for example, have line symmetry or rotational symmetry. In fourth grade, students explore line symmetry with transparent mirrors and rotational symmetry in a quilting project. Fifth graders investigate rotational symmetry in tessellations. Point and rotational symmetry are explored further in Grade 6.

For more on tessellations, see Section 5.10.

5.9 Coordinate Geometry

Coordinate geometry integrates numbers and geometry. The simplest coordinate geometry is a number line. A point on a number line is identified by a single number, the coordinate. For example, the point marked with an X on the number line to the right has coordinate –2.5.

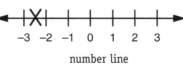
number line

Two perpendicular number lines that intersect at 0 form a rectangular coordinate system. The two number lines, called axes, make it possible to use pairs of numbers, called coordinates, to locate points. For example, point X on the coordinate plane in the margin is at (3, 2).

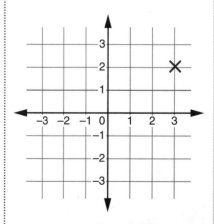
coordinate grid

For more on number lines, see Section 7.3.1 in the Reference Frames essay; for more on graphing, see Section 4.1.3 in the Data and Chance essay and Section 9.1.4 in the Patterns, Sequences, Functions, and Algebra essay.

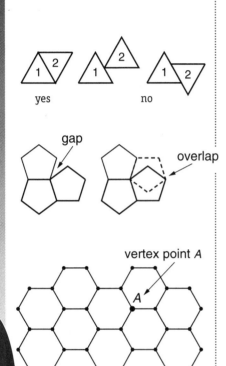

The ancient Egyptians and Romans used rectangular coordinates to survey fields. In the early seventeenth century, the French philosopher and mathematician René Descartes (1596–1650) made significant advances in coordinate geometry. Today, rectangular coordinates are often called Cartesian coordinates.

Since Descartes, coordinate geometry has been a powerful tool for advances in many areas of mathematics. In *Everyday Mathematics,* the serious study of coordinate geometry begins in fourth grade. Before that, work with coordinate geometry is restricted mostly to number lines and graphing data.

5.10 Tessellations

In mathematics, a **tessellation** is a pattern formed by repeated use of polygons or other figures to cover a surface without gaps or overlaps. The Latin root of the noun *tessellation* and the verb *tessellate* is *tessella,* referring to the small, square stones used in creating mosaics. Real-life examples of tessellations include honeycombs and checkerboards.

In a tessellation formed from polygons, the sides of the polygons coincide. A point where vertices of the polygons meet is called a **vertex point** of the tessellation. Notice that in order that there be no gaps or overlaps, the sum of the measures of the angles around every vertex point of a tessellation must be 360°.

Which regular polygons tessellate the plane? The key to answering this question is the fact that the sum of the angles around any vertex point is 360°. For a regular polygon to tessellate the plane, the measure of its angles must exactly divide 360°.

Consider the simplest regular polygon, an equilateral triangle. Each angle of an equilateral triangle is 60°. Since $\frac{360°}{60°}$ is 6, an equilateral triangle can tessellate the plane, with 6 triangles meeting at each vertex point.

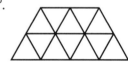

To determine if another regular polygon can tessellate, the first step is to determine the measure of one interior angle (they are all equal). If this measure divides 360° evenly, the polygon will tessellate the plane.

To find the measure of an interior angle of a regular polygon, first draw diagonals from one vertex to all the other non-adjacent vertices. This dissects the polygon into triangles. Then use the fact that the sum of the angles of any triangle is 180° to find the sum of all the angles in the polygon. Finally, divide by the number of angles in the polygon to find the measure of one angle.

For example, to find the number of degrees in each angle of a regular pentagon, draw both diagonals from any vertex. The resulting figure consists of three triangles, each with angle measures totaling 180°, so the total of the angle measures of the pentagon is $3 * 180°$, or $540°$. Because all five angles of a regular pentagon are equal in measure, the measure of each angle is $\frac{540°}{5}$, or $108°$.

The following chart applies this method to regular polygons with up to ten sides.

Regular Polygon		Total Interior Angle Measure	Measure of Each Interior Angle
Triangle		$1 * 180° = 180°$	$180°/3 = 60°$
Square		$2 * 180° = 360°$	$360°/4 = 90°$
Pentagon		$3 * 180° = 540°$	$540°/5 = 108°$
Hexagon	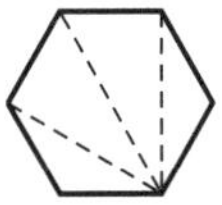	$4 * 180° = 720°$	$720°/6 = 120°$
Heptagon	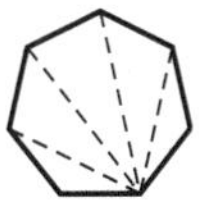	$5 * 180° = 900°$	$900°/7 = 128\frac{4}{7}°$
Octagon	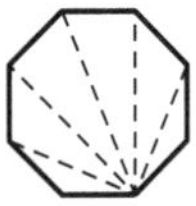	$6 * 180° = 1080°$	$1080°/8 = 135°$
Nonagon		$7 * 180° = 1260°$	$1260°/9 = 140°$
Decagon		$8 * 180° = 1440°$	$1440°/10 = 144°$

Note the pattern in the center column of the chart. In any convex polygon, the number of triangles formed by drawing diagonals from one vertex to each of the other vertices is 2 less than the number of sides. So the total of the angle measures is equal to $180°$ times 2 less than the number of sides. If the polygon is regular, the measure of each angle is equal to this total divided by the number of sides. Using variables, this says the measure of one interior angle of a regular n-gon is $(n - 2) * \frac{180°}{n}$.

A regular dodecagon has 12 sides. By the formula, each of its interior angles has measure

$$(12 - 2) * \frac{180°}{12} = 10 * \frac{180°}{12} = 150°$$

Notice that $150°$ does not divide $360°$ evenly: $2 * 150° < 360° < 3 * 150°$. This means that there will either be a gap or an overlap

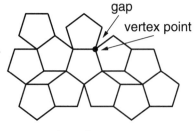

gap
vertex point

A regular pentagon
does not tessellate.

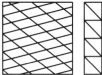

Figure B

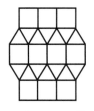

A semipure tessellation
named 3.3.3.4.4.

when regular dodecagons are arranged around a point. Hence, the regular dodecagon does not tessellate the plane.

From the chart, you can see that only equilateral triangles, squares, and regular hexagons have interior angles that are factors of 360°. They are the only regular polygons that tessellate the plane. The drawing in the margin shows how a regular pentagon does *not* tessellate.

5.10.1 Classifying Tessellations

A tessellation made with equilateral triangles is an example of a **same-tile** or **pure tessellation,** which consists of the same figure repeated over and over. Same-tile tessellations made with regular polygons are called **regular tessellations.** Figure A shows all three regular tessellations and their mathematical names, which list the number of sides of the polygons that meet at each vertex point.

Figure A. The names of the regular tessellations above are 3.3.3.3.3.3, 4.4.4.4, and 6.6.6.

Examples of irregular same-tile tessellations are shown in Figure B.

Semipure tessellations consist of at least two different kinds of polygons arranged in the same way around each vertex point. Again, the sum of the angles at each vertex point must equal 360°. Consider the tessellation in the margin, in which three equilateral triangles and two squares meet at each vertex point. The sum of measures of the angles around each vertex point is $3 * 60° + 2 * 90°$, which is equal to 360°.

If the polygons in a semipure tessellation are all regular, and the angles around any vertex point are congruent to the angles around any other vertex point, the tessellation is called **semiregular.** There are eight semiregular tessellations, made up of the following sets of regular polygons. The numbers in parentheses indicate the numbers of sides of the polygons that meet at a vertex point and their order.

- Four triangles and a hexagon (3.3.3.3.6)
- Three triangles and two squares (3.3.3.4.4)
- Triangle, square, hexagon, square (3.4.6.4)
- Square and two octagons (4.8.8)
- Triangle, hexagon, triangle, hexagon (3.6.3.6)
- Two triangles, square, triangle, square (3.3.4.3.4)
- Triangle, two dodecagons (3.12.12)
- Square, hexagon, dodecagon (4.6.12)

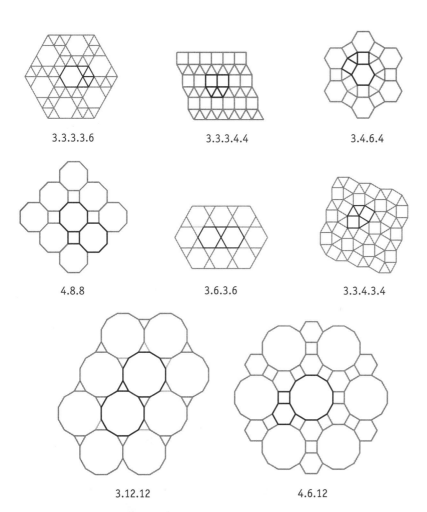

3.3.3.3.6

3.3.3.4.4

3.4.6.4

4.8.8

3.6.3.6

3.3.4.3.4

3.12.12

4.6.12

Demiregular tessellations are made with regular polygons, but the arrangements of angles around vertex points are not all the same. The figure in the margin is a demiregular tessellation with two different arrangements, 3.4.6.4 and 3.4.4.6.

Tessellations appeared as early as 4000 B.C. in Sumerian art. Persians and Romans decorated buildings with colorful mosaic tessellations. Islamic designs with tessellations can be found in the Alhambra, a Moorish palace built about A.D. 1300 in Granada, Spain.

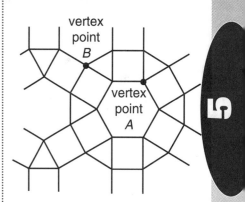

The name of this demiregular tessellation is 3.4.6.4/3.4.4.6.

Adam Woodfit/CORBIS 2

Adam Woodfit/CORBIS 3

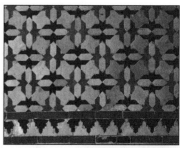

John Heseltine/CORBIS

5

Essay 5 Geometry **189**

translation

reflection

rotation

For more on slides, flips, and turns, see Section 5.6.1.

M. C. Escher, an artist born in 1898 in the Netherlands, was interested in the process of filling space with snugly fitting pieces. He was inspired by the decorations at the Alhambra. Escher's goal was to discover how shapes could fill a plane in a systematic manner. He concluded that the geometric motions of translation, rotation, and reflection could reproduce exact shapes. Each snugly fitting piece in Escher's tessellations evolves from one of six geometric shapes: parallelogram, rectangle, square, triangle, sixty-degree rhombus, and regular hexagon.

Students first encounter same-tile and regular tessellations in *Fifth Grade Everyday Mathematics*. Sixth graders investigate semiregular tessellations and get a taste of constructing Escher-type translation tessellations, in which one side of a polygon with an even number of sides is somehow manipulated and the result is translated onto the opposite side. Different manipulations can be done with each pair of opposite sides, as the example below shows. The procedure works for square and regular hexagon tessellations and certain irregular variations, such as parallelogram tessellations.

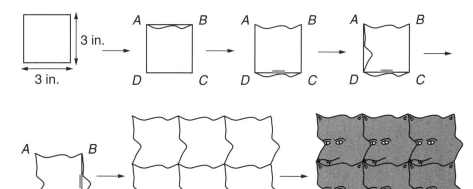

a translation tessellation

5.11 Topology

In the final lessons of Grade 6, students are introduced to **topology,** a flourishing branch of mathematics with roots in classical geometry and analysis (the study of functions). Topology is the study of properties of sets of points that remain unchanged under bending, stretching, squeezing, and other types of transformational mayhem. Because of this, topology is sometimes called rubber-sheet geometry. If you imagine an object made of a rubber sheet and then imagine all the shapes you could stretch and squish the object into without ripping, tearing, or puncturing it, you are thinking about **topological transformations.**

Two objects are said to be **topologically equivalent** if one can be transformed into the other via topological transformations. A die and a baseball, for example, are topologically equivalent to each other and to a bowling ball. (The "holes" in a bowling ball aren't really holes because they don't go all the way through; they are really just dents that can be smoothed out.) A sphere and a donut, or torus, are not topologically equivalent because of the hole in the donut. A donut and a coffee cup, however, are topologically equivalent—both have exactly one hole. The illustration below shows how you might imagine the transformation of a coffee cup into a donut.

To a topologist, in fact, holes are among the more interesting features of geometric shapes. The genus of a shape is the number of holes it contains. For example, a hockey puck has genus 0 because it has no holes; a coffee cup has genus 1; and the Geometry Template has genus 64. Geometric features such as parallel and perpendicular lines, angle measures, and areas are not so interesting to topologists. None of these features remain unchanged under topological transformations.

Sixth Grade Everyday Mathematics provides a brief introduction to topology in which students investigate topological transformations and find examples of topologically equivalent shapes.

5.12 Compass-and-Straightedge Constructions

Around 300 B.C., a Greek named Euclid wrote *The Elements,* the work for which he is most famous. In it he presented the basis for what we now call **Euclidean Geometry,** which is the geometry still taught in high school. According to mathematics historian Howard Eves,

> With the unique exception of the Bible, no work has been more widely used, studied, or edited, and for over two millennia it has dominated all teaching of geometry. More than a thousand editions of the work have appeared since the first printed one in 1482. Its content and its form have made a tremendous impact on the development of both the subject matter and the logical foundations of mathematics.
>
> (Howard Eves. *Great Moments in Mathematics: Before 1650.* Mathematical Association of America, 1983, pp. 70–71.)

Actually, more than half of *The Elements* is about number theory and algebra. It is his organization of the study of geometry, however, that has made Euclid a legend.

NOTE: Recent computer software for manipulating images mimics the rubber-sheet geometry of topology. Such software lets the user stretch, squish, twist, and otherwise mangle an image on the screen. This technique is often seen in movies and on television where things not only appear to change shape but babies wink and animals seem to speak.

Perhaps Euclid's most important contribution was his **axiomatic method** of doing mathematics. Basically, this method requires that anything to be proved must be deduced logically from previously proven results (theorems) or from "self-evident" truths called axioms. Euclid identified a number of axioms, such as

Things which are equal to the same thing are also equal to one another.

The whole is greater than the part.

A straight line segment can be drawn joining any two points.

All right angles are congruent.

Axioms such as these are unprovable ideas that we have to accept to get started doing mathematics. Over the millennia, other axioms have been added or substituted for some of Euclid's, but the axiomatic method he pioneered is still the basis of mathematical proof today.

The logical approach of the axiomatic method is not appropriate for elementary school students. Elementary school geometry should be more inductive, more like science than formal axiomatic mathematics. Axiomatic geometry should be reserved for high school or even college.

Another aspect of Euclid's geometry, however, is appropriate for elementary school students: compass-and-straightedge constructions, which are introduced in *Fourth Grade Everyday Mathematics*. Many of Euclid's geometric proofs can be illustrated by constructions that produce specific geometric objects. In a sense, a compass-and-straightedge construction is a step-by-step algorithm that proves a geometric theorem.

The *Student Reference Books* for Grades 4–6 include selected classic compass-and-straightedge constructions. For example, the following algorithm from sixth grade describes how to copy a triangle with a compass and a straightedge.

Copying a Triangle

Step 1: Draw a triangle *ABC*. Draw a line segment that is longer than $\overline{AB}$. Copy line segment $\overline{AB}$ onto it. Label the endpoints of the copy *A'* and *B'* (read as "*A* prime" and "*B* prime").

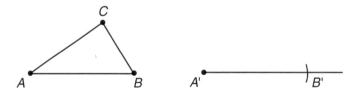

Step 2: Place the compass anchor at *A* and the pencil point at *C*. Without changing your compass opening, place the compass anchor on *A'* and draw an arc.

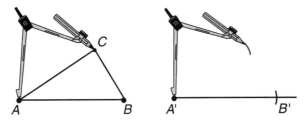

Step 3: Place the compass anchor at *B* and the pencil point at *C*. Without changing your compass opening, place the compass anchor on *B'* and draw another arc. Label the point where the arcs intersect *C'*.

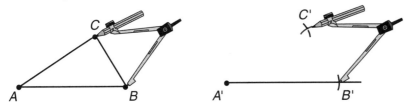

Step 4: Draw line segments $\overline{A'C'}$ and $\overline{B'C'}$.

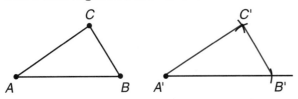

Triangles *ABC* and *A'B'C'* are **congruent.** That is, they are the same size and shape.

As geometry computer software becomes available in elementary schools, algorithms for drawing and manipulating figures will necessarily become important new topics. Two such computer programs, *Cabri Geometry* and the *Geometer's Sketchpad,* each have ways for students to define their own algorithms: In *Cabri* these algorithms are called *macros;* in the *Sketchpad,* they are called *scripts.* They are "written" simply by turning on a recorder and carrying out a series of actions in order. Turn off the recorder, name the algorithm, and you can use the algorithm whenever you like in the future.

5.13 Teaching Geometry

Children in *Kindergarten Everyday Mathematics* play with models of shapes, manipulate pattern blocks, cut shapes out of paper, and look for shapes in their everyday environment. This informal approach is intended to let children's curiosity lead them toward recognizing features of polygons and other geometric figures. Vocabulary is introduced as necessary in order to identify groups of shapes by name. Many common shapes that young children recognize are embedded in solids: A square is a face on a cube; a rectangle is a face on a box; a circle is the shape on the end of a can, and so on.

This approach—concrete manipulations leading to the recognition of key features and the naming of objects—continues throughout the grades. Children in Grade 3 reach a point where they know the names of most common polygons. They are also able to classify triangles and quadrilaterals by important characteristics such as parallel sides, equal sides, right angles, and equal angles. In Grade 4, students explore properties of angles, polygons, and solids; classify quadrilaterals using a hierarchical scheme similar to the one in Section 5.4.2; and begin to work with compass-and-straightedge constructions and transformations.

Work with classification and definition continues in *Fifth Grade Everyday Mathematics*. Students also explore tessellations, the effects of similarity transformations on area, perimeter, and angles, and transformations on the coordinate grid. In sixth grade, students classify tessellations, explore cross sections of geometric solids, and investigate the relationships among the angles formed when parallel lines are cut by a transversal. As in the primary grades, students in Grades 4–6 use a variety of geometric tools and concrete models. At these levels, however, the focus increasingly shifts from merely identifying and naming shapes to informal reasoning and the analysis of geometric properties and relationships.

5.13.1 The Van Hiele Levels

The *Everyday Mathematics* curriculum is based on research that has been carried out by the authors and others over several decades. In geometry, some of the most important research was done in the late 1950s by two Dutch researchers, Dina and Pierre van Hiele.

The van Hieles identified five stages in the development of geometric understanding. During the first stage, children approach shapes holistically. A triangle is a triangle because its overall shape is like other objects that are also called triangles. At this stage, shapes are not broken down into parts; line segments, vertices, and angles of the triangle are not considered separately. Instead, the child grasps the whole figure at once. At this stage, the visualization stage, children can benefit from hands-on work with pattern blocks, geometric solids, geoboards, straws and connectors, and real objects from their everyday environment.

During the second stage, children begin to notice the individual elements that make up geometric figures. They see that a triangle has three sides and three corners; they see that a square has four sides all the same length and four right angles. At this stage, children should continue hands-on work and begin to compare, measure, sort, and describe shapes. They can also begin to learn the names for the parts of geometric figures: side, angle, face, edge, and so on.

In the third stage, students begin to move beyond the analysis of single shapes and start thinking about relationships among different shapes. They can, for example, understand that squares are rectangles since they meet the minimal requirements: four sides and four right angles. Students also begin to understand hierarchical classification schemes like the one for quadrilaterals in Section 5.4.2. They should also be formulating simple chains of reasoning. If the context is not too abstract, students at this stage can work with definitions of geometric objects and properties. This is also the stage of informal proof, which is the highest level in elementary school geometry.

Beyond the informal proof stage, the van Hieles identified two further levels. One is the level of deductive reasoning, the level at which high school geometry is traditionally taught. The highest level is the formal axiomatic geometry of professional mathematicians, a level most of us would not even recognize as geometry.

5.13.2 Solid vs. Plane Geometry

Which is less abstract, a cube or a square? In a purely mathematical sense, both are equally abstract. But in a practical sense, a cube is less abstract than a square. Good, concrete models for cubes are commonplace: a sugar cube, a die, or a lump of clay pressed into shape are all excellent representations of a cube. A square, on the other hand, is not so easily modeled. The face of a cube is a model for a square region, not a square. We can use straws to build a model of the square, but everyday objects that are good models of squares (or circles, triangles, and other plane figures) are hard to find.

So, odd as it may sound, solid geometry is more concrete than plane geometry. For this reason, *Everyday Mathematics* includes work with spheres, prisms, cylinders, and other 3-dimensional figures much earlier than has been traditional.

5.13.3 Geometric Tools

The study of geometry in *Everyday Mathematics* involves many hands-on experiences, such as manipulating pattern blocks and attribute blocks, tracing shapes from templates, working with geoboards, cutting out shapes, folding shapes, drawing shapes with straightedges or compasses, constructing shapes out of straws, and constructing 3-dimensional figures from 2-dimensional nets (flat figures that can be folded to form closed, 3-dimensional solids).

For more on tools used for geometry in *Everyday Mathematics*, see page 43 in the Management Guide.

ESSAY

Measurement

outline

Measurement is one of the most widespread uses of mathematics in daily life. Even very young children show considerable interest in measure. *How tall is my block building? How long can we make this block train? How much water until the sink overflows?* and *How long until lunchtime?* are common questions spontaneously pursued by preschool and primary-grade children. Older students continue to be curious about how much, how long, how far, and the like. Many become fascinated with measures and ways of determining them, whether it is the height of a tall building or the amount of water in a swimming pool. *Everyday Mathematics* recognizes and capitalizes on the student's natural curiosity about measures and measurement. Throughout the grades, students engage in interesting and purposeful tasks as they learn how to measure and how to interpret other people's measures. Measurement tasks become more complex as students gain experience.

Measurement is the source of many of the numbers that we use in everyday life. Measures, along with their units, tell "how much" of something there is. We can perform arithmetic operations with measure numbers and obtain results that make sense. For example, a 6-pound cabbage weighs twice as much as a 3-pound cabbage, and someone who spends 30 minutes on homework spends twice as much time as someone who spends 15 minutes on homework. Quantifying and comparing are common quests of childhood (adulthood, too), and both are important when exploring measurement. Furthermore, because all measures are estimates, knowing how to measure means knowing how to approximate and deal with error. This topic is discussed later in this essay, in Section 6.3.1.

Sections 6.1 and 6.2 discuss measurement systems and units, including personal measures, the metric system, and U.S. customary measures. Section 6.3 highlights some measurement tools and their uses. Sections 6.4 through 6.6 address measurement in one, two, and three dimensions (length, area, and volume), while Section 6.7 discusses weight and mass. Angle measures, elapsed time, and money are discussed in Sections 6.8 through 6.10. Section 6.11 is devoted to the use of measures in geography, an important and interesting application of measurement that is a focus throughout *4–6 Everyday Mathematics*.

6.1 Personal Measures

Units for measures of length appeared relatively early in human history and were based on things familiar to people—namely, their bodies. Just as many early number systems were based on ten—probably because humans have ten fingers—many early linear measures were based on the lengths of certain body parts. This is the origin of such measures as foot, digit, span, and hand—each of which was, or still is, a commonly used unit for measuring length.

The problem with a measurement system based on body parts is that bodies differ. Who is to say *whose* cubit (a measure based on the distance between the elbow and fingertips) is *the* cubit to measure by? Without agreement, how do buyers know that they are getting their money's worth when someone sells them 56 cubits of cloth? In ancient Egypt, this problem led to the creation of a royal master cubit. The royal master cubit, which was made of black granite, became the standard against which every cubit stick in the land was periodically matched. The thousands of cubit sticks used to build the Great Pyramid of Cheops at Giza were made so precisely that the length of any one side of the pyramid differs only 0.05% from the mean length of all four sides. Eventually, nations established their measures by agreeing on standards against which all measurement implements were compared.

Another problem arose when members of two or more groups that had been isolated—because of distance, geography, or politics—came into contact with one another. In the medieval trade fairs of Europe, for example, merchants from many nations gathered to sell their wool cloth. Most agreed to measure their cloth in ells, but the length of an ell differed among the various nations' merchants. Therefore, an iron standard ell of two feet, six inches was made and left with the Keeper of the Fair. Each participating merchant was required to use this ell in all business dealings at the fair.

In England, cheating and abuse of measures became so common that a few years after the signing of the Magna Carta in 1215, the *Assize of Weights and Measures* was drawn up. The Assize defined and standardized a broad list of units, which lasted for almost 600 years. One of these units, "The Iron Yard of Our Lord the King," was divided into 3 feet of 12 inches each. Eventually, all kinds of measures became standardized in some way, and many national systems of measures came into being. Nearly all of these systems were replaced in Europe by the metric system during the nineteenth century. Britain and its former colonies in America kept to their old ways until well into the twentieth century. The United States still uses the old system.

The origins of some of our common measures give us a good way to approximate various lengths. The list below describes some common measures based on dimensions of the adult human body. For students, these personal measurements are likely to be smaller than the standards.

hand span The distance from the end of the thumb to the end of the little finger in an outstretched hand; a useful way to measure smaller things. The span has been standardized at 9 inches.

cubit A very old unit of measure, based on the distance between the elbow and the extended fingertips. The Egyptians used the cubit as early as 3000 B.C. to build their pyramids. The cubit has been standardized at various times at values between 18 and 22 inches.

yard The distance from the tip of the nose to the tips of the fingers; often used to measure cloth. A yard has been standardized at 3 feet (36 inches).

fathom The distance from fingertip to fingertip of the outstretched arms; said to be derived from an Anglo-Saxon word meaning "embrace." Fathoms are often used to measure the depth of water. Perhaps this is because the "leadsman" on a boat or ship in the days before electronic depth finders would drop a lead weight on the end of a rope until it hit bottom and then count the number of fingertip-to-fingertip measures as he gathered in his line. A fathom has been standardized at 6 feet (2 yards).

digit The width of a finger. A division of the royal master cubit in ancient Egypt.

hand The width of the palm. Horses are said to be so many "hands" high. The hand has been standardized at 4 inches.

Units of length too long to be measured conveniently with the body tended to vary widely from country to country before the adoption of the metric system. For example, where we used a mile (5,280 feet), the Russians used a verst (about 3,500 feet or about 1 kilometer).

Beginning in Kindergarten, children measure various items or parts of their classrooms with parts of themselves and discuss which body parts are more appropriate for which objects—a predecessor to choosing measurement tools and units that "fit" the measuring task. These activities are expanded in first grade as children learn techniques for measuring with their body-part units, such as putting the measuring device end to end to measure larger objects. They are also asked to make a habit of labeling their measures with appropriate "units." This habit is important not only for the act of measuring itself but as an important part of learning to solve number stories. From second grade on, students continue to use personal reference measures, but the focus shifts to finding body parts that approximate customary or metric units. These parts can then be used to estimate measures without using a ruler, tape measure, or other standardized measuring device. For example, the width of a finger may be about 1 centimeter, or a child's foot may be about 8 inches long. Body-part estimation activities continue in Grades 4–6; as students grow they need to adjust their personal reference measures.

6.2 Measurement Systems

The standardized measurement systems that we use today are the U.S. customary system and the metric system, both of which are discussed below. By "customary" measures we mean the ones commonly used in the United States. If you have students from other countries in your class, though, the metric system may be customary to them, so be sure to make the difference clear.

There are also several types of measures in common use that are neither metric nor U.S. customary: measures of angles, elapsed time, and monetary value, to name a few. *Everyday Mathematics* includes many activities to engage students in understanding these types of measures, as discussed later in this essay.

6.2.1 U.S. Customary System

The U.S. customary system is adapted from the English system, which was developed around the thirteenth century. Although most people in the United States are relatively comfortable with the U.S. customary system, it has definite drawbacks compared to the metric system. For one thing, because they evolved gradually out of specific, often local, needs, customary units of length, weight, and capacity are largely independent of one another. Another drawback is that the relationships between units are cumbersome. For example, a foot is $\frac{1}{3}$ of a yard, but an inch (the next-smaller standard unit) is $\frac{1}{12}$ of a foot. A quart is $\frac{1}{4}$ of a gallon, but a pint (the next-smaller standard unit) is $\frac{1}{2}$ of a quart.

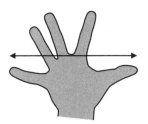

hand span

cubit

yard

fathom

digit

hand

6.2.2 Metric System

The metric system, on the other hand, was deliberately developed by scientifically-minded people in France at the end of the eighteenth century. Metric units of length, area, volume, capacity, and weight are interrelated. For example, a liter is a measure of capacity equal to 1 cubic decimeter, and a cubic decimeter is equal to the volume of 1 kilogram of distilled water at $4\,^{\circ}\text{C}$.

The basic unit of length in this system is the meter. Originally, the meter was defined as one ten-millionth of the distance from the North Pole to the equator along the global meridian through Paris. These days, the meter is defined as the distance light will travel in a vacuum in $\frac{1}{299,792,458}$ second. In the metric system, many units are defined relative to the meter. Next-smaller or next-larger units differ by a power of 10 and are, thus, easily converted from one to another. For example, a decimeter is one-tenth (or 0.1) of a meter, and a centimeter is 0.1 of a decimeter.

6.2.3 Converting between Measures

Because the United States uses both metric and customary measures, being able to convert between these systems can sometimes be important. For example, Minnesota, a neighbor of metric-using Canada, has posted road signs proclaiming that 55 miles per hour is 88 kilometers per hour. It is also important to be able to convert from one unit to another within a system. Knowing how many inches are in a foot, feet in a yard, yards in a mile, and so on provides the power to convert numbers from one unit to another, which can be handy in many situations.

In the early grades of *Everyday Mathematics,* students learn what U.S. customary and metric measures are, how to estimate them generally, and how to approximate them using measuring tools. Students in *K–3 Everyday Mathematics* do not convert units from one system to the other; they convert only within a given system. Converting between measurement systems is first addressed in *Fourth Grade Everyday Mathematics,* and students in Grades 5 and 6 continue to practice and apply this skill.

Measures can be converted by multiplying by unit fractions. A **unit fraction** is a fraction with 1 in the numerator. The unit fractions used in making conversions between measurements have numerators and denominators that name equal quantities but have different units. Such unit fractions are equivalent to 1. For example, the numerator and denominator in the unit fraction $\frac{1\ \text{ft}}{12\ \text{in.}}$ name the same quantity in different units, so $\frac{1\ \text{ft}}{12\ \text{in.}} = 1$.

Multiplying any number by 1 yields a product that is equal to the original number. Hence, multiplying a measurement by a series of unit fractions that are each equal to 1 yields a product that is equal to the original measurement. (Multiplying a measurement by reciprocals of unit fractions equal to 1 also yields a product equal to the original measurement.)

$$\frac{1\ \text{ft}}{12\ \text{in.}} \quad \frac{1\ \text{mi}}{5,280\ \text{ft}} \quad \frac{1\ \text{yd}}{36\ \text{in.}}$$

$$\frac{1\ \text{in.}}{2.54\ \text{cm}} \quad \frac{1\ \text{m}}{100\ \text{cm}} \quad \frac{1\ \text{km}}{1,000\ \text{km}}$$

unit fractions for converting between measures

To change 36,000,000 inches to miles, for example, multiply by unit fractions involving inches, feet, and miles:

$$36{,}000{,}000 \text{ in.} * \frac{1 \text{ ft}}{12 \text{ in.}} * \frac{1 \text{ mi}}{5{,}280 \text{ ft}}$$

The inches and feet divide out (as indicated by the slash marks below) leaving only the mile. Dividing 36,000,000 by 63,360 on a calculator yields an answer that is approximately equal to 570 miles.

$$36{,}000{,}000 \text{ in.} * \frac{1 \text{ ft}}{12 \text{ in.}} * \frac{1 \text{ mi}}{5{,}280 \text{ ft}} = \frac{36{,}000{,}000 \text{ mi}}{63{,}360} \approx 570 \text{ mi}$$

Because both metric and U.S. customary measures are used in the United States, and because almost all of the rest of the world is metric, being able to convert between systems is useful, especially for travelers. Precise conversions are seldom necessary, although it helps to know that, by definition, 1 inch = 2.54 centimeters. Here are other helpful conversion tips:

A centimeter is about $\frac{3}{8}$ inch.

A meter is about 10% longer than a yard.

A kilometer is about 0.6 mile; a mile is about 1.6 kilometers.

A liter is a little more than a quart.

A kilogram is about 10% more than 2 pounds.

More precise conversions between systems can be made in the same way as within a system. For example, to change 1 kilometer or 1,000 meters to miles, choose unit fractions so that meters, centimeters, inches, and feet divide out.

$$1{,}000 \text{ m} * \frac{100 \text{ cm}}{1 \text{ m}} * \frac{1 \text{ in.}}{2.54 \text{ cm}} * \frac{1 \text{ ft}}{12 \text{ in.}} * \frac{1 \text{ mi}}{5{,}280 \text{ ft}} \approx 0.62 \text{ mi}$$

In the unit-fraction approach to conversions described above, unit names in quotients and products are treated as though they behave in the same way as numbers. This method works for all types of measures, not just linear ones as in the examples. It is part of what is called *units analysis* or *dimensional analysis* and is an important technique in doing scientific calculations. A long-time concern of science educators has been the neglect of units analysis in mathematics instruction. *Everyday Mathematics* is committed to teaching students about the meaning and use of measurement units.

6.3 Measurement Tools and Techniques

No matter which system or unit is being used, measuring tools provide ways to attach numbers to many common and uncommon things in everyone's life. There are measuring tools to measure in any unit or system; some tools even provide help with conversions. The history of science is very much intertwined with the development of improved measuring instruments. New scientific discoveries often hinge on new and more precise measuring tools, and verification or rejection of theories often depends on increasingly precise measurements. Much of modern industry and technology depends on using very precise measures that are standardized throughout the world. Students learn that the measuring tools that we all use are based on mutually agreed-upon standards and that our own measurements are mere approximations, as the following paragraph explains.

6.3.1 Measurements as Estimates

Physical measurements are never exact. Even measures that seem exact are actually estimates that are "close enough" for practical considerations. We can never line up the precise edge of an object with a precise point on a measuring tool. For example, this page is not exactly 11 inches long. If you look at its edge under a microscope you will see that it is not exactly even and straight. Also, no matter how small the subdivisions on a ruler, there are always unmarked spaces between the marked lines. Thus, when students learn to measure—with inexact body measures in Kindergarten, or to the nearest half-inch, quarter-inch, or centimeter in later grades, for example—they also are learning to approximate and deal with error.

6.3.2 Measuring Sticks and Tapes

Along with weighing scales and balances, rulers and tape measures are among the first tools for practical everyday measurements, both in human history and in the lives of students. In the early grades, children learn to give "ballpark" estimates of heights and lengths; then, over the years, they get progressively more sophisticated in their use of measuring instruments to find approximate lengths. Carpenters' rules are important tools for applying the "half" fractions in later grades ($\frac{1}{2}$, $\frac{1}{4}$, $\frac{1}{8}$, and so on—each fraction being half the previous one); and meter sticks and centimeter rulers are instructive when teaching about decimals.

If your students are using the retractable tape measures, teach and enforce the "2-inch, 5-centimeter no-zap rule" (do not "zap" the tape measure until no more than 2 inches or 5 centimeters show). This will extend the life of these tools, as well as make your own life quieter and easier.

6.3.3 Scales and Balances

A scale is another "early" measuring tool. Scales are used to measure how heavy something is according to a standard weight. (See Section 6.7 for a discussion of weight.) There are many different kinds of scales. Some of the ones that *Everyday Mathematics* students will become most familiar with are highlighted below.

The ***balance*** scale was the first device for weighing. It was used in Egypt about 3500 B.C. and made use of a simple lever. In ancient

Egypt, gold dust was used as currency and needed to be weighed very precisely in order to determine its value.

Balances with the fulcrum (the support on which a lever moves) at the center of a horizontal bar are called **equal-arm balances.** The material being weighed is placed in a pan at one end, and known weights are placed in a pan at the other end until a pointer at the fulcrum indicates that the pans are balanced. Balances with unequal arms, known as steelyards, were developed by the ancient Romans. The object to be weighed is placed on the shorter arm, and a weight is moved along the longer arm until it balances the load.

Beam scales use a counterweight that is moved along the beam until the load is balanced. Calibrations on the beam give the weight. Health-care providers use this type of scale to weigh patients. Similarly, **platform** scales use a system of levers, so that a heavy object can be balanced by a relatively small counterweight on the beam. Truck and railroad scales are often of this type.

Spring scales, such as bathroom scales, use linkages to stretch or compress one or more springs. One spring causes the weight indicator to move and automatically give the weight. With simple spring scales, a pan or hook at the bottom of the spring holds the object to be weighed. This type is often seen hanging from ceilings in the produce sections of supermarkets.

Electronic scales were first commercially used in the 1950s and are now seen everywhere. They use a device called a strain-gauge load cell, which measures the stress an object puts on a mechanical element. The measurement is converted into an electrical signal and transferred to an electronic weight indicator, which gives the weight reading. Some high-precision scales determine weight by measuring the magnetic force needed to counter the downward pull of gravity and support the load on the scales.

Different scales are designed to measure different amounts of weight. There are scales with a variety of capacities and a variety of increments. High-precision scales can measure the weight of a piece of hair or a dose of medicine in increments as small as 0.001 gram or 0.000001 pound. Some platform scales can weigh trucks as large as 100 tons or railroad cars of 825 tons.

Scales have a variety of uses. In the kitchen, they are used to weigh food for cooking and for monitoring diets. Bathroom, nursery, and doctor's scales help monitor personal health. All kinds of scales are used by businesses that sell produce, meat, fish, and bakery items. The post office and other delivery services determine shipping prices based on package weight. Scales are used to weigh trucks to determine the amount of tax that drivers must pay for using the roads. Scales are also used to count pieces, such as the number of nails in a box or pennies in a bag. Scales may give the weight on a dial or digital display in U.S. customary units, metric units, or both.

balance scale

doctor's beam scale

spring scale

market scale

6.4 Length

Distances along 1-dimensional objects, or along paths, are measured with linear measures. Like all measures, a linear measure consists of a value and a unit. For example, to say, "The edge of my desk is about 3.5 long" makes no sense. Saying, "The edge of my desk is about 3.5 feet long" provides both the approximate length and a unit of measure. Some of the most common tools for measuring length—measuring sticks and tapes—were discussed in Section 6.3.2 and on pages 47–49 of the Management Guide.

The two most common linear measures are length (the distance between two points on a line or arc) and perimeter (the distance around an object). The perimeter of a circle is called the **circumference** of the circle.

Formulas for Linear Measures There is not a great need for formulas for most linear measures because they can be found easily enough with a direct measurement or by a direct measurement on a blueprint, map, or other model followed by a conversion. There are, however, four formulas involving linear measures in *Everyday Mathematics.*

2 inches

2 inches

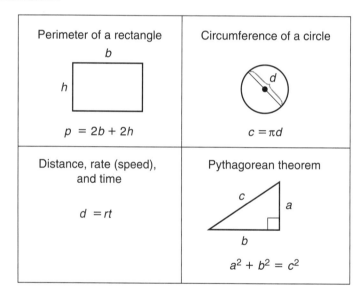

Perimeter of a rectangle $p = 2b + 2h$	Circumference of a circle $c = \pi d$
Distance, rate (speed), and time $d = rt$	Pythagorean theorem $a^2 + b^2 = c^2$

Students in *Fourth* and *Fifth Grade Everyday Mathematics* develop formulas for the perimeter of a rectangle and the circumference of a circle. The latter is approached by measuring diameters and circumferences of various circles and looking at their ratios to approximate π—an activity third graders performed with tin cans to get an approximation of "about 3" for π. Students are also given the formula relating distance traveled, rate of travel (speed), and time of travel, and they look at a graph of points for a fixed rate. In these activities, the focus is on the use of variables and equations as models, not so much on the value or necessity of the formula itself.

The Pythagorean theorem is included because the variables all represent distances—the lengths of the sides of a right triangle. The theorem is most useful in finding the length of one of the sides

NOTE: The Pythagorean theorem is used for solving indirect measurement problems in *Sixth Grade Everyday Mathematics.* Indirect measurement problems are those in which clues to a measurement are given in the form of related measures.

when the other two side lengths are known. To calculate the length of the hypotenuse c, for example, a useful variation of the equation is the following:

$$c = \sqrt{a^2 + b^2}$$

The Pythagorean theorem is introduced in part to help sixth graders understand the inverse relationship between squaring and taking square roots.

Just as 1-dimensional objects can be thought of as building blocks for 2- and 3-dimensional objects, so is length a building block for 2- and 3-dimensional measures. These are called area and volume, respectively. They are discussed in the following sections.

For more on the Pythagorean theorem, see Section 5.4.2 of the Geometry essay.

For applications of linear measures in geography, see Section 6.11.1.

6.5 Area

Just as length and perimeter are measures of a finite distance along a path, **area** is a measure of a finite amount of a 2-dimensional surface. This surface may lie in a single plane (for example, the interior of a rectangle), or it may exist in 3-dimensional space (for example, the curved surface of a cylinder or cone). The latter type of area is called **surface area**.

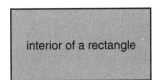

interior of a rectangle

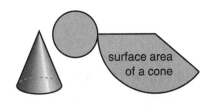

surface area of a cone

Like other numerical measures, a measure of area always includes both a number (a value) and a unit. Units of area are typically square units based on linear units (for example, square inches, square centimeters, square yards, and square meters). Some traditional units of area are not square units; for example, an acre of land is said to have been based, a long time ago, on the amount of land a farmer could plow in one day.

Discrete Conception of Area In most schoolbooks, the definition of area is based on the idea of "tiling," or covering a surface with identical unit squares, without gaps or overlaps, and then counting those units. This conception of area is "discrete" because it involves separate, countable parts. If the surface is bounded by a rectangle, it is natural to arrange the tiles in an array and to multiply the number of tiles per row by the number of rows. The usual formulas, $A = l * w$ and $A = b * h$, are then easily linked to array multiplication: Area is the number of square-unit tiles in one row (equal to the length of the base in the appropriate linear unit) times the number of rows (equal to the width, or height, in that same linear unit). For other surfaces, defined by regular or irregular boundaries, the tiling with square units can be thought of as (or actually done by) laying a grid of appropriate square units on the region and counting, estimating, or calculating how many squares or partial squares it takes to cover the region.

40 square units

about 21 square units

Continuous Conception of Area Tiling activities develop a *discrete* conception of area, as described above. In later grades, though, students touch on a *continuous* conception of area. Imagine rolling a paint roller 1 foot wide on the floor of a rectangular room. For every foot the roller travels, a square foot of the floor is painted.

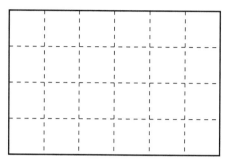

a discrete model of area

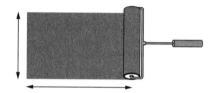

a continuous model of area

Now imagine that the room is 20 feet wide and that you use a roller the width of the room (a 20-foot-wide roller). Then, for every foot the roller travels, 20 square feet of floor will be painted. When the roller reaches the other side of the room, the entire floor will be painted.

If you think of the floor as the interior of a rectangle, then the area of the rectangle is obtained not by counting squares (a discrete conception) but by sweeping the width of the rectangle across the interior of the rectangle, parallel to its base (a continuous conception). The area is simply the product of the length of the base by the width of the rectangle. This can be shown by rubbing the long part of a piece of chalk on the chalkboard to mark a rectangular region—the farther it is swept along, the bigger the rectangle and the greater the area.

Students of *Everyday Mathematics* have experience with area throughout the program. Younger students focus on manipulating discrete conceptions of area through tiling activities. Beginning in Grade 4, students use formulas to model area symbolically. All students are asked to estimate area measures, and sometimes they check them by actually measuring. In Grades 4 and 5, students estimate areas of land and research areas of states, countries, and continents in the World Tour and American Tour.

Area Formulas Formulas for area measures are the first formulas seen by students of *Everyday Mathematics*. Rather than simply

For applications of area in geography, see Section 6.11.2.

being given formulas, fourth graders are asked to develop their own by doing experiments. The following are five useful area formulas.

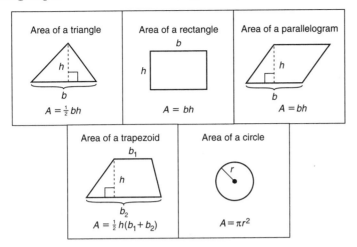

The formula for the area of a rectangle is fairly easy for students to discover. Area formulas for a parallelogram and a triangle are found with a little more guidance, using paper-folding techniques and grid paper. The area of a circle can be estimated quite closely; eventually, π is defined, and fifth graders are given the formula.

Sixth graders find the area of a trapezoid by dividing it into a rectangle and one or two triangles and then adding the areas of the pieces. The formula in the chart above is a shortcut you may wish to show students who are ready. (It makes a good end-of-year challenge that reviews many ideas in *Sixth Grade Everyday Mathematics*.) In the shortcut, b_1 is the length of one of the parallel bases of the trapezoid, b_2 is the length of the other base, and h is the height or altitude, as shown in the margin.

If the trapezoid is partitioned into two triangles and a rectangle as shown, then the area A of the trapezoid is equal to the sum of the areas of the triangles and rectangle, as follows:

$$A = \tfrac{1}{2}xh + \tfrac{1}{2}yh + b_1 h$$

This is equivalent to

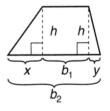

$$A = \tfrac{1}{2}xh + \tfrac{1}{2}yh + \tfrac{2}{2}b_1 h$$

By the distributive property,

$$A = \tfrac{1}{2}h(x + y + 2b_1)$$

This is equivalent to

$$A = \tfrac{1}{2}h(x + y + b_1 + b_1)$$

But $x + y + b_1$ is the length of the bottom base, b_2. The formula can be written as

$$A = \tfrac{1}{2}h(b_1 + b_2)$$

The formula shows that the area of a trapezoid is equal to the average of the two bases, $\tfrac{1}{2}(b_1 + b_2)$, times the height, h.

6.6 Volume

Volume is the measure of a finite amount of 3-dimensional space. As with measures in one and two dimensions, all measures of volume require a unit, and all are approximate. Volume units are typically cubic units based on linear measures, such as cubic inches, cubic centimeters, cubic yards, and cubic meters.

Discrete and Continuous Conceptions of Volume The concept of volume can be given a discrete meaning by building 3-dimensional shapes with identical cubes (or filling shapes completely with such cubes) and then counting the cubes. If the shape is a rectangular prism, a natural strategy is to build one layer of cubes, count the number of cubes in that layer, then multiply that number by the number of layers needed to fill the prism. Since the number of cubes in one layer corresponds to the area of the base (often represented by the formula $A = l * w$), this process can be linked to either of the two standard formulas for the volume of rectangular prisms: $V = l * \text{w} * h$ (the product of the length and width of the rectangular base and the height perpendicular to that base) or $V = B * h$ (the product of the area of the base and the height perpendicular to that base).

The formula $V = l * w * h$ is commonly used in elementary textbooks and on standardized tests. $V = B * h$ is used in many mathematics courses and technical applications. The latter captures a concept of volume as continuous, similar to the "sweeping out" of area. For example, imagine the base of a box as a rectangular region. Then imagine "sweeping" this rectangular region through the height of the box, filling the space. Or imagine gradually filling the box with water: the surface of the water is rectangular, like the base of the box. The higher the water level, the more space it occupies, and the greater the volume. This leads to a general formula for the volume of prisms and cylinders: the area of the base multiplied by the height. Unlike $V = l * w * h$, the formula $V = B * h$ works no matter what the shape of the base.

Both concepts of volume are used throughout *Everyday Mathematics,* with a discrete approach dominating Kindergarten through second grade as young students fill objects with cubes. In Grades 3 and 4, they experiment with a continuous approach by filling objects with water or sand. In Grades 5 and 6, students focus more on the use of variables in formulas to model volume symbolically.

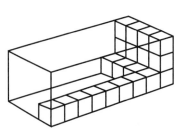

Filling a box with cubes is a discrete model of volume.

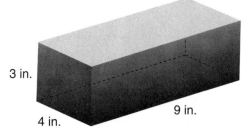

3 in.

4 in.

9 in.

a continuous model of volume

Volume Formulas Volume formulas are developed out of informal activities begun in *Third Grade Everyday Mathematics*. Fourth graders review box-packing experiments and generalize them into a formula for the volume of a rectangular prism. Fifth graders expand this formula to one for any prism or cylinder, and they develop formulas for the volume of any pyramid or cone.

It should be emphasized that the formula of choice is the more informal "area of base times height" formula, rather than the specific ones shown below. If students remember the informal formula, then they can construct any of the others by knowing the area formulas for polygons and circles. The following are seven useful volume formulas.

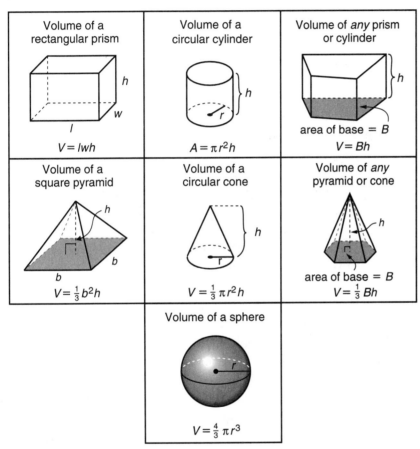

Volume of a rectangular prism	Volume of a circular cylinder	Volume of *any* prism or cylinder
$V = lwh$	$A = \pi r^2 h$	area of base $= B$ $V = Bh$
Volume of a square pyramid	Volume of a circular cone	Volume of *any* pyramid or cone
$V = \frac{1}{3} b^2 h$	$V = \frac{1}{3} \pi r^2 h$	area of base $= B$ $V = \frac{1}{3} Bh$

Volume of a sphere

$V = \frac{4}{3} \pi r^3$

6.6.1 Capacity

Sometimes we need to know amounts of things such as liquids or small grains of sand or sugar—things that take the shapes of their containers and can't be measured by their lengths, widths, and heights to get a volume. For these cases, we use measures of capacity. Capacity is a measure of how much a container can hold. Units of capacity are special types of volume units. For example, to determine how much milk or sugar is needed for a particular recipe or how much gasoline a car's tank will hold, we would use measures of capacity. (Dry ingredients, such as sugar, are sometimes measured by weight. This is common in recipes from other countries and when talking about bulk amounts.)

Some familiar units of capacity in the U.S. customary system are fluid ounces, cups, quarts, and gallons. A fluid ounce is defined as 1.804 cubic inches. The liter and milliliter are the most commonly used units of capacity in the metric system. A liter is defined as 1,000 cubic centimeters.

6.6.2 Linking Area and Volume

The idea of dimension is at the heart of area and volume, and understanding dimension requires plenty of experience with 1-, 2-, and 3-dimensional figures—both individually and in relation to one another. This is one reason why measuring actual objects for their 1-dimensional attributes, such as length or perimeter; 2-dimensional attributes, such as area and surface area; and 3-dimensional attributes, such as volume and capacity, is such an integral component of *Everyday Mathematics* beginning in Kindergarten.

By fourth grade, students should be comfortable identifying attributes of 1-, 2-, and 3-dimensional figures and their measures. They will also have had many informal experiences relating objects in different dimensions. For example, each edge of a 3-D cube is a 1-D line segment; the four edges of each face form a 2-D square. In *4–6 Everyday Mathematics,* students explore relationships between the dimensions through the continuous conceptions of area and volume described in the previous sections. The movement of a point to trace out a path shows the change from 0 to 1 dimension. The movement of a line segment shows the change from 1 to 2 dimensions. Moving a plane figure to generate a 3-dimensional object with volume shows movement from 2 to 3 dimensions.

6.7 Weight and Mass

Mass is a measure of the amount of matter in an object. *Weight* is the force of gravity on an object. If you took a trip around the solar system and weighed yourself on each planet, you would find your weight changing drastically depending on the size of the planet. You would weigh more on big planets because their gravitational pull is stronger. On small planets you would weigh less because they don't exert as much pull. Your mass, however, would remain the same regardless of the planet you were on because the amount of matter in your body is not affected by gravity.

This distinction between weight and mass is noted for you, but because most of us and the objects we weigh are firmly planted on Earth, it is not of everyday practical consequence. With young students, it is neither necessary nor appropriate to make any distinction between weight and mass. Some older students may be able to appreciate the difference.

Weight is measured using a variety of scales. A balance scale compares an object's mass to a standard mass set. A spring scale measures the pull of gravity as evidenced by an object's push or pull on a spring.

For more on dimension, see Section 5.1 of the Geometry essay.

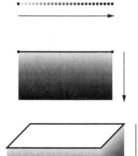

moving between dimensions

For more on scales, see Section 6.3.3.

6.8 Angle Measure

Angular measures quantify turns or rotations. In Kindergarten through third grade, students measure angles as fractions of a circle: a right angle is a quarter-turn; a straight angle is a half turn; and so on.

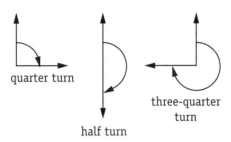

quarter turn

half turn

three-quarter turn

Students in *Fourth Grade Everyday Mathematics* start using protractors to measure angles in degrees. A degree is $\frac{1}{360}$ of a full rotation and is the angle measure used in most practical situations. In Grades 5 and 6, angle measure is often a part of contexts for problem-solving activities. In later mathematics courses, students will learn about other angle measures, especially the radian. (2π radians $= 360°$)

For more on tools used to measure angles, especially the percent circle and the protractor, see page 43 of the Management Guide.

For more on angles and rotations, see Section 5.4.1 of the Geometry essay.

6.9 Elapsed Time

Numbers are used both to mark time and to measure it. We mark time by establishing reference frames, such as a calendar year and the number of days in a month. Events are then described by locations on one or more of these frames—for example, "She was born August 15, 1989, at 2:00 A.M." These numbers are not "measures" because, unlike measures, they cannot be added or subtracted with any meaning. For instance, 2:00 P.M. plus 3:00 P.M. is not 5:00 P.M.. Nor is April 12 plus April 15 equal to April 27. The reference labels *P.M.* and *April* are not units of measure.

Once reference frames have been established, however, there are reference units that can be used as measures. For example, the play lasted 68 minutes; he finished the race in 3.9 seconds; the past 4 years have been warm. The use of time units to measure the duration of an event or the time between events is called elapsed time.

For more on reference frames, see the Reference Frames essay.

Our units of time have the longest history of any measuring units. The 24-hour day comes from the ancient Egyptians, who divided the period from sunrise to sunset into 12 equal parts and the period from sunset to sunrise into 12 equal parts as well. (Because the times of sunrise and sunset vary, the lengths of these two kinds of "hours" changed daily.) The seven-day week is credited to the Babylonians, who observed seven moving celestial bodies—the Sun, the Moon, and five planets. Also, the Babylonians used a numeration system based on 60 (probably because 60 can be divided evenly by many whole numbers), which led to the 60-second minute and the 60-minute hour.

Students use time measures frequently throughout *Everyday Mathematics,* most often in the context of number stories. As students learn new arithmetic skills, elapsed-time applications of these skills are developed. For example, in first and second grades, students use addition and subtraction to figure out elapsed times. ("What time was it 2 hours ago?" "What time will it be in 3 hours?") Beginning in third grade, students answer ratio questions about time, such as "What fraction of a year is 9 months?" In Grades 4–6, time measurements are important parts of rate problems in which students figure out gallons per minute of water flow, an animal's speed in feet per second, or calculations per millisecond by a computer, to name a few examples.

6.10 Money

See Essay 7 for a discussion of reference frames.

Money may be viewed as a reference frame because it is an arbitrary scale used to establish the values of goods and services. Like the variations in the linear measure "foot" before standardization, however, different people place different values on the same goods or services. To make matters even more complicated, the differences are not just physical but emotional, spiritual, and intellectual in nature. Even an individual's perceived value of something changes with time and experience.

In everyday life, though, money is more a measure of relative value than a reference frame. We measure the value of one thing versus another or of one thing now versus that thing yesterday or last year. Statements such as "This TV costs $50 more now than it did three months ago" and "Bananas are up 17 percent this season" indicate how we use arithmetic to compare monetary values. This is a sign that money behaves like a measure, and so it is categorized as such in *Everyday Mathematics.*

Young students are exposed to money, prices, buying and selling on a daily basis, but few have experience with money details. That is, students see money transactions, are given an exact amount to spend, or hand over coins and accept change without checking. Although there are exceptions, many first grade students are unable to distinguish among coins (nickels and quarters are often confused), and relatively few beginning first graders know the exchanges among coins or their links to the basic dollar unit.

Experience with money is important because of its inherent usefulness and, like most measures, because of the context it provides for number stories. Additionally, our base-ten monetary system is an excellent vehicle for the study of place value, fractions, and decimal notation. In *Everyday Mathematics,* we provide students with early experiences to develop their knowledge about the details of money. We then make use of the familiar context of money to make it easier for students to become acquainted with fractions and decimals at earlier ages than they would in a traditional mathematics curriculum.

In Grades K–3, money is a focus of instruction in *Everyday Mathematics*. By fourth grade it is assumed that most students have a good understanding of money and can use it in number and variable stories without explicit coverage or review.

6.10.1 Money Facts

Talking about coins and bills also provides a unique opportunity to bridge various curriculum areas. Money lore contains interesting facts about the history of our country, about the science of metals, and about symbols in our heritage. Use these facts liberally in your teaching about coins and bills in the *Everyday Mathematics* money lessons and at other times during the year. Some selected definitions follow.

alloy A mixture of two or more chemical elements, at least one of which is a metal.

denomination The official value of a coin.

E Pluribus Unum The original motto of the United States; translated from Latin as "From many, one." This motto is required by an 1873 law to appear on any coin that contains an eagle. In fact, it appears on all U.S. coins.

In God We Trust A motto that was permitted, but not required, on coins by the 1873 law; a 1955 law required that the motto be placed on all coins and bills. In 1956, President Dwight D. Eisenhower signed a law making "In God We Trust" the official motto of the United States.

intrinsic value The actual worth of the metal in a coin.

obverse The face or "front" of a coin; "heads."

reverse The back or "rear" of a coin; "tails."

rim The edge of a coin, which is quite functional because it allows the coin to be stacked and protects the design from damage. U.S. coins with values of more than 5 cents each have always had rims that are ornate, lettered, or reeded (that is, with parallel grooves that are perpendicular to the face of the coin, as in our dime and quarter). This was intended to discourage the scraping of the coin edges to steal some of their metal; it also makes it easier to identify coins by touch, which is necessary for people with visual impairments and useful for pulling a specific amount of change out of your pocket without looking.

New designs for coins and bills are adopted periodically, putting currency in the United States in a constant (albeit slow) state of flux. For example, at this writing, the U.S. Treasury Department was producing a new series of quarters and has put a new one-dollar coin into circulation. If desired, you can go into great detail about individual coins and their designs with your students, touching upon history, metallurgy, and architecture in the process. An example of the type of information you might want to share with your students is included below for the nickel.

Nickels

Until 1866, five-cent pieces were called half-dimes. The word *nickel* comes from the metal in the coin. Currently, nickels are made of an alloy of 75% copper and 25% nickel.

Obverse The Jefferson bust was designed by Felix O. Schlag, whose initials, FS, appear between the rim and the bottom of the bust on nickels produced after 1965.

Information about Thomas Jefferson	
Born	April 13, 1743; Shadwell (now Albemarle County), Virginia
Died	July 4, 1826; at Monticello in Albemarle County, Virginia. Jefferson died on the 50th anniversary of the signing of the Declaration of Independence. (The second President of the United States, John Adams, died on the same day.)
Occupations	Lawyer; delegate to the Continental Congress; author of the Declaration of Independence; Governor of Virginia; ambassador to France; Vice President; President; founder of the University of Virginia; farmer; architect
Important Dates	1797 elected Vice President under President John Adams 1801 inaugurated as 3rd President 1803 Louisiana Purchase 1804 reelected President

Reverse Monticello, Jefferson's home in Virginia, appears on the reverse, along with its name. This coinage design was suggested by President Franklin D. Roosevelt in 1938.

Information about Monticello	
Location	Albemarle County, Virginia
Architect	Thomas Jefferson
Built	1st version 1769–1793 2nd version 1793–1809

6.10.2 Money History

The history of money in our country is also quite interesting. The first coin used extensively in the American colonies was the Spanish milled dollar, a silver coin referred to as a piece of eight because it was worth 8 *reales* (pronounced ray-al-ays). The coin was also called a peso. Even today, our $ symbol is the same as that for the Mexican *peso*. The milled dollar was often cut into eight pieces to allow for smaller denominations. Each of the eight pieces was called a *real* or a *bit*. Thus, for many years, a dollar was referred to as eight bits, a half-dollar as four bits, and a quarter as two bits.

When the United States began to produce its own coins, it used the Spanish milled dollar as its model. The first U.S. dollars, which weighed exactly as much as the Spanish coins, were made of an alloy

NOTE: Cheers like "Two bits, four bits, six bits, a dollar!...All for U.C., stand up and holler!" continue to carry the early terms for coins into the present. "Shave and a haircut, two bits" may be dying out, but the rhythm behind the saying lives on.

composed of fifteen parts silver to one part gold. In 1792, Congress passed the first coinage act for the new country and authorized the production of coins in various denominations: an eagle ($10), a half-eagle ($5), coins with the modern values, and a half-cent. With the exception of the cent and the half-cent, these early coins did not show their denominations. This oversight was corrected by an 1837 Act of Congress. Until 1909, the heads, or busts, of all people represented on U.S. coins were abstractions (for example, Liberty) or generic figures (for example, an Indian). In 1909, the first coin picturing a real person—Abraham Lincoln—appeared.

The American Eagle, which appears by law on all coins with a value of more than 10 cents, is the likeness of an actual eagle—"Peter the Mint Bird," the mascot of the Philadelphia Mint in the 1840s and 1850s. After his death, Peter was stuffed and is, to this day, preserved in a glass case in the Philadelphia Mint.

References

Information about U.S. coins and bills and the history of money can be found on the U.S. Treasury's Web site: http://www.ustreas.gov and in books such as the following:

Barabas, Kathy. *Let's Find Out About Money*. New York: Scholastic. 1997.

Doty, Richard. *America's Money, America's Story*. Iola, Wisc.: Krause. 1988.

Yeoman, R. S. *Guide Book of United States Coins*. New York: Golden Books Adult. Issued yearly.

6.11 Measures in Geography

The use of measures in geography is a special focus throughout *Everyday Mathematics*. Geographic measurements are obtained directly, by applying measuring methods to Earth itself, or are obtained indirectly, by applying measuring methods to maps, aerial photos, satellite images, and so on.

6.11.1 Linear Measures in Geography

Linear (1-dimensional) measures have been culturally and politically important since humans began keeping records of territory. Linear measures can be of vertical (above or below sea level) or horizontal distances. The mean (average) sea level—a level agreed upon after many measurements—is called the **datum plane.** These measurements can be refined by reflecting laser beams from satellites. The following are important linear geographical measures:

Elevation of a city A benchmark with this measurement, established by the U.S. Geological Survey, is set in concrete somewhere in the downtown area of major cities. The vertical distance from the datum plane, correct to the nearest foot, is determined by stair-step surveying (leveling) as shown by the diagram in the margin.

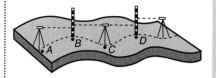

stair-step surveying

Elevations can be measured by leveling. An instrument with a horizontal line of sight is set at point A of known elevation. It is aligned with a graduated pole at point B of unknown elevation. The reading on the pole is used to find the elevation of B. The process can continue by moving the instrument to another point, C, taking a reading from the pole at B, and using it to find the elevation of point C. The elevation of point C can be used to find the elevation of point D, and so on.

Height of a mountain pass This is the measurement of the pass at its highest point. Nearby benchmarks are used, with stair-step surveying reaching upward from them, often from both sides of the pass. Rugged terrain and adverse atmospheric conditions may affect the accuracy of the measurement.

Depth of an ocean Sonar signals are sent to the ocean floor and reflected back. The total time is recorded and corrections made for water temperature and other factors. The final result, often accurate to the nearest ten feet, requires precise measurement of the position above or below the datum plane of the apparatus used to send the signal.

Depth of a lake or inland sea The same techniques and difficulties apply as those described for measurement of the lowest point from the surface of an ocean. The only difference is that each inland body of water is assigned its own datum plane, representing an average water level.

Length of a river This measurement is usually made on a map developed from satellite photography and perhaps other sources. The measurement is made by guiding a hand-held instrument about the size of a ball-point pen slowly and steadily along the full length of the river as represented on the map. This instrument has a very small wheel rather than a ball at its tip. It has a meter that counts the number of wheel rotations. The count along with the map scale are used to compute a measurement that is acceptable initially as the length of the river. Since the initial measurement results from a tracing on a level plane, corrections are made to take into account the slope of the river from its source to its mouth. Accuracy may be expected within 0.1% of the actual length. Variations may be due to disagreement on which of several headwater streams is the river proper and whether or not the river changed course since the mapping was made.

6.11.2 Area in Geography

Area measurements are based on accurate maps. Important applications include the following:

Area of a country Even though most countries have irregular shapes, their areas can be estimated by laying transparent graph paper or projecting a grid on an accurate map. The whole squares that fit within a country's boundaries are counted. Smaller squares or triangles are used to refine the measurement. The count and the map scale are used to calculate the area. Reported areas vary from reference book to reference book and should be accepted with caution. *Everyday Mathematics* mostly uses figures from the *World Almanac and Book of Facts.*

Also, figures regarding area are not accurate because of the following:

- There may not be agreement on a country's boundaries or claims to territorial waters.

- Measuring the area of a country as if its entire surface were a horizontal plane understates the land surface in mountainous territory.

Area of an ocean, sea, or lake This measurement relies on agreement as to a mean water level. For any given level, there is a shoreline that becomes the boundary for the area to be calculated. As with the area of a country, the area of a body of water is found by covering a carefully produced map with squares. Since the world's oceans are separated from each other by arbitrary boundaries rather than shorelines, ocean area figures—even those rounded to the nearest 100 square miles—should be accepted with caution.

Area of a continent The square-counting process is also used for this measurement. The same cautions about other published geographic areas also apply: Use of a horizontal plane results in understated areas in mountainous territory, and there may be uncertainty in identifying shorelines. Another consideration is whether to include the continental shelf, which extends out under water from the shoreline. The standard figures for continental areas typically use shoreline limits but can be overstated by including offshore land. For example, one source's area for North America includes Greenland and the islands of the Caribbean and gives an approximation rounded to the nearest 100,000 square miles.

Area of a desert Although the measurement of desert area uses the same square-counting process, finding desert area is challenging because of two factors:

- There are different definitions of a desert. *Desert* generally refers to land where there is no agriculture without irrigation because rainfall is insufficient. Sometimes *desert* refers to land where there is no grazing. (In this case, tundras—very cold places where the water is always frozen—would be considered deserts.)

- The edges of deserts are unstable because of climatic change or overuse by humans.

In Grades 4–6 of *Everyday Mathematics,* students discuss in their own language the appropriateness (validity) and the quality (reliability) of geographical area measures. For example: *Which is more appropriate for measuring the area of Texas, square centimeters or square miles? Is any reliable estimate of the water level of the Black Sea possible since the level rises and falls?* As with all measurements, geographical ones are estimates and should be taken as such.

6.11.3 Geography between Dimensions

Studying many different 1-dimensional measures (height, depth, length) in the context of geography may help students see the similarities among linear measurements (feet, miles, and so on) rather than the obvious differences in size. It also provides a strong, informal experience that may help some interested students investigate **fractal geometry** in later grades. Fractal geometry is a relatively new branch of mathematics (it got its name only in the 1970s). A part of fractal geometry was developed when investigators were trying to measure the length of the coastline of England to a greater degree of accuracy than before. Benoit Mandelbrot, an IBM scientist, determined that the dimension of a mathematical model of a coastline is somewhere *between* 1 and 2 dimensions! This **fractional dimensional** property led to the name **fractal.**

The crumpling of a sheet of aluminum foil can be used to demonstrate a fractal dimension. Think of the sheet of foil as 2-dimensional. If it were crumpled into a ball, it would be 3-dimensional. During the crumpling, the foil has many indentations and irregularities, allowing us to consider the foil as being between two and three dimensions.

Fractal geometry is now a major focus of mathematicians, who use sophisticated computers to study the roughness, brokenness, or irregularity of objects or events as well as to make fascinating graphical designs. You have probably seen fractals on computer screens and in science-fiction movies. Fractal designs demonstrate order and pattern in apparently highly irregular designs.

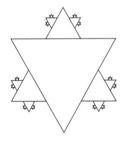

Basically, a fractal is a figure created by endlessly repeating a defining algorithm. For example, the figure in the margin shows the beginning of the so-called Sierpinski Snowflake. Each side of an equilateral triangle is divided into equal thirds, and an equilateral triangle is constructed on the middle third. The outward-pointing sides of the new triangles are divided into thirds, and new equilateral triangles are constructed on the middle thirds. The process is repeated (theoretically) without end.

The computer graphics image to the right, titled "A Birth of Lightning," is derived from the Mandelbrot set, one of the most famous fractal images. The definition of a Mandelbrot set involves complex numbers and iterated functions and is therefore beyond the scope of this book. But you can get an idea of how the set is defined by imagining a Frames-and-Arrows diagram with the arrow rule "Square and add c," where c is a complex number. A point is in the Mandelbrot set if the numbers in the Frames-and-Arrows diagram that starts with that point do not get infinitely large.

A group of complex numbers are plotted as coordinates and each point is assigned a color depending on the results of a series of repeated mathematical operations.

Such "chaotic" operations can be used to model real-world phenomena such as stock-market prices or population dynamics.

This illustration is a computer graphics representation of a detail from a figure in the Mandelbrot set, plotted from complex number coordinates.

Reference Frames

Reference frames are something of an oddity in mathematics. Unlike measurements or counts, numbers in reference frames locate things only within definite systems or contexts. Examples of numbers in reference frames include dates, times, Celsius and Fahrenheit temperatures, and coordinates on maps. The numbers in reference frames are set arbitrarily. For example, the year 2000 in our calendar system is not the same as the year 2000 in the traditional Chinese calendar system, and the Celsius temperature scale is quite different from the Fahrenheit scale.

Almost all reference frames have a *zero point,* leading to the use of positive and negative numbers to describe locations on one side of zero or the other. Zero in a reference frame means something different from zero as a count or a measure. In counts and measures, zero indicates nothingness: a measure or count of zero means that there is none of whatever is being measured or counted. In contrast, the zero point within a reference frame is an arbitrary starting point; it does not necessarily correspond with nothingness or the lowest possible value. As a result, numbers in reference frames may not be governed by the same mathematical rules that other numbers are.

Arithmetic operations cannot always be performed on numbers in reference frames to obtain results that make sense. For example, no meaningful result is obtained by adding the year 1930 to the year 1990; 30°C is not 3 times as warm as 10°C; and 3:00 P.M. plus 2:00 P.M. does not equal 5:00 P.M. On the other hand, the numbers in reference frames can be used to find the distance from one point to another in the same reference frame. For example: 1930 was 60 years earlier than 1990; 30°C is 20 degrees warmer than 10°C; and 5:00 P.M. is 2 hours later than 3:00 P.M.

©1989 Thaves. Reprinted with permission.

In *Everyday Mathematics,* students learn about a variety of contemporary and historical reference frames. This essay will discuss reference frames used to establish temperature (Section 7.1) and time (Section 7.2). It will also discuss coordinate systems (Section 7.3) and maps (Section 7.4), which are often based on coordinate grids.

7.1 Temperature

The temperature systems that we are most familiar with—Fahrenheit and Celsius—are reference frames that help us quantify hotness or coldness. Both establish an arbitrary zero point and an interval scale, with each interval being equal to a degree in that system. The Fahrenheit and Celsius scales have different zero points and different-size intervals from one another: 0° Fahrenheit does not feel the same as 0° Celsius, and a change of one degree Fahrenheit is not equal to a change of one degree Celsius.

Fahrenheit This scale was invented in the early 1700s by the German physicist D. G. Fahrenheit. The zero point of this scale (0°F) is the freezing point of a saturated salt and water solution at sea level. Pure water freezes at 32°F and boils at 212°F. The normal temperature for the human body is 98.6°F. The Fahrenheit scale is used primarily in the United States.

Celsius This scale was developed in 1742 by the Swedish astronomer Anders Celsius. The zero point for this scale (0°C) is the freezing point of pure water at sea level. Pure water at sea level boils at 100°C. The Celsius scale divides the span between these two points into 100 equal parts, each equal to one Celsius degree. For this reason it is also called the *centigrade scale.* The normal temperature for the human body is 37°C. The Celsius scale is standard for most people living outside of the United States and for most scientists everywhere.

NOTE: The Kelvin scale, suggested in 1848 by British physicist Lord Kelvin, is used in science and engineering. It is not a reference frame, because its zero point is not set arbitrarily but is based on the scientifically determined point at which the atoms and molecules in any substance have minimum energy. Thus there are no negative temperatures on the Kelvin scale. Pure water at sea level freezes at 273.15 K and boils at 373.15 K. The zero point of this scale (0 Kelvins or 0 K) is called absolute zero. The Kelvin interval is the same as the Celsius degree.

Thermometers have been evolving since the late sixteenth century. The first known thermometer, an inaccurate device called a thermoscope, was built by Galileo in about 1592. In 1709, D. G. Fahrenheit made an accurate thermometer using alcohol. In 1714, he built a mercury thermometer like those we use today. In 1954, U.S. Army Colonel George T. Perkins invented an electronic thermometer.

Because thermometers are used to measure[1] in reference frames, the zero point and the size of the intervals on a thermometer vary according to the temperature system(s) being used. The designs of thermometers also vary, depending on the temperature scale(s) they intend to display and the range of temperatures of interest. Common thermometers include those used for cooking (candy, deep-frying, oven), health (body parts), machines (automobile engine and climate control), and air temperature. Many thermometers have circular scales, but the straight-line scale is still popular. Thermometers with digital readouts are also available. The zero point and scale intervals are often not evident on the latter, making them less desirable as learning tools than the circular and straight-line designs.

Three common types of thermometers are described below:

Mercury or colored alcohol When the temperature rises, the volume of most liquids increases. So if a liquid is contained in a little bulb attached to a thin, straight tube with a sealed end, the liquid will rise in the tube as the temperature increases. Both alcohol and mercury are commonly used in thermometers. Mercury freezes at a little above −40°F or −40°C (the Celsius and Fahrenheit scales are equal at −40°). To display temperatures lower than that, alcohol is used. These liquid-in-glass-type thermometers are the least expensive and most popular. They are the kind we often use to determine whether we have a fever or to measure how warm or cold it is outside.

Bimetallic When the temperature rises, most solids expand, but different solids expand by different amounts. For example, brass expands about twice as much as iron when heated. If a bar is made by fastening a strip of brass next to a strip of iron, the bar will bend as the temperature rises. The bend will be toward the iron side, which expands less. If one end of the bar is fixed in place, the other end can act as a pointer on a scale. Most home thermostats contain such bimetallic thermometers.

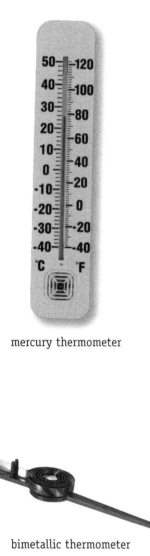

mercury thermometer

bimetallic thermometer

---

[1] Technically, one should probably not use the term *measure* to determine a number in a reference frame, since these numbers differ from actual measures. ("Locating," "establishing," or "reading" a number in a reference frame would be more proper.) Once a reference frame has been established, however, many locations are commonly treated as measures. In *Everyday Mathematics,* we follow this convention and will often refer to measuring time or a temperature and to time and temperature measurements. You and your students should do the same.

Thermocouple A thermocouple contains a loop made by joining two wires of different materials, such as copper and iron, at their ends. If the temperatures at the two joints are different, a voltage is created that is proportional to the difference. One joint is placed where the temperature is to be taken, while the other is kept at a constant lower temperature. The voltage is read by a measuring device and translated into a temperature reading.

thermometer with circular scale

Each of the above types of thermometers can be calibrated to quantify temperature in degrees Celsius or Fahrenheit.

In the early grades of *Everyday Mathematics,* students participate in various daily routines that enable them to practice reading temperatures, learn about the temperature scales, and become familiar with what various temperatures "feel" like. In first grade, the Fahrenheit temperature scale is emphasized. In the second and third grades, both Fahrenheit and Celsius scales are used.

In all grades of *Everyday Mathematics,* temperature is the context for number stories, data exploration, and graphical displays. Starting in fourth grade, students begin to use formulas, and two good examples are the formulas for converting from degrees Fahrenheit (F) to degrees Celsius (C) and vice versa:

$$C = \frac{5}{9}(F - 32) \text{ and } F = \frac{9}{5}(C + 32).$$

To find the Celsius equivalent of $72\,°F$, for example, replace F in the first formula with 72 to get

$$C = \frac{5}{9}(F - 32) = \frac{5}{9}(72 - 32) = \frac{5}{9}(40) \approx 22.$$

So $72\,°F$ is about $22\,°C$.

One must be careful about doing arithmetic with temperatures. The formulas above can be used to convert temperatures between the Fahrenheit and Celsius scales, but Fahrenheit temperatures and Celsius temperatures cannot be combined in any meaningful way. $30\,°F$ plus $20\,°C$ does not add up to anything. Temperature changes can be calculated within one scale but not across different scales. For example, knowing that it was $58\,°F$ this morning and the temperature rose 30 Fahrenheit degrees to the high for the day allows you to conclude that the high was $58 + 30 = 88$ degrees Fahrenheit.

The limitations of doing arithmetic with reference frame numbers can be a difficult concept. Although some students will grasp it intuitively, others will need to work with numerous examples over time before they understand when reference frame numbers cannot be manipulated like other numbers and when they can be meaningfully added and subtracted.

7.2 Time

As with all reference frames, locating an event or a point in time requires a zero point and a unit interval. Both of these depend on the context in which time is being examined. Calendars and

> NOTE: Pressure and volume affect the temperatures at which physical events occur. If pressure decreases, temperature decreases for a fixed volume. For example, the higher you go in elevation (where there is less air pressure), the lower the temperature you need to boil water. Increasing pressure on a fixed volume increases the temperature. This is how pressure cookers work—they cook at higher pressures and, therefore, higher temperatures.

timelines (discussed in Sections 7.2.2 and 7.2.3) help us keep track of broad expanses of time, from days to millennia. Clocks (see Section 7.2.1) help us track short-term time passage. And as with units in other reference frames, it does not always make sense to compute with numbers pertaining to time. For example, June 8 plus June 13 is not June 21; and 8:30 P.M. minus 1:20 P.M. is not 7:10 P.M. Within one reference frame, however, you can calculate elapsed time as a difference (or distance) between two times.

In Grades K–3 of *Everyday Mathematics,* students engage in many everyday activities with clocks and calendars that help them develop a "time sense" and become familiar with the language of time. Older students are expected to be comfortable with clocks and calendar reference frames; they use them as a context for number stories, investigations, and other problem-solving situations.

7.2.1 Clocks

Clock time is a reference frame with second, minute, and hour intervals that, though logical to most adults, can seem quite arbitrary and confusing to students. Learning to tell time accurately on an analog clock is one of the objectives of *K–2 Everyday Mathematics.* For older students, elapsed time is a common context for number and variable stories.

Clocks have been important in the development of many human enterprises, such as navigation, business, and science. Three important types of clocks are analog, digital, and atomic. Students of *K–3 Everyday Mathematics* practice telling time using both digital and analog clocks.

Analog Clocks Analog clocks are clocks with hands, what used to be called simply clocks before the invention of digital clocks. In general, analog refers to any system that measures a continuously changing quantity—in this case, time—with continuously varying markers of some kind. The first analog clocks may have been trees with markers showing where their shadows fell at different times during the day. These were precursors to sundials, which worked on the same principle. For thousands of years, water clocks were the standard for telling time (they worked even when the sun was down or behind a cloud). In a water clock, the water flows from one vessel to another, the flow being the analog for the time. In the late Middle Ages, the first successful mechanical clocks were constructed, a development that has thoroughly transformed our culture. Nowadays, most people use the term *analog clock* to refer to the type with hands on a round face. The first of these, with only an hour hand on it, is credited to the German inventor Henry de Vick in the 1300s. More advanced features came along in the 1700s, including minute and second hands and a pendulum. Electric analog clocks use an alternating current that vibrates sixty times per second to keep the clock on time.

Digital Clocks Digital clocks are not analog because time is not displayed in a continuous manner. Instead, every digital clock has a smallest increment of time that it displays without changing until the next increment is reached. Commonly, the increment is minutes. The clock display 10:10, for example, does not change for one minute. On some digital clocks, the colon in the time display blinks on and off once per second to indicate that time is still passing (or perhaps just to let you know the clock is still working). Most digital clocks work on alternating current.

Atomic Clocks Atomic clocks keep time according to the vibrations of atoms or molecules. The vibrations are so reliable that an atomic clock may lose or gain only a few seconds in 100,000 years. There are both analog and digital versions of atomic clocks.

7.2.2 Calendars

There are many different calendric systems, each one its own reference frame for marking the passage of time. The word *calendar* has roots in the Latin word *kalendae,* meaning "first of the month." *Kalendae,* in turn, was rooted in the word *calare,* which means "to call out solemnly." This etymology points to the importance that people have always placed on keeping track of months and marking their beginning and passing.

In the earliest times, the lunar month of 29.5 days was an important measure because of its close association with seasonal planting and harvesting schedules. Unfortunately, no whole number of lunar months coincides with a solar year of 365 days, 5 hours, 48 minutes, and 46 seconds (about 365 and one-fourth days). Twelve lunar months are 354 days; thirteen lunar months are 383.5 days. The fact that these important, naturally occurring cycles can't easily be reconciled has led to the peculiar natures of the calendar systems used throughout history. According to *The World Book Encyclopedia,* some noteworthy calendars include the following:

Babylonian This ancient Middle-Eastern calendar was based on a now-unknown zero point and a lunar month interval. The calendar had alternating 29- and 30-day months, with an extra month added three times every 8 years to make up for error.

Egyptian This ancient calendar had a zero point at the annual flooding of the Nile when the Dog Star, Sirius, first appeared. The year was broken into twelve 30-day months, with 5 days added at the end of the year. Because the extra one-fourth of a day per year wasn't accounted for, the calendar slowly got out of whack over the years. It has been calculated that the earliest recorded date on this calendar corresponds to 4236 B.C. on our current Gregorian calendar.

Roman According to legend, Romulus, the founder of Rome, introduced the earliest Roman calendar in the eighth century B.C. It came from the Greeks and was made up of 10 months and a

304-day year. The zero point was March 1 (by our current calendar). It is not clear how the other 61-odd days were accounted for. The names of eight of our current months came from the names for the ten Roman months: *Martius, Aprilis, Maius, Junius, Quintilis, Sextilis, September, October, November,* and *December.* Quintilis through December came from the numbers 5 through 10. The name *Martius* came from Mars, the Roman god of war; *Junius* from Juno, a Roman goddess; and *Maius* from Maia, a Greek goddess. It is thought that *Aprilis* may derive from the Latin word *aperire,* meaning "to open," referring to the unfolding of buds and blossoms during this month; though another possibility is from Aphrodite, the Greek goddess of love and beauty. Every two years a 22- or 23-day month was added to account for error with the solar year. Later, two more months, *Januarius* and *Februarius,* were added to the end of the year. *Januarius* was likely named from Janus, the Roman god of gates and doorways, and *Februarius* took its name from Februa, a Roman festival of purification held on the 15th day of this month.

Julian In 46 B.C. (known as the "year of confusion" because of calendar reform), Julius Caesar acted on suggestions from his astronomer Sosigenes to upgrade the Roman calendar. A system close to our own was implemented, including what we now know as the leap day in February every fourth year. To accommodate the fact that the Roman calendar was three months out of line with the seasons, Caesar made 46 B.C. 445 days long. Later, *Quintilis* was renamed July for Julius Caesar and *Sextilis* was named August to honor Emperor Augustus Caesar.

The Christian version of the Julian calendar was invented in A.D. 532 by an abbot named Dionysius Exiguus—Dennis the Short. In his plan, the Christian era was to begin January 1st of the year after Christ was born. He called the beginning year the Year of Our Lord, or Anno Domini (A.D.) 1. The Christian version of the calendar was not taken up immediately by church authorities but became widely used in Western Europe beginning in the eleventh century. The abbreviation B.C. for "Before Christ" was introduced later. As is well known, however, Dennis got the year of Christ's birth wrong. It now seems likely that Christ was born in 4 B.C., if not earlier. The abbreviations C.E. (Common Era) and B.C.E. (Before the Common Era) are sometimes used instead of A.D. and B.C.

Gregorian By 1582, the Julian calendar was off by about 10 days (because of the slight difference between $365\frac{1}{4}$ days and 365 days, 5 hours, 48 minutes, and 46 seconds); so Pope Gregory XIII dropped 10 days from October. He then decreed that February should continue to get an extra day every four years, as in the Julian calendar, except in century years that were not divisible by 400. This calendar is so accurate that, more than 400 years later, we are only about 26 seconds off. Most of the Western World uses the Gregorian calendar.

Hebrew The zero point for the Hebrew calendar is Creation, which has been calculated at 3,760 years and 3 months before the Christian era began. To find a year on the Hebrew calendar, add 3,760 or 3,761 to the year in the Gregorian calendar. (This conversion is presented as a formula in *Fifth Grade Everyday Mathematics.*) The Hebrew year is based on the moon and usually has 12 months, each 29 or 30 days long. Seven times every 19 years, an extra 29-day month is added.

Islamic The zero point for the Islamic calendar is Muhammad's flight from Mecca to Medina in A.D. 622 on the Gregorian calendar. This calendar is also lunar, with 12 months alternating between 29 and 30 days long. The months do not keep to the same seasons relative to the sun each year, and so the Islamic New Year moves backward through the seasons. Nineteen of every 30 years have 354 days each, and the other 11 years have an extra day each.

There are groups that advocate standardizing all calendars around the world. Three such calendars have been proposed: The Thirteen-Month calendar, with 13 months each 4 weeks long; the World calendar; and the Perpetual calendar. The latter two propose variations on a 12-month, 30- or 31-day-per-month design. And according to *Star Trek,* by the twenty-fourth century, the calendar will be metric.

This historical background is included for your information. You may want to share some of it with your students, who would benefit from knowing that other calendar systems exist. They also might enjoy hearing how calendars originated and have evolved.

7.2.3 Timelines

Timelines are also reference frames. They are number lines labeled with time units. Their zero points and unit intervals vary according to their purposes. A timeline designed to track the development of Earth may have "The Big Bang" as its zero point and use a large interval (millions or perhaps billions of years) to allow for a display over billions of years. A family history timeline might use generational intervals and mark its zero point with the most distant known relative. A timeline of someone's life might use the person's birth date as its zero point and track in one-year intervals corresponding to the person's age. For example, a timeline of a young child's landmarks might include such events as rolling over at about $\frac{1}{2}$ year, learning to walk at age 1, having a sibling when she was 3, and going to Kindergarten shortly after her 5th birthday. (A timeline such as this could also include numbers that refer to the Gregorian dates for the above events, for example, birth (1999), walking (2000), sibling (2002), and Kindergarten (2004), but it would not need to include these dates if birth was established as the zero point and age intervals were the specified unit.) Keep in mind that in each instance above, times "before" the chosen zero point exist. This is true with most reference frames.

You may have timelines associated with social studies or science units, or your colleagues teaching different grades may have them. If they are available and appropriate, it would be instructive to review them with your students from a reference-frame point of view. Ask, "What is the zero point? What is the unit interval? Why did they choose this zero point and these intervals for this timeline?" Students can make their own timelines to demonstrate or reinforce knowledge in other content areas—especially social studies. Because timelines are visual, they are a very useful tool for many students as they learn about history.

7.3 Coordinate Systems

For more on coordinate systems, see Section 5.9 in the Geometry essay.

Coordinate systems are reference frames in which locations are specified by one or more numbers, called coordinates. The simplest coordinate system is a number line, on which each location is fixed by only one number, or coordinate. Number lines (and their relatives, number grids and number scrolls) are discussed in Sections 7.3.1. Section 7.3.2 will discuss 2- and 3-dimensional coordinate systems.

7.3.1 One-Dimensional Coordinate Systems: Number Lines

Making a **number line** requires a **line,** an **origin** or **zero point,** and a **unit interval.** Placement of the zero point is arbitrary. The choice of a unit interval depends on the situation being represented. Starting from the zero point, **tick marks** are usually drawn at unit-interval distances, or at some multiple of the unit interval. For example, every other unit-interval point might be marked and labeled by 2s; or every half-interval point might be marked and labeled by halves. (Students are often asked to solve incomplete-number-line problems that help them understand these concepts.) Like any line, a number line extends infinitely far in two directions; a drawing can show only part of a number line.

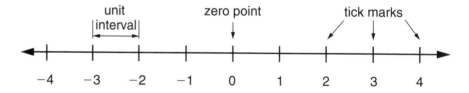

Any scale can be assigned to a number line. For example, the unit interval in the number line above could represent one mile on a map. It is also possible to have nonlinear scales on number lines. For example, slide rules and radio dials are based on logarithmic scales, which are beyond the scope of *Everyday Mathematics.*

For more on map scales, see Section 7.4.3.

The zero point on a number line need not be shown, but it must be somewhere. The zero point of the following number line is understood to lie off to the left. The broken line on the number line means that a piece of the line between 0 and 330 has been omitted. This device is often used in technical drawings to focus on important details and still show the reader that part of the object is missing. (There are a variety of broken-line symbols all meaning the same thing.)

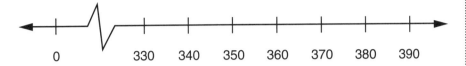

A number, or **coordinate,** can be associated with each point on a number line. Usually, coordinates of points to the right of the origin on a horizontal number line are positive, and coordinates of points to the left of the origin are negative.

Beginning in Kindergarten, students use number lines in context in counting and measuring activities. Both horizontal and vertical number lines appear. Number lines in coordinate graphing systems are introduced in third grade and are expanded upon and treated more formally in Grades 4–6. Number lines also continue to serve as one or more of the axes in data displays such as scatter plots, bar graphs, and line plots. In sixth grade, students use a real number line to order rational and irrational numbers.

Number Grids and Scrolls Number grids and scrolls are number lines with a different format. They were originally devised to manage the problem of number lines being infinitely long; number lines can be cumbersome even when stretched along a classroom wall, and it is nearly impossible to print them in books without breaking them into chunks. In *Everyday Mathematics,* number grids and scrolls are also used extensively to help students with pattern recognition and place-value concepts. Some number grid and number scroll activities that are common in *K–3 Everyday Mathematics* are described below. Some of these can be modified to reinforce more advanced numeration concepts for older students.

Number Grids

A **number grid** consists of rows of boxes, ten boxes in each row, containing consecutive whole numbers. Students are introduced to the number grid below for 0 to 110 in *First Grade Everyday Mathematics.*

									0
1	2	3	4	5	6	7	8	9	10
11	12	13	14	15	16	17	18	19	20
21	22	23	24	25	26	27	28	29	30
31	32	33	34	35	36	37	38	39	40
41	42	43	44	45	46	47	48	49	50
51	52	53	54	55	56	57	58	59	60
61	62	63	64	65	66	67	68	69	70
71	72	73	74	75	76	77	78	79	80
81	82	83	84	85	86	87	88	89	90
91	92	93	94	95	96	97	98	99	100
101	102	103	104	105	106	107	108	109	110

The grid lends itself to a number of activities that reinforce place-value concepts. By exploring the patterns in the digits in rows and columns, students discover that for a number on the number grid:

1 more is 1 square to its right.
1 less is 1 square to its left.
10 more is 1 square down.
10 less is 1 square up.

Number grids are useful as an aid for finding sums and differences. For example, to find the difference between 84 and 37, start at 37, count the number of tens going down to 77 (4 tens, or 40), and then count the ones going from 77 to 84 (7 ones, or 7). The difference between 84 and 37 is, thus, 47.

Number grids are used to explore number patterns. For example, students color the appropriate boxes as they count by 2s. If they start with 0, they will color the even numbers; if they start with 1, the odd numbers. If they count by 5s, starting at 0, they will color the boxes containing numbers with 0 and 5 in the ones place. Work with number patterns in grids helps students understand divisibility rules and factorizations in Grades 4–6.

Number grids may also be extended to negative numbers. This is especially useful when ordering negative numbers or finding differences.

a number grid puzzle

−19	−18	−17	−16	−15	−14	−13	−12	−11	−10
−9	−8	−7	−6	−5	−4	−3	−2	−1	0
1	2	3	4	5	6	7	8	9	10
11	12	13	14	15	16	17	18	19	20

Number Scrolls

A **number scroll** is an extension of a number grid. It is made by adding more single sheets of 100 numbers to existing ones—either forward (positively) or backward (negatively). Scrolls demonstrate patterns of the base-ten number system beyond 100: "101, 102, 103, ..." instead of continuing, as young students often do, with "200, 300, 400, ..." Teachers have found that many students get excited when they discover these patterns and realize the power they have of being able to write bigger and bigger numbers.

7.3.2 Two- and Three-Dimensional Coordinate Systems

Coordinate Grids Coordinate grids are reference frames defined by two or more number lines called **axes.** Axes are usually, but not always, perpendicular to each other, and intersect at a common point called the **origin.** (That is, the zero points of the axes coincide.) In a 2-dimensional coordinate grid in a plane, one axis is usually horizontal, the other vertical, and the axes usually have the same scale. A 3-dimensional coordinate grid in space begins with a coordinate grid in a plane, to which is added a third axis perpendicular to the other two, through the origin.

A major use of coordinate systems is to locate points by coordinates. On a number line, the coordinate is a single number. In a 2-dimensional coordinate system, or **coordinate plane,** points are identified by **ordered pairs** of numbers. By convention, the first number in the pair gives the position of the point along the horizontal axis. This axis is often called the **x-axis,** and the number is called the **x-coordinate.** The second number gives the position along the vertical axis. This axis is often called the **y-axis,** and the number is called the **y-coordinate.** The point (3, 2) is plotted and labeled in the drawing at the right.

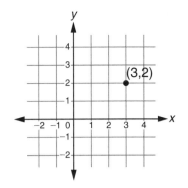
point (2,3) on a coordinate plane

Coordinate planes have many practical uses. For example, the streets in many cities and towns are laid out in a grid pattern and are sometimes numbered accordingly. Maps are also often based on coordinate planes, as is discussed in Section 7.4.

In a 3-dimensional coordinate system or **coordinate space,** points are identified by **ordered triples** of numbers. Imagine a coordinate plane with x- and y-axes on a table in front of you. Now imagine a vertical z-axis perpendicular to the coordinate plane and passing through its origin. A point in space can be identified by measuring along the x-axis, then the y-axis, and then the z-axis, in that order. The point (2, 3, 4) is plotted and labeled in the drawing in the margin. Three-dimensional coordinate spaces are beyond the scope of *Everyday Mathematics.*

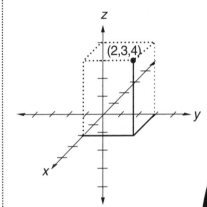
point (2,3,4) in a coordinate space

Distance on a Coordinate Grid On a number line, the difference between any two coordinates gives the **distance** between corresponding points on the line. For example, the distance from 3 to 8 on a number line is 8 − 3, or 5 units. The distance in the opposite direction, from 8 to 3, is 3 − 8, or −5 units. These are examples of **directed distance**—the positive number 5 indicates that 8 is right of 3 on the number line; the negative number −5 indicates that 3 is left of 8. Most often, however, one is interested in distance without concern for direction, and so the positive distance is used. In this case, distance is just 5 units. (Making the distance positive is an application of finding the absolute value of the difference.)

In a coordinate plane, there are two common ways to look at distance. In a city, the **practical distance** between two houses is measured along streets. So the shortest practical distance from the origin, (0, 0), to a house at (2, 2.5) is 4.5 blocks. The diagram shows one of several possible paths with length 4.5. Practical distance is sometimes called *taxicab distance.*

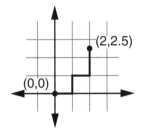
practical (taxicab) distance

For more on the Pythagorean Theorem, see Section 5.4.2 of the Geometry essay.

The **straight-line** distance between (0, 0) and the house at (2, 2.5)—or distance "as the crow flies"—does not follow streets. To calculate it requires using the Pythagorean Theorem, which is introduced in *Sixth Grade Everyday Mathematics.* In the following drawing, the length of the straight-line distance between the origin and the house is *d.* This path is the hypotenuse of a right triangle, with a horizontal leg 2 blocks long and a vertical leg 2.5 blocks long. By the Pythagorean theorem,

$$d = \sqrt{2^2 + 2.5^2} = \sqrt{10.25} \approx 3.2 \text{ blocks}$$

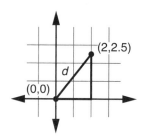

In secondary school, students will learn a general distance formula for the distance between any two points in the coordinate plane.

Coordinate Graphs Plotting points on coordinate grids is also called **coordinate graphing,** and a collection of plotted points is a **coordinate graph.** Coordinate graphing is a major topic in middle-school and high-school mathematics courses—particularly prealgebra and algebra. At these levels, graphs and tables of values are used to illustrate the behavior of functions given in equation form. Unfortunately, most first-time algebra students have had little previous experience with coordinate graphing and probably no experience at all with the relationships between stories, number models (equations and inequalities), tables of values, and graphs. *Everyday Mathematics* students will benefit from their relatively early exposure to these topics.

7.4 Maps

Maps are a common use of reference frames in *Everyday Mathematics.* Maps make use of reference frames to locate geographic points within a given region. In Kindergarten through Grade 6, mapping activities range from using maps to track steps going from room to room in the school to estimating distances between cities and towns to interpreting temperature contour maps. Maps also serve as rich supplies of ideas students can use to invent number stories.

7.4.1 Map Coordinates

Often, the reference frame for a map is a 2-dimensional, rectangular coordinate grid. One axis is usually horizontal, the other vertical; they usually have the same scale. Often, the full grid is not drawn on the map. Rather, points along each axis are labeled at the outer edges of the map. You can envision drawing horizontal and vertical lines across the page and through these points to complete the coordinate grid upon which the map is built.

For more on functions, see Sections 9.1.3, 9.1.4, 9.2, and 9.3 in the Patterns, Sequences, Functions, and Algebra essay. Also see Section 10.3 in the Problem-Solving essay.

For more on coordinate systems, see Section 7.3.2 of this essay and Section 5.9 of the Geometry essay.

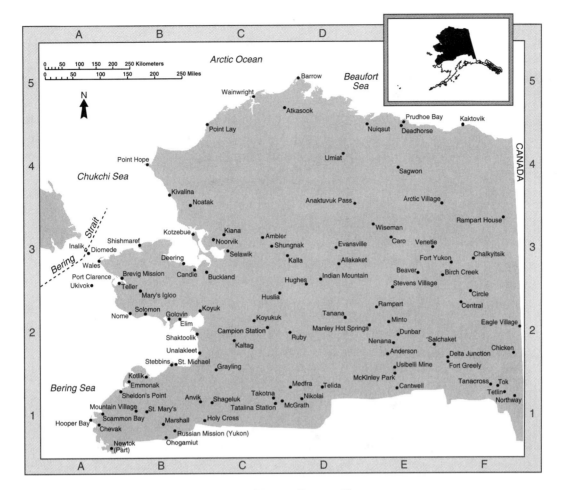

map with coordinate grid

You can easily locate a landmark on such a map according to its coordinates. For example, let's say that you know that the place you are looking for is at E4 or B3. (Many maps have an index that gives the coordinates for important locations on the map.) Find the point that is marked by the ordered pair (E, 4) or (B, 3) on the grid, and you have located that landmark (or a small region in which the landmark will be found) on the map. On the map above, Sagwon is located near (E, 4), and Deering and Shishmaref are located near (B, 3). Different maps label their coordinates differently—some with all numbers, some with letters and numbers, some with other markings. In each case, though, labels refer to points or regions within the coordinate grid.

Many cities and towns use a 2-dimensional coordinate grid to determine the address of each building in town. For example, 200 Third Avenue NE may locate a house two blocks north and three blocks east of the intersection (point zero) of two central roads in that town. Assuming that north is "up" on the vertical axis, east will be to the right of the zero point, and the position of the house could be given by the ordered pair (3, 2).

For more on 2- and 3-dimensional models, see Section 5.5.4 of the Geometry essay.

7.4.2 Contour Maps

Nearly everyone has seen temperature contours on daily weather maps in newspapers and on television. Many people have used contour maps that show elevations of mountains, hills, and valleys. Such 2-dimensional maps are much easier to produce and more convenient to put into a backpack or take to a construction job than a 3-dimensional model. With experience, a user can get as much information from a contour map as from a 3-dimensional model.

Average Yearly Precipitation in the U.S.

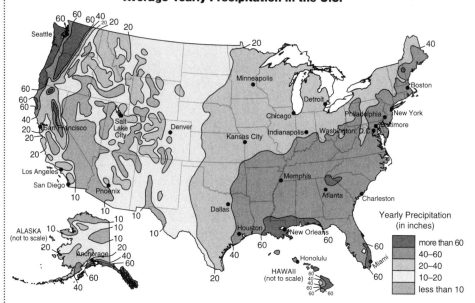

In *Fifth Grade Everyday Mathematics,* students investigate contour maps as part of the American Tour. The precipitation map above is from page 338 of the *Fifth Grade Student Reference Book.* The curves that separate the different colors are called **contour lines.** The numbers that are printed on or at the end of contour lines indicate inches of precipitation. Each contour line links points on the map with the same average annual precipitation, and so they might also be called "equal measure" or "equal value" lines.

Contour maps of the earth showing elevation above and below sea level are called **topographical maps,** meaning they show the shape of the landscape. Based on work of surveying parties led by John Wesley Powell, Ferdinand V. Hayden, and George Wheeler, the first detailed maps of the western United States were completed around 1875. The United States Geological Survey (USGS) was organized in 1879, and has been making detailed maps to the present day. On page 235 is a topographical map of part of northwest Indiana prepared by the USGS.

Most topographical maps are now made by computers, which trace contours on satellite and other aerial photographs.

See USGS internet sites http://mapping.usgs.gov and http://www.usgs.gov/index.html.

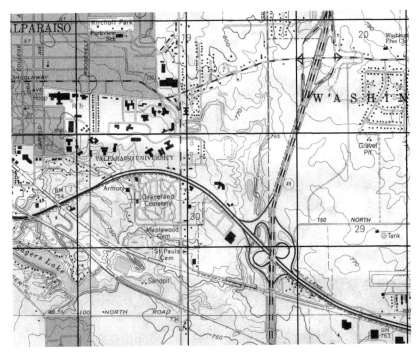

A topological map of an area in northwest Indiana

7.4.3 Map and Model Scales

A **scale** is an application of a size-change factor, usually where one of the figures is from real life and the other is a model. For example, a model train is a scaled-down version of a real train; a map is a scaled-down model of a real landscape. More precisely, a scale is a *ratio comparison*. It is a number used to quantify the relative sizes of two things being compared.

For example, a scale of 1:36,000,000 on a map means 1 map inch represents 36,000,000 real inches, or that a distance on the map is $\frac{1}{36,000,000}$ of the real distance. Note that a scale, as any ratio, has no unit. This example could be rewritten with the word *inch* replaced by *centimeter* or any other linear measure.

For clarity, scales on maps and other drawings often are accompanied by conversions. The scale in the margin (1:36,000,000) includes the phrase "One inch represents 570 miles." A student can check the accuracy of such information with a unit conversion like the following.

$$36,000,000 \text{ in.} * \frac{1 \text{ ft}}{12 \text{ in.}} * \frac{1 \text{ mi}}{5,280 \text{ ft}} \approx 568 \text{ mi}$$

Scales are often given graphically on a map, where the overall length of a line segment represents a map unit and real units are marked along the segment. You can simply mark a string (or the edge of a piece of paper) to show the length of the segment and then lay the string repeatedly on the map to determine distances in real units. Using string even allows you to follow winding roads with greater accuracy than is possible with a ruler.

scale 1:36,000,000
One inch represents 570 miles.

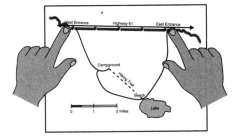

woodpecker (8 in.)
shown in $\frac{1}{4}$ scale

Other scale drawings follow conventions similar to those used in maps. For example, in architectural drawings, $\frac{1}{4}$ inch often represents 1 foot (so the scale is 1:48). A drawing of an insect might have the notation "2 times actual size," meaning that every linear measure in the drawing is twice the actual measure of the insect.

Map scales are introduced in *Third Grade Everyday Mathematics,* where students use them to estimate mileage between cities on a U.S. map. Fourth grade students review these skills and then work in the other direction to make scale drawings of their classroom. This exercise requires identifying key attributes of features in the classroom (e.g., positions of furniture, doors, and so on) and then choosing an appropriate scale to fit a drawing on a paper grid. In fifth grade, students continue to practice reading maps, and in sixth grade they work with scale in several contexts.

7.4.4 The Global Grid System

Students are introduced to the global grid system in *Fourth Grade Everyday Mathematics.* They make a model of a globe, including important grid markings, using an orange or other sphere. By applying their knowledge of geometry to construct the global grid, students develop a better understanding of the origins and functions of this reference frame.

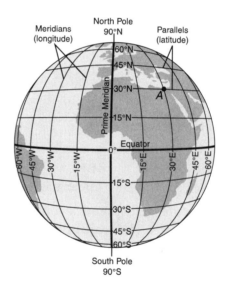

Point A is located at 30°N, 30°E.

Important components of the global grid system include the **North and South Poles, equator, prime meridian,** circles of **latitude,** and semicircles of **longitude.** Students begin by locating the North and South Poles on their spheres and drawing the equatorial circle. Then they mark the prime meridian semicircle connecting the North and South Poles and subdivide their model globes with longitude semicircles, first marking 90° quadrants and next subdividing these into 30° intervals. Students draw latitude circles parallel to the equator. They also find or describe places on the globe.

There are several important ideas to emphasize. Generally, it does not make sense to perform arithmetic operations on latitude and longitude readings. For example, it is not useful or meaningful to add the coordinates for Rome (12°E, 42°N) to those of Bombay (73°E, 18°N). As parts of a reference frame, however, global coordinates can be used for finding the distance from one point to another on a parallel or a meridian (using the measures of that frame, in this case degrees).

It is also important for students to understand that latitude is represented by complete circles in parallel planes and that longitude is represented by semicircles that are not parallel but approach each other as they near the poles. Students should also know why latitude and longitude readings must have two parts: a number of degrees and a direction with reference to the equator or prime meridian. By reconstructing the global grid system on their own models, students gain insight into the spherical geometry that ties this information together.

Estimation, Mental Arithmetic, and Fact Power

If you list everyday situations that involve arithmetic and identify the kind of answer and method of calculation that is most likely in each situation, you will probably end up with something like the following:

Situation	Kind of Answer	Most Likely Method
doubling a recipe	exact	mental arithmetic
making change	exact	mental arithmetic
deciding if you have enough money for a purchase	estimated	mental arithmetic
planning a daily schedule	estimated	mental arithmetic
balancing a checkbook	exact	calculator
computing gas mileage	estimated	mental arithmetic
comparing prices	estimated	mental arithmetic
calculating a discount percent	estimated	mental arithmetic
figuring income tax	exact	calculator
tipping	estimated	mental arithmetic

Of course, in certain situations you may seek a different kind of answer or use a different method than we have listed above, but in any case your list should reveal how common estimates and mental arithmetic are in everyday life. The practical importance of paper-and-pencil computation for daily living, never very great, is even further diminished in today's highly technological society. Sensible use of calculators and proficiency at mental arithmetic are more important than ever.

The diagram below displays six varieties of computation. The traditional school mathematics curriculum focuses almost exclusively on just one of these, obtaining exact answers with paper-and-pencil algorithms. The authors of *Everyday Mathematics* believe that students should be proficient in all six.

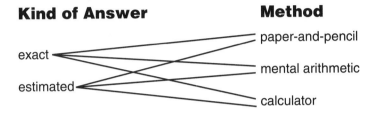

Kind of Answer   **Method**

exact

estimated

paper-and-pencil

mental arithmetic

calculator

The Algorithm essay (Essay 3) in this book discusses paper-and-pencil and calculator algorithms for finding exact answers. This essay (Essay 8) considers the other varieties of computation shown in the diagram above. The first part of the essay discusses why estimates may be necessary or desirable and how estimates may be obtained. The second part describes the *Everyday Mathematics* approach to mental arithmetic for exact and estimated answers. The last section is about basic facts, which must be mastered if facility at mental arithmetic and paper-and-pencil algorithms is to be achieved.

8.1 Estimation

Estimation is a major theme in *Everyday Mathematics* because of its importance in mathematics and everyday life. We estimate counts, measurements, and results of calculations. In practical matters, "ballpark" estimates are often as important as exact answers.

Despite its utility, many students and some adults feel that estimation is like cheating or lying. In reality, estimation is not a shoddy alternative to doing things right. Estimation requires good intuition about numbers, good understanding of problem situations, and a flexible repertoire of techniques.

The best estimators in any field are the experts in that field. Good estimation skills take years to develop but are worth striving for. Focusing on estimation can help students develop mental flexibility, good number sense, and confidence that mathematics makes sense.

The next section of this essay outlines the principal reasons for estimating. Later sections address "extreme" numbers, estimates in calculations, rounding, number sense, and mathematical connections.

NOTE: To recognize that calculators and computers have transformed the way people compute outside school is not to say that paper-and-pencil arithmetic is no longer important in the school mathematics curriculum. There are, in fact, good reasons for continuing to teach paper-and-pencil procedures for basic computations. See Section 3.1 of the Algorithms essay.

For more on using paper-and-pencil algorithms to find exact answers for addition, subtraction, multiplication and division problems, see the Algorithms essay.

NOTE: Many ideas and examples in this essay come from "Reasons for Estimating and Approximating" in *Applying Arithmetic* by Max Bell and Zalman Usiskin. *Applying Arithmetic* was published in 1983 by the University of Chicago and is available in three parts from ERIC: ED 264087, ED 264088, and ED 264089.

Educational Resources Information Center (ERIC) is a nationwide information storage and retrieval system for published and unpublished educational material.

8.1.1 Why Estimate?

Sometimes we use estimates because we must, other times because estimates are easier to understand than exact quantities, and still other times to help in solving problems.

Estimates May Be Necessary

Estimates are necessary in many situations because exact values are unobtainable.

A number may simply be unknown. Predictions about the future, guesses about the past, measurements of economic conditions, and even educated guesses about what groceries will cost are all examples of estimates necessitated by lack of precise knowledge.

A quantity may be different each time it is measured. Temperatures, populations, air pressures, and keyboarding speeds are examples of this type, as are situations involving random processes, such as the number of heads in 100 tosses of a coin.

Physical measurements are never exact. Even measures that seem exact are actually estimates, though they may be close enough for all practical purposes. For example, no sheet of paper is exactly 11 inches long, for if you look at the edge under a microscope, it will appear quite rough and uneven.

Getting an exact value may be too expensive. In many situations the numbers are so large that exact counts cannot be easily obtained. More often than not, large counts are estimated by taking samples and using statistics to generate results. Pollsters sample the viewing public to estimate how many people saw a particular TV program; they don't poll the entire television-watching public.

Decimal or fractional results may not make sense. For example, if candy bars are sold at a cost of 3 for $1, you do not pay $33\frac{1}{3}$¢ for each bar because there are no coins for fractions of pennies. Instead, you pay 34¢ for one bar and 33¢ for each of the other two bars.

Some situations require a built-in margin of error, so quantities are overestimated. For example, you overestimate the costs of items you are buying to make sure you have enough money to pay the cashier. Safety factors in new buildings are overestimated to more than meet the minimal requirements.

Numbers may not be in a form suitable for computation. For example, to add irrational numbers like $\sqrt{2}$ or π, you need to replace them with rational approximations.

In the situations above, there is no choice about whether to estimate. People who believe that estimates are inferior to exact answers are thus ignoring many situations in which it is necessary to estimate.

Estimates Are Easy to Understand

Estimates help us communicate by making numbers easier to understand.

Estimates may be clearer. A school budget of $148,309,563 for a school population of 62,772 students might be reported as "about $150 million for 63,000 students." A house on a lot whose width was surveyed as 40.13 feet would almost certainly be said to be on a "40-foot" lot. In such cases, estimates are easier to understand than more precise actual figures.

Sometimes we estimate other estimates to make them clearer. For example, the 3,849,674 square miles given in an almanac as the area of Canada is necessarily an estimate. Rounding this estimate to 3.8 million or 4 million square miles makes the measure easier to understand and communicate.

Students in *Everyday Mathematics* encounter many examples of estimates made for clarity. Many are found in the *World Tour* section of the *Fourth Grade Student Reference Book*, in the *American Tour* section of the *Fifth Grade Student Reference Book*, and in data analysis activities throughout the program.

Estimates may be used for greater consistency. Estimates for consistency are often prompted by a desire to show data uniformly in tables, charts, and graphs. For example, government unemployment reports often give a percent rounded to the nearest tenth. So, if 8 million of 99 million potential workers are unemployed, the government reports 8.1% unemployed rather than 8.08% or any closer approximation to 8.0808…%. Here an estimate is necessary because the original data are inexact, but the particular choice to report in tenths is done both to be consistent from month to month and to reflect the precision of the original data.

Results of calculations from physical measurements (all of which are estimates) should be recorded to a number of significant digits consistent with the precision of the original measurements. For example, if you measure two pieces of lumber to the nearest quarter-inch, then the sum of the two measures should be given to the nearest quarter-inch.

Sometimes the desire for consistency comes from tradition. For example, the batting average of a baseball player is found by dividing the number of hits by the number of times at bat. The answer is rounded to the nearest thousandth and is usually referred to as a percent in tables, even though it is shown as a 3-place decimal. A batting average is usually cited as if the decimal point were not there. For example, in 1941 Ted Williams made a hit in over 40 percent of his times at bat, when he hit "406" (which is usually pronounced "four oh six").

Everyday Mathematics does not emphasize the need for students to make their estimates consistent. Students see numbers all around them, however, that are written with just this goal in mind, so point out such instances when they arise.

For more on rounding, see Section 8.1.4.

NOTE: The important but difficult topic of significant digits is treated informally in *Everyday Mathematics* but is not taught explicitly. The basic idea is that computation cannot yield a result that is more precise than the least precise count or measure in the computation, as indicated by the "significant" (meaningful) digits in the counts or measures. For example, if one length is measured to the nearest centimeter (say 15 cm), another to the nearest half-centimeter (say 4.5 cm), and a third to the nearest millimeter (say 2.8 cm), their sum is best reported to the nearest centimeter (22 cm). If a rectangular wall is 3.6 meters by 4.8 meters, multiplication gives the area as 17.28 square meters. However, each dimension has only two significant digits; the area to two significant digits is 17 square meters. If the population of a city is estimated to the nearest thousand and the population of a second city to the nearest ten-thousand, the difference in population should be estimated to the nearest ten-thousand.

Estimates Can Help in Problem Solving

Estimation can be useful in solving problems, both before and after a solution is obtained. During the early phases of the problem-solving process, making an estimate can help in understanding the problem. Making an estimate helps clarify what is known and what is unknown and can provide guidance toward finding the solution. Even if an estimate near the beginning of the problem-solving process turns out to be rather inaccurate, making one can be helpful, especially for difficult problems.

Once a solution is obtained, an estimate can be useful for checking its reasonableness. Looking back over the problem-solving process is valuable, and estimating to verify the accuracy of a result is a good way to encourage such reflection. Estimating to check answers also emphasizes that results obtained in different ways should agree and, more generally, that mathematics makes sense.

8.1.2 Extreme Numbers

Students are interested in very big and very small numbers (they might be called **extreme numbers**). They appear in counts: the populations of countries, stars in galaxies, hairs on a head, cells in the brain, the national debt, and so on. They appear in measurements: distances between galaxies, years since the dinosaurs, the area of a continent, the speed of light, and so on.

Extreme numbers are difficult for most people to understand, and so relating them to familiar counts or measures can help. For example, it takes about 60 city blocks to cover one square mile. That means it would take about 6 million city blocks to cover the 104,000 square miles recorded as the area of Colorado. (104,000 square miles assumes that Colorado is flat.) Comparisons of a smaller, familiar measure to a larger, somewhat unfathomable one (and vice versa) are useful applications of the concepts of ratio comparison and similarity.

It can be difficult to compare large numbers to each other. Many people can visualize a comparison of 1 to 1,000 by comparing a 1-cm cube to a block 10 cm by 10 cm by 10 cm. Comparing 1,000,000 to 1,000,000,000, however, may not be quite as easy (unless the 1 cm cube is considered to represent 1,000,000). In Grades 4–6, students are encouraged to look at ratio comparisons of such numbers and to see 1 billion as 1,000 times 1 million—not as 1,000 more than 1 million, as many people imagine. Expressions such as "10 times as much," "10 times more (or less)," and "10 times as many (or fewer)" indicate ratio comparisons. Increasing or decreasing something by 10 times makes a big difference. Students experience an application of magnitude when examining the structure of the base-ten place-value system. Also, students are introduced to the concept of *order of magnitude* in which a ratio of two numbers is expressed as a power of 10.

NOTE: An increase in value of 10 times is sometimes called a *magnitude* by scientists. A magnitude estimate is an estimate of whether a count, measure, or result of an operation is in the tens, hundreds, thousands, ten-thousands, and so on.

For more on rate and ratio, see Section 2.1.2 in the Arithmetic Operations Essay.

Working with extreme numbers illustrates the need for estimating and approximating. Extreme numbers may need to be estimated if the things with which they are associated cannot be accurately counted or measured or if the number is a large product or a small quotient.

In third grade, students are exposed to numbers in the millions when they encounter population figures. In fourth grade, students extend the place-value system beyond millions and explore the relative sizes of millions, billions, and trillions. Students also compare big numbers by rounding to a consistent place value and by writing the results in exponential notation.

In fifth grade, students are asked to think about big numbers by using guess-and-test strategies. For example, they estimate how long it would take them to tap their fingers one million, one billion, or one trillion times. In sixth grade, students use big numbers in a project on the mathematical modeling of the solar system.

In many situations, the numbers are so large that exact counts or measurements cannot be obtained. The number of books in a large library at the end of a day is exact, but how would it be determined? How many grains of sand are on a beach? What is the population of the United States? Although the Census Bureau attempts to count every person in the United States every ten years, census takers miss people, may count incorrectly, or make other errors.

Large counts are often estimated by taking samples and using the techniques of statistics. In *Everyday Mathematics,* students explore many different ways of estimating large counts and measurements using surveys, polls, and experiments. Through class discussions, they are also encouraged to cultivate a healthy skepticism for claims that are based on such estimates.

8.1.3 Estimates in Calculations

When exact answers are not needed, we often make ballpark estimates to make calculations easier. In planning a trip and comparing costs of driving versus flying, for example, it is more realistic and easier to estimate. Your thinking might go like this: "The trip will be about 800 miles, my automobile gets about 25 miles per gallon, and gasoline costs about $1.80 per gallon; but there will be two days' extra driving and the motel will cost $80 and meals on the road about $50. On the other hand, the cheapest way to fly costs about $300, and I'll need to rent a car at the destination for five days at $60 per day…"

Even with calculators and computers taking much of the work out of computation, estimating may make things a lot easier with no important loss in the quality of the answers. In fact, answers derived using estimates may be more reasonable and more realistic than exact answers, as in planning a car trip.

Word Name	10^n
One million	10^6
One billion	10^9
One trillion	10^{12}
One quadrillion	10^{15}
One quintillion	10^{18}
One sextillion	10^{21}
One septillion	10^{24}
One octillion	10^{27}
One nonillion	10^{30}
One decillion	10^{33}
One undecillion	10^{36}
One duodecillion	10^{39}
One tredecillion	10^{42}
One quattuordecillion	10^{45}
One quindecillion	10^{48}
One sexdecillion	10^{51}
One septendecillion	10^{54}
One octodecillion	10^{57}
One novemdecillion	10^{60}
One vigintillion	10^{63}
One googol	10^{100}
One googolplex	10^{googol}

NOTE: Add the suffix -*th* to any of the word names to name the corresponding very small number. For example, 10^{-18} is "one quintillionth."

Brief Times	Seconds
One millisecond	10^{-3}
One microsecond	10^{-6}
One nanosecond	10^{-9}
One picosecond	10^{-12}
One femtosecond	10^{-15}
One attosecond	10^{-18}

In situations where exact answers are required and a calculator is used to find them, estimation can help check the results. Most of us have heard the story about the cashier at the fast-food restaurant who entered the price for an item incorrectly but couldn't tell that the total was incorrect. This story is often used to support the argument that people depend too much on machines and, therefore, that calculators should be banned from the classroom and students should master the traditional paper-and-pencil algorithms.

This argument misses the point entirely. Few people would want the cashier to stop using a machine and do the work on paper. What the cashier needs are estimation skills to check whether the machine total was reasonable. If it wasn't, then it should have been recalculated. In the cashier's defense, most traditional mathematics curricula don't teach estimation skills in conjunction with arithmetic operations. In fact, such skills are sometimes reviled as being merely trial and error. *Everyday Mathematics,* on the other hand, sees them as an integral component of a comprehensive and balanced approach to computation. Students are encouraged to compute either exactly or approximately, working mentally, with paper and pencil, or with a calculator, depending on what is most appropriate for each situation.

In Grades 4–6, students use estimation to forecast sums and differences, extending the practice to bigger and smaller numbers than the ones they encountered in earlier grades. They also estimate products, quotients, and powers, beginning with simple activities, such as making magnitude estimates that predict whether a product is in the thousands, ten-thousands, hundred-thousands, and so on. Students should use calculators extensively to find exact products and quotients of multidigit numbers. A general awareness of the magnitude of the results is especially important in providing a check for calculator computations.

Everyday Mathematics students encounter estimation in division informally and naturally through probability activities. These are often used to estimate the likelihood of future events. Students predict events in two different ways. First, they make educated guesses about common events such as how a coin might land and test their guesses with experiments. Second, they use data collection techniques and concepts from statistics and probability when predicting answers to less intuitive questions, such as: What might a population or wage be in the future? In *Fifth Grade Everyday Mathematics,* such estimation problems are presented as periodic challenges.

8.1.4 Rounding

Estimation is a reasoned guess at an unknown or unknowable value. Rounding is an algorithm for approximating known numbers. Usually, we round either up or down to a number that is close to a known number but easier to understand or work with, where "close" and "easier" are determined by the context of a problem.

Students in *Everyday Mathematics* often round when they deal with large numbers. For example, as part of the World Tour in Grade 4, students are asked to critically evaluate and use big numbers given for populations and land or water areas. Many times, numbers need to be rounded to a common place for ease of comparison or simply to make the numbers easier to understand or talk about. After rounding, power-of-ten or scientific notation can be used to further simplify reading, writing, and comparing the numbers.

All calculators round decimals to fit the display screen. Calculators capable of scientific notation may also round whole numbers. Most calculators round to the nearest place, but some older ones always round down. Almost all calculators hold more digits accurately in memory than they display. Understanding the principles and effects of rounding is important when using a calculator.

Some calculators have a **fix** option that enables you to fix the number of decimal places displayed to the right of the decimal point. For example, keying in [FIX] [0.01] would result in all numbers being rounded and displayed to the nearest hundredth.

An algorithm for rounding numbers to the nearest value of a given decimal place, taught in Grades 4–6, is shown in the following table.

> NOTE: You are probably familiar with the term *rounding* in the sense of rounding numbers to specified places. Although rounding is an important skill, it is even more important to develop good judgment about how precise an estimate is possible or reasonable in various circumstances.

For more on calculators, see Section 3.4 of the Algorithms essay.

Here is an algorithm to round a number to a given place:	Example 1: Round 4,538 to the nearest hundred	Example 2: Round 26,781 to the nearest thousand	Example 3: Round 5,295 to the nearest ten	Example 4: Round 3.573 to the nearest tenth
Step 1: Find the digit in the place you are rounding to.	4,538	26,781	5,295	3.573
Step 2: Rewrite the number, replacing all digits to the right of this digit with zeros. This is the lower approximation.	4,500	26,000	5,290	3.500
Step 3: Add 1 to the digit in the place you are rounding to. If the sum is 10, write 0 and add 1 to the digit to its left. This is the higher approximation.	4,600	27,000	5,300	3.600
Step 4: Is the original number closer to the lower approximation or to the higher approximation?	lower approximation	higher approximation	halfway	higher approximation
Step 5: Round to the closer of two numbers. If it is halfway between the higher and the lower number, round to the higher number.	4,500	27,000	5,300	3.600 = 3.6

Rounding is often used to make estimation easier, as in the following example:

You want to buy 4 cans of tennis balls that cost $2.59 a can. Estimate the least number of dollar bills you need in order to pay for your purchase.

Solution 1: Rounding up to $3 per can, a reasonable estimate for the cost of 4 cans is 4 * $3 = $12. Since you rounded up, however, you will definitely not need more than $12. So 12 $1 bills will be enough.

Solution 2: Rounding down to $2.50, a closer estimate to the cost of 4 cans is $11, because 4 * $2.50 = $10. However, 4 * $2.59 is a bit more than $10, so you will need at least 11 $1 bills.

Which solution is right? Both are good applications of rounding. Although the second solution is closer to the exact cost, it is not necessarily a better estimate. Both solutions might be suggested and then compared to each other. A discussion may show that to estimate a calculation to a nearest dollar, you don't necessarily want to round to the nearest dollar first.

8.1.5 Estimation, Number Sense, and Mathematical Connections

Students should be encouraged to estimate answers in problem situations in which exact solutions are unnecessary. Because students are often uncomfortable with estimates, it is important to discuss the differences between exact and estimated answers and to identify situations in which an estimate is good enough or even makes more sense than an exact answer. For example: "I have 75¢. I want to buy an eraser for 29¢ and a notebook for 39¢. Do I have enough money?" Sharing strategies can help students develop their estimation skills. Students should become aware that there is no single "correct" estimate; the purpose of estimation is to find a reasonable answer, not the exact answer.

At the beginning of each school year, it is recommended that in addition to the basic lessons, you set aside at least two 10–15 minute periods each week for this kind of interaction. Continue until students feel comfortable sharing their strategies and are able to talk about them fluently and to listen to one another attentively.

It is perhaps the single greatest goal of *Everyday Mathematics* that students completing the program acquire number sense. People with **number sense:**

• Have good mental arithmetic skills as well as reliable algorithms and procedures for finding results they can't produce mentally;

• Are flexible in thinking about numbers and arithmetic and will look for "shortcuts" to make their efforts as efficient as possible;

• Can use their number and arithmetic skills to solve problems in everyday situations;

- Are familiar with a variety of ways to communicate their strategies and results; and

- Can recognize unreasonable results when they see them in their own work, in everyday situations, or in the media.

Number sense develops only with wide mathematical experience, including instruction and practice in specific techniques. But good number sense also depends on attitudes and beliefs, especially the belief that mathematics makes sense. That is, people with good number sense expect their mathematical knowledge to connect with the rest of what they know, including their common sense and whatever they know about the situation at hand. Number sense thus depends on making connections between various kinds of mathematical knowledge and between mathematics and other subjects.

Everyday Mathematics helps students develop number sense in the contexts of data analysis, geometry, and elementary explorations of functions and sequences. In *Everyday Mathematics,* students make connections across mathematical topics and come to view mathematics as a coherent, consistent discipline, rather than a hodge-podge of disconnected procedures and skills.

Number sense also involves making connections between mathematics and other subjects in the curriculum. Many activities in *Everyday Mathematics* are designed to show how number sense applies to science, social studies, and geography. Throughout *Everyday Mathematics* there are connections between mathematics and history, including both the history of mathematics and how mathematics has shaped human endeavors.

Finally, *Everyday Mathematics* connects mathematics to the community through efforts to share with parents the authors' commitment to number sense. Family Letters explain how *Everyday Mathematics* introduces students not only to the traditional mathematics parents expect but also to a richer mathematics curriculum that older family members may not have experienced. Study Links enable parents to see the kinds of mathematics their students do in school and pass along some interesting ideas for parent involvement as well.

8.2 Mental Arithmetic

Although people frequently associate mental arithmetic with estimation, it is also useful for finding exact answers. In many situations, an exact answer is required but no tools are readily available. In such situations, mental arithmetic is the most convenient alternative. Even most paper-and-pencil computation involves mental arithmetic for exact answers. Paper-and-pencil division, for instance, is likely to require addition, multiplication, and subtraction, much of which is done mentally.

In *Everyday Mathematics,* students practice mental arithmetic to learn useful techniques, to develop flexible thinking, and to gain fact power. These skills contribute to students' number sense, which includes a flexible understanding both of numbers and of operations on those numbers. *Everyday Mathematics* emphasizes number sense because calculators and computers have actually increased the importance of estimation and mental arithmetic. Complicated paper-and-pencil computation has become relatively less important, while mental arithmetic and skillful use of calculators have become relatively more important. *Everyday Mathematics* reflects this shift.

An important part of being a flexible problem solver is to add continually to a personal toolkit of mental arithmetic skills. Some of these mental arithmetic skills should become automatic so they can be used reflexively, almost without thinking.

NOTE: Of these reflexive skills, the most important is automatic recall of the basic addition and multiplication facts, what *Everyday Mathematics* calls *fact power.*

For more on fact power, see Section 8.3.

Mental arithmetic skills are developed throughout the *Everyday Mathematics* curriculum as an integral part of the program. In Kindergarten through Grade 3, *Minute Math* and *Minute Math +* provide many activities for practicing mental arithmetic and problem-solving skills. Whenever students use calculators, they must verify that the calculator answer makes sense, or they may estimate an answer before using the calculator. Each lesson in first through sixth grades begins with a brief set of oral or slate exercises called Mental Math and Reflexes.

Perhaps the most important part of the process is to have students share their solution strategies after they solve a problem. Sharing strategies requires students to verbalize their thinking, thus making them conscious of a process that is often intuitive. Students also get insights into alternative approaches from their fellow students, sharpen their mental arithmetic skills, and develop creative and flexible thinking processes. Most importantly, students learn that common sense applies to mathematics and that they can solve difficult problems by thinking things through for themselves. Strategy sharing is vitally important throughout *Everyday Mathematics.*

There are many strategies and techniques for mental arithmetic. Some are formally introduced in *Everyday Mathematics;* students develop others on their own. The main goals are for students to be exposed to many techniques, to learn how they work, to master a few, and to build some into reflexes. A few examples of strategies follow. All may be justified mathematically, but we describe them here briefly in terms you may hear in the classroom.

Round

Techniques include rounding to the nearest ten, hundred, thousand, and so on, as appropriate, and computing with rounded numbers. For example, 647 + 284 is approximately 600 + 300 = 900, or perhaps 650 + 280 = 930.

Adjust the Numbers

A sum is unchanged if one addend is increased by a given amount and the other addend is decreased by the same amount. For example, $86 + 37 = 90 + 33 = 123$. This might be called the "Opposite Change Rule for Addition."

A similar rule is the "Same Change Rule for Subtraction," which states that a difference is unchanged if the same amount is added to or subtracted from the original numbers—the minuend and subtrahend. For example, $54 - 37 = 57 - 40 = 17$.

Look for Easy Combinations

For example, in $17 + 25 + 3 + 15$, add 3 to 17 ($= 20$) and 15 to 25 ($= 40$). So $17 + 25 + 3 + 15 = 20 + 40 = 60$.

Estimate, Then Adjust

An approximate answer is obtained first and then adjusted to make it more accurate. For example, $647 + 284$ is approximately $640 + 280$ ($= 920$); add $7 + 4$ ($= 11$) to that ($= 931$).

For Multiplication of Whole Numbers (only), Attach Zeros

To multiply by a multiple of 10, 100, 1,000, …, multiply the nonzero part of the factors and append as many zeros to the result as there are zeros in the factors.

For Division of Whole Numbers (only), Cross Out Zeros

To divide multiples of 10, 100, 1,000, …, cross out the same number of ending zeros in the divisor as in the dividend.

Estimate Magnitude

As a useful check for answers found another way, ask: Is a reasonable answer in the tens? Hundreds? Thousands? …

Quick Division by a Single-Digit Number

Break up the dividend into a sum of extended facts of the divisor.

For example, to calculate $364 / 7$ mentally:

Break up 364 into extended 7s facts:	$364 = 350 + 14$
Divide each part:	$364 / 7 = (350 / 7) + (14 / 7)$
	$= 50 + 2$
Add the results:	$= 52$

Note that quick division is an application of the distributive property. The strategy also works for problems that do not divide evenly. For example, to calculate $727 / 4$:

Break up 727 into extended 4s facts:	$727 = 400 + 320 + 7$
Divide each part:	$727 / 4 = (400 / 4) + (320 / 4) + (7 / 4)$
	$= 100 + 80 + 1\ 3 / 4$
Add the results:	$= 181\ 3 / 4$

For more on divisibility, see Section 1.2 of the Numeration and Order essay.

Miscellaneous Strategies

There are many other useful strategies. For example:

- To multiply a whole number by 10, append one zero to the result; to multiply by 100, append two zeros; ....

- To multiply a decimal by 10, move the decimal point one place to the right; to multiply a decimal by 100, move the decimal point two places to the right; ....

- To divide a decimal by 10, move the decimal point one place to the left; to divide a decimal by 100, move the decimal point two places to the left; ....

- To rename a decimal as a percent, move the decimal point two places to the right and append a percent sign; reverse the process to rename a percent as a decimal.

- To multiply a whole number by 5, multiply by 10 and find half of the result.

- To determine whether a number is divisible by 3, find the sum of its digits. If the sum is divisible by 3, then the number is divisible by 3. For example, 117 is divisible by 3, because the sum of the digits, 9, is divisible by 3. 117 is also divisible by 9 because the sum of the digits is divisible by 9.

- To multiply a two-digit number by 11, add the two digits and write the sum between the two digits. For example:

To find 11 * 34, add the two digits in 34 and place the sum between the 3 and 4.

$$3 + 4 = 7, \text{ so } 11 * 34 = 374.$$

To find 11 * 69, add the two digits in 69. Since $6 + 9 = 15$, add 1 to the first digit and place the 5 between 7 and 9. So 11 * 69 = 759.

8.3 Fact Power

"Knowing" the basic number facts is as important to learning mathematics as "knowing" words by sight is to reading. This has not gone unnoticed. Benjamin Bloom has written at length on the importance of automaticity as part of any complex talent; Max Bell has long emphasized the importance of number-fact reflexes; and Pamela Ames makes an analogy between number facts and finger exercises for the piano. Students are often told that habits—good and bad—come from doing something over and over until they do it without thinking. Developing basic number-fact reflexes can be likened to developing good habits.

In *Everyday Mathematics,* good fact habits are referred to as **fact power.** Students in Grades 1–3 keep Fact Power tables of the facts they know. By the end of the school year, most second graders should master the addition and subtraction facts. In third and fourth grades, the emphasis shifts to learning the multiplication and division facts. Although some students may not be able to demonstrate mastery of all these facts, they should be well on their

way to achieving this goal by the end of
fourth grade. Our expectations for the basic
number facts are shown in the table at the
right.

8.3.1 Key Reflexes

Students in *Everyday Mathematics* are
expected to develop other mathematical
reflexes, beyond fact power, that will serve
them in school mathematics and everyday
life. By the end of Grade 6, students are
expected to have well-grounded, automatic
responses in the following areas:

- Recalling arithmetic facts;
- Rounding, estimating, and doing simple
  mental arithmetic;
- Computing with 10, 100, 1,000, and other
  powers of 10;
- Finding many equivalent names for
  fractions;
- Identifying equivalencies between
  important fractions, decimals, and
  percents, especially halves, thirds, fourths,
  eighths, and other fractions found in
  everyday situations;
- Manipulating symbols in algebraic
  expressions and equations.

The following are useful skills but are not stressed in the program:

- Naming squares of whole numbers through 15;
- Giving approximations for the square roots of 2, 3, and 5;
- Naming multiples of 11, 12, 15, 20, and 25.

8.3.2 Practice

Practicing the facts is often tedious and traditionally involves many
pages of drill-and-practice problems. In *Everyday Mathematics,*
most fact practice is in the form of choral drills, games, and puzzles.
Teachers have had success with the following alternative methods
that avoid much of the tedium associated with building fact power.

Number Games

Many games are suggested in which numbers are generated by dice,
dominoes, number cards, spinners, egg-carton shakers, or other
random-number generators. Fact-power games help in the learning
of the basic facts. For conversions between fractions, decimals, and
percents, students play *Frac-Tac-Toe* on gameboards showing a
variety of related fractions, decimals, and percents. It is hoped that
you will supplement these games with some of your own.

Everyday Mathematics
Expectations for Basic Facts

	grade level				
	K	1	2	3	4
Addition					
easy facts	b	d/s	s		
hard facts		b/d	d/s		
Subtraction					
easy facts	b	d/s	s		
hard facts		b	d/s		
Multiplication					
easy facts			b	d/s	s
hard facts			b	d/s	s
Division					
easy facts			b	d/s	s
hard facts				b/d	d/s

B Beginning. Most children are learning the meaning of the
operation and are developing strategies for solving facts.
Basic-fact work occurs most often in problem contexts.
There is no emphasis on speed.

D Developing. Most children are learning efficient ways to
answer fact problems, including recall from long-term
memory and other strategies. Speed practice might be
appropriate for many children.

S Secure. Although a few children may be slower on some
facts, most children have achieved automatic recall.

50-Facts Multiplication Drills

In fourth grade, students take part in a multiplication facts drill on a regular basis. They take a one-minute, 50-item test about every third week and graph their scores. The tests encourage students to practice their multiplication facts at home. The drill routine also includes exposure to graphing, fractions, and percents.

Labels

Because numbers in real life nearly always occur in some context, *Everyday Mathematics* recommends that you frequently remind your students to think of labels for the numbers they are working with. The kind and number of labels you need depend on the operation. In addition and subtraction, only one label is needed. For example, if you think of the label "boxes," the problem $7 + 9 = ?$ becomes 7 boxes + 9 boxes = 16 boxes.

In multiplication and division, two or three related labels are needed. For example, for the problem $5 * 8 = ?$, you might choose the labels "boxes," "pounds per box," and "pounds." Then the problem becomes 5 boxes * 8 pounds per box = 40 pounds. (5 boxes, each weighing 8 pounds, weigh a total of 40 pounds.)

In some instances, the factors in multiplication have the same label. For example, for area, 5 feet * 8 feet = 40 square feet; on the other hand, 5 hats * 8 hats does not make sense.

Labels can be true-to-life or fanciful, serious or just plain silly. They can be units of measure (centimeters, minutes, pounds) or objects (cats, hats, ribbons). Although the main purpose for using labels is to keep numbers from becoming too abstract, labels are also important in other curriculum areas, especially in science.

Fact Families

The authors of *Everyday Mathematics* have found that young students not only can understand the inverse relationships between arithmetic operations (addition "undoes" subtraction, multiplication "undoes" division, and vice versa), they can often "discover" them on their own. A fact family is a collection of four related facts linking two inverse operations. For example, the following four equations symbolize the fact family relating 3, 4, and 12 by multiplication and division.

$$3 * 4 = 12 \qquad 4 * 3 = 12 \qquad 12 / 3 = 4 \qquad 12 / 4 = 3$$

You may recognize that the two multiplication facts in this family are instances of the commutative property of multiplication. Although *Everyday Mathematics* does not require students to learn mathematical names for properties, occasionally it is handy to have some name to use. The **turn-around rule for multiplication** is the name used in *Everyday Mathematics* for the commutative property of multiplication. From a practical point of view, the turn-around rule means that any time you learn a new multiplication fact, you get a second one for free! Note that there is no turn-around rule for either subtraction or division; for example, $7 - 4 \neq 4 - 7$ and $12 / 4 \neq 4 / 12$.

For more on basic fact families, including Fact Triangles, see page 50 of the Management Guide essay.

A major reason for teaching fact families is to give students ways to solve problems that may seem new or difficult by rewording or rewriting one of the facts in the family. For example, faced with 56 / 8 = ?, a fourth grader may think, "Hmm, I don't know. What times 8 is 56? Ah, that's easy! It's 7."

Students start to learn the basic multiplication and division facts and fact families in *Second Grade Everyday Mathematics*. In all grades, new facts are usually introduced through concrete manipulations, drawings, games, and connections to previously known facts.

Fact Extensions

Fact extensions are powerful mental arithmetic strategies for all operations with larger numbers. They appear in first grade and are extended throughout the program. For example, if students know 3 + 4 = 7, they also know 30 + 40 = 70, and 300 + 400 = 700.

If students know 6 * 5 = 30, they also know 60 * 5 = 300, 600 * 5 = 3,000, 3,000 ÷ 600 = 5, and so on.

8.3.3 Games

Frequent practice is necessary for students to build and maintain strong mental-arithmetic skills and reflexes. Although drill has its place, much of the practice in *Everyday Mathematics* is in game format. Games are not an attractive add-on: they are an essential component of the complete *Everyday Mathematics* program.

Drill and games should not be viewed as competitors for class time, nor should games be thought of as time-killers or rewards. In fact, games satisfy many, if not most, standard drill objectives—and with many built-in options. Drill tends to become tedious and, therefore, gradually loses its effectiveness. Games relieve the tedium because students enjoy them. Indeed, students often wish to continue to play games during their free time, lunch, and even recess.

Drill exercises aim primarily at building fact and operation skills. Practice through games shares these objectives, but at the same time, games often reinforce calculator skills, logical thinking, geometric intuition, and intuition about probability and chance (because many games involve numbers that are generated randomly).

Using games to practice number skills also greatly reduces the need for worksheets. Because the numbers in most games are generated randomly, the games can be played over and over without repeating the same problems. Many of the *Everyday Mathematics* games come with variations that allow players to progress from easy to more challenging versions. Games practice, therefore, offers an almost unlimited source of problem material.

Patterns, Sequences, Functions, and Algebra

Patterns can be found in sounds, in movements, in shapes, in numbers, in graphs, in data. Indeed, patterns can be found almost anywhere. Patterns are especially important in mathematics. Some people even define mathematics as the science of patterns.

Most of mathematics deals with patterns that are predictable. This means objects, colors, or numbers that are arranged so that you can predict what comes next. You can "see" or continue such patterns, and in many cases, it is possible to find a rule that underlies a given pattern. The first part of this essay deals with such patterns, including sequences and functions.

The second part of the essay begins with a description of the origin of common arithmetic symbols. This leads to a discussion of number models and number sentences, including open number sentences.

The essay ends with a discussion of variables and solving open number sentences. In keeping with the *Everyday Mathematics* emphasis on multiple solution methods, several approaches are outlined.

Patterns and algebra are closely related. Pattern tasks involve many mathematical processes that are fundamental in algebra. Among these are looking for patterns; making, testing, and proving conjectures about patterns; and representing patterns in several ways. Looking for patterns helps students develop modeling skills, which are crucial to many applications of algebra. By making and justifying conjectures about patterns, students develop habits of generalization and verification that will serve them well in algebra and beyond. Finally, working with multiple representations for functions—function machines, tables, rules, graphs, words, and symbols—will help students build the conceptual understandings that will eventually support the symbol-manipulation skills so necessary for success in algebra.

9.1 Patterns, Sequences, and Functions

Most of the patterns in *Everyday Mathematics* are either visual patterns or number patterns.

The program includes many activities involving visual patterns. Many of these activities help students focus on geometric properties of shapes. These visual patterns are discussed in other sections of this manual. For example, pattern-based classifications of polygons are discussed in the Geometry essay. Visual patterns in graphs are discussed in the essay on Data and Chance.

In the following sections, most of the attention is on number patterns and the arithmetic rules that generate them. We especially focus on two types of number patterns that are so important throughout mathematics that they have names: functions and sequences. Mathematics provides us with a rich set of tools for examining these patterns concretely, symbolically, and visually.

For more on classification of polygons, see Section 5.4.2 of the Geometry essay. For more on patterns, see Sections 4.1.4 and 4.2.3 of the Data and Chance essay.

9.1.1 Number Patterns

For centuries people have studied number patterns in a branch of mathematics called **number theory**. In this section we address perhaps the simplest of these patterns, odd and even numbers.

Odd and even numbers are simple but can lead to generalizations that are genuinely mathematical and are of fundamental importance in number theory. For example, it is easy to observe that odd numbers of things always have one left over after pairing. Building on this simple observation, some students discover relationships such as the following:

- The sum of any two even numbers is even (there are no leftover pieces).
- The sum of an even number and an odd number is odd (the leftover piece remains).
- The sum of any two odd numbers is even (the leftovers pair up).

If *difference* is substituted for *sum* above, the statements are still true. That is, the difference of any two even numbers is even, and so on.

Similar relationships exist for the products and quotients of odd and even numbers, though students are less likely to discover these relationships on their own, particularly for division. A product is even if at least one of the factors is even. If none of the factors is even, then the product will be odd. For example, $3 * 7 * 5$ will be odd since all the factors are odd. $27 * 3 * 4$ will be even since one of the factors is even.

Division is a bit trickier. A quotient will be even if the dividend is "more even" than the divisor; otherwise the quotient will be odd. For example, 12 / 6 is even since 12 has two 2s (12 = 2 * 2 * 3) and 6 has only one 2 (2 * 3 = 6). But 24 / 8 is odd since both 24 and 8 have three 2s (24 = 2 * 2 * 2 * 3 and 8 = 2 * 2 * 2). Note that this discussion assumes the quotient "comes out even." Odd and even do not apply when there is a remainder.

Odd numbers of people or things are often seen as a nuisance. If there is an odd number of people, it is impossible to get the same number on each of two teams. Similarly, an odd number of objects that cannot be broken apart, such as marbles, cannot be shared equally by two people. On the other hand, it is easier to find the middle value (median) of an odd number of measurements, such as heights and weights, because with an even number of data points, there is no single middle value.

Making generalizations based on observations of patterns is fundamental to mathematics and science, and so when students discover and "prove" simple relationships about odd and even numbers, they are learning powerful ways of thinking that will serve them throughout their mathematical careers.

9.1.2 Sequences

A number sequence is a list of numbers. Many sequences are important enough to have names:

- whole numbers: 0, 1, 2, 3, 4, 5, 6, ...
- odd numbers: 1, 3, 5, 7, 9, 11, ...
- even numbers: 2, 4, 6, 8, 10, 12, ...
- prime numbers: 2, 3, 5, 7, 11, 13, ...
- square numbers: 1, 4, 9, 16, 25, 36, ...

Sequences of numbers, in a way, are similar to visual patterns in that both number sequences and shape or color sequences often have a rule that governs what the next number or object in the sequence is. For number sequences, the rule usually involves one or more arithmetic operations. The counting numbers, for example, can be generated by starting with 1 and repeatedly applying the rule "Add 1." The even numbers can be generated by starting at 2 and applying the rule "Add 2."

Many number sequences can be linked to visual patterns. The square numbers, for example, can be modeled by a sequence of square arrays. The even numbers and triangular numbers can also be modeled by sequences of dot shapes. The interplay of number sequences and visual patterns is fertile ground for investigations in elementary school mathematics.

Heights (in inches):
48 48 49 51 51 52 54

median = 51 inches

Weights (in pounds):
65 68 70 72 73 75

median = (70 + 72) / 2
= 71 pounds

For more on landmarks, see Section 4.1.4 in the Data and Chance essay.

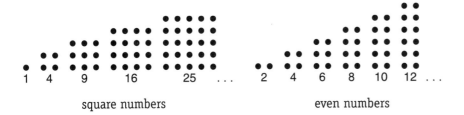

square numbers   even numbers

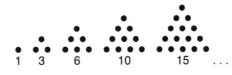

triangular numbers

Patterns in many number sequences are accessible to students of any age. Starting in *Kindergarten Everyday Mathematics,* students use Frames-and-Arrows diagrams to make up or complete sequences or to find the rule for a given sequence. (A sequence may be governed by more than one rule.) In the early grades, students also begin filling in missing numbers on a number line. In later grades, these number-line activities are extended to sequences of fractions, decimals, and negative numbers, as shown in the following examples:

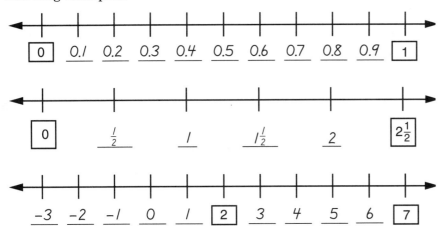

As this work with number lines is carried on, students will discover a rather amazing fact: that between any two points (numbers) on the number line, at least one more point (number) can always be found.

9.1.3 Functions

Function is one of those everyday words that mathematicians use in a special way. Later in this section we will explain the mathematical definition of *function,* but first we want to outline how *Everyday Mathematics* approaches this powerful idea in ways that even kindergartners can understand.

Function Machines

Perhaps the best initial metaphor for understanding functions is the function machine. A function machine is an imaginary device that receives inputs and generates outputs. In the margin, for example, is a function machine that doubles any number put into it.

For more on number lines, see Sections 1.3, 1.4, 1.6, 1.7, and 1.9 in the Numeration and Order essay.

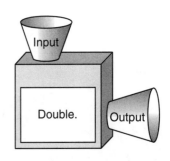

One can imagine putting a number into this machine, waiting a moment, and then getting another number out. For example, if 1 is put in, then 2 will come out. If 5 is put in, then 10 will come out. Whatever number goes in, twice that number will come out.

The inputs and outputs from a function machine can be recorded in a table. Each line in the table is an ordered pair in which the first number is the input and the second number is the output. Here is a table for the doubling function machine.

Rule: Double	
Input	Output
1	2
2	4
3	6
5	10
638	1276

doubling function

One important feature of a function machine is that it should always give the same output for a given input number. If two rows in an input-output table have the same number in the input column, then they must also have the same number in the output column.

Note It is not required that every input number have a different output number. Often this is the case—it is for the doubling machine above, for example—but not always. For example, a function machine might always output the same number, no matter what is put in. Such functions are called constant functions and are perfectly legitimate, if a bit dull.

Rule: Always output 3	
Input	Output
1	3
2	3
3	3
5	3
638	3

constant function

The function machine metaphor captures the key features of the functions that are studied in pre-college mathematics: There is a set of inputs, a set of outputs, and a rule associating each input with exactly one output.

In the first four grades, *Everyday Mathematics* uses function machines and tables of values to study functions. Function machines help students visualize how a rule associates each input value with an output value. A principal activity for developing this concept further is called "What's My Rule?"

"What's My Rule?"

In a "What's My Rule?" problem, two of the three parts (input, output, and rule) are known. The goal is to find the unknown part. There are three basic kinds of problems.

1. The rule and some input numbers are known. Find the corresponding output numbers.

Rule: +10	
In	Out
39	
54	
163	

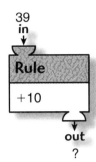

2. The rule and some output numbers are known. Find the corresponding input numbers.

Rule: −6	
In	Out
	6
	10
	20

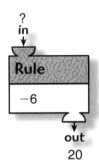

3. Some input and output numbers are known. Find the rule.

Rule: ?	
In	Out
55	60
85	90
103	108

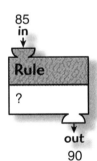

You can combine more than one type of problem in a single table. For example, you could give a partially completed table with an unknown rule. If you give enough input and output clues, students can fill in blanks as well as figure out the rule, as in the problem below.

Rule: ?	
In	Out
15	25
4	14
7	
	63

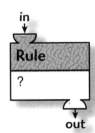

What Is a Function?

Like many ideas in mathematics, the concept of a function is simple yet powerful. Also like many ideas in mathematics, the definition of *function* seems at first to be rather odd. According to a dictionary of mathematics, "A function is a set of ordered pairs (x, y) in which each value of x is paired with exactly one value of y." A few examples may help clarify what this means:

- doubling: {(1, 2), (2, 4), (3, 6), (4, 8), ...}
- squaring: {(1, 1), (2, 4), (3, 9), (4, 16), ...}
- adding 1: {(1, 2), (2, 3), (3, 4), (4, 5), ...}

In each of these sets of ordered pairs, the first number is paired with exactly one second number. According to the definition, then, each of these sets is a function.

This definition includes all the functions discussed so far in this essay, but you will note that there is no mention of a rule. The pairings in a function don't have to follow any rule; the only requirement is that each first value be paired with exactly one second value. If, for example, you matched every number less than 100 with a randomly chosen number less than 100, then you would have a function.

- a function with no rule: {(1, 82), (2, 15), (3, 74), ..., (99, 17), (100, 92)}

Such a function isn't very useful, but it is still a legitimate function. A more interesting example of a function with no rule is one that takes a date as the input and gives the closing price of IBM stock as the output. If you could find a rule for such a function, you could get rich. Unfortunately, economists have proved no such rule can exist because if such a rule did exist, someone would figure it out, use it to make money, and in the process invalidate the rule. The only way to find the closing price of IBM is to wait and see what it is.

Don't worry too much about functions without rules. Most interesting functions are interesting precisely because they do have rules. All the functions in *Everyday Mathematics* are associated with rules that are either given or may be deduced. To keep them interesting to students, many of them are based on real life.

Also missing from the mathematical definition of function is any mention of numbers. In fact, functions do not have to involve numbers at all—all that is required is a set of inputs and a set of outputs. A function might take polygons in and output "triangle," "quadrangle," "pentagon," and so on. Another function might take triangles in and output "acute," "right," or "obtuse." All that is required for a function is a set of inputs that are allowed (you can't put a polygon into a "subtract 3" machine) and a set of outputs. A rule for associating a specific output with each input makes the function interesting, but as noted above, such a rule is not strictly required.

Many real-world situations behave like functions. A bathroom scale is a function machine: Stand on it and it outputs your weight. A gasoline pump has a built-in function machine: Input an amount of gasoline and out comes the total cost, including tax. One way to think about science is as a search for functions that relate real-world variables.

Sequences can also be considered to be functions. Some sequences can be thought of as iterative functions, in which an output comes from applying a rule to the previous output (that is, to the previous number in the sequence) rather than to any arbitrary input value. For example, to get the next even number, just add 2 to the previous even number. Other sequences can't be approached in this way because there is no rule that gives the next term from the previous terms. (Mathematicians call the numbers in a sequence the terms of the sequence.) The sequence of closing prices for IBM stock is an example of a sequence for which knowing all the previous terms is not enough to determine the next term.

Another way to think of sequences as functions is to number the terms. The even numbers, for example, correspond to the function in the table to the right. Thinking of a sequence in this way can sometimes lead to a rule that will give any term in the sequence without having to find all the previous terms. Studying the table, for example, leads to a rule for finding any even number: To find the nth even number, simply double n.

Input	Output
1	2
2	4
3	6
4	8
5	10

even numbers function

In *Everyday Mathematics,* sequences are not treated as functions—it's easier to think of sequences as lists of numbers, often with a rule for generating the next term, as in Frames-and-Arrows diagrams. Activities with sequences, however, are quite helpful for developing students' understanding of functions.

9.1.4 Functions and Representations

Students of *Everyday Mathematics* approach functions concretely, pictorially, verbally (usually orally), and symbolically. Concrete activities include those in which students sort objects according to some measure or attribute. Lining up people by height and ordering pattern blocks by shape, for example, are concrete activities in which students explore patterns leading to functions.

Frames-and-Arrows problems, incomplete number lines, and function machines are pictorial representations of functions and sequences. Graphs are particularly important pictorial representations that are investigated extensively in *4–6 Everyday Mathematics.* In Grade 3 students get their first exposure to graph models when they plot ordered pairs on a coordinate grid.

> NOTE: Functions are not restricted to a single input variable and a single output variable. For example, a function with two input variables and one output variable would be one that takes in the number of gallons of gasoline and the price per gallon and outputs the total cost. In Everyday Mathematics, however, we restrict ourselves to functions that involve only two variables.

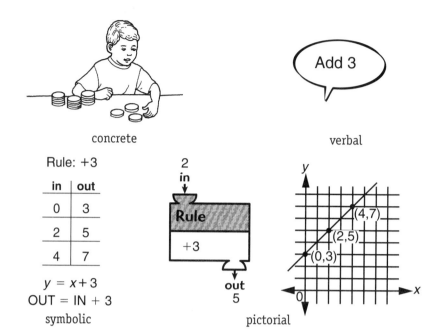

concrete

verbal

Rule: +3

in	out
0	3
2	5
4	7

$y = x + 3$
OUT = IN + 3

symbolic

pictorial

Tables of values are an important kind of representation of functions in *K–3 Everyday Mathematics*. Many functions in real life are given as tables: The sports and business sections of the newspaper are filled with tables that represent functions of various sorts. The input could be a baseball team, for example, and the output the team batting average as of the date of the newspaper. Sports standings, financial tables, weather tables, and so on can all be considered to be functions. A great deal of the tabular information in almanacs and other reference books can also be thought of as functions.

Verbal representations for functions include rules like "double" or "add 5." These verbal representations can often be made more concise by using symbols like "+3" or "Output = Input + 3" or even "$y = x + 3$." The symbolic representation of functions as equations is explored extensively in fourth through sixth grades.

Everyday Mathematics provides three kinds of activities that reinforce the link between these several representations.

x	y
0	2
1	3
2	3
1	1

FRED's vertices

1. Given a graph, students read the coordinates of points and make a table of values. The graph may consist of a set of discrete points, or it may be a graph of a continuous line or curve. For example, given the graph of polygon *FRED* shown to the right, students make a table of values for the vertices. Or, given the graph of the function $y = 2x$, they make a table of values by picking several values for x and finding the corresponding values for y.

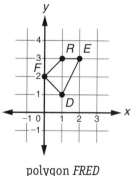

polygon *FRED*

2. Given a table of values, students interpret it as a set of ordered pairs and graph the pairs as a set of discrete points. For example, given the table of polygon *FRED*'s vertices, they plot them and connect the dots.

3. Given a rule for a function in equation form, students make a table of values by choosing several values for x and calculating the corresponding values for y. Then they graph these values and connect the points with a smooth, continuous line.

For more on reading and writing number sentences, see Section 9.2.2.

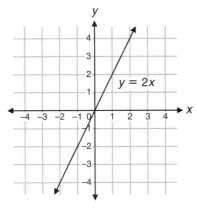

graph of $y = 2x$

x	y
-2	-4
1	2
1.5	3

points on $y = 2x$

For more on graphing, see Section 7.3.2 of the Reference Frames essay.

Of course, students develop these skills gradually. Simple "What's My Rule?" games begin in Kindergarten. Number sentences to model number stories are introduced in Grade 1. In third and fourth grades, students graph sets of ordered pairs, such as those found in tables of values, on a coordinate plane. Starting in fifth grade, the connection between rules, tables, and graphs is explored through investigations of patterns in data. Students also use ordered pairs to define the vertices of polygons and to examine the effects on these polygons when the coordinates are operated on arithmetically. Also beginning in fifth grade, students examine "mystery graphs" in the coordinate plane to identify which graphs best represent given behaviors.

Here are two examples of activities that focus on multiple representations of a function.

In Grade 5, students use the distance formula $d = 8t$ to calculate the distance d an airplane travels in t minutes at a rate of 8 miles per minute. They fill out a table of values using the formula and then plot the points and connect the dots to make a continuous line graph. Finally, they use the graph to answer questions about distances and times not included in their table, which they can check using the formula.

Time (min) (t)	Distance (mi) (8 * t)
1	8
2	16
3	24
4	32
5	40
6	48

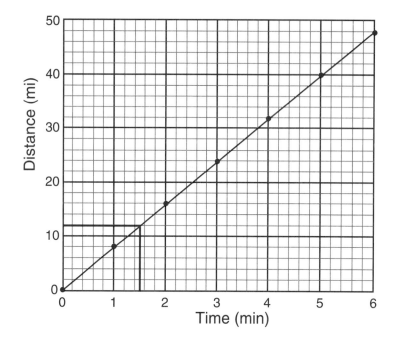

In a similar manner, Grade 6 students investigate the formula $d = 16t^2$, which gives the distance d, in feet, that an object will fall in t seconds under Earth's gravity (ignoring air resistance).

The authors expect that *Everyday Mathematics* students will enter middle and high school mathematics courses with a strong, informal understanding of graphs and their relationships to tables of values and variable models. This will prepare them for the study of techniques used to solve the following kind of problem:

> Given a table of values or graph, write a rule in equation form that describes the relationship between the input and the output of the function.

9.2 Arithmetic Symbols and Number Sentences

Number sentences are equations or inequalities such as $10 = 7 + 3$ or $12 / n = 6$ or $14 > 3$. Number sentences have a left-hand side, a relation symbol, and a right-hand side. Symbols for numbers, unknowns, and operations can appear on either side of the relation symbol.

Number sentences can be true, false, or neither true nor false. Number sentences that are neither true nor false are called **open.** The sentence $5 + 3 = 8$ is true; the sentence $5 + 4 = 8$ is false; the sentence $5 + \_ = 8$ is open.

A **number model** is a number sentence that fits some real or hypothetical situation. For example, $7 + 3 = 10$ is a number model that fits the situation, "Gupta had 7 pennies and got 3 more. Then he had 10 pennies." Number models can be based on stories made up by students, on situations invented by the teacher, or on information from everyday life.

In *Everyday Mathematics*, number models are symbolic shorthand for the oral statements, concrete actions, and pictures that are used to state and represent problems. In the first years of the program, problem representations emphasize the concrete, the verbal (usually oral), and the pictorial. Number models, however, are often present, usually written by the teacher on the chalkboard or overhead projector with blank response lines to represent or hold the place of unknown numbers. Symbols for operations ($+$, $-$, $\times$, and so on) and relations ($=$, $>$, $<$, and so on) are introduced informally. In second and third grades, the students take on more responsibility for writing the number models. In fourth through sixth grades, students learn to use number sentences not simply to represent situations but also to solve problems.

Writing number sentences is similar to writing English sentences. Both written English and written mathematics have rules and conventions about grammar, syntax, punctuation, and usage. These rules clarify thinking and make communication easier. The following sections address first the arithmetic symbols themselves and then how they are used in number sentences.

9.2.1 Arithmetic Symbols

Many people feel that mathematics has too many symbols. Symbols, however, are vitally important to mathematics. They make the language of mathematics more concise and, ultimately, easier to understand. Symbols, by relieving the mind of unnecessary work and leaving it free to focus on more advanced problems, can increase our mathematical power.

Writers of school mathematics programs face a dilemma. On the one hand, an efficient set of symbols is needed so that activities may progress smoothly in the classroom. But symbols, especially if they are introduced too early, may pose an obstacle to the understanding of a concept. With this in mind, the authors of *Everyday Mathematics* have been careful to avoid introducing symbols (and mathematical vocabulary in general) prematurely; symbols are introduced only when they help students communicate more efficiently.

The curriculum must introduce both the symbols needed for classroom activities and the symbols required for real-world general knowledge. Symbols for classroom activities can be introduced on an ad hoc basis and could be restricted to a small and efficient set. But the need for students to understand mathematics within a broader social context means the curriculum must include a more expansive list of symbols. Each group in society—grocers, scientists, engineers, advertisers, journalists, and so on—has a different set of symbols it considers necessary. Even the way we write numbers can spark debate: Should it be .1 or 0.1? Is 1/2 better than $\frac{1}{2}$, or is $\frac{1}{2}$ the best? Should we write -3, -3, or $^{-}3$?

Calculators and computers, which might have been expected to help standardize notation, have actually increased the need for understanding that different symbols can mean the same thing. For example, there are several alternative symbols for multiplication, division, powers, and opposites (inverses). *Everyday Mathematics* provides activities to help make students aware of these alternative notations so they can adapt to different situations as necessary. The program employs several notations for certain operations so students will become familiar with all common symbols.

Addition and Subtraction Symbols

There are no symbols for addition and subtraction other than $+$ and $-$. Although the ideas behind the operations are thousands of years old, the symbols first appeared in print in 1498 in a book by the German mathematician Johann Widman. Widman's symbols gradually caught on and are now universally accepted. The words we use for these symbols, however, do vary: *plus, add,* and *positive* all refer to $+$; *minus, take away,* and *negative* all refer to $-$.

Students of *Everyday Mathematics* see these symbols only after they have informal experiences with the underlying operations. Kindergarten students, for example, hear the words "add" and "subtract" as they put lumps of modeling dough on or remove them from a pan balance, yet they do not need symbols to describe the activity. One of the first encounters that Kindergarten students have with the addition symbol occurs when they use the [+] key on their calculators in a counting-on activity. Establishing this informal connection between the $+$ symbol and counting supports later use of the $+$ symbol for paper-and-pencil representations of addition and the understanding of a rule such as "+ 3" in "What's My Rule?" and Frames-and-Arrows activities. Similar counting-back activities use the [−] key.

Multiplication and Division Symbols

Multiplication and division can each be represented by several symbols. All of the symbols are discussed in the *Everyday Mathematics Teacher's Lesson Guide,* but to standardize symbolic representation in the materials, some choices have been made that should be clarified here.

Mathematics textbooks traditionally use the symbol $\times$ ("times" or "multiplied by") to indicate multiplication. The Englishman William Oughtred invented this symbol in 1631. When multiplication models are introduced in *Second* and *Third Grade Everyday Mathematics,* the $\times$ symbol is used. One disadvantage of $\times$ is that it can be confused with the addition symbol ($+$). Another disadvantage is that it does not appear on a standard computer or typewriter keyboard, though it is standard on most calculator keypads. Finally, $\times$ can easily be mistaken for the letter *x,* which becomes a problem in fourth grade when letter variables begin to be used more frequently. One solution to this problem is to use a raised dot for multiplication ($5 \cdot 6$ rather than 5×6). Gottfried Leibniz, one of the inventors of calculus, introduced this notation in 1698. But an obvious difficulty with a raised dot is confusion with the decimal point. In fact, in some countries a raised dot is used as the decimal point.

After much consideration, the authors of *Everyday Mathematics* decided to use ∗ as the usual symbol for multiplication beginning in fourth grade. It is always the multiplication symbol on computer keyboards, and it is frequently used in print. It is also found on some calculators. The symbol is easy to write or type and is not likely to be confused with other symbols. Using ∗ for multiplication prepares students for the present as well as the future in a world of computers. A disadvantage is that ∗ is less familiar than × to teachers and parents.

Eventually, students learn to indicate multiplication by juxtaposition; that is, by writing symbols next to each other: writing $(15)(23)$ to mean 15×23, $2a$ to mean $2 \times a$, ab to mean $a \times b$, and so on. Juxtaposition to indicate multiplication is common in formulas, which are among the earliest uses of letter variables that *Everyday Mathematics* students encounter. For example, the area A of a rectangle with width w and length l is written as $A = lw$. In fact, almost the only place where this formula would be written as $A = l \times w$ is an elementary school mathematics textbook.

Historically, symbols for division have included $\div$, $\overline{)}$, /, :, and the fraction bar. Their inventors were, respectively, the Swiss Johann Rahn in 1659; the German Michael Stifel in 1544; the Mexican Manuel A. Valdes in 1784; the German Gottfried Leibniz in 1684; and the Arab al-Ḥaṣṣâr in the twelfth century.

In second and third grades, *Everyday Mathematics* uses $\div$. Unfortunately, $\div$ shares two disadvantages with the multiplication symbol ×: it can easily be misread as +, and it does not appear on standard computer or typewriter keyboards. On the other hand, it is the symbol for division on almost all calculators.

Beginning in fourth grade, *Everyday Mathematics* uses / and the fraction bar, as well as $\div$, to indicate division. The / has been used for centuries. It appears on some calculators, is easy to write, and is found on computer and typewriter keyboards. The use of / and the fraction bar for indicating division has an additional, most important advantage: the forms a/b and $\frac{a}{b}$ reinforce the relation between division and fractions. The fraction notation also prepares students for the division symbols they are likely to see in middle and high school mathematics and beyond.

Writing division with a remainder can be a bit of a problem. Consider what can happen if equal signs are used:

$$12 \div 5 = 2 \text{ R}2$$

$$102 \div 50 = 2 \text{ R}2$$

Since the right-hand sides of the two equations above are the same, it appears that the left-hand sides should be equal too. Hence we should be able to write:

$$12 \div 5 = 102 \div 50$$

Unfortunately, if you do the division, the problem becomes apparent:

$$12 \div 5 = 2.4$$

$$102 \div 50 = 2.04$$

The answers are *not* equal. The problem is that 2 R2 is not really a number, and so using it in equations can lead to trouble. Since 102 ÷ 50 is a number, but 2 R2 is not a number, they cannot possibly be equal. To eliminate this problem, *Everyday Mathematics* uses arrows in number models for divisions with remainders:

$$102 \div 50 \rightarrow 2 \text{ R2}$$

This notation, though nonstandard, will not mislead students as using = may. Later, when students learn to show remainders as fractions or decimals, the problem disappears altogether:

$$12 \div 5 = 2\frac{2}{5}$$

$$102 \div 50 = 2\frac{2}{50}$$

The symbol $\overline{)}$ is closely linked to the traditional long-division algorithm. Actually, it is really more like a template for carrying out a procedure than a mathematical symbol. Using it, therefore, may suggest the use of the long-division algorithm when another method is warranted. It can be useful, however, for recording answers to division problems with remainders.

Other Arithmetic Symbols

Many other symbols in addition to those discussed above are used in arithmetic.

In addition to all the conventional symbols that students should learn to use, they should also be encouraged to create their own notations. While these invented notations may not be much good for formal mathematical communication, they can be useful for clarifying complicated situations. We must remember that every standard notation we use today began as someone's creation.

9.2.2 Reading and Writing Number Sentences

Just as English words become meaningful when they are arranged into sentences, mathematical symbols become meaningful when they are arranged into sentences. And just as proper punctuation and grammar make written English easier to read, rules and conventions in number sentences ease mathematical communication.

A number sentence has three parts: a left-hand side, a relation symbol, and a right-hand side. In the sentence 4 + 3 = 7, for example, "4 + 3" is the left-hand side, "=" is the relation symbol, and "7" is the right-hand side. Number sentences in which the relation symbol is = ("equals" or "is equal to") are called **equations**. Sentences in which the relation symbol is < ("is less

For more on symbols for numbers, see Sections 1.3 and 1.4 of the Numeration and Order essay.

For more on symbols for numerical relations, see Section 1.9.2 of the Numeration and Order essay.

For more on symbols for powers and exponents, see Section 2.2 of the Arithmetic Operations essay.

than"), > ("is greater than"), ≤ ("is less than or equal to"), ≥ ("is greater than or equal to"), or ≠ ("is not equal to") are called **inequalities**. A number phrase with a variable but no relation symbol, such as $3 + y$, is called an **algebraic expression** or simply an **expression**. A number phrase with no variable, such as $74 + 3$, is an expression. A single number or a product of a constant and one or more variables is a **term**. Terms are what are added and subtracted in expressions. For example, in the expression $75 + 3x$, the terms are 75 and $3x$.

A number sentence that is neither true nor false because it contains a variable or unknown, such as $14 = t - 9$ or $(81 + c) * 10 < 100$, is called an **open sentence**. Any number can replace the variable. Depending on which number replaces the variable, the resulting number sentence will be true or false. Any number that makes an open sentence true is called a **solution** of the sentence. Finding a value for a variable that makes a number sentence true is called solving the sentence.

For more on symbols and variables, see Section 9.3.1.

In *Everyday Mathematics*, children in first grade encounter unknowns in situation diagrams. These diagrams display the numbers in number stories so that the quantitative relationships are easier to understand. The empty cell in a diagram represents the unknown—the variable.

For more on the use of variables, see Section 9.3.

In first grade, the teacher also writes open sentences to model number stories. Beginning in second grade, students write their own number models. At first, a blank or question mark is used for the unknown ($4 + \_\_ = 12$ or $4 + ? = 12$); by fourth grade, letter variables are used ($4 + N = 12$). Inequalities are introduced in fourth grade. The terms *expression* and *equation* are introduced in fifth grade. In fifth and sixth grades, students begin to learn to solve open number sentences by algebraic manipulations. Various forms of variables and names for open sentences are used so students become familiar with a variety of mathematical symbols and with algebraic language.

For more on situation diagrams, see Section 2.1 in the Arithmetic Operations essay.

Grouping Symbols

The ordinary operations of arithmetic—addition, subtraction, multiplication, and division—are called "binary operations" because they are carried out on two numbers at a time. (Addition and multiplication can certainly involve more than two numbers, but the final product or sum is obtained by repeatedly adding or multiplying pairs of numbers.) When only two numbers and one operation are involved, there is no need for grouping symbols. Similarly, no grouping symbols are needed in adding several numbers or in multiplying several numbers, because these operations may be performed in any order.

For more on solving open sentences, see Section 9.3.2.

However, in situations involving several numbers with subtraction, division, or a combination of operations, you may obtain different results depending on the order in which the operations are performed. The value of 4 + 3 * 5, for example, is 35 if the addition is done first and 19 if the multiplication is done first.

To avoid such ambiguity, you can insert parentheses to indicate the order in which the operations are to be performed. The operations within the parentheses are carried out first. If the addition is to be done first, the expression should be written (4 + 3) * 5; if the multiplication is to be done first, it can be written 4 + (3 * 5).

Parentheses may be **nested**, meaning there are parentheses within parentheses. For example, in 2 * (3 + (2 − 1)), the (2 − 1) group is nested within the (3 + (2 − 1)) group. In nested parentheses, you always begin with the innermost set of parentheses. Sometimes different symbols are used to help distinguish between sets of grouping symbols. In the previous example, square brackets could be used for either set of parentheses: 2 * [3 + (2 − 1)] or 2 * (3 + [2 − 1]) are equivalent. Sometimes braces { } are used. Computers and calculators commonly use only parentheses (not brackets or braces), so it is not necessarily helpful in everyday experience to require the use of more than one kind of symbol in nested groups.

A horizontal fraction bar, known as a vinculum, is also a grouping symbol. You can imagine a set of parentheses around the entire numerator of a fraction and another set around the entire denominator. For example, an expression such as

$$\frac{22 - (5 + 4)}{1 + (9 - 3) * 2}$$

is equivalent to

$$(22 - (5 + 4)) / (1 + (9 - 3) * 2) = (22 - 9) / (1 + 6 * 2)$$
$$= 13 / (1 + 12)$$
$$= 13 / 13$$
$$= 1$$

Brief exercises with parentheses are worth repeating throughout each year. Most students find such exercises to have an appealing, game-like quality. Moreover, students learn something of importance that in the past was postponed, unaccountably, until secondary school mathematics. Such exercises also provide students with practice with basic number facts and their extensions, reminders of the effect of multiplying by or adding zero, and practice with expressing solutions in games such as *Name That Number*.

The Order of Operations

Beginning in Grade 2, students are encouraged to use grouping symbols, particularly parentheses, to make their number sentences clearer. Once they begin to use variables and scientific calculators, however, students need to understand the mathematical convention called the **order of operations,** which is also known as the algebraic order of operations. The order of operations specifies the sequence in which the operations in an expression are to be performed. Grouping symbols are used only for greater clarity or to specify an order different from the conventional order.

An understanding of the order of operations is assumed in most of the mathematics that students will encounter in middle school and beyond. The order of operations is formally introduced in *Fifth Grade Everyday Mathematics*. In *K–4 Everyday Mathematics*, grouping symbols, such as parentheses and brackets, are used to avoid confusion.

The order of operations is:

1. Do the operations inside **parentheses**. Work from the innermost grouping symbols outward. Within grouping symbols, follow Rules 2–4.

2. Calculate all expressions with **exponents**.

3. **Multiply** and **divide** in order, from left to right. Neither operation has priority over the other—just do them in order from left to right.

4. **Add** and **subtract** in order, from left to right. Neither operation has priority over the other—just do them in order from left to right.

According to this convention,

$$4 + 3 * 5 = 19$$

$$8 / 2^2 - 12 / 4 + 7 * (9 - 3) = 41$$

A mnemonic for the order of operations is *Please Excuse My Dear Aunt Sally*: Do work inside the Parentheses first, and then Exponentiation, and then Multiplication and Division, and finally Addition and Subtraction.

Simplifying Expressions

Students use expressions throughout *Everyday Mathematics* but have no need to call them by that name until Grade 5. Also, in their explorations of number models, students seldom need to focus on an expression by itself—expressions are usually parts of number models that fit number stories drawn from real life.

In preparation for solving the more challenging equations of secondary school mathematics, Grade 6 students are introduced to **simplifying expressions**. For example, in each equation below, the expression on the left-hand side simplifies to the expression on the right-hand side.

$$11x + 5 - 6x + 4 = 5x + 9$$

$$2x + 12 - 3y + 7y + x = 3x + 4y + 12$$

Each of the preceding equations illustrates **combining like terms**. Like terms are terms that have exactly the same variables.

- A **constant term** is a single number, such as 5, 4, or 9 in the first equation above. All constant terms are like terms.
- A **variable term** contains one or more variable factors. For example, $2x$, $3x$, xy, and simply x are variable terms. A number factor in a variable term is called the **coefficient** of the term. Variable terms with the same variable factor or factors are like terms.

Combining like terms relies on the order of operations and properties of the rational number system—especially the distributive property, which is described below. Sometimes like terms "cancel" each other, as in the following equation:

$$2 - x + 3x - 2x = 2$$

When the three variable terms on the left-hand side, $-x$, $3x$, and $-2x$, are combined, the result is $0x$ or 0, which is not written on the right-hand side.

The Distributive Property

Students in *Everyday Mathematics* are exposed to the distributive property beginning in Grade 4, but it is first formally named in Grade 6. The following is the **distributive property of multiplication over addition:**

For any three numbers a, b, and c, $a(b + c) = ab + ac$.

The following is the **distributive property of multiplication over subtraction:**

For any three numbers a, b, and c, $a(b - c) = ab - ac$.

"The distributive property" commonly refers to both of these properties.

Rewriting an expression using the distributive property from left to right as shown above is called **expanding** the expression, or distributing a over $b + c$ or $b - c$. The property also applies when there are more than two terms inside the parentheses. For example, $2(x + y + z) = 2x + 2y + 2z$.

The distributive property also applies in the "other direction":

$$ab + ac = a(b + c) \qquad ab - ac = a(b - c)$$

When the property is used in this "direction," the process is called factoring a from the other two terms. This is because a is a factor of both terms, and therefore a is a factor of the whole expression. Also, because of the turn-around rule for multiplication, the property could be written:

$$ab + ac = (b + c)a \qquad ab - ac = (b - c)a$$

Simplifying expressions often makes use of the distributive property for factoring, even though it may not be obvious. In the following simplifications, steps have been added to highlight how the property is used.

$$11x + 5 - 6x + 4 = 11x - 6x + 5 + 4$$
$$= (11 - 6)x + 9$$
$$= 5x + 9$$
$$2x + 12 - 3y + 7y + x = 2x + x - 3y + 7y + 12$$
$$= (2+1)x + (-3 + 7)y + 12$$
$$= 3x + 4y + 12$$

In a sense, students use the distributive property beginning in Kindergarten, when they add and subtract counts. For example,

6 bananas + 8 bananas = (6 + 8) bananas = 14 bananas

Beginning in Grade 3, *Everyday Mathematics* students use the distributive property to:

- Invent mental arithmetic procedures. For example, "To find 15 times 6, I can take 10 sixes and add 5 sixes."
- Play the *Multiplication Wrestling* game, which applies the distributive property twice, as shown in the margin.
- Use the partial-products algorithm and lattice multiplication.
- Add and subtract fractions with common denominators.

The distributive property is connected beautifully to geometry by an area model illustrated in sixth grade. For the figure below, the area of the big rectangle is given by the product of the overall dimensions, $5 * (3 + 7)$, or by the sum of the areas of the two smaller rectangles, $(5 * 3) + (5 * 7)$. In other words, $5 * (3 + 7) = (5 * 3) + (5 * 7)$.

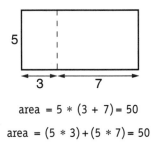

area = $5 * (3 + 7) = 50$

area = $(5 * 3) + (5 * 7) = 50$

Teaching with Number Models and Number Sentences

When they are first introduced in *Everyday Mathematics*, number models usually appear after a problem has been solved. A typical instructional sequence might be this:

1. The teacher poses a problem.

2. The students solve the problem.

3. The students share their solutions, and the teacher makes a record of them on the board. During the discussion of solutions, the teacher writes number models and draws situation diagrams on the board. There are no blanks in the number models or situation diagrams.

Multiplication Wrestling

$27 * 32$
$= (20 + 7) * (30 + 2)$
$= (20 * 30) + (20 * 2) + (7 * 30) + (7 * 2)$
$= 600 + 40 + 210 + 14$
$= 864$

Partial-Products Algorithm

$$\begin{array}{r} 27 \\ *32 \\ \hline 600 \\ 210 \\ 40 \\ 14 \\ \hline 864 \end{array}$$

Adding Fractions

$\frac{1}{5} + \frac{3}{5} = \frac{1}{5}(1+3) = \frac{1+3}{5} = \frac{4}{5}$

A bit later, the sequence might be as follows:

1. The teacher poses a problem.

2. The teacher and students discuss the problem and write a number model or diagram that corresponds to the problem. The number model or diagram includes a blank or a question mark for the unknown quantity.

3. Students solve the problem. They may use the number model or diagram to help them, or they may use another method entirely.

4. Students share their solutions, and the teacher records them on the board. During the discussion of the solutions, the teacher fills in the blanks in the number model or diagram.

Number models in the primary grades are not a method for solving problems. Rather, they are used to represent and clarify the quantitative relationships in problem situations. For example, before solving the number story "Marie has 55¢. She wants to buy a candy bar that costs 89¢. How much more does she need?" a child might write the number model $55 + N = 89$. The model shows the relationships between the quantities in the story and may suggest finding the answer by counting up. After solving the story by counting up or some other method, the child might write $55 + 34 = 89$ to summarize the work. Learning to use number models to represent number stories helps students learn the mathematical symbol system that is the foundation of algebra.

In third and fourth grades, more complicated equations are treated informally through puzzles such as "I am the number x in $6 + 5 * x = 16$. What number am I?" Solving this puzzle requires knowing that the order of operations dictates that x be multiplied by 5 before 6 is added. Students are encouraged to clarify this by rewriting the left-hand side of the number sentence as $6 + (5 * x) = 16$. Students solve such puzzles by trial and error or by working backward.

Solving equations by formal algebraic manipulations is taken up in *Fifth* and *Sixth Grade Everyday Mathematics*.

9.3 Algebra and Uses of Variables

Most adults in the United States probably remember algebra as a junior or senior high school course devoted to learning how to manipulate equations containing variables. But algebra is actually far more than just symbol manipulation. Algebra can be thought of as generalized arithmetic, as a set of powerful problem-solving procedures, as a study of numerical relationships, or as a study of the structure of mathematics. The authors of *Everyday Mathematics* believe these are all valid descriptions of algebra. Accordingly, although the formal study of algebraic syntax is not appropriate for most elementary school students, *Everyday Mathematics* students engage in many activities involving algebra.

Algebra is the branch of mathematics that deals with variables and operations on variables. So, in a sense, as soon as first graders

For more on solving equations, see Section 9.3.2.

encounter problems like $8 + \_\_ = 12$ they are beginning algebra because the blank is a kind of variable. Later in *Everyday Mathematics*, students experience variables as unknowns ($5 + x = 8$), in formulas ($A = lw$), in statements of mathematical properties ($a + b = b + a$), and in functions ($y = x + 5$). This experience with variables prepares students for eventual success in algebra.

Two major topic strands in *Everyday Mathematics* are devoted to algebra: Algebra and Uses of Variables; and Patterns, Functions, and Sequences. Algebra also has an important link to the problem-solving theme. The diagram in the margin identifies four problem-solving representations. To represent problems symbolically, students need to understand the usefulness of algebraic notation and variables.

For more on common uses of variables, see Section 9.3.1.

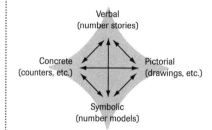

9.3.1 Uses of Variables

A letter or other symbol that stands for a number is called a **variable**. In Grades 4–6 of *Everyday Mathematics*, variables are used in several distinct ways.

Variables as Unknowns

As students write number sentences to fit problem situations, they often find that they need to represent numbers that are unknown. For example, the problem "There are 24 students in our class, but today only 18 are here. How many are not here?" might be modeled as $24 - ? = 18$, or as $18 + ? = 24$, or as $24 - 18 = ?$ Alternatively, a letter, a response line, or a box can be used to indicate the unknown number: $24 - n = 18$, or $18 + \_\_ = 24$, or $24 - 18 = \boxed{}$. All four symbols ($?$, n, $\_\_$, and $\boxed{}$) are variables.

In *K–3 Everyday Mathematics*, variables are used primarily as unknowns in open sentences, and so introducing the term *variable* is unnecessary. Also, in sentences such as $5 + N = 13$, the unknown is a single number that doesn't vary, and so explaining the root of *variable* (*vary*) is not helpful.

Besides being used to represent single unknown numbers, such as x in $48 / x = 6$, variables can represent more than a single unknown number in certain situations. For example, "I'm thinking of a number less than 10" can be modeled as $x < 10$, which has whole-number solutions 0, 1, …, 9, and many more solutions if fractions, decimals, or negative numbers are allowed.

There can also be more than one unknown in situations modeled by equations. For example, "What pairs of whole numbers have 8 as their sum?" can be modeled as $m + n = 8$; solutions are pairs 0 and 8, 1 and 7, 2 and 6, and so on. Students in Grades 4–6 use more than one unknown when they write and interpret open sentences for "What's My Rule?" problems.

Variables in Formulas

A **formula** uses variables to state concisely a relationship that would otherwise require many words to describe. For example, "The area of a rectangle can be found by multiplying the length of the rectangle times the width" may be written as the formula $A = l * w$, or simply $A = lw$. Area relationships for triangles, parallelograms, and other figures can be expressed similarly, as can volume and many other relationships.

It is important to keep track of the units of measure or count that go with the numbers represented by the variables and to make sure those units are consistent with the relationship expressed by the formula. For example, an area formula will not give a correct result if the length is measured in feet and the width in meters. In Kindergarten through Grade 3, students use *unit boxes* to help them develop the habit of thinking about units. In Grades 4 and 5, students use a *whole box* to name the entire quantity, or 100%, being considered.

In formulas with three variables, such as $A = lw$, if any two numbers are known, the third number can be found. A similar rule applies to relationships expressed with a greater number of variables.

Formulas are introduced in Grade 4 and revisited frequently in Grade 5, where students use formulas to find areas of plane figures and volumes of right rectangular prisms. Students are also introduced to the connection between formulas, tables, and coordinate graphs when they explore the relationship $d = rt$ for a fixed rate.

For more on multiple representations, see Section 9.1.3.

In *Sixth Grade Everyday Mathematics*, students continue to use formulas given to them, but they also develop some of their own, such as a formula used to calculate the number of bricks needed to build a wall. They also expand their study of connections between formulas, tables, and graphs by exploring a formula for the distance traveled by a freely falling object. Yet another use of formulas in sixth grade is in the context of using a spreadsheet.

Variables in Properties of Numbers and Operations

Variables are also used to express basic mathematical properties. For example, the "turn-around rule" for addition says that two numbers can be added in either order and the sum will be the same. Expressed with variables, the turn-around rule becomes "$m + n = n + m$" or, more formally, "For any two numbers m and n, $m + n = n + m$."

Properties of numbers and operations express patterns. Describing a pattern with variables and algebraic notation can, with practice, make the pattern much clearer than descriptions of the same pattern with specific numbers or words. Students of *Fifth* and *Sixth Grade Everyday Mathematics* practice describing patterns with variables.

Consider, for example, the following special cases and general pattern. Which is more concise? Which is clearer?

Special Cases: $1 * 1 = 1$ General Pattern: $1 * n = n$
                   $1 * 2 = 2$
                   $1 * 5 = 5$
                   $1 * 20 = 20$

This use of variables differs from variables in formulas. The level of generality is much higher. There is no specific physical or mathematical situation underlying the property as there is for an area or volume formula.

Variables in Functions

Another important use of variables, at least in higher mathematics, is their use in functions. In its simplest form, a function is a rule that gives a certain output for a given input. For example, "add 2" is a simple function. Using variables, this function could be written OUTPUT = INPUT + 2 or $y = x + 2$.

In *K–3 Everyday Mathematics*, students explore functions through function machines and by playing "What's My Rule?" In fourth through sixth grades, the comparable activity is to make tables of "in" and "out" values for relationships such as $y = x + 2$, where x represents "in" numbers and y represents "out" numbers. Then students graph the ordered pairs from the table and connect the points to get a picture of the relationship.

The equation $y = x + 2$ expresses an important mathematical relationship called a function. The simplest type of function is a rule that matches each number in one set (all the values of the variable x) with exactly one number in a second set (all the values of the variable y).

For more on functions, see Section 9.1.3.

Variables as Storage Locations

In computer programs, variables serve as names for memory locations where values are stored. Computer variables may consist of more than one letter; often they name the quantity being stored. For example, PRICE might name the location of the current price of an item. INPUT PRICE in certain computer languages means to place a value into the storage location PRICE. To find a price plus 8% sales tax, the computer could calculate $1.08 * $ PRICE.

9.3.2 Solving Open Sentences

Open sentences are number sentences that are neither true nor false because they contain variables. In *Everyday Mathematics*, students begin to learn about open sentences as they work with situation diagrams, which display the relationships among the quantities in simple number stories. The empty part of a situation diagram represents an unknown number, or variable. Beginning in first grade, the teacher may write an open sentence for a problem after it has been modeled in a situation diagram. Open sentences are introduced as another way to represent the quantitative relationships in the problem situation.

For more on situation diagrams, see Section 2.1 in the Arithmetic Operations essay and Section 9.2.2.

Number Story: "Twelve girls and 18 boys are in school today. How many students are here today?"

Situation Diagram:

Students	
?	
girls	boys
12	18

Number Model: $12 + 18 =$ ___

By third grade, the responsibility for writing simple sentences using the four basic operations and grouping symbols is in the students' hands. In fourth grade, students begin to move from writing informal open sentences with blanks, spaces, or question marks for unknowns to a more consistent use of letter variables.

For the first several years of the program, number models are used for two main reasons. First, they are useful for representing relationships among quantities in problem situations. Once students understand these relationships in a problem, they can generally work out a solution, perhaps by carrying out an algorithm, making a drawing, or doing mental arithmetic. Number models with variables can help students understand and therefore solve problems better.

The second reason for working with number models in the primary grades is to familiarize students with the mathematical symbol system that is used in algebra and beyond. In the primary grades, students are not expected to manipulate the number models in order to solve problems. But through repeated exposures, students will gradually learn the rudiments of a mathematical language that will eventually become a powerful tool for solving problems.

Informal Methods

The simplest strategy for solving equations, and the usual method in Grades K–3 of *Everyday Mathematics*, is **trial and error** (or "guess and check"): Simply substitute a trial value for the variable in an open sentence to see if it makes the sentence true. If the trial value makes the sentence true, then it is a solution and the problem is solved. If the trial value is not a solution, adjust it and check whether the new trial value is a solution. Repeat until a solution is found.

Example: Solve $37 +$ ___ $= 83$ by trial and error.

Try 40: $37 + 40 = 77$.

Try 50: $37 + 50 = 87$.

Try 45: $37 + 45 = 82$.

Try 46: $37 + 46 = 83$.

The solution to $37 +$ ___ $= 83$ is 46.

Obviously, trial and error is not very efficient in this case. But short-term efficiency is not our only goal, and the experience of solving equations by trial and error can develop students' number sense and their understanding of operations and equations. Trial and error is also actually a very powerful strategy in higher mathematics. When problems are too hard to be solved by direct methods, trial and error is often the only practical approach.

A more systematic approach to solving equations is called the **cover-up method**. This method can be used to solve more challenging equations, but it is equally useful with even the simplest equations. For example, to solve $8 * (11 - c) = 72$, you might write it on the chalkboard, cover up the expression $11 - c$, and ask, "What times 8 is 72?" (9) Then write $11 - c = 9$. Now cover up the c and ask, "Eleven minus what number is 9?" (2) So $c = 2$.

Trial and error and the cover-up method are used by students in Grades 4 through 6, but other strategies are also introduced.

Pan-Balance Problems

Building on work with pan balances in earlier grades, *Fifth Grade Everyday Mathematics* introduces students to a pan-balance representation for equations. The problems are first presented concretely, with objects of different weights distributed on both sides of a pan balance. Students attempt to keep the pans balanced while removing weights. This leads to the idea of applying the same operation to both sides of an equation in order to put it into a form in which a solution is obvious.

For example, the pan-balance representation of the equation $3x + 14 = 23$ is shown by Figure 1 in the margin. A square represents x and a circle represents 1.

Removing 14 circles from each pan should keep the pans balanced and is equivalent to subtracting 14 from each side of the equation. The pan balance now represents the equation $3x = 9$, as shown in Figure 2.

Finally, by equal sharing, each square in the left pan must balance three circles in the right pan. This is equivalent to division by 3. The resulting equation, $x = 3$, is represented by the pan balance in Figure 3.

In *Fifth* and *Sixth Grade Everyday Mathematics*, students solve many pan-balance problems. The problems become progressively more complicated, leading to problems with two separate balances that are equivalent to systems of equations. Pictures of objects in the pans are eventually replaced by letter variables, so that students are essentially solving linear equations in one and two variables.

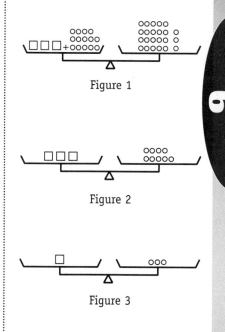

Figure 1

Figure 2

Figure 3

A Systematic Method for Solving Equations

In *Sixth Grade Everyday Mathematics*, work with pan-balance problems leads to a systematic method for solving the simplest algebraic equations, linear equations in one unknown such as $3x + 8 = x + 24$. Building on their experience with pan-balance problems, students learn to transform an equation in which the variable and constants appear on both sides of the equal sign into an equivalent equation in which the variable appears only on one side and the constants appear only on the other side. Students also combine like terms and remove parentheses by using the distributive property. Once the equation has been suitably transformed, the solution is obvious.

The following example is from the *Sixth Grade Student Reference Book*. It illustrates the method.

Example: Solve $5(b + 3) - 3b + 5 = 4(b - 1)$.

	Step	Equation
1	Copy the equation.	$5(b + 3) - 3b + 5 = 4(b - 1)$
2	Use the distributive property to remove parentheses.	$5b + 15 - 3b + 5 = 4b - 4$
3	Combine like terms.	$2b + 20 = 4b - 4$
4	Subtract 2*b* from both sides. (*S* 2*b*).	$\begin{aligned} 2b + 20 &= 4b - 4 \\ -2b &\quad -2b \\ \hline 20 &= 2b - 4 \end{aligned}$
5	Add 4 to both sides. (*A* 4)	$\begin{aligned} 20 &= 2b - 4 \\ +4 &\quad +4 \\ \hline 24 &= 2b \end{aligned}$
6	Divide both sides by 2. (*D* 2)	$\begin{aligned} 24 / 2 &= 2b / 2 \\ 12 &= b \end{aligned}$

Solving an equation in this way involves transforming the original equation into a series of equivalent simpler equations. This requires a step-by-step undoing of the operations in the original equation. A major goal of algebra courses in middle school and high school is for students to become proficient at this process. We are confident that your students will find the equation solving in those courses easy because of the solid foundation provided in *Fifth* and *Sixth Grade Everyday Mathematics*.

Solving Proportions

A **proportion** is a number sentence that states that two fractions are equal. Proportions can be used to model a wide range of situations, including rate, ratio, and other multiplication and division situations. Students learn to model problems with proportions beginning in fifth grade. The following example from the *Fifth Grade Student Reference Book* illustrates the approach.

Example:

Jack earned $12. He bought a can of tennis balls that cost $\frac{1}{3}$ of his earnings. How much did he spend?

Write a proportion for the cost of the tennis balls and Jack's earnings.

$$\frac{\text{cost of tennis balls}}{\text{total earnings}} = \frac{1}{3}$$

Jack's total earnings were $12. Substitute 12 for "earnings" in the proportion.

$$\frac{\text{cost of tennis balls}}{12} = \frac{1}{3}$$

These two fractions are equivalent. To name $\frac{1}{3}$ as an equivalent fraction with a denominator of 12, multiply the numerator and denominator of $\frac{1}{3}$ by 4. The cost of the tennis balls was $4.

$$\overset{* \, 4}{\underset{* \, 4}{\frac{\text{cost}}{\$12} = \frac{1}{3}}}$$

If you know any three numbers in a proportion, then you can find the fourth number. Finding a missing number in a proportion is called **solving the proportion**. Students in *Everyday Mathematics* learn to solve proportions in several ways.

One way to solve a proportion is to use the multiplication and division rules for equivalent fractions.

Example: Solve $\frac{2}{3} = \frac{n}{15}$.

The denominators, 3 and 15, are related by multiplication: $3 * 5 = 15$. The multiplication rule for equivalent fractions tells you the numerators must be related in the same way.

$$\frac{2 * 5}{3 * 5} = \frac{n}{15}$$

So $n = 2 * 5$, or 10.

Example: Solve $\frac{6}{15} = \frac{x}{5}$.

The denominators, 5 and 15, are related by division: $5 = 15 \div 3$. The division rule for equivalent fractions tells you the numerators must be related in the same way.

$$\frac{6 \div 3}{15 \div 3} = \frac{x}{5}$$

So $x = 6 \div 3$, or 2.

For more on multiplication and division rules for equivalent fractions, see Sections 3.3.4 and 3.3.5 of the Algorithms essay.

You may find diagrams like those below helpful when you solve proportions using rules for equivalent fractions.

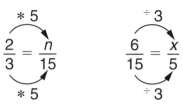

In *Sixth Grade Everyday Mathematics*, students learn to solve proportions by using cross multiplication. **Cross multiplication** is the process of finding **cross products**. The **cross products** of two fractions are found by multiplying the numerator of each fraction by the denominator of the other fraction.

Example: Find the cross products of $\frac{2}{3}$ and $\frac{1}{4}$.

The cross products are $2 * 4 = 8$ and $3 * 1 = 3$.

Example: Find the cross products of $\frac{5}{6}$ and $\frac{10}{12}$.

The cross products are $5 * 12 = 60$ and $6 * 10 = 60$.

Using cross multiplication to solve proportions depends on the following fact:

> If two fractions are equivalent, then the cross products are equal. If two fractions are not equivalent, then the cross products are not equal.

In the first example above, $\frac{2}{3}$ and $\frac{1}{4}$ are not equivalent, and their cross products are not equal. In the second example above, $\frac{5}{6}$ and $\frac{10}{12}$ are equivalent, and their cross products are equal.

The fact above can be proved with a bit of algebra. Suppose $\frac{a}{b}$ and $\frac{c}{d}$ are equivalent fractions. Then,

$$\frac{a}{b} = \frac{c}{d}$$

Multiplying both sides by bd yields

$$\frac{a}{b} * bd = \frac{c}{d} * bd$$

$$ad = bc$$

This shows that if two fractions are equivalent, then their cross products are equal. Working backward from $ad = bc$ to $\frac{a}{b} = \frac{c}{d}$ shows that if the cross products are equal, then the fractions are equivalent.

To solve a proportion by using cross multiplication involves several steps.

Step 1: Find the cross products of the two fractions in the proportion.

Step 2: Write an equation setting the two cross products equal.

Step 3: Solve the equation from Step 2.

Example: Solve $\frac{3}{4} = \frac{z}{20}$ by cross multiplication.

Step 1: Cross multiply. Note that the cross product of 4 and z is $4 * z$, or $4z$.

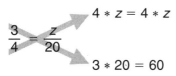

$$4 * z = 4 * z$$

$$3 * 20 = 60$$

Step 2: Since the two fractions in the proportion, $\frac{3}{4}$ and $\frac{z}{20}$, are equivalent, the two cross products must be equal. Write an equation setting them equal:

$$60 = 4 * z$$

Step 3: Solve the equation from Step 2 by dividing both sides by 4:

$$60 / 4 = 4 * z / 4$$

$$15 = z$$

ESSAY

10

Problem Solving

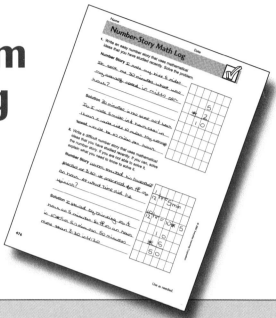

In 1977, the National Council of Supervisors of Mathematics issued a position paper on basic skills. The first basic skill listed was problem solving: "Learning to solve problems is the principal reason for studying mathematics" (NCSM, 1977, p. 20). Ever since, problem solving has remained at the top of the school mathematics agenda.

This essay is about problem solving and how *Everyday Mathematics* teaches it. Section 10.1 surveys various definitions of problem solving and explains what problem solving means in *Everyday Mathematics*. Section 10.2 discusses various ways mathematical ideas can be represented (concretely, pictorially, verbally, or symbolically) and what such representations have to do with problem solving. Section 10.3 explains what mathematical modeling is and its relationship to problem solving. Finally, Section 10.4 provides further details about teaching problem solving in *Everyday Mathematics*.

10.1 What Is Problem Solving?

In elementary school mathematics books, "problem solving" often refers only to finding answers to printed "word problems." But problem solving is much more than that. In the NCSM position paper cited above, problem solving is defined as "the process of applying previously acquired knowledge to new and unfamiliar situations." In *Principles and Standards for School Mathematics,* the National Council of Teachers of Mathematics (NCTM) states that problem solving "is finding a way to reach a goal that is not immediately attainable" (NCTM, 2000, p. 116). George Polya, whose book *How to Solve It* is a classic, wrote, "Solving a problem is finding the unknown means to a distinctly conceived end" (1988, p. 1).

These broader definitions of problem solving are not restricted to arithmetic and certainly not to arithmetic "word problems." Central to all of them is the idea that solution methods are not known in advance. A problem is not a problem if the problem solver knows exactly what to do right away. Problems for which the solution method is known ahead of time may be useful exercises. Indeed, a comprehensive curriculum like *Everyday Mathematics* must include many such exercises so students can practice essential skills. But they are not genuine problems in the sense implied here.

In *Everyday Mathematics*, problem solving is broadly conceived. Number stories (word problems) have their place, but problem solving permeates the entire curriculum. Students solve problems both in purely mathematical contexts, such as "What's My Rule?" tables, and in real situations from the classroom and everyday life. Students also create and solve problems using information from the materials, the teacher, and their own experiences and imaginations.

Everyday Mathematics defines problem solving as the process of modeling everyday situations using tools from mathematics. Mathematical modeling is discussed in detail in Section 10.3, but in a nutshell it means that expert problem solvers generally do one or more of a small number of things:

- identify what the problem is
- analyze what they know and seek out further data as necessary
- play with the data to discover patterns and meaning
- identify and apply mathematical techniques to find a solution
- look back after finding a solution and ask whether it makes sense and whether the method can be applied to other problems

10.2 Problem Representations

Often the key step in solving a problem is simply looking at it in the right way. Consider this problem: "How many handshakes are there when five people shake hands with one another?" One approach to solving this problem would be to find five people and have them shake hands, being careful to count each handshake. This approach is, to say the least, not very convenient. Another approach would be to make a list. If the people are represented by the letters A, B, C, D, and E, the handshakes could be listed as follows: A–B, A–C, A–D, A–E, B–C, B–D, B–E, C–D, C–E, and D–E. Although this is practical for five people shaking hands, it would be troublesome for much larger numbers. One might easily make a mistake in listing all the handshakes. Still another approach is to draw a picture of a pentagon with all its diagonals. Each corner stands for a person, and each line connecting two people stands for a handshake. Finding a

<table>
<tr><td>

NOTE: In mathematics, the word *solution* has two related meanings. One meaning is "the answer." The other is "how the answer was obtained; the solution method." Usually the context makes clear which meaning is intended.

</td></tr>
</table>

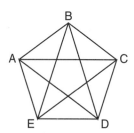

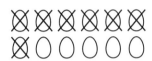

mistake in such a figure may be easier than in a long list, though it might be a nuisance to draw the figure for a large number of people.

Each of these solutions to the handshake problem depends on a different way of looking at the problem. One way used real people; another way involved a list; the third way made use of a drawing. Different ways of looking at a problem are called "problem representations."

Everyday Mathematics focuses on four basic kinds of problem representations: concrete, verbal, pictorial, and symbolic. Suppose, for example, you need a dozen eggs to make egg salad, but when you take out your eggs, you drop the carton on the floor. That's a concrete situation. A verbal description might make certain details explicit, such as the fact that seven of the eggs are broken. A simple picture could show the unfortunate eggs, and a number model could sum it up in symbols: $12 - 7 = 5$.

These varieties of problem representations can be diagrammed as shown below. Note that arrows connect each kind of representation with each of the other kinds. Students and adults use all of these representations at one time or another, depending on the situation at hand.

Four Problem-Solving
REPRESENTATIONS

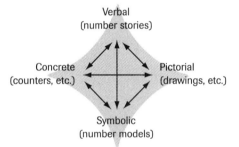

Representations are used both to give problems and to model solutions. Different students have different talents for and preferences among the representations, so each student benefits from repeated exposures to all four varieties. One of the aims of *Everyday Mathematics* is to increase students' facility with representations. Variations and extensions of the four basic kinds of representations are featured as students move beyond third grade. Symbolic representations, including number models with variables, and pictorial representations with graphs become increasingly important in Grades 4–6.

Another objective in *Everyday Mathematics* is to help students make easy translations among various ways of representing problems. Representations are closely related to solution strategies: Translating a problem into another representation is often the key to solving it. Discussion of different representations and solutions exposes students to methods they may like to try and reinforces the important message that there are many ways to solve problems.

As you discuss problems and solutions, compare various representations and ask students to translate from one to another. For example, the problem "If Jean rode her bike for 2.5 hours at an average speed of 8 miles per hour, how far did she travel?" might be presented orally by a teacher or a student or written in a Math Message or on a journal page. Solutions might be found and shared using representations such as a rate diagram or graph (pictorial), a number model (symbolic), or in words by a student who did the problem mentally (verbal). You might ask a student who did the problem mentally to write a number model. Or you might ask students to compare a number model and a graph for the problem. By encouraging such multiple representations and translations among representations, you can help students develop into more powerful problem solvers.

For more on graphing, see Section 5.9 in the Geometry essay and Section 4.1.3 in the Data and Chance essay.

For more on situation diagrams, see Section 2.1 in the Arithmetic Operations essay.

For more on number models, see Section 1.2.1 and 1.3.3 in the Numeration and Order essay.

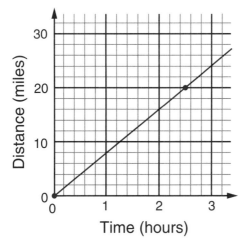

hours	miles per hour	miles
2.5	8	(20)

2.5 hours * 8 miles per hour = 20 miles

Jean traveled 20 miles because 8 25s is 200 so 8 2.5s is 20.0.

As you observe students working with various representations, you can also determine their problem-solving strengths and weaknesses, which can, in turn, help you adjust activities to meet individual needs. You might observe, for example, that a certain child never uses letter variables in number models, preferring blanks instead. This might lead you to suggest a number model such as "2.5 hours * 8 miles per hour = d miles" for the bicycle problem above. A student who is having difficulty understanding rate tables might benefit from a suggestion to try drawing a graph.

NOTE: Using pictures to represent problems and solutions can be especially helpful for students who are having difficulty. Use simple pictures and diagrams to illustrate classroom discussions as much as possible.

10.3 Mathematical Modeling

A mathematical model is something mathematical that corresponds to something in the real world. A sphere is a model for a basketball. The number sentence "22 + 1 = 23" is a model for the number of students in a classroom when a new student arrives. The formula "d = (5 hours) * (50 miles/hour)" is a model for the distance a car travels in 5 hours at 50 mph, and the formula $d = rt$ is a model linking distance, rate (speed), and time more generally. Specialists in science and industry spend much of their time building and testing mathematical models of real-world systems. People do mathematical modeling whenever they use mathematics to solve a problem.

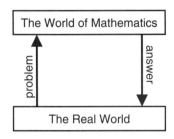

The World of Mathematics

problem

answer

The Real World

NOTE: The word *model* can also mean something in the real world that illustrates something mathematical. In this sense, a basketball is a model of a sphere. When people speak of mathematical modeling, however, the model is the mathematical object and the thing that is modeled is something in the real world.

For more on representing data in graphs, see Section 7.3.2 of the Reference Frames essay.

Mathematical modeling is the process of translating a real or hypothetical situation into the language of mathematics. After the situation is translated into mathematics, a solution is found using mathematical techniques; finally, the solution is translated back into the real world as the answer to the original problem. This process is illustrated in the margin.

The figure in the margin is an oversimplification. Mathematical modeling is often more complicated and involves some or all of the following steps:

- Formulate or confront a problem. Try to understand your problem. What do you want to find out? Imagine what the answer would look like if you had one.
- Study the information that is given and seek additional data as necessary. Discard unnecessary information. Sort the data you have.
- Explore the data. Represent the data in various ways, perhaps by drawing a picture, making a graph, or writing a number model. Play with the data.
- Do the math. Do the arithmetic, algebra, geometry, statistics, or whatever else is necessary to find an answer.
- Check the answer to see if it makes sense. Compare your answer to someone else's or to an answer you obtain in another way. Think about the method you used. Can the same method be used to solve other problems? Is there another method that would work for this problem? Compare various solutions and methods.

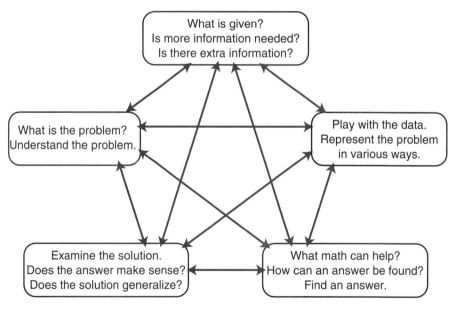

The process of mathematical modeling can actually begin anywhere and go anywhere. The lines in the figure above illustrate this. Often, for example, mathematical modeling begins with data. Suppose you are a baseball fan and are studying tables of baseball statistics. As you explore the data, you might notice that it appears that in inter-league games, National League teams win more often than American League teams. This might lead you to ask whether this is actually true. By adding up the total wins for each league you might find that the National League does win more often. If you wished, you could test your answer by making a prediction about the next set of inter-league games.

This baseball situation involves all five phases of the mathematical modeling process, though not quite in the order that they appear in the list on page 288. Sometimes, only a few of the phases are involved. An expert problem solver (or a student!) might see the solution to a problem instantly and simply have to check that it's correct. Sometimes it may be necessary to cycle repeatedly among phases—playing with the data, finding more data, playing with the new data, and so on—before a solution can be found.

Mathematical modeling involves abstraction. The number model "$100 - 79 = 21$" is an abstraction from the action of buying a 79¢ candy bar with a dollar bill. The modeling process involves both a real situation and an abstract mathematical model of that situation. (Even a mathematical model that uses concrete physical objects, such as base-10 blocks, is abstract in the sense that it omits many details of the original situation.) Because it is abstract, a single mathematical model can fit many different real-world situations. For example, the formula for the area of a rectangle, $A = lw$ (area equals length times width), applies to all real-world rectangles. This versatility is part of what makes mathematics such a powerful problem-solving tool.

Because they are abstract, however, mathematical models can become disconnected from the situation they are meant to model. Sometimes, students work their way through a mathematical process, arrive at an answer that makes no sense, and are completely unconcerned that they have produced nonsense. Making frequent connections between the real situation and the abstract model can help keep the process on track. Students should ask themselves questions such as these: *What does this number refer to? What does this graph say about the problem situation? Does this solution make sense?*

One reason for making ballpark estimates is to keep the problem-solving process on track. If a solution doesn't agree with the estimate, then something is wrong either with the estimate or with the solution. Making ballpark estimates helps reinforce connections between mathematical abstractions and real-world situations.

10.4 Teaching Problem Solving

Often when you are trying to learn something complicated, it is a good idea to focus on just one part. A pianist might play a difficult passage over and over again; a chef might practice making a roux until it's just right; a golfer might spend hours working on eight-foot putts. Practicing just one part at a time helps develop component skills that are essential for mastery of the entire complex activity, whether it's piano, cooking, or golf.

NOTE: In *Everyday Mathematics,* the problem-solving process often begins with information from a journal or *Student Reference Book* page. Students use the information to make up their own problems, which they or their classmates solve.

For more about reasons for estimating and the importance of estimation in problem solving, see Section 8.1.1 in the Estimation, Mental Arithmetic, and Fact Power essay.

As the mathematical modeling diagram illustrates, problem solving is a complex activity that can be broken down into parts—formulating problems, playing with data, and so on—each of which students can practice separately. Many of the exercises in *Everyday Mathematics* aim to provide practice in specific parts of the problem-solving process. For example, students become skilled at counting, measuring, calculating, estimating, looking up information, and many other specific skills that are useful in solving problems. During their years in school, students thus learn how to be effective in each separate phase of the mathematical-modeling process.

Such instruction is effective in teaching students how to manage each individual phase of the process, but successful problem solving in real life requires experience in navigating among the phases, just as cooking a fine meal requires successfully orchestrating many separate steps. It takes years of experience to become proficient at navigating among the phases. Knowing when to abandon an approach that's not working and go back to playing with the data, for example, is a skill that develops only with experience.

As students progress through *Everyday Mathematics*, they confront or pose problems that are more interesting and less routine, that make use of more sophisticated skills and concepts, and that require more complicated navigation around the mathematical-modeling diagram.

10.4.1 Number Stories

Everyday Mathematics aims to help students deal with real, age-appropriate problems. The authors' research shows that young students have impressive but largely untapped problem-solving abilities. One way *Everyday Mathematics* works to expand these abilities is through the use of number stories.

Number stories are stories that involve numbers and a question. The stories may be written, oral, pictorial, or even dramatic. Number stories may be created by the teacher or by the students. Stories may be designed to practice specific problem-solving techniques—the teacher might tell a rate story, for example, in order to introduce or practice the rate diagram—or may arise spontaneously from classroom situations.

Starting with *Kindergarten Everyday Mathematics*, students create number stories based on everyday experiences. In Grades K–3, many of the students' stories are based on journal pages that present a range of numerical data related to real situations (animal measures, shopping for groceries, vending machines, and so on). Beginning in fourth grade, students also write and tell stories based on reference materials, sections of the *Student Reference Book,* including the World Tour and American Tour sections, and data from experiments they perform.

For more on types of problem situations common in number stories, see Section 2.1 in the Arithmetic Operations essay.

NOTE: Some teachers say a number story involves numbers and has an "ending" rather than a question. This allows stories that give the answer.

Problem posing—making up problems—is a part of the problem-solving process that is often ignored in school mathematics, yet identifying and defining the problem is often the crucial first step toward a solution. Problem posing also leads to a high level of enthusiasm and involvement because students feel they have ownership of the problems they create themselves. Since the information presented tends to cover a wide range of difficulty, all members of the class will have opportunities to participate.

Students enjoy hearing and telling number stories. You might consider devoting an occasional language arts lesson to working with number stories. Creating, sharing, and discussing number stories can help develop students' communication and listening skills as well as their problem-solving abilities. The careful reading required for solving number stories helps students develop skills that will serve them well when they deal with technical text as they grow older.

The following description of what Kindergarten and first grade students do in *Everyday Mathematics* is included here for teachers in later grades who may be interested in the backgrounds of their students, or who have students entering the program without previous experience with *Everyday Mathematics*.

Number stories provide a bridge from natural to symbolic language. Children in Kindergarten and Grade 1 can be helped across that bridge by following these steps:

- Introduce number stories. Use a situation that is familiar to the students. Keep the stories short and the language simple. (When students tell their own stories, this is not always easy to do!) Whenever possible, draw pictures or diagrams to illustrate the stories. Modeling with concrete objects is effective with all ages and essential with younger students.

- Begin to include occasional mathematical terms in your comments on students' stories. For example, "You told an addition story. You had 5 candies and then you added 3 more."

- Begin writing number models beneath your illustrations as you discuss the stories. Relate the numbers and other symbols $(+, -, =)$ in the number models to quantities and actions in the stories. (For example, "This '5' is for the candies you started with. '+ 3' means you got three more, '8' tells how many you ended up with, and '=' means that 8 is the same as 5 and 3 more.") Help students understand how the symbols fit the problem situation. Explain that by using symbols you can write a number story more quickly and easily. If you wrote it in words, it would take a long time and might fill the board.

- Students may begin writing number models to fit stories. Often more than one number model can fit a given number story. Some first grade students may begin to use diagrams for parts-and-total, change, and comparison stories, though this is not expected until second grade.

10

When students begin to write number stories depends on their writing skills. Many first grade teachers report that their students enjoy trying to put their stories into words. For most students, it appears that skill at writing stories develops later than the ability to write number models using +, −, and =. Although you may give students the opportunity to write number stories at an early age, do not expect this from most of them until second or third grade. Younger students can tell or dictate stories before they can write them themselves or they can draw pictures and write a few words or numbers for their stories.

From third grade on, students write, swap, and solve stories for each other. By fourth grade, students should be using variables in number models for number stories. In fifth grade, students are encouraged to communicate with one another and with the teacher using more writing than in previous grades. Writing provides opportunities for students to analyze their own thinking, to reflect upon their thoughts, and to organize information for themselves. It also gives the teacher a great additional way to assess students' understanding of ideas and concepts.

Students use a variety of methods to solve one another's number stories, but *Everyday Mathematics* encourages using mental arithmetic whenever possible. This does not mean restricting students to doing the arithmetic entirely in their heads. Instead, students should develop a variety of flexible solution strategies that use whatever means are familiar and comfortable—manipulatives, jumps on a number line, doodles, diagrams, and so on. The emphasis is on solving problems in the students' own ways, on being open to a variety of approaches, and on choosing the approach that is most appropriate for a particular problem situation.

10.4.2 Sharing Strategies and Solutions

Research indicates that students develop a variety of problem-solving strategies if they are given the opportunity to share their ideas with their peers. If this sharing takes place in an open, receptive environment, students will learn that inventing creative, innovative ways of solving problems is acceptable in mathematics. The practice of gathering together to share solutions after individual or group problem solving continues throughout *Everyday Mathematics*.

Number stories are an excellent context for developing habits of sharing. Students should share their strategies and record their solutions, both correct and incorrect, on the board, using pictures and number models to illustrate their solutions. Students develop a better understanding of various mathematical processes when asked to think and strategize rather than when they are merely asked to repeat the steps of a standard written algorithm.

Discussing students' solutions can be extremely valuable, but care should be taken to ensure that students are not embarrassed if their

For more on variables and open number sentences, see Sections 9.3.1 and 9.3.2 in the Patterns, Sequences, Functions, and Algebra essay.

efforts fall short. Students with correct answers are usually happy to share their models and their strategies with the class, but discussing incorrect answers can also be very instructive. Below are several suggestions for dealing with wrong answers:

- Emphasize that it is OK to make mistakes. In fact, errors are inevitable. What is not OK is failing to learn from one's mistakes.

- Frame discussions of incorrect solutions by saying, "Some students in last year's class did _____ [Describe the incorrect approach.] Why do you think they did that? How would you help them see their mistake?"

- Emphasize that answers obtained using different methods should agree, so if there is not agreement, something must be wrong. Press students to resolve the dilemma.

- Compare and contrast different strategies and help students see advantages and disadvantages of each. An incorrect method may have some good ideas that can be used to improve another method.

At the beginning of each school year, *Everyday Mathematics* builds in specific occasions for this kind of interaction. Many other opportunities materialize over the course of the year. Eventually, with practice, students will become comfortable sharing their strategies and will be able to talk about them freely and fluently, listen to one another attentively, and revise their own strategies and adopt new ones based on these discussions.

10.4.3 Basic Problem-Solving Strategies

The diagram of the problem-solving process on page 288 fits what experts actually do when they solve problems, but it is too complicated to be of much help for beginners. On the other hand, many elementary school mathematics textbooks include long lists of strategies and tips—but these lists are often little help even with simple real-life problems and are essentially useless for dealing with complicated problems of public policy or in the workplace.

Students need a guide that is more useful than a list of tips but simpler than a diagram of expert behavior. To this end, *Everyday Mathematics* includes general guidelines for managing problem solving, such as the one in the margin, which is taken from the *Fourth Grade Student Reference Book*.

Because problems from everyday life are usually complicated, often the first need is to simplify the situation and figure out exactly what is known and what is to be found out. Problem situations in daily life, for example, often contain many irrelevant numbers. Sometimes relevant information is missing and must be inferred or derived from what is known. Often the problem solver must deal not only with just a few counts or measures but with large sets of data. Considerable effort may be required to make the data consistent in format and to devise a display that suggests useful patterns or interesting questions. The process seldom follows one predictable step after another.

1. Understand the problem.
2. Plan what to do.
3. Carry out the plan.
4. Look back.

10.4.4 Results

Teachers who have used the approach to problem solving described report very positive results, as have researchers and program evaluators who have studied problem solving in *Everyday Mathematics*. These teachers and researchers find that students develop strong, flexible, and independent calculation skills and problem-solving strategies. After using mental arithmetic with interesting number stories and relatively small numbers, students become able to operate with much larger numbers than they would normally have been able to handle. Students also develop an understanding of various mathematical processes that many students do not attain when using standard written algorithms.

Blair Chewning, an *Everyday Mathematics* teacher from Virginia, provides an example of the powerful results that this approach can yield. Ms. Chewning read an article in the *Richmond Times-Dispatch* with the headline "State, national math scores add up to poor report card." The picture painted was bleak, charging that on a recent national mathematics test, 40 percent of eighth grade students failed to perform at even a basic level. The following problem was given as an example of a "basic problem" for Grade 8:

> Jill needs to earn $45 for a class trip. She earns $2 each day on Mondays, Tuesdays, and Wednesdays. She earns $3 each day on Thursdays, Fridays, and Saturdays. She does not work on Sundays. How many weeks will it take her to earn $45?

Ms. Chewning was teaching second grade at the time, using *Everyday Mathematics*, and decided to see how her students would handle this problem. This is what she reported:

> Every single student attempted the problem, which was presented as optional. Such risk-takers they have become! Two students, using mental math only, presented me with the correct answer by the time I had completed writing the number story on the board. A total of 82% of the students, using a variety of strategies (see page 295), successfully solved the problem in less than five minutes. Of the three students who struggled, two were right on track, making only minor computational errors, and the third achieved success after extensive trial and error.

> Needless to say, I was astounded. While I had expected them to be successful to some extent, I had not anticipated the speed and comfort with which they approached the task.

> Thank you, *Everyday Mathematics*. The skills your program fosters empowered my second graders to soar higher than they or their teacher thought possible. They wore the "hats" of eighth graders quite proudly that day and would seem to suggest that our math future is anything but bleak.

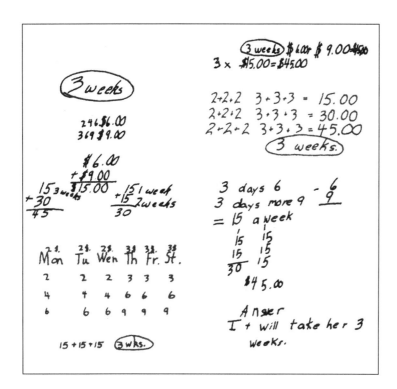

References

National Council of Supervisors of Mathematics. (1977). Position paper on basic skills. *Arithmetic Teacher* 25 (1): 19–22.

National Council of Supervisors of Mathematics. (1988). *Essential mathematics for the 21st century: The position of the National Council of Supervisors of Mathematics*. Minneapolis: Author.

National Council of Teachers of Mathematics. (1980). *An Agenda for Action: Recommendations for School Mathematics of the 1980s*. Reston, VA: Author.

National Council of Teachers of Mathematics. (1989). *Curriculum and Evaluation Standards for School Mathematics*. Reston, VA: Author.

National Council of Teachers of Mathematics. (2000). *Principles and Standards for School Mathematics*. Reston, VA: Author.

Polya, George. *How to Solve It*. Princeton University Press. 1988.

Glossary

absolute value The absolute value of a number is the distance between the number and 0 on the number line. The absolute value of a number is the larger of the number and its opposite. The absolute value of a positive number is the number itself, and the absolute value of a negative number is the opposite of the number. The absolute value of 0 is 0. The notation for the absolute value of n is $|n|$.

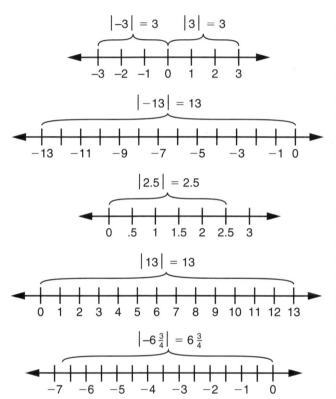

abundant number A number for which the sum of all the proper factors is greater than the number itself. For example, 12 is an abundant number because the sum of its proper factors is $1 + 2 + 3 + 4 + 6 = 16$, and 16 is greater than 12. Compare *to deficient number* and *perfect number.*

account balance An amount of money that you have or that you owe. See *"in the black"* and *"in the red."*

accurate As near as possible to a true result. For example, an accurate measure or count is one with little or no error. Compare to *precise.*

acre In the U.S. customary system, a unit of area equal to 43,560 square feet, roughly the size of a football field. A square mile is 640 acres. See the Tables of Measure. See Section 6.5 of the Measurement essay.

acute angle An angle with a measure greater than 0° and less than 90°. See *angle.* See Section 5.4 of the Geometry essay.

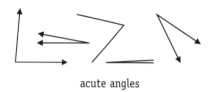

acute angles

acute triangle A triangle having three acute angles. See *triangle.* See Section 5.4 of the Geometry essay.

addend One of two or more numbers that are added. For example, in $5 + 3 + 1$, the addends are 5, 3, and 1. See *addition.*

addition A mathematical operation based on putting together two or more quantities. Numbers being added are called *addends;* the result of addition is called the *sum.* For example, in $12 + 33 = 45$, the addends are 12 and 33 and the sum is 45. Subtraction "undoes" addition: $12 + 33 = 45$ can be "undone" by either $45 - 12 = 33$ or $45 - 33 = 12$. See Section 2.1 of the Arithmetic Operations essay and 3.2 of the Algorithms essay.

addition fact Two 1-digit numbers and their sum, such as $9 + 7 = 16$. See *arithmetic facts.* See Section 2.1 of the Arithmetic Operations essay and 8.3 of the Estimation, Mental Arithmetic, and Fact Power essay.

additive inverses Two numbers whose sum is 0. The additive inverse of a number is also called its *opposite*. For example, 3 and −3 are additive inverses because 3 + (−3) = 0.

address In a spreadsheet, a letter-number pair, such as A5, used to identify a cell.

address box In a spreadsheet, a place where the address of a cell is shown when the cell is selected.

add−up subtraction A subtraction procedure in which the difference is found by adding up from the smaller number. For example, to solve 87−49, start at 49, add 30 to reach 79, and then add 8 more to reach 87. The difference is 30 + 8 = 38. See Section 3.2 of the Algorithms essay for further discussion and other subtraction algorithms.

adjacent angles Two angles with a common side and vertex that do not otherwise overlap. See Section 5.4 of the Geometry essay.

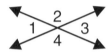

Angles 1 and 2, 2 and 3, 3 and 4, and 4 and 1 are pairs of adjacent angles.

algebra (1) A school subject, usually first studied in eighth or ninth grade. (2) The use of letters of the alphabet to represent numbers in equations, formulas, and rules. (3) A set of rules and properties for a number system. See Section 2.1 of the Arithmetic Operations essay and Section 9.3 of the Patterns, Sequences, Functions, and Algebra essay.

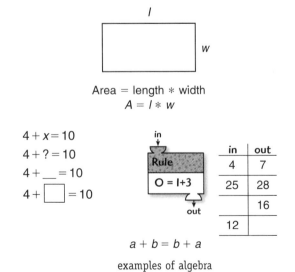

Area = length ∗ width
$A = l * w$

$4 + x = 10$
$4 + ? = 10$
$4 + \_\_ = 10$
$4 + \boxed{} = 10$

in	out
4	7
25	28
	16
12	

Rule
O = I+3

$a + b = b + a$

examples of algebra

algebraic expression An *expression* that contains a variable. For example, if Maria is 2 inches taller than Joe and if the variable *M* represents Maria's height, then the algebraic expression $M − 2$ represents Joe's height. See *algebra*. See Section 2.1 of the Arithmetic Operations essay and Sections 9.2 and 9.3 of the Patterns, Sequences, Functions, and Algebra essay.

algebraic order of operations Same as *order of operations*.

algorithm A set of step-by-step instructions for doing something, such as carrying out a computation or solving a problem. The most common algorithms are those for basic arithmetic computations, but there are many others. Some mathematicians and many computer scientists spend a lot of time trying to find more efficient algorithms for solving problems. See Sections 3.1–3.3 of the Algorithms essay.

altitude (1) In a geometric figure, the shortest line segment from any vertex to the line containing the opposite side or to the plane containing the opposite face. (2) The length of this segment. (3) The perpendicular distance from one side of a figure to a parallel side or from a vertex to the opposite side; the height. See *height of a parallelogram*, *height of a prism or cylinder*, *height of a pyramid or cone*, and *height of a triangle*. See Sections 5.4 and 5.5 of the Geometry essay.

Altitudes of 2-D figures are shown in blue.

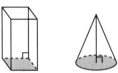

Altitudes of 3-dimensional figures are shown in blue.

(4) Geography: Distance above sea level. Same as *elevation*.

analog clock A clock that shows the time by the positions of the hour and minute hands. Compare to *digital clock*. See Section 7.2 of the Reference Frames essay.

-angle A suffix meaning *angle*, or corner.

angle A figure formed by two rays or two line segments with a common endpoint. The common endpoint is called the *vertex of the angle*. The rays or segments are called the *sides of the angle*. An angle is measured by a number of degrees between 0 and 360, which can be thought of as the amount of rotation around the vertex from one side to the other. Angles can be represented by rotating one side while the other is kept stationary. Angles are named either by a single capital letter naming the vertex or by three letters, two naming points on the sides with the vertex letter between them. See *acute angle*, *obtuse angle*, *reflex angle*, *right angle*, and *straight angle*. See Section 5.4 of the Geometry essay.

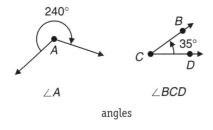

angles

anthropometry The study of human body sizes and proportions.

apex In a pyramid or cone, the vertex opposite the base. In a pyramid, all the non-base faces meet at the apex. See Section 5.5 of the Geometry essay.

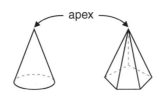

apex

arc Part of a circle, from one point on the circle to another. For example, a semicircle is an arc with endpoints that are the endpoints of a diameter of the circle. An arc is named by its endpoints.

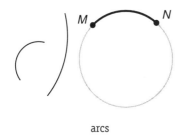

arcs

area A measure of a bounded surface. The boundary might be a triangle or rectangle in a plane or the boundaries of a state or country on the earth's surface. Area is expressed in square units such as square miles, square inches, or square centimeters, and can be thought of as the approximate number of non-overlapping squares that will "tile" or "cover" the surface within the boundary. See Section 6.5 of the Measurement essay for a discussion of area.

40 square units

21 square units

The area of the United States is about 3,800,000 square miles.

area model (1) A model for multiplication in which the length and width of a rectangle represent the factors and the area of the rectangle represents the product. See Section 2.1.

area model for 3 * 5 = 15

(2) A model for fractions that represents parts of a whole. The whole is a region, such as a circle or a rectangle, representing the number ONE. See Section 1.3.

area model for $\frac{2}{3}$

arithmetic facts The basic arithmetic facts are the addition facts (addends 9 or less); subtraction facts that are the inverses of these; multiplication facts (factors 9 or less); and division facts that are inverses of these, except there is no division by zero. See Section 8.3. There are:

100 addition facts, from $0 + 0 = 0$ to $9 + 9 = 18$
100 subtraction facts, from $0 - 0 = 0$ to $18 - 9 = 9$
100 multiplication facts, from $0 \times 0 = 0$ to $9 \times 9 = 81$
90 division facts, from $0/1 = 0$ to $81/9 = 9$

An *extended fact* involves a multiple of 10 (or 100, 1,000,...) of one or both addends or factors in a basic fact or use of a basic fact to get a relatively simple new result.

$2 + 3 = 5$ so $20 + 30 = 50$, $500 - 300 = 200$
$4 \times 6 = 24$, so $400 \times 6 = 2,400$, $240/60 = 4$
$5 + 7 = 12$, so $15 + 7 = 22$

arm span The distance from fingertip to fingertip of a person's outstretched arms. Same as *fathom*. A fathom is standardized at 6 feet, or 2 yards. See Section 6.1 of the Measurement essay.

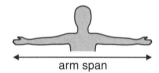
arm span

array An arrangement of objects in a regular pattern, usually rows and columns. Arrays can be used to model multiplication. See Section 2.1 of the Arithmetic Operations essay and Section 6.5 of the Measurement essay.

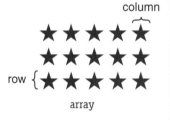
column
row
array

associative property A property of addition and multiplication (but not subtraction or division) that says that changing the grouping of the elements being added or multiplied will not change the sum or product. See Section 1.5.

For addition:
$(a + b) + c = a + (b + c)$, so $(4 + 3) + 7 = 4 + (3 + 7)$

For multiplication:
$(a * b) * c = a * (b * c)$, so $(4 * 3) * 7 = 4 * (3 * 7)$

astronomical unit The average distance from Earth to the Sun. It is used as a unit of measure to express distances in space. One astronomical unit is about 93 million miles or 150 million kilometers.

attribute A feature of an object or common feature of a set of objects. Examples of attributes include size, shape, color, and number of sides. Same as *property*.

average (1) A central, or typical, value of a set of numbers. In statistics, and in *Everyday Mathematics*, several different averages are defined, including the mean, the median, and the mode. (2) In common usage, "average" is usually assumed to refer to the mean, which is determined by finding the sum of all the numbers in a set and then dividing the sum by the number of numbers in the set.

axis (1) Either of the two number lines used to form a coordinate grid. Plural: *axes*.

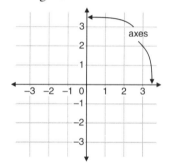
axes

(2) A line about which a solid figure rotates.

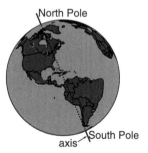
North Pole
axis
South Pole

ballpark estimate A rough estimate. A ballpark estimate can serve as a check on the reasonableness of an answer obtained through some other procedure, or it can be made when an exact figure is unnecessary or is impossible to obtain. See Section 8.1 of the Estimation, Mental Arithmetic, and Fact Power essay and Section 10.2 of the Problem Solving essay.

bank draft A written order for the exchange of money. $1000 bills are no longer in existence so $1,000 bank drafts are issued. People can exchange $1,000 bank drafts for smaller bills (for example, 10 bills of $100 each).

glossary

bar graph A graph that shows relationships in data by the use of bars to represent quantities. See Section 4.1 of the Data and Chance essay.

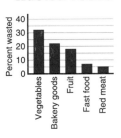

Wasted Foods

Source: The Garbage Product

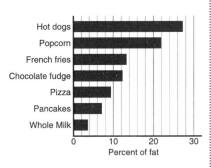

Fat Content of Foods

Source: The New York Public Library Desk Reference

base (1) Geometry: A side of a polygon, usually used for area computations along with the "altitude" or height perpendicular to it. See *base of a parallelogram*, *base of a triangle*, *height*, and *altitude*. See Section 5.4 of the Geometry essay.

Bases are shown in blue, altitudes in gray.

(2) Geometry: Either of two parallel and congruent faces that define the shape of a prism or cylinder, or the face that defines the shape of a cone or pyramid. See *base of a prism or cylinder* and *base of a pyramid or cone*. See Section 5.5 of the Geometry essay.

Bases are shown in blue.

(3) Arithmetic: See *exponential notation*. See Section 2.2 of the Arithmetic essay. (4) Arithmetic: The foundation number for a numeration system. For example, our usual way of writing numbers is a base-ten place-value system, with 1, 10, 100, 1,000 and other powers of 10 as the values of the places in whole numbers. In electronics and computers, bases of two, eight, or sixteen are usual, instead of base ten. See Sections 1.7 and 2.2.

$$356 = 300 + 50 + 6$$

expanded notation for a base-ten number

baseline A set of data used for comparison with subsequent data. Baseline data can be used to judge whether an experimental intervention is successful.

base of a parallelogram One of the sides of a parallelogram; also, the length of this side. In calculating area, the base is used along with the height, or altitude, which is measured on a perpendicular to the side opposite this base. See *altitude* or *height of a parallelogram*. See Section 5.4 of the Geometry essay.

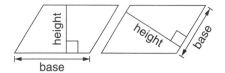

base of a prism or cylinder Either of the two parallel, congruent faces of a prism or cylinder that define its shape and are used to determine its name and classification. In a cylinder, the base is a circle or ellipse. See *altitude* or *height of a prism or cylinder*.

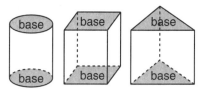

base of a pyramid or cone The face of a pyramid that defines its shape and is used to name and classify the pyramid. The base of a pyramid is the face opposite the apex, which is the vertex where all the other faces meet. The base of a cone is a circle. See *altitude* or *height of a pyramid or cone*.

base of a triangle The side of a triangle to which an altitude is drawn; also, the length of this side. The height, or altitude, is the length of the shortest line segment from the base to the vertex opposite the base; the height is perpendicular to the base. See *altitude* or *height of a triangle*. See Section 5.4 of the Geometry essay.

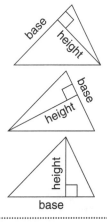

base ten The characteristic of our standard numeration system that results in the value of each "place" being 10 times the value of the place to its right. The base-ten numeration system (also called the decimal numeration system or standard notation) consists of the ten digits 0, 1, 2, ..., 9 and a method of assigning values to those digits depending on where they appear in a numeral (ones place, tens place, hundreds place, and so on, to the left of the decimal point; tenths place, hundredths place, and so on, to the right of the decimal point).

base-ten shorthand In *Everyday Mathematics*, a system used to represent base-10 blocks. See Section 1.7 of the Numeration and Order essay and Section 2.1 of the Arithmetic Operations essay.

Name	Base-10 block	Base-10 shorthand
cube	⬠	▪
long	▯	│
flat	▦	▢
big cube	▧	◰

benchmark An important count or measure that can be used to evaluate the reasonableness of other counts, measures, or estimates. A benchmark for land area is that a football field is about one acre. A benchmark for length is that the width of a man's thumb is about one inch. See Section 6.1 of the Measurement essay.

big cube In *Everyday Mathematics*, the term for the base-10 block cube that measures 10 cm by 10 cm by 10 cm. A big cube is worth 1,000 1-cm cubes. See Base-10 Blocks, pages 49-50, in the Tools section of the Management Guide.

billion In American usage, 1 billion is 1,000,000,000 or 10^9. In British, French, and German usage, 1 billion is 1,000,000,000,000 or 10^{12}.

bisect To divide a segment, angle, or figure into two parts of equal measure.

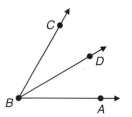

Ray *BD* bisects angle *ABC*.

braces See *grouping symbols*.

brackets See *grouping symbols*.

broken−line graph Same as *line graph*. See Section 4.1 of the Data and Chance essay.

calibrate To divide or mark something, such as a thermometer, with gradations.

calorie A unit for measuring the amount of energy a food will produce when it is digested by the body. One calorie is the amount of energy required to raise the temperature of 1 liter of water 1° Celsius. (Technically, this is the "large calorie" or kilocalorie. The "small calorie" is one thousandth of the large calorie.)

capacity (1) A measure of how much a container can hold, usually in such units as *quart*, *gallon*, *cup*, or *liter*. See *volume*. See Section 6.6 of the Measurement essay. (2) The maximum weight a scale can measure.

cartographer A person who makes maps.

cell In a spreadsheet, a box formed where a column and a row intersect. A *column* is a section of cells lined up vertically. A *row* is a section of cells lined up horizontally.

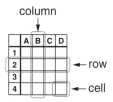

Celsius The temperature scale on which pure water at sea level freezes at 0° and boils at 100°. The Celsius scale is used in the metric system. A less common name for this scale is "centigrade", because there are 100 units between the freezing and boiling points of water. Compare to *Fahrenheit*. See Section 7.1 of the Reference Frames essay.

census An official count of population and the recording of such data as age, sex, income, education, and so on.

cent (1) Sometimes means one-hundredth, as with a penny; $\frac{1}{100}$ of a dollar. The word comes from the Latin word *centesimus*, which means a hundredth part. (2) Sometimes a prefix meaning one-hundred, as in century.

center Of a circle: The point in the plane of a circle equally distant from all points on the circle. See Section 5.4 of the Geometry essay. Of a sphere: The point equally distant from all points on the sphere. See Sections 5.4 and 5.5 of the Geometry essay.

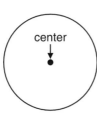

centi- In the metric system, a prefix meaning one hundredth. For example, a centimeter is $\frac{1}{100}$ of a meter. (*Centi-* can also mean one hundred, as in "centipede," an arthropod with many legs.)

centimeter (cm) In the metric system, a unit of length equivalent to 10 millimeters, $\frac{1}{10}$ of a decimeter, and $\frac{1}{100}$ of a meter. See the Tables of Measure. See Section 6.2 of the Measurement essay.

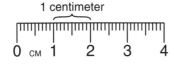

chance The possibility of an outcome occurring in an uncertain event. For example, in tossing a coin there is an equal chance of getting heads or tails. See Section 4.2 of the Data and Chance essay.

change diagram In *Everyday Mathematics*, a diagram used to represent situations in which quantities are either increased or decreased. The diagram includes the starting quantity, the ending quantity, and the amount of change. Change diagrams can be helpful in solving many one-step addition and subtraction problems. See *situation diagram*. See Section 2.1 of the Arithmetic Operations essay, Sections 9.2 and 9.3 of the Patterns, Sequences, Functions, and Algebra essay, and page 20 of the Management Guide.

change diagram for 14 − 5 = 9

change of sign key The $\boxed{\pm}$ key on certain calculators. This key changes the sign of the number in the display. It will change a positive number to a negative number and a negative number to a positive number. To enter a negative number on such calculators, the key is pressed after the digits have been keyed in. For example, to find 35.4 + (−12.8) you would key in 35 $\boxed{.}$ 4 $\boxed{+}$ 12 $\boxed{.}$ 8 $\boxed{\pm}$ $\boxed{=}$.

change-to-less story A number story that describes a change situation in which the ending quantity is less than the starting quantity. A number story about spending money is an example of a change-to-less story. Compare to *change-to-more story*.

change-to-more story A number story that describes a change situation in which the ending quantity is more than the starting quantity. A number story about earning money is an example of a change-to-more story. Compare to *change-to-less story*.

circle The set of all points in a plane that are equally distant from a given point in the plane called the *center* of the circle. The distance from the center to the circle is the *radius*. The circle is the boundary only. A circle together with its interior is called a *disk* or a *circular region*. See Section 5.4 of the Geometry essay.

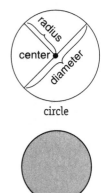

circle

circular region

circle graph A graph in which a circle and its interior are divided into parts to represent the parts of a set of data. The whole circle represents the whole set of data. Same as *pie graph*. See Section 4.1 of the Data and Chance essay.

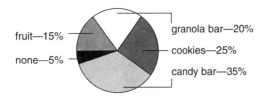

circumference The distance around a circle or the maximum distance around a sphere. See Sections 5.4 and 5.5 of the Geometry essay.

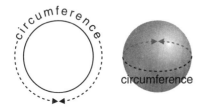

Class Data Pad In *Everyday Mathematics*, a large pad of paper where data collected by the class can be stored for use (and reuse) throughout the year. Data recorded on the Class Data Pad can be used for analysis, graphing, and generating number stories. See Section 4.1 of the Data and Chance essay. See the Organizing Routines and Displays section, pages 31–33, in the Management Guide.

clockwise A rotation in the same direction that the hands of a standard analog clock move; turning to the right.

column (1) A vertical arrangement of objects or numbers in an array or a table.

(2) A section of cells lined up vertically in a spreadsheet. See *cell*.

column addition An addition procedure in which the addends' digits are first added in each place-value column separately, and then 10-for-1 trades are made until each column has only 1 digit. Lines may be drawn to separate the place-value column. See Section 3.2 of the Algorithms essay for further discussion and for information on other addition algorithms.

common denominator Any nonzero number that is a multiple of the denominators of two or more fractions. For example, the fractions $\frac{1}{2}$ and $\frac{2}{3}$ have common denominators 6, 12, 18, and so on. See *denominator*. See Section 3.3.

common factor Any number that is a factor of two or more numbers. The common factors of 18 and 24 are 1, 2, 3, and 6. See *factor*.

common fraction A fraction in which the numerator and the denominator are both integers. Compare to *decimal fraction*.

commutative property A property of addition and multiplication (but not division or subtraction) that says that changing the order of the elements being added or multiplied will not change the sum or product.

For addition: $a + b = b + a$, so $5 + 10 = 10 + 5$
For multiplication: $a \times b = b \times a$,
so $5 \times 10 = 10 \times 5$.

See *turn-around facts*. See Section 1.5 of the Numeration and Order essay.

comparison diagram In *Everyday Mathematics*, a diagram used to represent situations in which two quantities are compared. Comparison diagrams can be helpful in solving certain one-step addition and subtraction problems. See *situation diagram*. See Section 2.1 of the Arithmetic Operations essay, Sections 9.2 and 9.3 of the Patterns, Sequences, Functions, and Algebra essay, and page 20 of the Management Guide.

Quantity
12

Quantity	
9	?

difference

Quantity
12

Quantity	Difference
9	?

comparison diagrams for $12 = 9 + N$

comparison story A number story that describes a comparison situation between two quantities, focusing on the difference between them. A number story about the difference in amounts of two things is an example of a comparison story.

compass (1) A tool used to draw circles and arcs and copy line segments. Certain geometric figures can be drawn using only a compass and a straightedge. See *compass-and-straightedge construction*.

(2) A tool used to determine geographic direction.

compass-and-straightedge construction A drawing of a geometric figure made using only a compass and a straightedge. See Section 5.12 of the Geometry essay.

compass rose Same as *map direction symbol*.

complementary angles Two angles whose measures total 90°. See Section 5.4 of the Geometry essay.

Angles 1 and 2 are complementary angles.

composite number A whole number that has more than two factors. For example, 10 is a composite number because it has four factors: 1, 2, 5, and 10. A composite number is divisible by at least three whole numbers. Compare to *prime number*.

compound unit A quotient or product of units. For example, miles per hour (mi/hr, mph), square centimeters (cm²), and person-hours are compound units.

concave polygon A polygon in which at least one vertex is "pushed in." A line may intersect a concave polygon at more than two points. The term "nonconvex" is a more formal synonym for concave. Compare to *convex polygon*. See Section 5.4 of the Geometry essay.

concave polyhedron A polyhedron in which at least one vertex is "pushed in." If a polyhedron is concave, it is possible to find two points on it that can be connected with a line segment that passes outside the polyhedron. A line may intersect a concave polyhedron at more than two points. A more formal term for concave is "nonconvex."

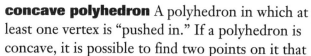

concave polyhedron with segment

concentric circles Circles that have the same center but radii of different lengths. See Section 5.4 of the Geometry essay.

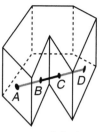

concentric circles

cone A 3-dimensional shape having a circular base, a curved lateral surface, and one vertex, called the *apex*. See Section 5.5 of the Geometry essay.

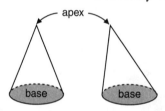

congruent Having the same size and shape. Two figures are congruent if a combination of slides, flips, and turns can be used to move one of the figures so that it exactly fits "on top of" the other figure. In diagrams of congruent figures, the congruent sides may be marked with the same number of tick marks. The symbol ≅ means "is congruent to."

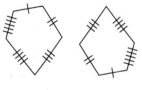

congruent pentagons

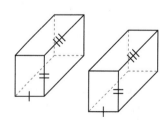

congruent prisms

consecutive Following one another in an uninterrupted order. For example, A, B, C, and D are four consecutive letters of the alphabet; 6, 7, 8, 9, and 10 are five consecutive whole numbers.

consecutive angles Two angles in a polygon that share a common side. See Section 5.4 of the Geometry essay.

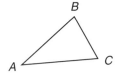

Angles *A* and *B, B* and *C,* and *C* and *A* are pairs of consecutive angles.

constant A value that does not change. For example, the ratio of the circumference of a circle to the diameter is a famous constant, π. In the number sentence $3x = y$, 3 is a constant.

contour line A curve on a map through places where a measurement (such as temperature, elevation, air pressure, or growing season) is constant.

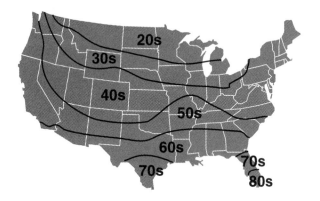

contour map A map that uses contour lines to delineate areas according to a particular feature, such as elevation or climate. See *contour line.*

conversion fact A fixed relationship, such as 1 yard = 3 feet or 1 inch = 2.54 centimeters, that can be used to convert measurements within or between systems of measurement. See Section 6.2 of the Measurement essay.

convex polygon A polygon in which all vertices are "pushed outward." A line segment connecting any two points on different sides of a convex polygon lies entirely within the polygon. Compare to *concave polygon.* See Section 5.4 of the Geometry essay.

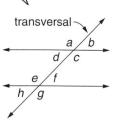

convex polygon

convex polyhedron A polyhedron that is everywhere "pushed out." Any line segment connecting any two points on different faces of a convex polyhedron is contained completely inside the polyhedron. Compare to *concave polyhedron.*

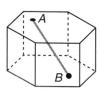

convex polyhedron

coordinate A number used to locate a point on a number line, or one of two numbers used to locate a point on a coordinate grid. See Section 5.9 of the Geometry essay.

coordinate grid A device for locating points in a plane by means of ordered pairs of numbers. A rectangular coordinate grid is formed by two number lines that intersect at right angles at their zero points. See Section 5.9 of the Geometry essay and Section 7.3 of the Reference Frames essay.

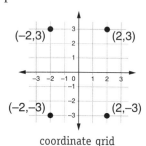

coordinate grid

corner Same as *vertex.*

corresponding angles (1) Of angles in figures: two angles in the same relative position. Corresponding angles can be marked with the same number of arcs or slashes.

(2) Of angles formed by lines cut by a *transversal:* Two angles in similar locations in relation to a transversal intersecting two lines. In the diagram, $\angle a$ and $\angle e$, $\angle b$ and $\angle f$, $\angle d$ and $\angle h$, and $\angle c$ and $\angle g$ are corresponding angles. If any two corresponding angles are congruent, then the lines are parallel.

transversal

corresponding sides Two sides in the same relative position in two figures. Corresponding sides are marked with the same number of slash marks.

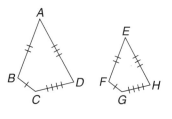

glossary

corresponding vertices Two vertices in the same relative position in two similar figures.

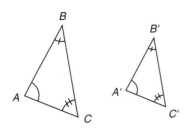

A and A′, B and B′, and C and C′ are corresponding vertices.

counterclockwise A rotation in the opposite direction as that of the hands of a standard analog clock; turning to the left.

counting numbers The numbers used to count things. The set of counting numbers is {1, 2, 3, 4, ...}. Sometimes 0 is included. Counting numbers are also in the set of whole numbers, the set of integers, the set of rational numbers, and the set of real numbers, but those sets also include numbers that are not counting numbers. See Section 1.1 of the Numeration and Order essay.

cover−up method A method for finding the solution of an equation by covering up a part of the equation containing a variable.

credit An amount, such as a deposit, added to an account balance.

cross section A shape formed by the intersection of a plane and a geometric solid. See Section 5.5 of the Geometry essay.

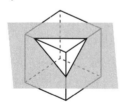

cube (1) A polyhedron with six square faces. One of the 5 regular polyhedra. See *regular polyhedron*. See Section 5.5 of the Geometry essay.

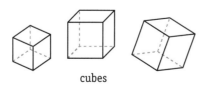

cubes

(2) In *Everyday Mathematics*, the term for the smaller cube of the base-10 blocks, measuring 1 cm on each edge. See Base-10 Blocks pages 49–50, in the Tools section of the Management Guide.

cube of a number The product of a number used as a factor three times. For example, the cube of 5 is $5 * 5 * 5 = 5^3 = 125$.

cubic centimeter (cc or cm³) A metric unit of volume; the volume of a cube that is 1 centimeter on a side. 1 cubic centimeter is equal to 1 milliliter. See the Tables of Measure. See Sections 6.2 and 6.6 of the Measurement essay.

cubic unit A unit used in measuring volume. Common cubic units include cubic centimeters, cubic inches, cubic feet, and cubic meters. See Section 6.6 of the Measurement essay.

cubit An ancient unit of length, measured from the point of the elbow to the end of the middle finger. The cubit has been standardized at various times to be between 18 and 22 inches. The Latin word *cubitum* means "elbow." See Section 6.1 of the Measurement essay.

cup In the U.S. customary system, a unit of capacity equal to 8 fluid ounces; $\frac{1}{2}$ pint. See the Tables of Measure. See Sections 6.2 and 6.6 of the Measurement essay.

curved surface A surface that does not lie in a plane; for example, a sphere or the lateral surface of a cylinder. See Section 5.5 of the Geometry essay.

customary system of measurement The measuring system used most often in the United States. Units for length include inch, foot, yard, and mile; units for weight include ounce and pound; units for capacity (amount of liquid or other pourable substance a container can hold) include cup, pint, quart, and gallon; units for temperature include degrees Fahrenheit. See Section 6.2 of the Measurement essay.

cylinder A 3-dimensional shape having a curved surface and parallel congruent circular or elliptical bases. The points on the curved surface of a cylinder are on straight lines connecting corresponding points on the bases. See Section 5.5 of the Geometry essay.

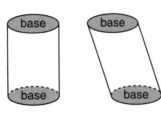

data Information that is gathered by observing, counting, or measuring. Strictly, *data* is the plural of *datum*, but *data* is often used as a singular word. See Section 4.1 of the Data and Chance essay.

debit An amount, such as a withdrawal, subtracted from a bank balance.

deca- Prefix meaning ten.

deci- Prefix meaning one-tenth.

decimal A number written in standard notation containing a decimal point, as in 2.54. See *repeating decimal* and *terminating decimal*. See Section 1.3 of the Numeration and Order essay.

decimal fraction A fraction whose denominator is a power of 10. Also, a decimal. This term is not used in *Everyday Mathematics*. Compare to *common fraction*.

decimal point The mark that separates the whole number from the fraction in decimal notation; in expressing money, it separates the dollars from the cents. In the United States, a period is used; in Europe and elsewhere, a comma is used.

decimeter (dm) In the metric system, a unit of length equivalent to $\frac{1}{10}$ meter or 10 centimeters.

deficient number A number greater than the sum of all its proper factors. For example, 10 is a deficient number because the sum of its proper factors is $1 + 2 + 5 = 8$, and 8 is less than 10. Compare to *abundant number* and *perfect number*. See *proper factor*.

degree (°) (1) A unit of measure for angles based on dividing one complete circle (rotation) into 360 equal parts. See Section 5.4 of the Geometry essay. (2) A unit for temperature on either the Celsius or Fahrenheit scale. See Section 7.1 of the Reference Frames essay. The small, raised symbol ° is called the degree symbol.

degree Celsius (°C) Unit for marking Celsius thermometers or for measuring differences in temperature in the metric system. On the Celsius scale, pure water at sea level freezes at 0° and boils at 100°. See *Celsius*. See Section 7.1 of the Reference Frames essay.

degree Fahrenheit (°F) Unit for marking Fahrenheit thermometers or measuring differences in temperature in the U.S. customary system. On the Fahrenheit scale, pure water at sea level freezes at 32°F and boils at 212°F, and a saturated salt solution freezes as 0°F. See *Fahrenheit*. See Section 7.1 of the Reference Frames essay.

denominator In a fraction, the number written below the line or to the right of the slash. In the fraction $\frac{a}{b}$ or *a/b*, *b* is the denominator. In a part-whole fraction, the denominator is the number of equal parts into which the whole (or ONE) has been divided. See *part-whole fraction*. Compare to *numerator*. See Section 1.3 of the Numeration and Order essay.

density A rate that compares the mass of an object with its volume. For example, suppose a ball has a mass of 20 grams and a volume of 10 cubic centimeters. To find its density, divide its mass by its volume: 20 g/10 cm³ = 2 g/cm³ (2 grams per cubic centimeter).

diagonal (1) A line of objects or numbers from upper left to lower right or from lower left to upper right in an array or a table:

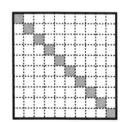

(2) A line segment joining two non-adjacent vertices of a polygon. See Section 5.4 of the Geometry essay. (3) A line segment joining two vertices of different faces of a polyhedron. See Section 5.5 of the Geometry essay.

diameter A line segment that passes through the center of a circle or sphere and has endpoints on the circle or sphere; also, the length of such a line segment. The diameter of a circle or sphere is twice the length of the radius. See *circle* and *sphere*. See Sections 5.4 and 5.5 of the Geometry essay.

difference The amount by which one number is greater or less than another number; the result of subtracting one number from another. For example, in $12 - 5 = 7$, 7 is the difference between 5 and 12. See *subtraction*.

digit In the base-ten numeration system, one of the symbols 0, 1, 2, 3, 4, 5, 6, 7, 8, 9, which can be used to write any number. For example, the numeral 145 is made up of the digits 1, 4, and 5.

digital clock A clock that shows the time with numbers to represent hours and minutes, with a colon separating the two. Compare to *analog clock*. See Section 7.2 of the Reference Frames essay.

dimension (1) A measure in one direction of an object, especially length, width, or height. The dimensions of a box might be 24 cm by 20 cm by 10 cm. (2) The number of coordinates necessary to fix a point in a geometric space. Thus, a line has one dimension since one coordinate suffices to locate a point on a line. A plane or the surface of a sphere has two dimensions since two coordinates are necessary to locate a point. Space has three dimensions because three coordinates are required to locate a point in space. See Section 5.1 of the Geometry essay.

direction symbol Same as *map direction symbol* and *compass rose*.

discount The amount by which the regular price of an item is reduced, expressed as a fraction or percent of the original price. For example, a $4.00 item that is on sale for $2.00 is discounted by 50 percent or by $\frac{1}{2}$. Or, when a $10.00 item has a discount percent of 10% (or the equivalent discount fraction of $\frac{1}{10}$) its sale price is $9.00.

disk A circle and its interior region.

displace To move something from one position to another.

display bar In a spreadsheet, a place where data or formulas entered from the keyboard are shown.

distributive property A property that relates two operations on numbers, usually multiplication and addition or multiplication and subtraction. This property gets its name because it "distributes" the factor outside the parentheses over the terms within the parentheses. See Section 9.2.

For multiplication over addition:
$a * (x + y) = (a * x) + (a * y)$,
so $2 * (5 + 3) = (2 * 5) + (2 * 3) = 10 + 6 = 16$
For multiplication over subtraction:
$a * (x - y) = (a * x) - (a * y)$,
so $2 * (5 - 3) = (2 * 5) - (2 * 3) = 10 - 6 = 4$

dividend In division, the number that is being divided. For example, in $35 \div 5 = 7$, the dividend is 35. See *division*.

divisibility test A procedure to determine whether a whole number can be divided evenly by another whole number, without actually doing the division. To check whether a number is divisible by 3, for example, check whether the sum of its digits is divisible by 3. Since the sum of the digits of 51 is divisible by 3 ($5 + 1 = 6$, which is divisible by 3), 51 passes the divisibility test for 3, so we know that 51 is divisible by 3. To check that a number is divisible by 5, see if the ones digit is either 0 or 5. Since 51 does not end in 0 or 5, it does not pass the divisibility test for 5, so we know that 51 is not divisible by 5.

divisible One whole number is divisible by another whole number if there is no remainder when the larger number is divided by the smaller numbers. For example, 28 is divisible by 7, because 28 divided by 7 is 4 with remainder 0. If a number *n* is divisible by a number *d,* then *d* is a factor of *n.* Every whole number except 0 is divisible by itself. See *factor.*

division The operation used to solve equal-sharing, equal-grouping, and certain other problems; the inverse of multiplication. For example, 24/4 can mean *How many 4s in 24?* and is an inverse of the product $6 * 4 = 24$. If *a/b* results in a whole number, *a* is said to be *divisible* by *b,* as in the example 24/4. Otherwise, depending on the nature of the problem being solved, *a/b* can be expressed using fractions, decimals, or as a whole number quotient and a remainder. See the examples below. See *dividend, divisor,* and *quotient.* See Section 2.1 of the Arithmetic Operations essay.

$$25 / 4 = 6\tfrac{1}{4} \qquad 6\tfrac{1}{4} * 4 = 25$$
$$25 / 4 = 6.25 \qquad 6.25 * 4 = 25$$
$$25 / 4 \rightarrow 6 \text{ R1} \qquad 6 * 4 + 1 = 25$$

dividend / divisor = quotient

$$\frac{\text{dividend}}{\text{divisor}} = \text{quotient}$$

dividend / divisor → quotient with remainder

division of fractions property A rule for dividing: Division by any number is equivalent to multiplication by the number's reciprocal. If the divisor is a fraction, the reciprocal is obtained by exchanging the numerator and the denominator, so $n \div \frac{c}{d} = n * \frac{d}{c}$. If both the dividend and the divisor are fractions, the rule becomes $\frac{a}{b} \div \frac{c}{d} = \frac{a}{b} * \frac{d}{c}$. Examples:

$$5 \div 8 = 5 * \frac{1}{8} = \frac{5}{8}$$
$$15 \div \frac{3}{5} = 15 * \frac{5}{3} = \frac{75}{3} = 25$$
$$\frac{1}{2} \div \frac{3}{5} = \frac{1}{2} * \frac{5}{3} = \frac{5}{6}$$

division symbols The number *a* divided by the number *b* is expressed in print in a variety of ways: $a \div b$; $\frac{a}{b}$ and *a/b* are used in *Everyday Mathematics*; $b\overline{)a}$ is used to set up a "long division" algorithm; *a:b* is sometimes used in Europe; $a \div b$ is rarely used except in school mathematics text books. See Section 9.2.

divisor In division, the number that divides another number (the dividend). For example, in $35 \div 7 = 5$, the divisor is 7. See *division.*

$$\overset{\text{divisor}}{\underset{\text{dividend} \qquad \qquad \text{quotient}}{35/5 = 7}}$$

$$\overset{\text{divisor}}{\underset{\text{dividend} \qquad \qquad \text{quotient}}{40 \div 8 = 5}}$$

quotient → 3
divisor → $12\overline{)36}$ ← dividend

dodecahedron A polyhedron with 12 faces. If each face is a regular pentagon, it is one of the 5 regular polyhedra. See *regular polyhedron.* See Section 5.5 of the Geometry essay.

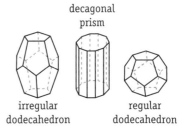

decagonal prism

irregular dodecahedron   regular dodecahedron

double Two times an amount; an amount added to itself.

doubles fact An addition or multiplication fact without a turn-around partner. A doubles fact names the sum or product of a one-digit number added to or multiplied by itself, such as $4 + 4 = 8$ or $3 * 3 = 9$.

edge A line segment where two faces of a polyhedron meet. See Section 5.5 of the Geometry essay.

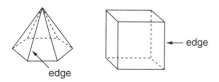

elevation A height above sea level. Same as *altitude*.

ellipse A closed, oval plane figure. An ellipse is the path of a point that moves in a plane so that the sum of its distances from two fixed points in the plane is constant. Each of the fixed points is called a focus of the ellipse.

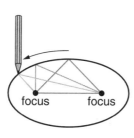

embedded figure A figure entirely enclosed within another figure.

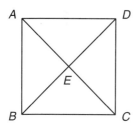

Triangle *ADE* is embedded in Square *ABCD*.

endpoint A point at the end of a line segment or ray. A line segment is normally named using the letter labels of its two endpoints. "Segment *LT*" or "segment *TL*" is the line segment between L and T. See *ray* and *line*. See Section 5.3 of the Geometry essay.

enlarge To increase the size of an object or figure. See Section 5.6 of the Geometry essay.

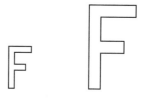

equal chance When none of the possible outcomes of a random process is more likely to occur than any other, it is an equal-chance situation.

equal-grouping story A number story involving separating something into equal groups. In these problems, the total and the number in each group are known. For example, "How many tables seating 4 persons each are needed for 52 people?" is an equal-grouping story. Often division can be used to solve equal-grouping stories. See *measurement division* and *quotitive division*. See Section 2.1 of the Arithmetic Operations essay.

equal groups Sets with the same number of elements, such as cars with 5 passengers, rows with 6 chairs, boxes each containing 100 clips, and so on. See Section 2.1 of the Arithmetic Operations essay.

equal groups notation A way to denote a number of equal-sized groups. The size of the groups is shown inside square brackets and the number of groups is written in front of the brackets. So, for example, 3 [6s] means 3 groups with 6 in each group. More generally, *n* [*b*s] means *n* groups with *b* in each group.

equal-sharing story A number story involving sharing something equally. In these problems, the total and the number of groups are known. For example: "There are 10 brownies to share equally among 4 children. How many brownies will each child get?" is an equal-sharing story. Often division can be used to solve equal-sharing stories. See *partitive division*. See Section 2.1 of the Arithmetic Operations essay.

equation A mathematical sentence that asserts the equality of two quantities. See Section 9.2.

equator An imaginary circle around Earth halfway between the North Pole and the South Pole. The equator is the 0° line for latitude. See *latitude*.

equidistant marks A series of marks separated by a constant space.

equidistant marks

equilateral polygon A polygon in which all sides are the same length. See Section 5.4 of the Geometry essay.

equilateral triangle A triangle in which all three sides are the same length and all three angles are the same measure. See *triangle*. See Section 5.4 of the Geometry essay.

equivalent Equal in value, though possibly different in form. For example, $\frac{1}{2}$, 0.5, and 50% are all equivalent. See Section 1.9 of the Numeration and Order essay.

equivalent equations Equations that have the same solutions. For example, $2 + x = 4$ and $6 + x = 8$ are equivalent equations; their solution is 2. See Section 9.3.

equivalent fractions Fractions that have different denominators but represent the same number. See Section 1.3 of the Numeration and Order essay.

equivalent names Different ways of naming the same number. For example; $2 + 6$, $4 + 4$, $12 - 4$, $18 - 10$, $100 - 92$, $5 + 1 + 2$, eight, VIII, and ~~HHT~~ /// are all equivalent names for 8. See *name-collection box*.

equivalent ratios Ratios that make the same comparison. Equivalent ratios can be expressed by equivalent fractions. For example, $\frac{1}{2}$ and $\frac{4}{8}$ are equivalent ratios. See *equivalent fractions*. See Section 1.3 of the Numeration and Order essay.

estimate (1) A close, rather than exact, answer; an approximate answer to a computation; a number close to another number. (2) To make an estimate. See the Estimation essay.

European subtraction A subtraction procedure common in Europe and in certain parts of the United States. The method involves increasing the smaller number rather than regrouping. The method is as efficient as the traditional procedure once children have practiced using it. See Section 3.2 of the Algorithms essay for further discussion and other subtraction algorithms.

evaluate (1) An algebraic expression: To replace each variable in an algebraic expression with a particular number and then calculate the value of the expression. (2) A numerical expression: To carry out the operations in a numerical expression to find the value of the expression. (3) A formula: To find the value of one variable in the formula when the values of the other variables are given.

even number A whole number that can be evenly divided by 2. Compare to *odd number*. See Section 9.1 of the Patterns, Sequences, Functions, and Algebra essay.

event In probability, the result of a random process such as rolling a die or tossing a coin. For example, the dice throw of 5 is an event, as is a coin landing heads-side up when tossed. See Sections 4.2 and 4.3 of the Data and Chance essay.

expanded notation A way of expressing a number as the sum of the values of each digit. For example, in expanded notation, 356 is written $300 + 50 + 6$. Compare to *standard notation*, *scientific notation*, and *number-and-word notation*.

expected outcome The average outcome over a large number of repetitions of a random experiment. For example, the expected outcome of rolling one die is the average number of spots showing over a large number of rolls. Since each face of a fair die has equal probability, the expected outcome will be $(1 + 2 + 3 + 4 + 5 + 6)/6 = 21/6 = 3\frac{1}{2}$. This means that the average of many rolls of a fair die will be about $3\frac{1}{2}$. (More formally, the expected outcome is defined as an average over infinitely many repetitions.)

Exploration In *Everyday Mathematics*, an independent or small-group activity that may involve concept development, manipulatives, data collection, problem solving, games, and skill reviews. See page 23 in the Management Guide for more information.

exponent See *exponential notation*. See Section 2.2 of the Arithmetic Operations essay.

exponential notation A way of representing repeated multiplication by the same factor. For example, 2^3 is exponential notation for $2 * 2 * 2$. The small, raised 3, called the *exponent*, indicates how many times the number 2, called the *base*,

glossary

is used as a *factor*. See Section 2.2 of the Arithmetic Operations essay.

$$2^3 = 2 * 2 * 2 = 8$$
$$4^5 = 4 * 4 * 4 * 4 * 4 = 1{,}024$$

exponential notations

expression A group of mathematical symbols (numbers, operation signs, variables, grouping symbols) that represent or can represent a number if values are assigned to any variables that the expression contains. See Sections 9.2 and 9.3 of the Patterns, Sequences, Functions, and Algebra essay.

$$2 + 3$$
$$\sqrt{2ab}$$
$$\pi r^2$$

expressions

extended fact A variation of a basic arithmetic fact involving multiples of 10, 100, and so on. For example, $30 + 70 = 100$, $40 * 5 = 200$, and $560/7 = 80$ are extended facts. See *arithmetic facts*.

face (1) Any of the polygonal regions that form 3-dimensional prisms, pyramids, or polyhedra. Some special faces are called bases. (2) Curved surface that forms part or all of a cylinder, cone, sphere or other geometric solid. See Section 5.5 of the Geometry essay.

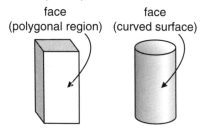

face
(polygonal region)

face
(curved surface)

fact See *arithmetic facts*. See Section 8.3.

fact extensions Calculations with larger numbers using knowledge of basic facts. For example, knowing the basic fact $5 + 8 = 13$ makes it easy to solve problems like $50 + 80 = ?$ and $65 + ? = 73$. Fact extensions can also be applied to basic subtraction, multiplication, and division facts.

fact family A collection of related addition and subtraction facts, or multiplication and division facts, made from the same numbers. For 5, 6, and 11, the addition/subtraction fact family consists of $5 + 6 = 11$, $6 + 5 = 11$, $11 - 5 = 6$, and $11 - 6 = 5$. For 5, 7, and 35, the multiplication/division fact family consists of $5 * 7 = 35$, $7 * 5 = 35$, $35/7 = 5$, and $35/5 = 7$. See *number family*. See Section 8.3.

fact habits In *Everyday Mathematics*, a term used to refer to number-fact reflexes; automaticity in knowing basic addition, subtraction, multiplication, and division facts. See Section 8.3.

factor (1) A number being multiplied in a multiplication number model. In the number model $6 * 0.5 = 3$, 6 and 0.5 are factors and 3 is the product. See *multiplication*. (2) A whole number that can divide another whole number without a remainder. For example, 4 and 7 are both factors of 28 because 28 is divisible by both 4 and 7. (3) To represent a number as a product of factors. To factor 21, for example, is to write it as $7 * 3$. See Section 1.2.

factorial A product of a whole number and all smaller whole numbers except 0. An exclamation point, !, is used to denote factorials. For example:
$$3! = 3 * 2 * 1 = 6$$
3! is read as "three factorial."
$$4! = 4 * 3 * 2 * 1 = 24$$
4! is read as "four factorial."
For any number N,
$N! = N * (N - 1) * (N - 2) * ... * 1$ and $N!$ is read as "N factorial."

factor pair Two whole-number factors of a number whose product is the number. A number may have more than one factor pair. For example, the factor pairs for 24 are 1 and 24, 2 and 12, 3 and 8, and 4 and 6. See Section 1.2.

factor rainbow A way to show factor pairs in a list of all the factors of a number. A factor rainbow can be used to check whether a list of factors is correct.

factor rainbow for 24

factor string A name for a number written as a product of at least two whole-number factors other than 1. For example, a factor string for the number 24 is $2 * 3 * 4$. This factor string has three factors, so its length is 3. By convention, the number 1 is not allowed in factor strings. For example, $1 * 2 * 3 * 4$ is not a factor string for 24 because it contains the number 1.

factor tree A method used to obtain the prime factorization of a number. The original number is represented as a product of factors, and each of those factors is represented as a product of factors, and so on, until the factors are all prime numbers. Factor trees are drawn upside down, with the root at the top and the leaves at the bottom. See *prime factorization* and *tree diagram*. See Section 1.2.

factor tree for 30

fact power In *Everyday Mathematics*, a term that refers to the ability to recall basic number facts automatically without having to figure them out. See Section 8.3 of the Estimation, Mental Arithmetic, and Fact Power essay.

Facts Table A chart of rows and columns showing arithmetic facts. An Addition/Subtraction Facts Table shows addition and subtraction facts. A Multiplication/Division Facts Table shows multiplication and division facts.

Fact Triangle A triangular flash card labeled with the numbers of a fact family that students can use to practice addition/subtraction and multiplication/division facts. The two 1-digit numbers and their sum or product (marked with a dot) appear in the corners of each triangle. See *fact family*. See Section 8.3. See page 50 in the Management Guide.

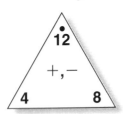

Fahrenheit The temperature scale on which pure water at sea level freezes at 32° and boils at 212°. The Fahrenheit scale is widely used in the U.S. but in few other places. Compare to *Celsius*. See Section 7.1 of the Reference Frames essay.

fair Free from bias. Each of the six sides of a fair die should come up about equally often. Each section of a fair spinner should come up in proportion to its area. On a fair coin, heads and tails should come up about equally often.

fair game A game in which every player has the same chance of winning. If any player has an advantage or disadvantage at the beginning (for example, by playing first), then the game is not fair. See Section 4.2 of the Data and Chance essay.

false number sentence A number sentence that is not true; a number sentence in which the relation symbol does not accurately relate the two sides. For example, $8 = 5 + 5$ is a false number sentence. Compare to *true number sentence*.

fathom A unit used mainly by people who work with boats and ships to measure depth of water and lengths of cables. A fathom is 6 feet, or 2 yards. Same as *arm span*. See Section 6.1 of the Measurement essay.

figurate numbers Numbers that can be shown by specific geometric patterns. Square numbers and triangular numbers are examples of figurate numbers.

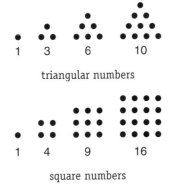

flat In *Everyday Mathematics*, the term for the base−10 block consisting of 100 cm cubes. See Tools for Numeration and Operations section of the Management Guide, pages 49–50.

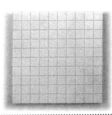

flip An informal name for a reflection transformation. See *reflection* and *transformation*. See Section 5.6 of the Geometry essay.

flowchart A diagram that shows a series of steps to complete a task. A typical flowchart is a network of frames and symbols connected by arrows that provides a guide for working through a problem step by step.

fluid ounce In the U.S. customary system, a unit of capacity equal to $\frac{1}{16}$ of a pint. One fluid ounce is 29.574 milliliters. See the Tables of Measure. See Sections 6.2 and 6.6 of the Measurement essay.

foot (ft) In the U.S. customary system, a unit of length equivalent to 12 inches or $\frac{1}{3}$ of a yard. See the Tables of Measure. See Section 6.2 of the Measurement essay.

formula A general rule for finding the value of something. A formula is often written symbolically using letters, called variables, to stand for the quantities involved. For example, a formula for distance traveled can be written as $d = s * t$, where d stands for distance, s for speed, and t for time. See Section 9.3.

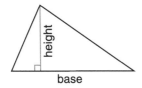

Area of triangle = 1/2 base * height
$A = 1/2 \, b * h$

fraction A number in the form $\frac{a}{b}$ or a/b, where a and b are whole numbers and b is not 0. Fraction notation is used in many contexts: to name part of an object or part of a collection of objects, to compare two quantities, and to represent division. For example, $\frac{12}{6}$ can mean 12 divided by 6, and $\frac{2}{3}$ can be thought of as 2 divided by 3. See Section 1.3 of the Numeration and Order essay and Section 3.3 of the Algorithms essay.

fraction stick A diagram used in *Everyday Mathematics* to represent simple fractions. See pages 50–51 of the Management Guide.

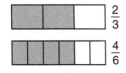

Frames and Arrows In *Everyday Mathematics*, diagrams used to represent number sequences— lists of numbers often generated by one or more rules. The diagrams consist of *frames* in which numbers are written and *arrows* that represent the rule(s) for moving from one frame to the next. Frames-and-Arrows diagrams are also called "chains." See Section 9.1 of the Patterns, Sequences, Functions, and Algebra essay.

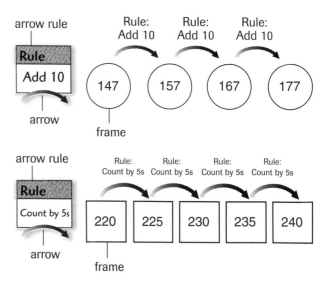

frequency (1) The number of times a value occurs in a set of data. See Section 4.1 of the Data and Chance essay. (2) The number of vibrations per second of a sound wave; more generally, the number of repetitions per unit of time.

frequency graph A graph showing how often each value occurs in a data set. See Section 4.1 of the Data and Chance essay.

Colors in a Bag of Gumdrops

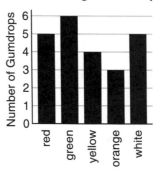

frequency table A chart on which data are tallied to record the frequency of given events or values. See Section 4.1 of the Data and Chance essay.

Color	Number of Gumdrops
red	ⅢⅡ
green	ⅢⅡ I
yellow	ⅢⅠ
orange	Ⅲ
white	ⅢⅡ

frieze pattern A geometric design in a long strip in which an element is repeated over and over again.

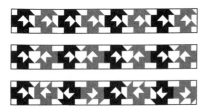

fulcrum (1) The center support of a pan balance.

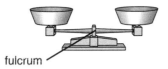

fulcrum

(2) The support on which a lever turns.

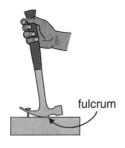

fulcrum

(3) The point on a mobile at which a rod is suspended.

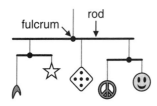

fulcrum   rod

function A set of ordered pairs of numbers, usually related by a rule, such that each first number is paired with exactly one second number. A function can be shown in a table, as points on a coordinate graph, or by a rule. For example, for a function with a rule of "double," 1 is paired with 2, 2 is paired with 4, 3 is paired with 6, and so on. See Section 9.1 of the Patterns, Sequences, Functions, and Algebra essay.

function machine In *Everyday Mathematics*, an imaginary machine programmed to process numbers according to a certain rule. A number (the *input*) is put into the machine and is then transformed into a second number (the *output*) through the application a rule. See *function*. See Section 9.1 of the Patterns, Sequences, Functions, and Algebra essay.

in	out
1	2
2	4
3	6
5	10
20	40
300	600

function machine with input/output table

furlong A unit of measure equal to one-eighth of a mile. Today, furlongs are most commonly used in horse racing.

gallon (gal) In the U.S. customary system, a unit of capacity equal to 4 quarts. See the Tables of Measure. See Sections 6.2 and 6.6 of the Measurement essay.

genus In *topology:* The number of holes in a geometric shape. Shapes with the same genus are topologically equivalent. See Section 5.11.

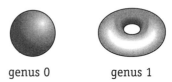

genus 0   genus 1

geometric solid A 3-dimensional shape bounded by surfaces. Common geometric solids include the *rectangular prism, square-based pyramid, cylinder, cone,* and *sphere*. Despite its name, a geometric solid in *Everyday Mathematics* is defined as the surface only (it is "hollow") and does not include the points in its interior. Sometimes, however, in informal discussion and in certain dictionaries, a solid is defined as both the surface and its interior. See Section 5.5 of the Geometry essay.

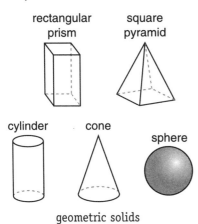

geometric solids

geometry The study of spatial objects and their properties and relationships. The word geometry is derived from the Greek words for "earth" and "measure." See the Geometry essay.

Geometry Template An *Everyday Mathematics* tool that includes a millimeter ruler, a ruler with sixteenth-inch intervals, a half-circle and a full-circle protractor, a percent circle, pattern-block shapes, and other geometric figures. Tiny holes at selected inch and centimeter marks allow the template to serve as a compass. See page 44 in the Management Guide.

girth The distance around a 3-dimensional object.

Golden Ratio A particular ratio, approximately equal to 1.618 to 1. The Golden Ratio is sometimes denoted by the Greek letter phi: ϕ.

The Golden Ratio is an irrational number equal to $\frac{1 + \sqrt{5}}{2}$. See Section 1.3.

Golden Rectangle
A rectangle in which the ratio of the longer side to the shorter side is the *Golden Ratio*, or about 1.618 to 1. A standard index card, 5 inches by 3 inches, is nearly a Golden Rectangle.

a Golden Rectangle

-gon A suffix meaning angle. For example, a hexagon is a plane figure with six angles—one at each vertex.

gram In the metric system, a unit of mass equal to $\frac{1}{1,000}$ of a kilogram. See the Tables of Measure.

graph key An annotated list of the icons and other symbols used in a graph. A graph key explains how to read the graph. Compare to *map legend*.

greatest common factor (GFC) The largest factor that two or more numbers have in common. For example, the common factors of 24 and 36 are 1, 2, 3, 4, 6, and 12. Thus, the greatest common factor of 24 and 36 is 12.

great span The distance from the tip of the thumb to the tip of the little finger (pinkie), when the hand is stretched as far as possible. The great span averages about 9 inches for adults. Same as *hand span*. Compare to *normal span*. See Section 6.1 of the Measurement essay.

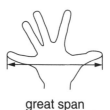

great span

grouping symbols Symbols such as parentheses ( ), brackets [ ], or braces { }, that indicate the order in which operations in an expression are to be done. For example, in the expression (3 + 4) * [(8 + 2)/5], the operations within the grouping symbols are to be done first, beginning with the innermost grouping symbols and proceeding outward. Thus, the expression above first becomes (3 + 4) * [10/5], then 7 * 2, and then 14. See Section 9.2.

half One of two equal parts.

hand span Same as *great span*.

height A measure of how tall something is. In geometry, height is the same as *altitude*. See Sections 5.4 and 5.5 of the Geometry essay.

height of a parallelogram The length of the shortest line segment between a base of a parallelogram and the line containing the opposite side. The height is perpendicular to the base. Also,

the line segment itself.
See *altitude* and *base of a parallelogram*. See Section 5.4 of the Geometry essay.

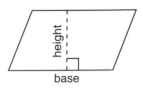

height of a prism or cylinder The length of the shortest line segment from a base of a prism or cylinder to the plane containing the opposite face.

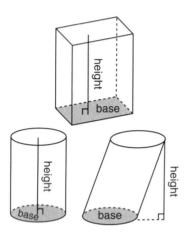

height of a pyramid or cone The length of the shortest line segment from the vertex of a pyramid or cone to the plane containing the base. See *altitude* and *base of a pyramid or cone*.

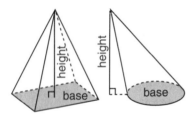

height of a triangle The length of the shortest segment from a vertex of a triangle to the line containing the opposite side. See *altitude* and *base of a triangle*. See Section 5.4 of the Geometry essay.

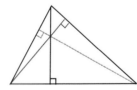

The heights of the triangle are indicated in blue.

hepta- A prefix meaning seven.

heptagon A 7-sided polygon. See Section 5.4 of the Geometry essay.

hexa- Prefix meaning six.

hexagon A 6-sided polygon. See Section 5.4 of the Geometry essay.

horizon Where the earth and sky appear to meet; if nothing is in the way, as when looking out to sea, the horizon looks like a line.

horizontal Positioned in a left-to-right orientation. Parallel to the line of the horizon.

hypotenuse In a right triangle, the side opposite the right angle. See Section 5.4.

icon A small picture or diagram, sometimes used to represent quantities. For example, an icon of a stadium might be used to represent 100,000 people on a *pictograph*. Icons are also used to represent functions or objects in computer operating systems and applications. See *pictograph*.

icosahedron A polyhedron with 20 faces. One of the five regular polyhedra is an icosahedron with triangular faces. See *regular polyhedron*. See Section 5.5 of the Geometry essay.

irregular icosahedron   regular icosahedron

image A figure that is produced by a transformation of another figure. See *transformation*. Compare to *preimage*. See Section 5.6 of the Geometry essay.

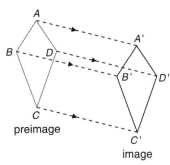

improper fraction A term for a fraction whose numerator is greater than or equal to its denominator. An improper fraction names a number greater than or equal to 1. For example, $\frac{4}{3}$, $\frac{5}{2}$, $\frac{4}{4}$, and $\frac{24}{12}$ are all improper fractions. In *Everyday Mathematics*, improper fractions are sometimes called "top-heavy" fractions.

inch (in.) In the U.S. customary system, a unit of length equal to $\frac{1}{12}$ of a foot and equivalent to 2.54 centimeters. See the Tables of Measure. See Section 6.2 of the Measurement essay.

index of locations A list of places together with a system for locating them on a map. For example, "Billings, D3," indicates that Billings can be found on a map in the rectangle to the right of the letter D and above the number 3 on the borders of the map. See Section 7.4 of the Reference Frames essay.

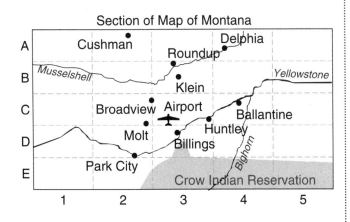

indirect measurement The determination of heights, distances, and other quantities that cannot be measured directly.

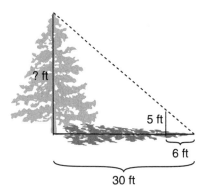

Using indirect measurement, the height of the tree is found to be 25 ft.

inequality A number sentence stating that two quantities are not equal, or might not be equal. Relation symbols for inequalities include $\neq$, $<$, $>$, $\leq$, and $\geq$. See Section 1.9.

input (1) A number inserted into an imaginary function machine, which processes numbers according to a designated rule. See *function machine*. Compare to *output*. (2) A number operated on by a function rule to produce an output. See *function*. See Section 9.1 of the Patterns, Sequences, Functions, and Algebra essay.

inscribed polygon A polygon whose vertices are all points on a circle.

inscribed polygon

integer A number in the set {... −4, −3, −2, −1, 0, 1, 2, 3, 4, ...}. All integers are rational numbers, but not all rational numbers are integers. (For example, $-\frac{1}{2}$ is a rational number but not an integer.) All whole numbers are integers, but not all integers are whole numbers. (For example, –3 is an integer, but not a whole number.) Compare to *whole number*, *rational number*, *irrational number*, and *real number*. See Section 1.4 of the Numeration and Order essay.

interest Money paid for the use of someone else's money. Interest is usually a percentage of the amount borrowed.

interior The set of all points in a plane "inside" a closed 2-dimensional figure, such as a polygon or circle. Also, the set of all points in space "inside" a closed 3-dimensional figure, such as a polyhedron or sphere. The interior is usually not considered to be part of the figure. See Sections 5.4 and 5.5 of the Geometry essay.

interior

intersect To share a common point or points.

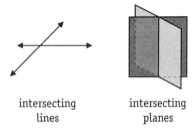

intersecting lines   intersecting planes

interval (1) A set of numbers between two numbers *a* and *b*, which may include one or both of *a* and *b*. (2) A part of a number line, including all numbers between two points.

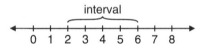

interval

0 1 2 3 4 5 6 7 8

"in the black" Having a positive balance; having more money than is owed.

"in the red" Having a negative balance; owing more money than is available.

irrational number A number that cannot be written as a fraction where both the numerator and denominator are integers and the denominator is not zero. For example, $\sqrt{2}$ and π are irrational numbers. An irrational number can be represented by a nonterminating, nonrepeating decimal. For example, the decimal for π, 3.141592653..., continues without a repeating pattern. The number 1.10100100010000... is also irrational; although there is a pattern in the decimal, it does not repeat. See Section 1.6 of the Numeration and Order essay.

irregular polygon A polygon with sides of different lengths or angles of different measures.

three irregular polygons

isometry transformation A transformation such as a translation (*slide*), a reflection (*flip*), a rotation (*turn*), or a combination of these that preserves distances between points and angle measures. As a result, isometries preserve both shape and size of figures, but not necessarily position or orientation. (From Greek *isometros*, of equal measure.) See *transformation*, *translation*, *reflection*, and *rotation*. See Section 5.6 of the Geometry essay.

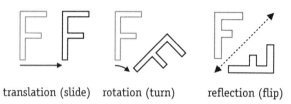

translation (slide)   rotation (turn)   reflection (flip)

isosceles trapezoid A trapezoid whose non-parallel sides are the same length. See *trapezoid*. See Section 5.4 of the Geometry essay.

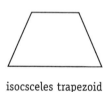

isocsceles trapezoid

isosceles triangle A triangle with at least two sides that are the same length and at least two angles that are the same measure. See *triangle*. See Section 5.4 of the Geometry essay.

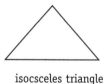

isocsceles triangle

juxtapose To place side by side in an expression. In mathematics, juxtaposition often indicates multiplication. For example, $5n$ means $5 * n$, and ab means $a * b$. See Section 9.2.

key sequence A set of instructions for performing a particular calculation or function with a calculator. See Section 3.4 and page 34 in the Management Guide.

kilo- A prefix meaning thousand.

kilogram In the metric system, the fundamental unit of mass; it is equal to 1,000 grams. The kilogram is defined in terms of actual objects stored in special vaults in Paris, Washington D.C., and elsewhere. 1 kilogram equals approximately 2.2 pounds. See *weight*. See the Tables of Measure. See Sections 6.2 and 6.7 of the Measurement essay.

kilometer In the metric system, a unit of length equal to 1,000 meters. One kilometer equals about 0.62 mile. See the Tables of Measure. See Sections 6.2 and 6.4 of the Measurement essay.

kite A quadrilateral with two adjacent sides of one length and two other sides of a different length. Both kites and parallelograms have pairs of equal-length sides, but in kites the equal-length sides are adjacent while in parallelograms the equal-length sides are opposite. The diagonals of a kite are perpendicular. See Section 5.4 of the Geometry essay.

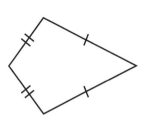

label (1) A descriptive word or phrase used to put a number or numbers in context. Using a label reinforces the idea that numbers refer to something. Flags, snowballs, and scary monsters are examples of labels. See Sections 2.1 and 2.3 of the Arithmetic Operations essay. (2) In a spreadsheet or graph, words or numbers used to provide information such as the title of the spreadsheet, the heading for a row or column, or the variable on an axis.

landmark A notable feature of a data set. Landmarks include *median*, *mode*, *maximum*, *minimum*, and *range*. See Section 4.1 of the Data and Chance essay.

latitude The angular distance north or south of the equator of a point on Earth's surface, measured on the meridian of the point. See *latitude lines*. Compare to *longitude*. See Section 7.4.

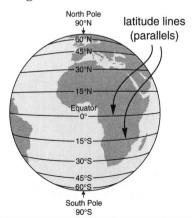

latitude lines Lines of constant latitude drawn on a map or globe. Lines of latitude are used to indicate the location of a place with reference to the equator. Latitude is measured in degrees, from 0° to 90°, north or south of the equator. Lines of latitude are also called "parallels," because they are parallel to the equator and to each other. Compare to *longitude lines*. See Section 7.4.

lattice method An algorithm for multiplying multidigit numbers. Lattice multiplication is a very old method, requiring little more than a knowledge of basic multiplication facts and the ability to add strings of 1−digit numbers. Once the lattice is drawn, the method is highly efficient and can be used to multiply very large numbers, including numbers too large to enter into calculators. See Section 3.2 of the Algorithms essay for further discussion and other multiplication algorithms.

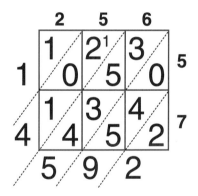

$256 \times 57 = 14{,}592$

least common denominator The least common multiple of the denominators of every fraction in a given collection. For example, the least common denominator of $\frac{1}{2}$, $\frac{4}{5}$, and $\frac{3}{8}$ is 40.

least common multiple (LCM) The smallest number that is a multiple of two or more given numbers. For example, while some common multiples of 6 and 8 are 24, 48, and 72, the least common multiple of 6 and 8 is 24.

left-to-right subtraction A subtraction procedure which works left to right in several steps. For example, to solve 94 −57, first subtract 50 from 94 to obtain 44, and then 7 from 44 to obtain 37. The method is especially suited to mental arithmetic. See Section 3.2 of the Algorithms essay for further discussion and other subtraction algorithms.

leg of a right triangle

A side of a right triangle that is not the hypotenuse. Compare to *hypotenuse*. See Section 5.4.

length of a factor string The number of factors in a factor string. See *factor string*.

length of a rectangle Usually, but not necessarily, the longer dimension of a rectangle or a rectangular object.

letter number pair An ordered pair in which one of the coordinates is a letter. See *ordered pair*.

like fractions Fractions with the same denominator.

like terms In an algebraic expression, either the constant terms or any terms that contain the same variable(s) raised to the same power(s). For example, $4y$ and $7y$ are like terms in the expression $4y + 7y - z$. To "combine like terms" means to rewrite the sum or difference of like terms as a single term. For example, $5a + 6a$ can be rewritten as $11a$, because $5a + 6a = (5 + 6)a = 11a$. Similarly, $16t - 3t$ can be rewritten as $13t$. See Section 9.2.

line A straight path that extends infinitely in opposite directions. See Section 5.3 of the Geometry essay.

line graph A graph in which data points are connected by a line or line segments. Same as *broken line graph*. See Section 4.1 of the Data and Chance essay.

line of reflection A line halfway between a plane figure (pre image) and its reflected image. The line of reflection is the perpendicular bisector of the line segments connecting points on the preimage

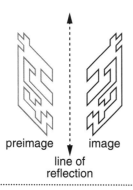

preimage   image

line of
reflection

with the corresponding points on the image. Also known as *mirror line*. See *reflection*. Compare to *line of symmetry*.

line of symmetry A line that divides a plane figure into two halves that are mirror images of each other. Each point in one of the halves of the figure is the same distance from the line of symmetry as the corresponding point in the other half. A figure may have any number of lines of symmetry. For example, a parallelogram that is not a rectangle has no lines of symmetry. A square has four lines of symmetry. A circle has infinitely many lines of symmetry. A line of symmetry can also be thought of as a line of reflection. Compare to *line of reflection*. See Section 5.8 of the Geometry essay.

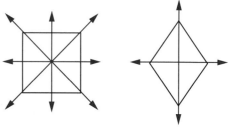

Lines of symmetry are shown in blue.

line plot A sketch of data in which check marks, Xs, or other symbols above a labeled line show the frequency of each value. See Section 4.1 of the Data and Chance essay.

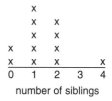

number of siblings

line segment A straight path joining two points, called the *endpoints* of the line segment. Line segments are often labeled for the letter labels of their endpoint. See Section 5.3 of the Geometry essay.

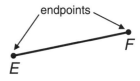

line symmetry A figure has line symmetry if a line can be drawn through it so that it is divided into two parts that look exactly alike but face in opposite directions. See *line of symmetry*. Compare to *rotational symmetry*. See Section 5.8 of the Geometry essay.

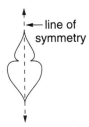
line of symmetry

liter (L) In the metric system, a unit of capacity equal to the volume of a cube that measures 10 centimeters on a side. 1 L = 1,000 mL = 1,000 cm³. A liter is a little larger than a quart. See the Tables of Measure. See Sections 6.2 and 6.6 of the Measurement Essay.

logic grid A grid of rows and columns used to organize information in a problem.

	1	2	3
Sam	X	✓	X
Jon	✓	X	X
Sara	X	X	✓

long In *Everyday Mathematics*, the term for the base-10 block consisting of 10 cm cubes. Sometimes called a "rod." See Base-10 Blocks, pages 49–50, in the Tools section of the Management Guide.

longitude A measure of how far east or west of the prime meridian a location on Earth is. Longitude is the measure, usually in degrees, of the angle formed by the plane containing the meridian of a particular place and the plane containing the *prime meridian*. Compare to *latitude*. See *longitude lines*. See Section 7.4.

longitude lines Lines of constant longitude; semicircles connecting the North and South Poles. Longitude lines are used to locate places with reference to the *prime meridian*. Lines of longitude are also called meridians. Compare to *latitude lines*.

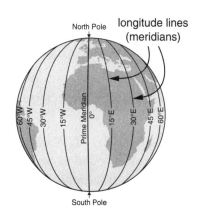

lowest terms Same as *simplest form*. See Section 1.3 of the Numeration and Order essay.

magnitude estimate A rough estimate of the size of a numerical result—whether it is in the 1s, 10s, 100s, 1,000s, and so on. For example, the U.S. national debt per person is in the tens of thousands of dollars. In *Everyday Mathematics*, children are often asked to give magnitude estimates for problems like "How many dimes in $200?" or "How many halves are in 30?" Same as *order of magnitude estimate*. See Section 8.1 of the Estimation, Mental Arithmetic, and Fact Power essay.

magnitude increase Same as *order of magnitude increase*.

majority More than half of a total amount.

map direction symbol A symbol on a map that identifies north, south, east, and west. Sometimes only north is indicated.

map legend A diagram that explains the symbols, markings, and colors on a map. Also called a *map key*.

map scale A device for relating distances on a map to corresponding distances in the real world. One inch on a map, for example, might correspond to 1 mile in the real world. A map scale is often represented by a labeled line segment, similar to a ruler; by a ratio of distances (for example $\frac{1}{63,360}$ when an inch represents a mile); or by an incorrect use of the = symbol (as in "1 inch = 1 mile"). See Section 7.4 of the Reference Frames essay.

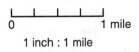
1 inch : 1 mile

mass A measure of the amount of material in an object. The mass of an object is the same on Earth as it is in outer space. Metric units for mass include grams and kilograms. These units are also used for weight. Compare to *weight*. See Section 6.7 of the Measurement essay.

Math Boxes In *Everyday Mathematics*, a format to provide review problems and to practice skills. A set of Math Boxes for each lesson is in the student Math Journals. See pages 10-11 in the Management Guide for more information.

mathematics A study of relationships among numbers, shapes, systems, and patterns. Among other things, mathematics is used to count and measure things, to discover similarities and differences, to solve problems, and to learn about and organize the world.

Math Journal In *Everyday Mathematics*, a student record of mathematical discoveries and experiences. Journal pages provide visual models for conceptual understanding, problem material, and activities for individuals and small groups.

Math Master In *Everyday Mathematics*, a page ready for duplicating. Most masters are used by students in carrying out suggested activities. Some masters are used more than once during the school year.

Math Message In *Everyday Mathematics*, an activity for students to complete before the start of a lesson. Math Messages may be problems that introduce the day's lesson, directions to follow, sentences to complete or correct, review exercises, or reading assignments. See page 11 in the Management Guide for more information.

maximum The largest amount; the greatest number in a set of data. Compare to *minimum*. See Section 4.1 of the Data and Chance essay.

mean A typical or central value for a set of numbers, often called the "average." The mean is calculated by finding the sum of all the numbers in the set and then dividing the sum by the number of numbers. See *average*. Compare to *median* and *mode*. See Section 4.1 of the Data and Chance essay.

measurement division A phrase often used in teacher training courses to indicate the use of division in equal-shares situations in which the total amount and the size of the shares are known and the number of shares is to be found. For example, "How many tables seating 4 people each are needed for 52 people?" is a measurement division problem. Same as *quotitive division*. In *Everyday Mathematics*, the term "equal-grouping story" describes measurement division problems. See *equal-grouping story*. Compare to *partitive division* and *equal-sharing story*. See Section 2.1 of the Arithmetic Operations essay.

measurement unit The reference unit used when measuring. Basic units include meters (length), grams (mass or weight), liters (capacity), seconds (elapsed time), and degrees Celsius (change of temperature). Compound units include square centimeters (area) and kilometers per hour (speed). See Section 6.2 of the Measurement essay.

median The middle value in a set of data when the data are listed in order from least to greatest (or greatest to least). If there is an even number of data points, the median is the mean of the two middle values. The median is also known as the *middle value*. Compare to *mean* and *mode*. See Section 4.1 of the Data and Chance essay.

memory keys Keys to manage a calculator's memory. The memory keys are labled differently on different calculators. See Section 3.4 of the Algorithms essay.

mental arithmetic Computations done by people "in their heads," either in whole or in part. In *Everyday Mathematics*, students develop a variety of strategies for doing arithmetic—calculating mentally, using paper and pencil, drawing pictures, counting jumps on a number grid, and so on. See Section 3.1 of the Algorithms essay, Section 8.2 of the Estimation, Mental Arithmetic, and Fact Power Sense essay, and Section 10.4 of the Problem Solving essay.

Mental Math and Reflexes In *Everyday Mathematics*, exercises (usually oral), suggested at the start of most lessons. They are designed to strengthen students' number sense and to review and advance essential basic skills. See Section 3.1 of the Algorithms essay and page 11 in the Management Guide.

meridian bar A device on a globe that shows degrees north and south of the equator.

meridians Same as *longitude lines*.

meter (m) In the metric system, the fundamental unit of length from which other metric units of length are derived. Originally, the meter was defined as $\frac{1}{10,000,000}$ of the distance from the North Pole to the equator along a meridian passing through Paris. From 1960 to 1983, the meter was defined as 1,630,763.73 wavelengths of orange-red light from the element krypton. Today, the meter is defined as the distance light travels in a vacuum in $\frac{1}{299,792,458}$ second. One meter is equal to 10 decimeters, 100 centimeters, and 1,000 millimeters. See Section 6.2 of the Measurement essay.

metric system A measurement system based on the base-ten numeration system and used in most countries around the world. Units for linear measure (length, distance) include millimeter, centimeter, meter, and kilometer; units for mass (weight) include gram and kilogram; units for capacity include milliliter and liter; and the unit for temperature change is degrees Celsius. See Section 6.2 of the Measurement essay and the Tables of Measure.

middle value Same as *median*. See Section 4.1 of the Data and Chance essay.

midpoint A point halfway between two other points.

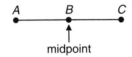

midpoint

mile (mi) In the U.S. customary system, a unit of length equal to 5,280 feet or 1,760 yards; about 1,609 meters.

milli- A prefix meaning one thousandth, especially in measures.

milliliter (mL) In the metric system, a unit of capacity equal to $\frac{1}{1,000}$ of a liter; 1 cubic centimeter. See Sections 6.2 and 6.6 of the Measurement essay.

millimeter (mm) In the metric system, a unit of length equivalent to $\frac{1}{10}$ of a centimeter or $\frac{1}{1,000}$ of a meter. See Section 6.2 of the Measurement essay.

millisecond (ms or msec) A unit of time equal to $\frac{1}{1,000}$ of a second.

minimum The smallest amount; the smallest number in a set of data. Compare to *maximum*. See Section 4.1 of the Data and Chance essay.

minuend The number that is reduced in subtraction. For example, in $19 - 5 = 14$, the minuend is 19. See *subtraction*.

mixed number A number that is written using both a whole number and a fraction. For example, $2\frac{1}{4}$ is a mixed number equal to $2 + \frac{1}{4}$.

Möbius strip or Möbius band A shape with only one side and one edge; named for mathematician August Ferdinand Möbius.

Möbius strip

modal Of or relating to the *mode*. See Section 4.1 of the Data and Chance essay.

mode The value or values that occur most often in a set of data. Compare to *median* and *mean*. In the data set 3, 4, 4, 4, 5, 5, 6, the mode is 4. See Section 4.1 of the Data and Chance essay.

multiples (1) Repeated groups of the same amount. Multiples of a number are the products of that number and the numbers 1, 2, 3, ... For example, the multiples of 7 are 7, 14, 21, 28, ... (2) Products of a number and an integer. The multiples of 7 are . . ., −21, −14, −7, 0, 7, 14, 21, ...

multiplication The operation used with whole numbers to find the total number of things in several equal groups or the number of things in a rectangular array. Multiplication is used with whole numbers, fractions, or decimals to find areas, enlargements or reduction of quantities, and to "check" division results. Numbers being multiplied are called factors; the result of multiplication is called the *product*. See Section 2.1 of the Arithmetic Operations essay and Section 3.2 of the Algorithms essay.

multiplication counting principle A way of determining the total number of possible outcomes for two or more separate choices. Suppose, for example, you roll a die and then flip a coin. There are 6 choices for which face of the die shows and 2 choices for which side of the coin shows. Then there are 6 * 2, or 12, possible outcomes all together: (1,H), (1,T), (2,H), (2,T), (3,H), (3,T), (4,H), (4,T), (5,H) (5,T), (6,H), (6,T).

multiplication diagram A diagram used to represent numbers in which several equal groups are being considered together. The diagram has three parts: a number of groups, a number in each group, and a total number. Also called "multiplication/ division diagram." See *rate diagram*.

rows	chairs per row	total chairs
15	25	?

multiplication fact The product of two 1−digit numbers, such as $6 \times 7 = 42$. See *arithmetic fact*. See Section 8.3.

multiplication symbols The number *a* multiplied by the number *b* is expressed in a variety of ways. Mathematics textbooks and *Second* and *Third Grade Everyday Mathematics* use " × " to indicate multiplication ($a \times b$). In fourth grade, *Everyday Mathematics* begins to use the ∗ symbol for multiplication ($a * b$). Other common ways to signify multiplication are through the use of a raised dot (for example, $a \cdot b$) and by juxtaposition (*ab*), which is common in formulas. See *juxtapose* and *multiplication*. See Section 9.2.

multiplicative inverses Two numbers whose product is 1. For example, the multiplicative inverse of 5 is $\frac{1}{5}$; the multiplicative inverse of $\frac{3}{5}$ is $\frac{5}{3}$. Multiplicative inverses are also called *reciprocals* of each other.

name-collection box In *Everyday Mathematics*, a box-like diagram tagged with a given number and used for collecting equivalent names for that number. See *equivalent names*. See Section 1.9 of the Numeration and Order essay and page 12 in the Management Guide.

25
37 − 12
20 + 5
~~HHt~~ ~~HHt~~ ~~HHt~~ ~~HHt~~ ~~HHt~~
twenty-five
veinticinco

name of a tessellation A numerical description of a tessellation, which gives, in order beginning with the smallest, the number of sides of the polygons that meet at each vertex point.

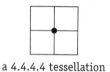

a 4.4.4.4 tessellation

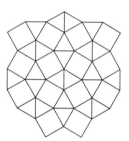

a 3.3.4.3.4 tessellation

natural numbers Same as *counting numbers*.

negative number A number less than 0; a number to the left of 0 on a horizontal number line or below 0 on a thermometer or other vertical number line. See Section 1.4 of the Numeration and Order essay.

negative power of 10 A number that can be written as a product using only 0.1, or 10^{-1}, as a factor. For example, 0.01 is a negative power of 10 because it is equal to 0.1×0.1, or 10^{-2}. See *power of 10*. Compare to *positive power of 10*. See Section 2.2.

negative rational numbers Numbers less than 0 that can be written as a fraction or a terminating or repeating decimal. For example, −24, −20.333..., and −2.45 are negative rational numbers. See *rational numbers*. See Section 1.4 of the Numeration and Order essay.

net score The final score of a turn or game after all operations have been completed.

net weight The weight of the contents of a container, not including the weight of the container.

***n*-gon** A polygon with *n* sides. For example, a 5-gon is a pentagon and an 8-gon is an octagon. Polygons with large numbers of sides are usually named only as *n*-gons such as 13-gon and 100-gon, etc. See Section 5.4 of the Geometry essay.

nona- A prefix meaning nine.

nonagon A nine-sided polygon.

nonconvex polygon Same as *concave polygon*.

normal span The distance from the end of the thumb to the end of the index (first) finger of an outstretched hand. For estimating lengths, many people can adjust this distance to approximately 6 inches or 15 centimeters. Same as *span*. Compare to *great span*.

n-to-1 ratio A ratio of a number to 1. Every ratio can be converted to an n-to-1 ratio. For example, to convert the ratio of 3 girls to 2 boys to an n-to-1 ratio, divide 3 by 2. The n-to-1 ratio is 1.5 to 1.

number-and-word notation A notation consisting of the significant digits of a number and words for the place value. For example, *27 billion* is number-and-word notation for 27,000,000,000. See *significant digits*.

number family Same as *fact family*. See Section 8.3.

number grid In *Everyday Mathematics*, a table in which consecutive numbers are arranged in rows, usually 10 columns per row. A move from one number to the next within a row is a change of 1; a move from one number to the next within a column is a change of 10. See Section 7.3 of the Reference Frames essay and pages 12–13 of the Management Guide.

									0
1	2	3	4	5	6	7	8	9	10
11	12	13	14	15	16	17	18	19	20
21	22	23	24	25	26	27	28	29	30
31	32	33	34	35	36	37	38	39	40
41	42	43	44	45	46	47	48	49	50
51	52	53	54	55	56	57	58	59	60
61	62	63	64	65	66	67	68	69	70
71	72	73	74	75	76	77	78	79	80
81	82	83	84	85	86	87	88	89	90
91	92	93	94	95	96	97	98	99	100
101	102	103	104	105	106	107	108	109	110

number grid

number-grid puzzle In *Everyday Mathematics*, a piece of a number grid in which some, but not all, of the numbers are missing. Number-grid puzzles are used for practice with place-value concepts. See Section 7.3 of the Reference Frames essay.

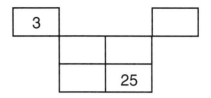

number-grid puzzle

number line A line on which points correspond to numbers, used as a frame of reference for counting and numeration activities. Every real number has a point on the line, and every point corresponds to a real number. See Sections 5.9 and 7.3.

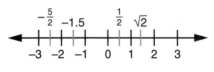

number line

number model A number sentence that models or fits a situation. For example, the situation *Sally had $5 and then she earned $8. How much did she have then?* can be modeled by the equation $5 + 8 = n$. See Section 2.1 of the Arithmetic Operations essay, Section 9.2 of the Patterns, Sequences, Functions, and Algebra essay, and Sections 10.3 and 10.4 of the Problem Solving essay.

number scroll In *Everyday Mathematics*, number-grid pages taped together. See *number grid*. See Section 7.3 of the Reference Frames essay.

number scroll

number sentence At least two numbers or expressions separated by a relation symbol ($=$, $<$, $>$, $\neq$, $\leq$, or $\geq$). Number sentences usually contain at least one operation symbol ($+$, $-$, $\times$, $*$, $\cdot$, $\div$, $/$). They may also have grouping symbols, such as parentheses. See *open sentence*. See Section 9.2 of the Patterns, Sequences, Functions, and Algebra essay.

$$5 + 5 = 10$$
$$a \times b \geq 16$$
$$(x + y) / 2 - 4 < 20$$

number sentences

number sequence A list of numbers, often generated by some rule. See *Frames and Arrows*, which generate number sequences. See Section 9.1 of the Patterns, Sequences, Functions, and Algebra essay.

1, 2, 3, 4, 5, 6, ...
1, 4, 9, 16, 25, 36, ...
1, 2, 1, 2, 1, 2, 1, 2, ...
1, 3, 5, 7, 9, 11, 13, 15, 17, ...

number sequences

number story A story that contains a problem that can be solved by using one or more of the four basic arithmetic operations or by sorting out relations, such as equals, is less than, or is greater than. See Section 10.4 of the Problem Solving essay.

numeration A method of numbering or of reading and writing numbers. In *Everyday Mathematics*, numeration activities include counting, writing numbers, identifying equivalent forms for name-collection boxes, exchanging coins (such as, 5 pennies for 1 nickel), and renaming numbers in computation.

numerator In a fraction, the number written above the line or to the left of the slash. In a part-whole fraction, where the whole is divided into a number of equal parts, the numerator names the number of equal parts being considered. In the fraction $\frac{a}{b}$ or a/b, a is the numerator. See *part-whole fraction*. Compare to *denominator*. See Sections 1.3 and 3.3.

obtuse angle An angle with a measure more than 90° and less than 180°. See *angle*. See Section 5.4 of the Geometry essay.

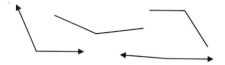

obtuse triangle A triangle with an angle larger than 90°. See *triangle*. See Section 5.4 of the Geometry essay.

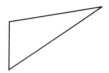

octa- A prefix meaning eight.

octagon An 8-sided polygon. See Section 5.4 of the Geometry essay.

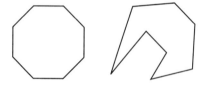

octahedron A polyhedron with eight faces. One of the five regular polyhedra is an octahedron with eight triangular faces. See *regular polyhedron*. See Section 5.5 of the Geometry essay.

odd number A whole number that cannot be evenly divided by 2. Compare to *even number*. See Section 9.1 of the Patterns, Sequences, Functions, and Algebra essay.

ONE In *Everyday Mathematics*, a way of denoting the unit whole in part-whole fractions and other similar situations. Same as *whole*, *unit whole*. See *part-whole fraction*. See Section 1.3 of the Numeration and Order essay.

one-dimensional (1-D) (1) A figure such as a line segment or part of a curve that has length, but no width or depth. (2) A figure such as a line in which one can locate any point with just one number in a coordinate system. Compare to *two-dimensional* and *three-dimensional*. See Sections 5.1, 5.3, and 5.9 of the Geometry essay.

open sentence A number sentence that is neither true nor false because one or more variables hold the place of missing numbers. For example, the number sentences 9 + __ = 15 and __ − 24 < 10 are open. As an introduction to algebra, *Everyday Mathematics* regards a ?, blank, or frame as a variable or "place holder," in, for example, "missing addend" problems. See Sections 2.1, 9.2, and 9.3.

$$9 + ? = 15 \qquad 5 - ? \geq 3$$
$$9 + \underline{\quad} = 15 \qquad 5 - \underline{\quad} \geq 3$$
$$9 + \boxed{\quad} = 15 \qquad 5 - \boxed{\quad} \geq 3$$
$$9 + x = 15 \qquad 5 - x \geq 3$$

open sentences

operation An action performed on one or two numbers producing a single number result. See *addition, subtraction, multiplication,* and *division* for definitions of the four basic "binary" operations. See *opposite of a number* and *square root of a number* for information on operations on single numbers that produce another single-number result. See Section 2.1 of the Arithmetic Operations essay.

operation diagram Same as *situation diagram.* See Section 2.1 of the Arithmetic Operations essay.

operation symbol A symbol used in number sentences to stand for a particular mathematical operation. The operation symbols most often used in school mathematics are:

+ for addition
− for subtraction
×, ∗, and • for multiplication
÷ and / for division

See Section 9.2 of the Patterns, Sequences, Functions, and Algebra.

OPP key The change-of-sign key on certain calculators. Pressing the OPP key changes the sign of the number in the display, making a negative number positive and a positive number negative. OPP stands for opposite.

opposite angles
(1) Of a quadrilateral: angles that do not share a common side.

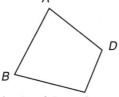

Angles *A* and *C* and Angles *B* and *D* are pairs of opposite angles.

(2) Of a triangle: an angle is opposite the side of a triangle that is not one of the sides of the angle.

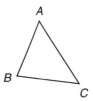

Angle *C* is opposite Side *AB.*

(3) When two lines intersect, the angles that do not share a common side are opposite angles. Opposite angles have equal measures. Also called *vertical angles.* See Section 5.4.

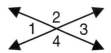

Angles 2 and 4 and Angles 1 and 3 are pairs of opposite, or vertical, angles.

opposite-change rule Same as *rename-addends algorithm.* See Section 3.2 of the Arithmetic Operations essay for further discussion and other addition algorithms. Compare to *same-change rule.*

opposite of a number A number that is the same distance from zero on the number line as the given number, but on the opposite side of zero. The opposite of a number *n* is written as (op)*n* or −*n*. If *n* is a negative number, (op)*n* or −*n* is a positive number. For example, if *n* = −5, then −*n*, or (op)*n*, is (op)−5 = 5. The sum of a number and its opposite is zero. Same as *additive inverse.* See Section 1.4 of the Numeration and Order essay.

opposite side (1) Of a quadrilateral: sides that do not share a common vertex. (2) Of a triangle: a side is opposite an angle of the triangle if it is not part of that angle. Compare to *opposite angles.*

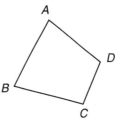

Sides *AB* and *CD* and Sides *AD* and *BC* are pairs of opposite sides.

order of magnitude estimate Same as *magnitude estimate*. See Section 8.1 of the Estimation, Mental Arithmetic, and Fact Power essay.

order of magnitude increase A ten-fold increase in a value. See Section 1.7 of the Numeration and Order essay and Section 8.1 of the Estimation, Mental Arithmetic, and Fact Power essay.

order of operations Rules that tell the order in which operations in an expression should be carried out. The conventional order of operations is:
1. Carry out operations inside parentheses and other grouping symbols. Work out from the innermost set of grouping symbols, using rules 2–4.
2. Carry out any exponentiation (raising to powers, such as 5^2).
3. Carry out multiplications and divisions in order from left to right.
4. Carry out additions and subtractions in order from left to right.

$$5^2 + (3 \times 4 - 2) \div 5 = 5^2 + (12 - 2) \div 5$$
$$= 5^2 + 10 \div 5$$
$$= 25 + 10 \div 5$$
$$= 25 + 2$$
$$= 27$$

See Section 9.2 of the Patterns, Sequences, Functions, and Algebra essay.

ordered pair (1) A pair of numbers used to locate a point on a coordinate grid. The first number corresponds to a position along the horizontal axis, and the second number corresponds to a position along the vertical axis. (2) Any pair of objects or numbers in a particular order. See Section 5.9 of the Geometry essay and Section 7.3 of the Reference Frames essay.

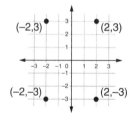

ordered pairs

orders of magnitude Positive powers of ten: 10, 100, 1,000, and so on. See Section 1.7 of the Numeration and Order essay and Section 8.1 of the Estimation, Mental Arithmetic, and Fact Power essay.

ordinal number A number used to express position or order in a series, such as first, third, and tenth. Generally, ordinal numbers are used in dates, as in "May fifth" (rather than "May five"). See Section 1.9 of the Numeration and Order essay.

origin The zero point in a coordinate system. In 2-dimensional Cartesian coordinates, the origin is the point at which the *x*-axis and *y*-axis intersect. See Section 5.9 of the Geometry essay and Section 7.3 of the Reference Frames essay.

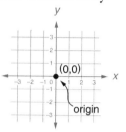

ounce (oz) (1) In the U.S. customary system, a unit of weight equal to $\frac{1}{16}$ of a pound. One ounce is about 28.35 grams. (2) In the U.S. customary system, a *fluid ounce* is a unit of capacity equal to $\frac{1}{16}$ of a pint. One fluid ounce equals 29.574 milliliters. See the Tables of Measure. See Sections 6.2, 6.6, and 6.7 of the Measurement essay.

outcome A possible result of a random process. Heads and tails are the two possible outcomes of tossing a coin. See Sections 4.2 and 4.3 of the Data and Chance essay.

output A number resulting from the application of a function rule to a given input number. See *function*. Compare to *input*. See Section 9.1 of the Patterns, Sequences, Functions, and Algebra essay.

pan balance A device used to weigh objects or compare their weights. See Section 6.3 of the Measurement essay.

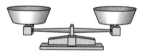

parabola The curve formed by the surface of a right circular cone when it intersects a plane which is parallel to a side of the cone. A parabola can also be defined as the curve formed by all of the points in a plane that are the same distance from a line in the plane and a point in the plane not on that line. See example on page 331.

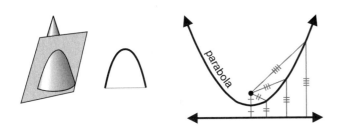

parallel Lines, rays, line segments, and planes that are equidistant at all points, no matter how far extended. See Section 5.7 of the Geometry essay.

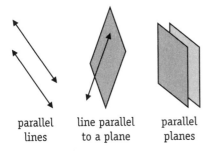

parallel lines | line parallel to a plane | parallel planes

parallelogram A quadrilateral that has two pairs of parallel sides and opposite sides that are congruent. All rectangles are parallelograms, but not all parallelograms are rectangles because parallelograms do not necessarily have right angles. See *opposite side* and *rectangle*. See Section 5.4 of the Geometry essay.

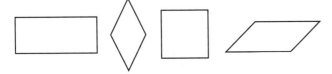

parallels Same as *latitude lines*.

parentheses See *grouping symbols*. See Section 9.2.

partial-differences method A subtraction procedure in which differences are computed for each place separately and then added to yield the final answer. See Section 3.2 of the Algorithms essay for further discussion and other subtraction algorithms.

$$
\begin{array}{r}
932 \\
-356 \\
\end{array}
$$

Subtract 100s: 900 − 300 ⟶ 600
Subtract 10s: 30 − 50 ⟶ − 20
Subtract 1s: 2 − 6 ⟶ − 4
Add the partial differences ⟶ 576
   (600 − 20 − 4, done mentally)

partial-products method A way to multiply in which the value of each digit in one factor is multiplied by the value of each digit in the other factor. The final product is the sum of these partial products. See Section 3.2 of the Algorithms essay for further discussion and other multiplication algorithms.

$$
\begin{array}{r}
67 \\
\times 53 \\
\end{array}
$$

50 × 60 ⟶ 3000
50 × 7 ⟶ 350
3 × 60 ⟶ 180
3 × 7 ⟶ + 21
3551

partial-quotients method A division procedure in which the quotient is found in several steps. In each step, a partial quotient is found. The partial quotients are then added to find the final quotient. See Section 3.2 of the Algorithms essay for further discussion and other division algorithms.

$$
\begin{array}{r}
22\overline{)400} \\
-220 \\
180 \\
-110 \\
70 \\
-44 \\
26 \\
-22 \\
4
\end{array}
$$

10 (10 [22s] in 400)
5 (5 [22s] in 180)
2 (2 [22s] in 70)
1 (1 [22] in 26)
18

400 / 22 → 18 R4

partial-sums method An addition procedure in which sums are computed for each place separately and then added to yield a final sum. See Section 3.2 of the Algorithms essay for further discussion and other addition algorithms.

$$
\begin{array}{r}
268 \\
+483 \\
\end{array}
$$

Add 100s: 200 + 400 ⟶ 600
Adds 10s: 60 + 80 ⟶ 140
Add 1s: 8 + 3 ⟶ + 11
Add partial sums. ⟶ 751

partitive division A phrase used in teacher training courses to indicate the use of division in equal-shares situations in which the total amount and the number of shares are known and the size of the shares is to be found. For example, "If $10 is shared by 4 people, how much does each person get?" is a partitive division problem. In *Everyday Mathematics*, the term "equal-sharing story" is used to describe partitive division problems. See *equal-sharing story*. Compare to *measurement division* and *equal-grouping story*. See Section 2.1 of the Arithmetic Operations essay.

parts-and-total diagram In *Everyday Mathematics*, a diagram used to represent problems in which two or more quantities are combined to form a total quantity. It is often used when the parts are known and the total is unknown. It can also be used when the total and one or more parts are known, but one part is unknown. See *situation diagram*. See Sections 2.1, 9.2, and 9.3.

13	
8	?

Total	
13	
Part	Part
8	*N*

parts-and-total diagrams for 13 = 8 + *N*

parts-and-total story A number story about a situation in which there is some whole that is made up of distinct parts. An example of a parts-and-total story is, "There are 15 girls and 12 boys in Mrs. Dorn's class. How many students are there in all?"

part-to-part ratio A ratio that compares a part of a whole to another part of the same whole. For example, the statement "There are 8 boys for every 12 girls" expresses a part-to-part ratio. See *ratio*. Compare to *part-to-whole ratio*. See Section 1.3.

part-to-whole ratio A ratio that compares a part of a whole to the whole. For example, the statement "8 out of 20 students are boys" expresses a part-to-whole ratio. The statement "12 out of 20 students are girls" also expresses a part-to-whole ratio. See *ratio*. Compare to *part-to-part ratio*. See Section 1.3.

part-whole fraction A fraction used when an object or a collection is divided into equal parts. In *Everyday Mathematics*, the object or collection is called the ONE, or the whole. Many common models for fractions are part-whole including pizzas, rectangles, and circles. See Section 1.3 of the Numeration and Order essay.

pattern A model or plan by which elements are arranged so that what comes next can be predicted. See Section 9.1 of the Patterns, Sequences, Functions, and Algebra essay.

penta- A prefix meaning five.

pentagon A 5-sided polygon. See Section 5.4 of the Geometry essay.

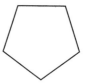

per In each or for each, as in *ten chairs per row* or *six tickets per family*.

per capita Per person.

percent (%) Per hundred, or out of a hundred. 1% means $\frac{1}{100}$ or 0.01. For example, "48% of the students in the school are boys" means that out of every 100 students in the school, 48 are boys. See Section 1.3 of the Numeration and Order essay.

Percent Circle A device on the Geometry Template used to measure or draw figures (such as circle graphs) involving percents. See *Geometry Template*.

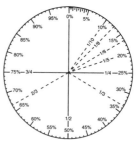

perfect number A number that equals the sum of its proper factors. For example, 6 is a perfect number because the sum of its proper factors is 1 + 2 + 3 = 6. Compare to *abundant number* and *deficient number*. See *proper factor*. See Section 1.2.

glossary

perimeter The distance around a closed plane figure or region. *Peri-* comes from the Greek word for "around," and *meter* comes from the Greek word for "measure"; perimeter means "around measure." See Section 6.4 of the Measurement essay.

perpendicular Rays, lines, line segments, or planes that form right angles are perpendicular to each other. See Section 5.7 of the Geometry essay.

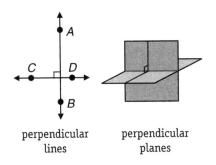

perpendicular   perpendicular
lines   planes

perpetual calendar A table that can be used to determine the correct day of the week for any date in a wide range of years.

personal measurement reference A convenient approximation for a standard unit of measurement. For example, many people have thumbs that are approximately one inch wide.

perspective drawing A method of drawing that realistically represents a 3-dimensional object on a 2-dimensional surface. See Section 5.1 of the Geometry essay.

per-unit rate A rate with 1 in the denominator. "2 dollars per gallon" is a per-gallon rate, "12 miles per hour" is a per-hour rate, and "4 words per minute" is a per-minute rate.

pi (π) The ratio of the circumference of a circle to its diameter. Pi, which is an irrational number approximately equal to 3.14, is the same for every circle. Pi is also the ratio of a circle's area to the square of its radius. Pi is usually written as the Greek letter π. The first twenty digits of π are:

3.1415926535897932384

See Section 5.4 of the Geometry essay.

pictograph A graph constructed with pictures or symbols. A pictograph makes it possible to compare at a glance the relative amounts of two or more counts or measures. See Section 4.1 of the Data and Chance essay.

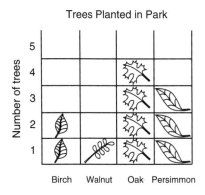

Trees Planted in Park

pie graph Same as *circle graph*. See Section 4.1 of the Data and Chance essay.

pint In the U.S. customary system, a unit of capacity equal to 2 cups or 16 fluid ounces. A handy saying to remember is "A pint's a pound the world around," which refers to the fact that a pint of water *weighs* about 1 pound (or 16 ounces). See the Tables of Measure. See Sections 6.2 and 6.6 of the Measurement essay.

place value The relative worth of each digit in a number, which is determined by its position. Each place has a value ten times that of the place to its right and one-tenth of the value of the place to its left.

thousands	hundreds	tens	ones	tenths	hundredths

a place-value chart

plane A 2-dimensional flat surface that extends forever. See Section 5.4 of the Geometry essay.

plane figure A figure that can be entirely contained in a single plane. For example, triangles, squares, pentagons, circles, and parabolas are plane figures; cones, cubes, and prisms are not. See *two-dimensional*. See Section 5.4 of the Geometry essay.

point An exact location in space. Points are usually labeled with capital letters. See Section 5.2 of the Geometry essay.

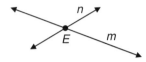

Lines *m* and *n* intersect at point *E.*

point symmetry The property of balance in a figure that can be rotated 180° about a point in such a way that the resulting figure (the image) exactly matches the original figure (the preimage). Point symmetry is rotational symmetry in which the turn is 180°.

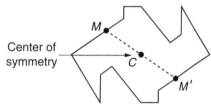

2-D shape with point symmetry

poly- A prefix meaning many.

polygon A closed plane figure formed by three or more line segments that meet only at their endpoints. Exactly two segments meet at each corner of a polygon. See Section 5.4 of the Geometry essay.

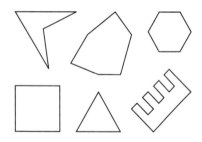

polyhedron A closed 3-dimensional shape, all of whose surfaces (faces) are flat. Each face consists of a polygon and its interior. See Section 5.5 of the Geometry essay.

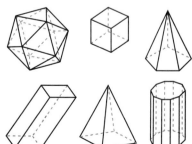

population (1) The total number of people living within a certain geographical area. (2) In data collection, the collection of people or objects that is the focus of study. The population is often larger than the target audience for a given survey, in which case a smaller, representative sample is considered. See *sample*. See Section 4.1.

population density The number of people living in a given area; usually given as a rate, such as "876 people per square mile."

positive number A number greater than 0; a number to the right of 0 on a horizontal number line or above 0 on a thermometer or other vertical number line. See Section 1.4 of the Numeration and Order essay.

positive power of 10 A power of 10 greater than 1. The positive powers of 10 are 10, 100, 1,000, and so on. See *power of 10*. Compare to *negative power of 10*. See Section 2.2.

positive rational numbers A number greater than 0 that can be written as a fraction or a terminating or repeating decimal. For example, 7, 4/3, 1/1,000, 0.01, 8.125, and 5.111… are positive rational numbers. See *rational number*. See Section 1.4 of the Numeration and Order essay.

poster In *Everyday Mathematics*, a page displaying a collection of numerical data. A poster may be used as a source of data for developing number stories in lessons following the lesson in which it is introduced.

pound (lb) In the U.S. customary system, a unit of weight equal to 16 ounces (oz) and defined as 0.45359237 kilograms. See the Tables of Measure. See Sections 6.2 and 6.7 of the Measurement essay.

power (1) The exponent to which a "base" number is raised in exponential notation; the number a in n^a, where n is the base. If n is any number and a is a positive whole number, a tells how many times to use n as a factor in a product. For example, $5^3 = 5 * 5 * 5 = 125$, and is read "5 to the third power." See *power of 10* for more examples, including examples in which a is a negative integer. (2) The result of a "powering" or "exponential" operation x^y. In mathematics beyond grades K–4, exponentiation goes beyond repeated multiplication, so that y can be a fraction or a decimal. See Section 2.2 of the Arithmetic Operations essay.

power of 10 (1) A whole number that can be written as a product using only 10 as a factor; also called a positive power of 10. For example, 100 is equal to 10 * 10, or 10^2. 100 can also be called ten squared, the second power of 10, or 10 to the second power. (2) More generally, any number that can be written as a product using only 10s or $\frac{1}{10}$s as factors. For example, 0.01 is equal to 0.1 * 0.1, or 10^{-2}. Other powers of 10 include $10^1 = 10$ and $10^0 = 1$. See *power*, *positive power of 10*, and *negative power of 10*. See Section 2.2.

powers key The [y^x] or [^] key on a calculator, used to calculate powers. Keying in 4 [^] 5 gives 4 raised to the fifth power, or 4^5, which equals $4 * 4 * 4 * 4 * 4$, or 1,024. See *power*.

precise In everyday language, a fine measurement or scale. The smaller the unit, or fraction of a unit used, the more precise the measurement or scale. For example, a measurement to the nearest inch is more precise than a measurement to the nearest foot. A ruler with $\frac{1}{16}$-inch markings is more precise than a ruler with $\frac{1}{4}$-inch markings. Compare to *accurate*.

predict To tell what will happen ahead of time; to make an educated guess about what might happen.

prediction line A line on a graph that can be used to make predictions about values that are not in the data set that was used to construct the graph. In statistics, prediction lines can be fit to data using regression analysis. In elementary mathematics, lines are usually drawn "by eye" so that they pass as close as possible to the given data points.

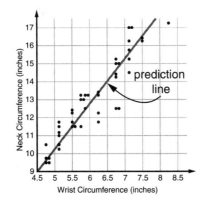

preimage A geometric figure that is operated on by a transformation—such as a reflection, rotation, or translation—to produce another figure. See *transformation*. Compare to *image*. See Section 5.6 of the Geometry essay.

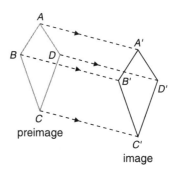

preimage

image

prime factorization A whole number expressed as a product of prime factors. Every whole number greater than 1 has a unique factorization. For example, the prime factorization of 24 is $2 \times 2 \times 2 \times 3$. See *prime number*. See Section 1.2.

prime meridian An imaginary semicircle on Earth, connecting the North Pole and South Pole through Greenwich, England. See *longitude* and *longitude lines*.

prime number A whole number greater than 1 that has exactly two whole-number factors, 1 and itself. For example, 7 is a prime number because its only factors are 1 and 7. The first five prime numbers are 2, 3, 5, 7, and 11. Compare to *composite number*. See Section 1.2.

prism A polyhedron with two parallel faces (bases) that are the same size and shape and other faces that are bounded by parallelograms. The points on the lateral faces of a prism are all on lines connecting corresponding points on the bases. In a right prism, the non-base faces are rectangles. Prisms are classified according to the shape of the two parallel bases. See Section 5.5 of the Geometry essay.

triangular prism   rectangular prism   hexagonal prism

probability A number from 0 to 1 that indicates the likelihood that an event will happen. The closer a probability is to 1, the more likely that the event will happen. The closer a probability is to 0, the less likely that the event will happen. For example, the probability that a fair coin will show heads is $\frac{1}{2}$. See *event*. See Section 4.2 of the Data and Chance essay.

Probability Meter In *Everyday Mathematics*, a tool used to show probabilities expressed as fractions, decimals, and percents.

probability tree diagram See *tree diagram*.

product The result of a multiplication. In the number model $4 \times 3 = 12$, the product is 12. See *multiplication*.

Project In *Everyday Mathematics*, a thematic activity to be completed in one or more days by small groups or by the whole class. Projects often involve collecting and analyzing data and are usually cross-curricular in nature. See page 14 in the Management Guide for more information.

proper factor Any whole-number factor of a number except the number itself. For example, the factors of 10 are 1, 2, 5, and 10, but the proper factors of 10 are 1, 2, and 5. See Section 1.2.

proper fraction The traditional term for a fraction in which the numerator is less than the denominator; a proper fraction names a number less than 1. For example, $\frac{3}{4}$, $\frac{2}{5}$, and $\frac{12}{24}$ are proper fractions. Compare to *improper fraction*. See Sections 1.3 and 3.3.

property Same as *attribute*.

proportion A number sentence, possibly including variables, that equates two fractions. Often the fractions in a proportion represent rates or ratios. Many problem situations can be modeled by proportions. For example, the problem, "Alan's speed is 12 miles per hour. At the same speed, how far can he travel in 3 hours?" can be modeled by the proportion:

$$\frac{12 \text{ miles}}{1 \text{ hour}} = \frac{n \text{ miles}}{3 \text{ hours}}$$

See Sections 1.3 and 9.3.

protractor A tool used for measuring or drawing angles. When measuring an angle, the vertex of the angle should be at the center of the protractor and one side aligned with the 0° mark. A half-circle protractor can be used to measure and draw angles up to 180°; a full-circle protractor can be used to measure and draw angles up to 360°. See Section 6.8.

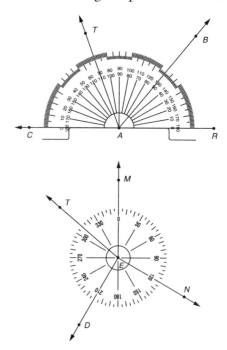

pyramid A polyhedron in which one face (the base) is a polygon and all other faces are triangles with a common vertex called the *apex*. Pyramids are classified according to the shapes of their bases. See Section 5.5 of the Geometry essay.

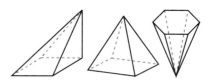

Pythagorean theorem The proposition that for any right triangle, the area of the square on the hypotenuse is equal to the sum of the areas of the squares on the other two sides. See Section 5.4.

Symbolically, the theorem

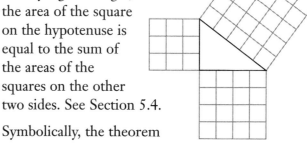

can be stated as follows: If the legs of a right triangle have lengths *a* and *b*, and the hypotenuse has length *c*, then $a^2 + b^2 = c^2$.

quad- A prefix meaning four.

quadrangle A polygon with four angles. Same as *quadrilateral*. See Section 5.4 of the Geometry essay.

quadrant Any of the four sections into which a rectangular coordinate grid is divided by the intersection of the *x*- and *y*-axes. The quadrants are numbered I, II, III, and IV beginning at the upper right (where *x*- and *y*-coordinates are positive) and going counterclockwise. See Sections 5.9 and 7.3.

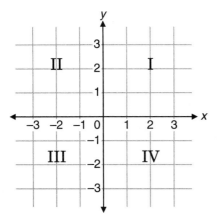

quadrilateral A polygon with four sides. Same as *quadrangle*. See Section 5.4 of the Geometry essay.

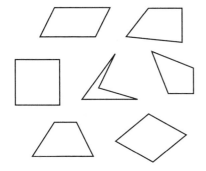

quadruple Four times an amount.

quart In the U.S. customary system, a unit of capacity equal to 32 fluid ounces, 2 pints, or 4 cups. See the Tables of Measure.

quick common denominator The product of the denominators of two or more fractions. The quick common denominator of $\frac{a}{b}$ and $\frac{c}{d}$ is $b * d$. For example, the quick common denominator of $\frac{3}{4}$ and $\frac{5}{6}$ is 4 * 6 or 24. See Section 3.3.

quotient The result of dividing one number by another number. In the division model $10 \div 5 = 2$, the quotient is 2. See *division*.

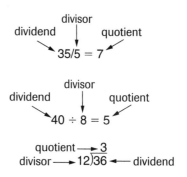

quotitive division Same as *measurement division*. See Section 2.1 of the Arithmetic Operations essay.

radius A line segment from the center of a circle (or sphere) to any point on the circle (or sphere); also, the length of such a line segment. See Sections 5.4 and 5.5 of the Geometry essay.

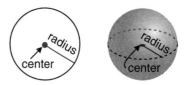

random Not predictable with respect to individual outcomes. Flipping a fair coin is a random process because the outcome of an individual flip cannot be predicted. See Section 4.2 of the Data and Chance essay.

random number A number produced by a random process, such as rolling a die or spinning a spinner. A random number has the same chance of appearing as any other possible number. See Sections 4.2 and 4.3 of the Data and Chance essay.

random sampling Selecting a sample from a population in a way that allows all members of the population the same chance of being included. See Section 4.1.

range The difference between the greatest and least values in a set of data. See Section 4.1 of the Data and Chance essay.

rank To put in order by size; to sort from smallest to largest or vice versa.

rate A comparison by division of two quantities with different units. For example, traveling 100 miles in 2 hours can be expressed as 100 mi/2 hr or 50 miles per hour. In this case, the rate compares distance (miles) to time (hours). Compare to *ratio*. See Section 1.3 of the Numeration and Order essay and Section 2.1 of the Arithmetic Operations essay.

rate diagram A tool used to represent rate situations. See *situation diagram* and *multiplication diagram*. See Section 2.1 of the Arithmetic Operations essay.

rows	chairs per row	chairs
6	4	?

rate table A means of displaying rate information. See *rate*.

miles	35	70	105	140	175	210
gallons	1	2	3	4	5	6

rate unit A unit, used to describe a rate, made up of two different units. For example, miles per hour, dollars per pound, and words per minute are all rate units. See *rate*. See Section 1.3 of the Numeration and Order essay.

ratio A comparison by division of two quantities with the same units. Ratios can be expressed as fractions, decimals, or percents, as well as in words. Ratios can also be written with a colon between the two numbers being compared. For example, if a team wins 3 games out of 5 games played, the ratio of wins to total games is $\frac{3}{5}$, 3/5, 0.6, 60%, 3 to 5, or 3:5 (read "three to five"). Compare to *rate*. See Section 1.3 of the Numeration and Order essay.

rational number Any number that can be represented in the form *a/b*, where *a* and *b* are integers and $b \neq 0$. A rational number can always be represented by either a terminating decimal or a repeating decimal. For example, 2/3, –2/3, 0.5, 20.5, and 0.333… are all rational numbers. See Sections 1.3–1.5 of the Numeration and Order essay.

ray A straight path that extends infinitely from a point, called its *endpoint*. See Section 5.3 of the Geometry essay.

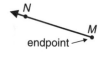

real number Any rational or irrational number. For every real number there is a corresponding point on the number line, and for every point on the number line there is a real number. See Section 1.7 of the Numeration and Order essay.

recall survey A survey in which data is gathered by asking people what they remember about a particular topic. For example, a recall survey might ask people to list what soft drinks they have consumed in the previous week.

reciprocal Same as *multiplicative inverse*.

rectangle A parallelogram whose angles are all right angles. See *parallelogram*. See Section 5.4 of the Geometry essay.

rectangle method A method for finding area in which one or more rectangles are drawn around a figure or parts of a figure. The sides of the rectangle(s), together with the sides of the original figure, define regions that are either rectangles or triangular halves of rectangles. The area of the original figure can be found by adding and subtracting the areas of these rectangular and triangular regions.

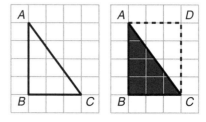

rectangular array A rectangular arrangement of objects in rows and columns such that each row has the same number of objects and each column has the same number of objects. See *x-by-y array*. See Section 2.1 of the Arithmetic Operations essay.

rectangular coordinate grid A system for locating points by means of perpendicular lines, called axes. See *coordinate grid*. See Sections 5.9 and 7.3.

glossary

rectangular prism (1) In common usage, a prism whose faces (including the bases) are all rectangles. Many packing boxes have the shape of rectangular prisms. (2) More generally, any prism with rectangular bases, some of the faces of which might be non-rectangle parallelograms. See Section 5.5 of the Geometry essay.

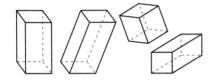

rectangular pyramid A pyramid whose base is a rectangle. See Section 5.5 of the Geometry essay.

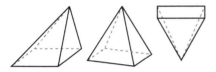

reduce (1) To make an object or shape smaller. (2) To reduce fractions: To put into simpler form. See *simplest form*. See Section 1.3 of the Numeration and Order essay.

reference frame A system for locating numbers within a given context, often with reference to an arbitrarily set 0-point. Examples of reference frames are number lines, timelines, calendar systems, temperature scales, and coordinate systems, including those on maps. See the Reference Frames essay.

reflection A transformation that "flips" a figure over a line or an object over a plane so that it becomes a mirror image of the original (preimage). Same as *flip*. See *transformation*. See Section 5.6 of the Geometry essay.

reflex angle An angle with a measure between 180° and 360°. See *angle*. See Section 5.4 of the Geometry essay.

regular polygon A polygon whose sides are the same length and whose angles are all equal. See Section 5.4 of the Geometry essay.

regular polyhedron A polyhedron whose faces are all congruent regular polygons and that has the same number of faces meeting at every vertex, all at the same angle. There are five regular polyhedra, known as the Platonic solids:

tetrahedron: 4 faces, each an equilateral triangle
cube: 6 faces, each a square
octahedron: 8 faces, each an equilateral triangle
dodecahedron: 12 faces, each a regular pentagon
icosahedron: 20 faces, each an equilateral triangle
See Section 5.5 of the Geometry essay.

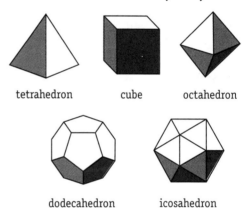

tetrahedron   cube   octahedron

dodecahedron   icosahedron

regular tessellation A tessellation made up of only one kind of regular polygon. There are only three regular tessellations. See *tessellation*. See Section 5.10.

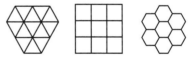

the three regular tessellations

relation symbol A symbol used to express a relationship between two quantities. Some relation symbols used in number sentences include: = for "is equal to," ≠ for "is not equal to," < for "is less than," > for "is greater than," ≤ for "is less than or equal to," and ≥ for "is greater than or equal to." See Sections 1.9 and 9.2.

remainder An amount left over when one number is divided by another. In the division number model 16 / 3 → 5 R1, the quotient is 5 and the remainder is 1. See Section 2.1 of the Arithmetic Operations essay.

rename-addends algorithm An addition procedure in which both addends are changed by equal amounts in opposite directions. For example, 73 + 29 = (73 − 1) + (29 + 1) = 72 + 30 = 102. Same as *opposite-change rule*. See Section 3.2 of the Algorithms essay for further discussion and other addition algorithms.

repeating decimal A *decimal* in which one digit, or a group of digits, is repeated without end. For example, 0.3333. . . and 0.$\overline{147}$ are repeating decimals. Compare to *terminating decimal*. See Section 1.3.

revolution Movement in a circle or a curve around some point. The planets revolve around the sun.

rhombus A parallelogram with all sides the same length. The angles may be right angles, in which case the rhombus is a square. See Section 5.4 of the Geometry essay.

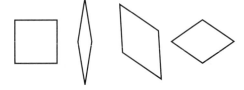

right (1) Of an angle: An angle whose measure is 90°. See *angle*. See Section 5.4 of the Geometry essay.

(2) Of a prism or cylinder: Having lateral faces or surfaces that are perpendicular to their bases. Compare to *slanted*.

a right circular cylinder and
a right triangular prism

(3) Of a pyramid or cone: Having an apex directly above the center of its base. Compare to *slanted*.

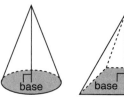

a right circular cone and a right square pyramid

(4) Of a triangle: Having a right angle. See *triangle*. See Section 5.4 of the Geometry essay.

Roman numerals Symbols from an ancient Roman system of numeration. Roman numerals are the letters that are used alone and in combination to represent numbers in this ancient system. Roman numerals are still found on clocks, building cornerstones, preliminary pages in books, and other places.

Roman Numerals

I = 1	X = 10	C = 100
II = 2	XX = 20 (2 tens)	CC = 200
III = 3	XXX = 30 (3 tens)	CCC = 300
IV = 4	XL = 40 (50 less 10)	CD = 400
V = 5	L = 50	D = 500
VI = 6	LX = 60 (50 plus 10)	CM = 900
VII = 7	LXX = 70 (50 plus 20)	M = 1,000
VIII = 8	LXXX = 80 (50 plus 30)	
IX = 9	XC = 90 (100 less 10)	

rotation A transformation that "turns" an object around a fixed point or axis. The point or axis, called the *center* or *axis of rotation*, can be inside or outside of the original image. Same as *turn*. See *transformation*. See Section 5.6 of the Geometry essay.

rotational symmetry (1) In a plane, a figure has rotational symmetry if it can be rotated less than one full turn around a point so that the resulting figure (the image) exactly matches the original figure (the preimage). Compare to *line symmetry*. See Section 5.8 of the Geometry essay.

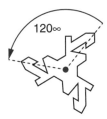

order 3 rotational symmetry

(2) A 3-D figure has rotational symmetry if it can be rotated less than a full turn around an axis so that the resulting figure exactly matches the original figure.

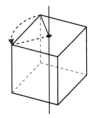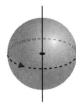

3-D shapes with rotational symmetry

round (1) Arithmetic: To express a number in a simplified way. Examples of rounding include expressing a measure of weight to the nearest pound and expressing an amount of money to the nearest dollar. See Section 3.2 of the Algorithms essay and Section 8.1 of the Estimation, Mental Arithmetic, and Fact Power essay. (2) Geometry: Circular in shape.

row (1) A horizontal arrangement of objects or numbers in an array or table. (2) A section of cells lined up horizontally in a spreadsheet. See *cell*.

same-change rule A subtraction procedure in which the same change is made to both numbers. For example,
$87 - 34 = (87 - 4) - (34 - 4) = 83 - 30 = 53$.
See Section 3.2 of the Algorithms essay for other subtraction algorithms.

sample A part of a population intended to represent the whole. See Section 4.1.

scale The ratio of the distance on a map, globe, or drawing to the actual distance. See *scale factor*. See Section 2.1 of the Arithmetic Operations essay and Section 7.4 of the Reference Frames essay.

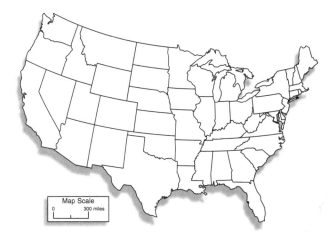

Map Scale
0   300 miles

(2) A number line on a thermometer used for measuring temperature. More generally, any number line on a measuring tool.
(3) An instrument for measuring weight.

scale drawing
A drawing that represents an object or area in fixed proportion to its actual size. The proportion is called the *scale factor*. For example, if an actual object measures 33 yards by 22 yards, a scale drawing of it might

woodpecker (8 in.) shown in $\frac{1}{4}$ scale

measure 33 centimeters by 22 centimeters, with all of the proportions between corresponding parts of the drawing and the actual object being the same. A map is a scale drawing of a geographical region. See *scale factor*. See Section 1.3 of the Numeration and Order essay, Section 2.1 of the Arithmetic Operations essay, and Section 7.4 of the Reference Frames essay.

scale factor The multiplier, or ratio, between an image and preimage (or between a scale drawing or model and an actual object). See *scale*, *scale drawing*, and *scale model*. See Section 2.1 of the Arithmetic Operations essay, and Section 5.6 of the Geometry essay.

glossary

scale model A model that represents an object or display in fixed ratio to its actual size. The ratio is called the scale factor. For example, many model trains or airplanes are scale models of actual vehicles. See *scale factor*. See Section 2.1 of the Arithmetic Operations essay.

scalene triangle A triangle with sides of three different lengths and angles of three different sizes. See *triangle*. See Section 5.4 of the Geometry essay.

scientific calculator A calculator that displays very large and very small numbers in scientific notation and has keys for powering and other advanced operations. Scientific calculators usually carry out operations in accordance with the conventional order of operations. See *scientific notation* and *order of operations*. See Section 3.4 and the section on calculators in the Management Guide.

scientific notation A system for representing numbers in which a number is written as the product of a power of 10 and a number that is at least 1 and less than 10. Scientific notation allows writing big and small numbers with only a few symbols. For example, 4,300,000 in scientific notation is $4.3 * 10^6$, and 0.00001 in scientific notation is $1 * 10^{-5}$. Compare to *standard notation* and *expanded notation*. See Section 2.2 of the Arithmetic Operations essay.

scroll To move through previous displays using the [up arrow] and [down arrow] keys on the calculator.

second (1) A unit of time. There are 60 seconds in a minute. (2) An ordinal number in the sequence first, second, third, …

sector A region bounded by an arc and two radii of a circle. A sector resembles a slice of pizza. The word wedge is sometimes used instead of sector. See Section 5.4 of the Geometry essay for a discussion of circles.

sector

semicircle Half of a circle, bounded by the circumference and the ends of a diameter. In common usage, the diameter is often included as a boundary of a semicircle, making it a closed figure that is half of a circular region. See *circle*. See Section 5.4 of the Geometry essay.

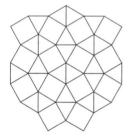

semi-regular tessellation A tiling in which every tile is a regular polygon and the angles around every vertex point are congruent to the angles around every other vertex point. A semi-regular tessellation must have more than one kind of regular polygon; otherwise it would be a regular tessellation. Every vertex in a semi-regular tessellation looks the same. There are eight semi-regular tessellations. Compare to *regular tessellation*. See *tessellation*, *tiling*, and *name of a tessellation*. See Section 5.10.

a 3.3.4.3.4 semi-regular tessellation

set A collection or group of objects, numbers, or other items.

side Any one of the line segments that make up a polygon. Sometimes a face of a 3-dimensional figure is called a side. See Section 5.4 of the Geometry essay.

side-by-side bar graph A bar graph that uses adjacent bars to show two related sets of data. The side-by-side bar graph shows both road miles and air miles from Los Angeles to different cities. See Section 4.1.

Miles from Los Angeles

(Bar graph showing distances "to Dallas", "to Chicago", and "to New York" with axis from 0 to 3,000 Miles, in intervals of 1,000.)

Key: ☐ Road Miles ■ Air Miles

Sieve of Eratosthenes A method for identifying prime numbers. The mathematician Eratosthenes (c. 276–194 B.C.) was the head librarian at the great library in Alexandria in Egypt.

To use the Sieve of Eratosthenes to find all prime numbers less than n, follow these steps:

1. List all the counting numbers from 2 to n.
2. Circle 2. Cross out all the multiples of 2 greater than 2.
3. Find the first number that is not already crossed out. Circle that number. Cross out all the higher multiples of that number.
4. Repeat step 3 until the first number that is neither crossed out nor circled is greater than the square root of n. At this point, the numbers that are not crossed out are all the prime numbers less than or equal to n.

Sieve of Eratosthenes for primes less than 25

significant digits The digits in a number that convey useful and reliable information. A number with more significant digits is more precise than a number with fewer significant digits. In general, calculations cannot produce results with more significant digits than the original numbers. For example, suppose a rectangular plot of ground, carefully measured to the nearest tenth of a meter, is 12.4 meters by 16.7 meters. Its area can be calculated as 207.08 square meters. However, each of the original numbers has only three significant digits; therefore only the digits 207 are significant and the area should be reported as 207 sq. m.. See *scientific notation*. See Section 8.1 of the Estimation, Mental Arithmetic, and Fact Power essay.

similar Having the same shape but not necessarily the same size. All squares are similar to one another. Compare to *congruent*. See Section 5.7 of the Geometry essay.

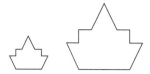

simpler form A fraction can be put in simpler form by dividing its numerator and denominator by a whole number that is greater than 1. For example, $\frac{18}{24}$ can be put in simpler form by dividing the numerator and the denominator by 2. The result, $\frac{9}{12}$, is in simpler form than $\frac{18}{24}$.

simplest form (1) Of proper fractions: Having numerator and denominator with no common factors (other than 1). For example, $\frac{10}{15}$ and $\frac{2}{3}$ are equivalent fractions. However, $\frac{10}{15}$ is not in simplest form because the numerator and denominator can each be divided by 5; $\frac{2}{3}$ is in simplest form because 2 and 3 have no common factors (other than 1). (2) Of mixed numbers and improper fractions: Being in mixed number form in which the fraction part is proper and in simplest form. For example, $1\frac{7}{3}$ is not in simplest form because the fraction part is not proper. Same as *lowest terms*. See Section 3.3. *Note:* Simplest form is not emphasized in *Everyday Mathematics* because other equivalent forms are often equally or more useful. For example, when comparing or adding fractions, fractions written with a common denominator are easier to work with than those in simplest form.

simplify (1) Of a fraction: To express in simplest form, or lowest terms. See *simplest form*. See Section 9.2. (2) Of an equation: To rewrite an equation by clearing parentheses and combining like terms and constants on each side of the equal sign. Equations that have been simplified are often easier to solve. (3) Of an expression: To rewrite by removing parentheses and by combining like terms. For example, $7y + 4 + 5 + 3y$ can be simplified as $10y + 9$ and $3(2y + 5) - y$ can be simplified as $5y + 15$.

glossary

situation diagram One of various diagrams used to organize information in simple problem situations. Same as *operation diagram*. See *change diagram, comparison diagram, parts-and-total diagram, multiplication diagram,* and *rate diagram*. See Sections 2.1, 9.2, and 9.3. See page 20 of the Management Guide.

size change An enlargement or reduction of an original. See Section 5.6.

size-change factor A number that indicates the amount of an enlargement or reduction. See *size change*. See Section 5.6.

skew lines Lines in space that do not lie in the same plane. Skew lines do not intersect and are not parallel. An east-west line on the floor and a north-south line on the ceiling are skew. See Section 5.7.

Skew lines can be modeled with 2 pencils.

slanted Of a cylinder, cone, prism, or pyramid: tilted. Slanted cylinders and prisms have lateral faces or surfaces that are not all perpendicular to their bases. Slanted cones and pyramids have apexes that are not directly above the centers of their bases. Also known as oblique or slant. Compare to *right prism or cylinder, right pyramid or right cone*. See Section 5.5 of the Geometry essay.

slanted cylinder, cone, prism, and pyramid

slate A lap-sized (about 8" by 11") chalkboard or whiteboard that students use in *Everyday Mathematics* for recording responses during group exercises and informal group assessments. See page 21 in the Management Guide for more information.

slide An informal name for a translation transformation. See *translation* and *transformation*. See Section 5.6 of the Geometry essay.

slide rule (1) A mechanical tool composed of a ruler and a sliding insert. Slide rules can be used to do many types of calculations but have been rendered obsolete by electronic calculators. (2) An *Everyday Mathematics* tool made of paper or cardstock that can be used for adding and subtracting integers and fractions.

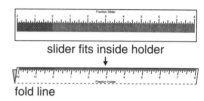

slider fits inside holder

fold line

slide rule

solution (1) Of an open sentence: A value or values for the variable(s) which make the sentence true. For example, the open sentence $4 + \_\_ = 10$ has the solution 6. See *open sentence*. See Section 9.3 of the Patterns, Sequences, Functions, and Algebra essay. (2) Of a problem: The answer or the method by which the answer was obtained.

solution set The set of all solutions of an equation or inequality. For example, the solution set of $x^2 = 25$ is {5, –5} since substitution of either 5 or –5 for x makes the sentence true.

span Same as *normal span*. Compare to *great span*.

speed A rate that compares distance traveled with the time taken to travel that distance. See *rate*. See Section 1.3 of the Numeration and Order essay.

sphere A 3-dimensional shape whose curved surface is, at all points, a given distance from its center point. A ball is shaped like a sphere.
A sphere is hollow; it does not include the points in its interior. See Section 5.5 of the Geometry essay.

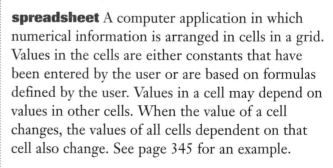

spreadsheet A computer application in which numerical information is arranged in cells in a grid. Values in the cells are either constants that have been entered by the user or are based on formulas defined by the user. Values in a cell may depend on values in other cells. When the value of a cell changes, the values of all cells dependent on that cell also change. See page 345 for an example.

glossary

	A	B	C	D
		budget for class picnic		
1				
2				
3	quantity	food items	unit price	cost
4	6	packages of hamburgers	2.79	16.74
5	5	packages of hamburger buns	1.29	6.45
6	3	bags of potato chips	3.12	9.36
7	3	quarts of macaroni salad	4.50	13.50
8	4	bottles of soft drinks	1.69	6.76
9			subtotal	52.81
10			8% tax	4.23
11			total	57.04

Class Picnic ($$)

spreadsheet

The name *spreadsheet* comes from ledger worksheets for financial records. Such sheets were often taped together and then spread out for examination.

square A rectangle whose sides are all the same length. See Section 5.4 of the Geometry essay.

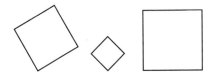

square number A number that is the product of a whole number and itself; a whole number to the second power. For example, 25 is a square number, because $25 = 5 \times 5$. A square number can be represented by a square array. See *array* and *rectangular array*. See Section 2.2 of the Arithmetic Operations essay.

square of a number The product of a number and itself. The square of a number is symbolized by a raised 2. For example, $3.5^2 = 3.5 \times 3.5 = 12.25$. See Section 2.2 of the Arithmetic Operations essay.

square pyramid A pyramid with a square base.

square root of a number The square root of a number n is a number that, when multiplied by itself results in the number n. For example, 4 is a square root of 16, because $4 \times 4 = 16$. Normally, square root refers to the positive square root, but the opposite of a positive square root is also a square root. For example, –4 is also a square root of 16 because $-4 \times -4 = 16$.

square root key The $\boxed{\sqrt{}}$ key on certain calculators. The $\boxed{\sqrt{}}$ key undoes the result of squaring a non-negative number.

square unit A unit used to measure area. A square unit represents a square with the measure of each side being a related unit of length. For example, a square inch is the area of a square that measures one inch on each side. See Section 6.5 of the Measurement essay.

square units

squaring key Many calculators have a special key for squaring numbers. Most often this key is labeled and is pressed after the number to be squared has been entered. For example, to square 24 on such a calculator, key in 2 4 $\boxed{x^2}$ $\boxed{\text{Enter}}$. To square numbers on calculators without a squaring key, use $\boxed{\wedge}$ 2 or repeated multiplication.

stacked bar graph A bar graph in which the bars are sub-divided to show additional information. A stacked bar graph can be used to show how a total is made up of several parts. See *bar graph*. Compare to *side-by-side bar graph*. See Section 4.1.

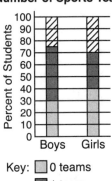

Number of Sports Teams

Key: 0 teams
1 team
2 or more teams

standard notation The most familiar way of representing whole numbers, integers, and decimals. Standard notation is base-ten place-value numeration. For example, standard notation for three hundred fifty-six is 356. Compare to *expanded notation*, *scientific notation*, and *number-and-word notation*. See Section 2.2 of the Arithmetic Operations essay.

standard unit A unit of measure that has been defined by a recognized authority, such as a government or a standards organization. For example, inches, meters, miles, seconds, pounds, grams, and acres are all standard units. See Section 6.2 of the Measurement essay.

glossary

stem-and-leaf plot A display of data in which digits with larger place values are "stems" and digits with smaller place values are "leaves." See Section 4.1 of the Data and Chance essay.

Stems 10's	Leaves 1's
2	4 4 5 6 7 7
3	1 1 2 2 6 6
4	1 1 3 5 8
5	0 2

step graph A graph that looks like steps because the values are the same for an interval and then change (or "step") for another interval. The horizontal axis of a step graph often represents time. See Section 4.1.

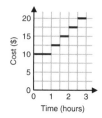

straight angle An angle measuring 180°. See *angle*. See Section 5.4 of the Geometry essay.

straightedge A tool used to draw line segments. A straightedge does not have measure marks on it, so if a ruler is used as a straightedge, the markings on it should be ignored. See Section 5.12.

Study Links In *Everyday Mathematics*, a suggested follow-up or enrichment activity to be done at home. See page 22 in the Management Guide for more information.

substitute To replace one thing with another; in a formula, to replace variables with numerical values. For example, if $b = 4.5$ and $h = 8.5$, then these values can be substituted in the formula $A = b \times h$ to yield $A = 4.5 \times 8.5 = 38.25$. See Section 2.1 of the Arithmetic Operations essay and Section 9.3 of the Patterns, Sequences, Functions, and Algebra essay.

subtraction The operation used to find how much remains when a given quantity is decreased, what the difference is between two quantities, and in various other situations. The number being subtracted is called the *subtrahend*; the number being subtracted from is called the *minuend*; and the result of the subtraction is called the *difference*. For example, in $45 - 12 = 33$, the minuend is 45, the subtrahend is 12, and the difference is 33. Addition "undoes" subtraction: $45 - 12 = 33$ can be "undone" by $12 + 33 = 45$. See Section 2.1 of the Arithmetic Operations essay and Section 3.2 of the Algorithms essay.

subtrahend In subtraction, the number that is being taken away from another. For example, in $15 - 5 = 10$, the subtrahend is 5. See *subtraction*.

sum The result of adding two or more numbers. For example, in $5 + 3 = 8$, the sum is 8. See *addition*.

supplementary angles Two angles whose measures total 180°. See Section 5.4 of the Geometry essay.

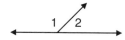

∠1 and ∠2 are supplementary angles.

surface (1) The outside boundary of an object; the part of an object that is next to the air. Common surfaces include the top of a body of water, the outermost part of a ball, and the topmost layer of ground that covers Earth. (2) A basic concept of geometry, usually thought of as a continuous set of points, flat or curved, without thickness; any 2-dimensional layer. A surface can be bounded (for example, a circle and its interior or the surface of a cylinder) or unbounded (for example, a plane).

surface area A measure of the surface of a 3-dimensional figure. The surface area of a polyhedron is the sum of the areas of its faces. See *area*. See Section 6.5 of the Measurement essay.

survey A study that collects data. Surveys are used to find out about people's characteristics, behaviors, interests, opinions, and so on. In *Everyday Mathematics*, surveys are used to generate data for graphing and analysis. See Section 4.1 of the Data and Chance essay.

symmetric Having symmetry. See *symmetry*, *line symmetry*, and *rotational symmetry*.

symmetry The property of exact balance in a figure; having the same size and shape reflected across a dividing line or plane or rotated around a point. See *line symmetry* and *rotational symmetry*. See Section 5.8 of the Geometry essay.

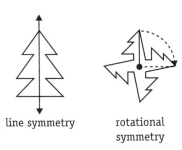

line symmetry   rotational symmetry

tally A mark (////) used to keep track of a count. See Section 4.1 of the Data and Chance essay.

tally chart A method for organizing data in a table in which tallies are made next to each value to show the frequency of that value in the data set.

Number of Pull-Ups	Number of Children
0	ⅧⅢ I
1	ⅧⅢ
2	////
3	//

tally chart

tangent (1) Of circles: Intersecting at exactly one point. The line connecting the centers of two tangent circles passes through the point of tangency.
(2) Of a line and a circle: Intersecting at exactly one point. A line tangent to a circle is perpendicular to the radius of the circle at the point of tangency.

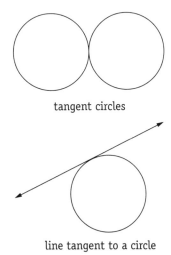

tangent circles

line tangent to a circle

temperature A gauge of how hot or cold something is, usually expressed in degrees Celsius or degrees Fahrenheit. The Celsius and Fahrenheit temperature scales are different reference frames for temperature. See *reference frame*. See Section 7.1 of the Reference Frames essay.

template In *Everyday Mathematics*, a sheet of plastic with geometric shapes cut out of it, used to draw patterns and designs. See *Geometry Template*. See Section 5.13 of the Geometry essay.

term (1) In an algebraic expression or equation, a number or a product of a number and one or more variables. For example, in the equation $5y + 3k = 8$, the terms are $5y$, $3k$, and 8. See Section 9.2 of the Patterns, Sequences, Functions, and Algebra essay. (2) An element in a sequence. In the sequence of square numbers, the terms are 1, 4, 9, 16, and so on.

terminating decimal A decimal that ends. For example, 0.5 and 0.125 are terminating decimals. A terminating decimal can be thought of as a repeating decimal in which only 0 repeats. Since 0.5 and 0.125 can be written with repeating 0s: 0.500... and 0.12500..., respectively, they 'terminate.' See *decimal*. Compare to *repeating decimal*. See Section 1.3.

tessellate (1) To make a tessellation or tiling. See *tessellation*. (2) To fit into a tessellation. Any quadrilateral will tessellate. See Section 5.10.

tessellation An arrangement of closed shapes that covers a surface completely without overlaps or gaps. Same as *tiling*. See *tile*. See Section 5.10.

test number A number used to replace a variable during the process of solving an equation by trial-and-error. Test numbers are useful for "closing in" on the exact solution of an equation. See *trial-and-error method*.

tetrahedron Same as *triangular pyramid*.

theorem A mathematical statement that can be proved to be true. For example, the Pythagorean theorem states that if the legs of a right triangle have lengths a and b and the hypotenuse has length c, then $a^2 + b^2 = c^2$. The Pythagorean theorem has been proved in hundreds of ways over the past 2,500 years.

three-dimensional (3-D) (1) A figure in space that cannot be contained in a plane. Examples include prisms, pyramids, and spheres, all of which have depth, width, and height. Other examples of 3-D shapes include pairs of perpendicular planes and sets of lines that are not all in the same plane. (2) A space in which any point can be located with three numbers. Compare to *one-dimensional* and *two-dimensional*. See Section 5.5 of the Geometry essay.

tile A shape used in a *tessellation*. If only one shape is repeated in a tessellation, the tessellation is called a "same-tile tessellation." See Section 5.10.

tiling An arrangement of closed shapes that covers a surface completely without overlaps or gaps. See *tessellation*. Also, the act of making a tessellation.

time graph A graph that is constructed from a story that takes place over time. A time graph shows what happened through a progression of time.

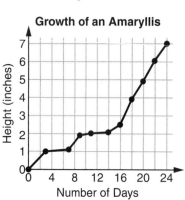
Growth of an Amaryllis

timeline A device for showing in sequence when events took place. A timeline is a number line with the numbers naming years, days, and so on. See *reference frame*. See Section 7.2 of the Reference Frames essay.

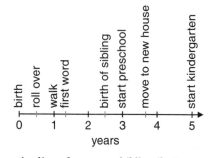
timeline of a young child's milestones

tool kit In *Everyday Mathematics*, a bag or a box containing a calculator, measuring tools, and manipulatives often used in the program. See page 33 in the Management Guide for more information.

top-heavy fraction Same as *improper fraction*.

topology The study of the properties of shapes that are unchanged by shrinking, stretching, twisting, bending, and similar transformations. (Tearing, breaking, and sticking together, however, are not allowed.) See Section 5.11.

trade-first subtraction A subtraction procedure in which all necessary trades are done before any subtractions are carried out. Doing so simplifies the algorithm since the user can concentrate on one thing at a time. See Section 3.2 of the Algorithms essay for further discussion and other subtraction algorithms.

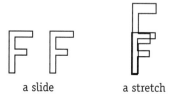

transformation An operation on a geometric figure that produces a new figure, called the image, from the original figure, called the preimage.

F   F   F

a slide   a stretch

Transformations are sometimes thought of as moving a figure from one place to another and sometimes changing its size or shape. The study of transformations is called *transformation geometry*. See *isometry transformation*, *reflection*, *rotation*, and *translation*. See Section 5.6 of the Geometry essay.

transformation geometry The study of the geometry of transformations. See *transformation*. See Section 5.6 of the Geometry essay.

translation The motion of "sliding" an object or picture along a line segment. Same as *slide*. See *transformation*. See Section 5.6 of the Geometry essay.

translation tessellation A tessellation created by translating (sliding) curves from one side of a figure (such as a square) to the opposite side. The resulting figure is then translated to create the interlocking pieces in the tessellation. M. C. Escher created many beautiful and elaborate translation tessellations. See *translation* and *tessellation*. See Section 5.10.

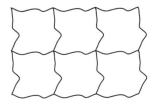

a translation tessellation

transparent mirror A piece of semitransparent plastic used to draw and study reflections. See page 46 of the Management Guide.

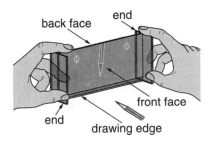

transparent mirror

transversal A line that intersects two or more other lines. See Section 5.7.

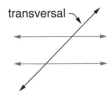

trapezoid A quadrilateral that has exactly one pair of parallel sides. No two sides need be the same length. See Section 5.4 of the Geometry essay.

tree diagram A network of points connected by line segments and containing no closed loops. One special point is the root of the tree. Tree diagrams are used to factor numbers and to represent

probability situations in which there is a series of events. The first tree diagram below shows the prime factorization of 30. The second tree diagram represents flipping one coin two times. See *factor tree*.

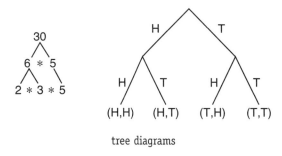

tree diagrams

tri- A prefix meaning three, as in triangle, tricycle, or triple.

trial-and-error method A method for finding the solution of an equation by trying a series of test numbers. See *test number*. See Section 9.3.

triangle A polygon with three sides and three angles. See *equilateral triangle, isosceles triangle, scalene triangle, acute triangle, right triangle,* and *obtuse*

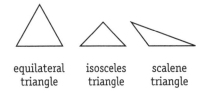

equilateral   isosceles   scalene
triangle   triangle   triangle

triangle. See Section 5.4 of the Geometry essay.

triangular numbers Figurate numbers that can be shown by triangular arrangements of dots. The triangular numbers are {1, 3, 6, 10, 15, 21, 28, 36, 45, ...}. See *figurate numbers*.

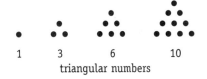

1   3   6   10
triangular numbers

triangular prism A prism whose bases are triangles. See Section 5.5 of the Geometry essay.

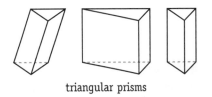

triangular prisms

triangular pyramid A pyramid in which all faces are triangles, any one of which can be called the base. If all of the faces are equilateral triangles, the pyramid is a regular tetrahedron and is one of the five regular polyhedra. See *tetrahedron* and *regular polyhedron*. See Section 5.5 of the Geometry essay.

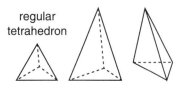

triangular pyramids

true number sentence A number sentence in which the relation symbol accurately reflects the relation between the two sides of the sentence. $75 = 25 + 50$ is a true number sentence. Compare to *false number sentence*. See Sections 9.2 and 9.3.

truncate (1) To replace all digits to the right of a particular place with 0s. For example, 3,654 can be truncated to 3,650 or 3,600 or 3,000. Truncation is similar to rounding but always makes the number smaller (unless all the truncated digits are 0s). (2) To cut off a vertex of a solid figure.

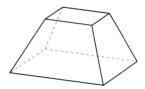

truncated pyramid

turn An informal name for a rotation transformation. See *rotation* and *transformation*. See Section 5.6 of the Geometry essay.

turn-around facts A pair of addition or multiplication (but not subtraction or division) facts in which the order of the addends or the factors is reversed. For example, $3 + 5 = 8$ and $5 + 3 = 8$ or $3 \times 9 = 27$ and $9 \times 3 = 27$. Turn-around facts illustrate the commutative properties of addition and multiplication. If a fact is known, its turn-around is also known. See *commutative property*. See Section 8.3.

turn-around rule A principle, based on the *commutative property*, for solving math fact problems. If you know, for example, that $6 \times 8 = 48$, then by the turn-around rule you also know that $8 \times 6 = 48$.

turn symmetry Same as *rotational symmetry*. See Section 5.8 of the Geometry essay.

twin primes Two prime numbers that are separated by just one number. For example, 3 and 5 are twin primes; 11 and 13 are also twin primes.

two-dimensional (2-D) (1) Contained completely within a plane but not entirely on a line. Two-dimensional objects have length and width but no thickness. (2) A surface on which one can locate any point with two numbers. Compare to *one-dimensional* and *three-dimensional*. See Sections 5.1 and 5.4 of the Geometry essay.

unfair game A game in which every player does not have the same chance of winning. Compare to *fair game*. See Section 4.2.

unit A label, descriptive word, or unit of measure used to put a number in context. Using units with numbers reinforces the idea that numbers refer to something. Fingers, snowballs, miles, and cents are examples of units. See Section 2.1 of the Arithmetic Operations essay and Section 6.2 of the Measurement essay.

unit box In *Everyday Mathematics*, a box displayed alongside a set of numbers or problems. It contains the unit or label for the numbers in use.

unit box

unit fraction A fraction whose numerator is 1. For example, $\frac{1}{2}, \frac{1}{3}, \frac{1}{12}, \frac{1}{8}$, and $\frac{1}{20}$ are all unit fractions. See Section 1.3 of the Numeration and Order essay and Section 6.2 of the Measurement essay.

unit percent One percent (1%).

unit price The price for one item or unit of measure. For example, if a 5-ounce package of something costs $2.50, then $0.50 per ounce is the unit price. Unit prices are often used to compare relative cost or value of similar things packaged in different amounts and with different prices.

glossary

unit ratio Same as *n-to-1 ratio*. See Section 1.3 of the Numeration and Order essay.

unit whole Same as the whole or ONE in specifying the basis for a multiple or fraction. See Section 1.3.

unlike (1) Of denominators: Being unequal. The fractions $\frac{2}{3}$ and $\frac{4}{5}$ have unlike denominators. (2) Of fractions: Having different denominators. Compare to *like fractions*.

U.S. customary system of measurement See *customary system of measurement*.

value A specific number or quantity represented by a variable. In the equation $y = 4x + 3$, if the value of x is 7, then the value of y is 31.

vanishing line A line in a perspective drawing connecting a point on a figure to the vanishing point. See *perspective drawing* and *vanishing point*.

vanishing point In a perspective drawing, the point at which parallel lines seem to converge on the horizon line. See *perspective drawing*, *vanishing line*, and *horizon*.

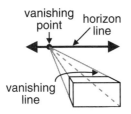

variable A letter or other symbol that represents a number. A variable need not represent one specific number; it can stand for many different values. For example, in the expression $2x + 3y$, x and y are variables, and in the equation $a + 12 = 2b + 6$, a and b are variables. See Section 9.3 of the Patterns, Sequences, Functions, and Algebra essay.

variable term A term that contains at least one variable. For example, in the equation $4b - 8 = b + 5$, $4b$ and b are variable terms. See *term*.

Venn diagram A picture that uses circles to show relationships among sets. See Section 4.1.

vertex The point at which the rays or line segments of an angle, the sides of a polygon, or the edges of a polyhedron meet. Same as corner. See Sections 5.3–5.5 of the Geometry essay.

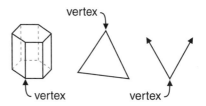

vertical Upright; perpendicular to the horizon. See *horizon*. Compare to *horizontal*.

vertical angles When two lines intersect, the angles that do not share a common side; the angles opposite each other. Vertical angles have equal measures. Same as *opposite angles (3)*.

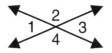

Angles 1 and 3 and Angles 2 and 4 are pairs of vertical angles.

volume A measure of the amount of space occupied by a 3-dimensional shape, generally expressed in "cubic" units, such as cm³, cubic inches, or cubic feet. See Section 6.6 of the Measurement essay.

weight A measure of how heavy something is. Weight is a measure of the force of gravity on an object, which depends on the object's mass and the strength of the gravitational field acting on it. Hence, the same object can have different weights depending on where it is. For example, a person who weighs 150 pounds in San Diego would have a different weight on the moon. Compare to *mass*. See Section 6.7 of the Measurement essay.

"What's My Rule?" In *Everyday Mathematics*, a routine that involves a set of number pairs in which the numbers in each pair are related to each other according to the same rule. "What's My Rule?" problems are usually displayed in table form in which two of the three parts (input, output, and rule) are known and the goal is to find the unknown part. See *function* and *function machine*. See Section 9.1 of the Patterns, Sequences, Functions, and Algebra essay.

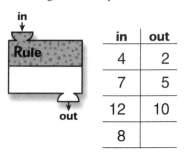

in	out
4	2
7	5
12	10
8	

"What's My Rule?" problem

whole The entire object, collection of objects, or quantity being considered; the unit; 100%. Same as the *ONE* and the *unit whole*. See Section 1.3 of the Numeration and Order essay.

whole number Any of the numbers 0, 1, 2, 3, 4, and so on. See Section 1.1 of the Numeration and Order essay.

width of a rectangle Length of one side of a rectangle or rectangular object; often the shorter side.

wind–chill temperature A measure of how cold the air feels, based on a combination of wind speed and air temperature.

x-by-y array A rectangular arrangement of elements having x rows with y elements per row. An x-by-y array can represent x sets with y objects in each set.

yard (yd) In the U.S. customary system, a unit of length equivalent to 3 feet or 36 inches. Historically, a yard was the distance from the tip of the nose to the tip of the longest finger. See the Tables of Measure. See Sections 6.2 and 6.4 of the Measurement essay.

zero fact The sum of two one-digit numbers when one of the addends is 0, as in $0 + 5 = 5$. If 0 is added to any number, there is no change in the number. Also, the product of two one-digit numbers when one of the factors is 0, as in $4 * 0 = 0$. The product of a number and 0 is always 0.

Reference

Symbols	
+	plus or positive
−	minus or negative
*, ×	multiplied by
÷, /	divided by
=	is equal to
≠	is not equal to
<	is less than
>	is greater than
≤	is less than or equal to
≥	is greater than or equal to
≈	is about equal to
x^n, $x^{\wedge}n$	nth power of x
$\sqrt{x}$	square root of x
%	percent
$\frac{a}{b}$, $a{:}b$, a/b	ratio of a to b or a divided by b or the fraction $\frac{a}{b}$
a [bs]	a groups, b in each group
$n/d \rightarrow a\,Rb$	n divided by d is a with remainder b
{ }, ( ), [ ]	grouping symbols
∞	infinity
$n!$	n factorial
°	degree
(a,b)	ordered pair
$\overleftrightarrow{AS}$	line AS
$\overline{AS}$	line segment AS
$\overrightarrow{AS}$	ray AS
∟	right angle
⊥	is perpendicular to
‖	is parallel to
△ABC	triangle ABC
∠ABC	angle ABC
∠B	angle B
≅	is congruent to
∼	is similiar to
≡	is equivalent to

Prefixes			
uni-	.one	tera-	.trillion (10^{12})
bi-	.two	giga-	.billion (10^{9})
tri-	.three	mega-	.million (10^{6})
quad-	.four	kilo-	.thousand (10^{3})
penta-	.five	hecto-	.hundred (10^{2})
hexa-	.six	deca-	.ten (10^{1})
hepta-	.seven	uni-	.one (10^{0})
octa-	.eight	deci-	.tenth (10^{-1})
nona-	.nine	centi-	.hundredth (10^{-2})
deca-	.ten	milli-	.thousandth (10^{-3})
dodeca-	.twelve	micro-	.millionth (10^{-6})
icosa-	.twenty	nano-	.billionth (10^{-9})

Rules for Order of Operations

1. Do operations within parentheses or other grouping symbols before doing anything else.

2. Calculate all powers.

3. Do multiplications or divisions in order, from left to right.

4. Then do additions or subtractions in order, from left to right.

Reference

Formulas	Meaning of Variables
Rectangles • Perimeter: $p = (2 * l) + (2 * w)$ • Area: $A = (b * h)$	p = perimeter; l = length; w = width A = area; b = length of base; h = height
Squares • Perimeter: $p = 4 * s$ • Area: $A = s^2$	p = perimeter; s = length of side A = area
Parallelograms • Area: $A = b * h$	A = area; b = length of base; h = height
Triangles • Area: $A = \frac{1}{2} * b * h$	A = area; b = length of base; h = height
Regular Polygons • Perimeter: $p = n * s$	p = perimeter; n = number of sides; s = length of side
Circles • Circumference: $c = \pi * d$, or $c = 2 * \pi * r$ • Area: $A = \pi * r^2$	c = circumference; d = diameter; r = radius A = area
Pick's Formula for the Area of Polygons • Area: $A = (\frac{1}{2} * P) + I - 1$	A = area; P = number of grid points on polygon; I = number of grid points in the interior
Polyhedrons • Euler's Formula: $e = (f + v) - 2$	e = number of edges; f = number of faces; v = number of vertices
Mobiles • Fulcrum at center: $W * D = w * d$ • Fulcrum not at center: $(W * D) + (R * L) = w * d$	W = weight of object farthest from fulcrum D = distance of this object from the fulcrum w = weight of object closest to fulcrum d = distance of this object from the fulcrum R = weight of rod L = distance from center to fulcrum

Reference

Formulas	Meaning of Variables
Rectangular Prisms • Volume: $V = B * h$, or $V = l * w * h$ • Surface area: $\quad S = 2 * ((l * w) + (l * h) + (w * h))$	V = volume; B = area of base; l = length; w = width; h = height S = surface area
Cubes • Volume: $V = e^3$ • Surface area: $S = 6 * e^2$	V = volume; e = length of edge S = surface area
Cylinders • Volume: $V = B * h$, or $V = \pi * r^2 * h$ • Surface area: $\quad S = (2 * \pi * r^2) + ((2 * \pi * r) * h)$	V = volume; B = area of base; h = height; r = radius of base S = surface area
Pyramids • Volume: $V = \frac{1}{3} * B * h$	V = volume; B = area of base; h = height
Cones • Volume: $V = \frac{1}{3} * B * h$, or $V = \frac{1}{3} * \pi * r^2 * h$	V = volume; B = area of base; h = height; r = radius of base
Spheres • Volume: $V = \frac{4}{3} * \pi * r^3$	V = volume; r = radius
Temperatures • Fahrenheit to Celsius conversion: $\quad C = \frac{5}{9} * (F - 32°)$ • Celsius to Fahrenheit conversion: $\quad F = (\frac{9}{5} * C) + 32°$	C = degrees Celsius; F = degrees Fahrenheit
Distances • $d = r * t$	d = distance traveled; r = rate of speed; t = time of travel

Properties of Rational Numbers

The following properties are true for all rational numbers. The variables *a, b, c,* and *d* stand for any rational numbers (except 0, if the variable stands for a divisor).

Properties

Binary Operations Property

When any two numbers are added, subtracted, multiplied, or divided, the result is a single number.

$a + b$, $a - b$, $a * b$, and $a \div b$ are equal to single numbers.

Commutative Property

The sum or product of two numbers is the same, regardless of the order of the numbers.

$a + b = b + a$

$a * b = b * a$

Associative Property

The sum or product of three or more numbers is the same, regardless of how the numbers are grouped.

$a + (b + c) = (a + b) + c$

$a * (b * c) = (a * b) * c$

Distributive Property

When a number is multiplied by the sum or difference of two or more numbers, the number is "distributed" over the numbers that are added or subtracted.

$a * (b + c) = (a * b) + (a * c)$

$a * (b - c) = (a * b) - (a * c)$

Addition Property of Zero

The sum of any number and 0 is equal to the original number.

$a + 0 = 0 + a = a$

Multiplication Property of One

The product of any number and 1 is equal to the original number.

$a * 1 = 1 * a = a$

Opposites Property

The opposite of a number, *a,* is normally written $-a$ or (OPP)*a*. Sometimes in *Everyday Mathematics,* we write (OPP)*a* for the opposite of *a.*

If *a* is a positive number, then (OPP)*a* is a negative number.

If *a* is a negative number, then (OPP)*a* is a positive number.

If $a = 0$, then (OPP)$a = 0$. Zero is the only number that is its own opposite.

Opposite of Opposites Property

The opposite of the opposite of a number is equal to the original number.

$(\text{OPP})(\text{OPP})a = (\text{OPP})(-a) = a$

Sum of Opposites Property

The sum of any number and its opposite is 0.

$a + (-a) = (-a) + a = 0$

Multiplication of Reciprocals Property

The product of any number and its reciprocal is 1.

$a * \frac{1}{a} = \frac{1}{a} * a = 1$

Properties of Rational Numbers

The following properties are true for all rational numbers. The variables *a, b, c,* and *d* stand for any rational numbers (except 0, if the variable stands for a divisor).

Properties (cont.)

Addition Property of Positive and Negative Numbers

The sum of two positive numbers is a positive number.

The sum of two negative numbers is the opposite of the sum of the "number parts" of the addends.

To find the sum of a positive number and a negative number, subtract the smaller from the larger "number part." The sum takes on the sign of the addend with the larger "number part."

Multiplication Property of Positive and Negative Numbers

The product of two positive numbers or two negative numbers is a positive number.

The product of a positive number and a negative number is a negative number.

Subtraction and Division Properties

All subtraction problems can be solved by addition, and all division problems can be solved by multiplication.

$$a - b = a + (-b)$$

$$\frac{a}{b} = a * \frac{1}{b}$$

$$a \div b = a * \frac{1}{b}$$

Equivalent Fractions Property

If the numerator and denominator of a fraction are multiplied or divided by the same number, the resulting fraction is equivalent to the original fraction.

$$\frac{a}{b} = \frac{a * c}{b * c} \qquad\qquad \frac{a}{b} = \frac{a \div c}{b \div c}$$

Addition and Subtraction of Fractions Properties

The sum or difference of fractions with like denominators is the sum or difference of the numerators over the denominator.

$$\frac{a}{c} + \frac{b}{c} = \frac{a + b}{c}$$

$$\frac{a}{c} - \frac{b}{c} = \frac{a - b}{c}$$

To add or subtract fractions with unlike denominators, rename the fractions so that they have a common denominator.

$$\frac{a}{b} + \frac{c}{d} = \frac{ad + bc}{bd}$$

$$\frac{a}{b} - \frac{c}{d} = \frac{ad - bc}{bd}$$

Multiplication of Fractions Property

The product of two fractions is the product of the numerators over the product of the denominators.

$$\frac{a}{b} * \frac{c}{d} = \frac{a * c}{b * d}$$

Division of Fractions Property

The quotient of two fractions is the product of the dividend and the reciprocal of the divisor.

$$\frac{a}{b} \div \frac{c}{d} = \frac{a}{b} * \frac{d}{c} = \frac{a * d}{b * c}$$

Powers of a Number Property

If *a* is any number and *b* is a positive whole number, then a^b is the product of *a* used as a factor *b* times.

$$a^b = \underbrace{a * a * a * ... * a}_{b \text{ factors}}$$

a^0 is equal to 1.

If *a* is any nonzero number and *b* is a positive whole number, then a^{-b} is 1 divided by the product of *a* used as a factor *b* times.

$$a^{-b} = \frac{1}{a^b} = \underbrace{\frac{1}{a * a * a * ... * a}}_{b \text{ factors}}$$

4–6 Games Correlation Chart

Skill and Concept Areas

Game	Grade 4 Lesson	Grade 5 Lesson	Grade 6 Lesson	Basic Facts	Operations	Calculator	Numeration	Geometry	Data	Algebra	Reference Frames	Mental Arithmetic	Strategy
Addition Top-It	2.5	2.3		■	■								
Algebra Election		4.6	6.7			■				■			■
Angle Tangle		3.6	5.1					■					
Baseball Multiplication	3.2	1.3	*	■	■							■	
Beat the Calculator	3.3	1.3		■	■							■	
Broken-Calculator Game	3.10	7.10	6.7			■				■		■	
Build-It		8.1					■						
Buzz			4.2		■								
Credits/Debits Game	10.6				■					■			
Credits/Debits Game (Advanced)	11.6	7.8	6.3		■					■			
Dart Game	10.2								■				
Division Arrays	3.4				■		■						
Division Dash	6.2	4.1	2.10		■							■	
Doggone Decimal			2.4		■								
Estimation Squeeze		5.5	*				■						
Exponent Ball		7.1	2.7		■				■				
Factor Bingo		1.9			■								
Factor Captor		1.4	*		■								
Factor Top-It		1.7		■	■								
First to 100		4.6	*	■	■							■	
500		7.7			■								
Frac-Tac-Toe		5.7	4.8		■	■							
Fraction Action, Fraction Friction		8.4	4.3		■				■				
Fraction Capture		6.9			■								
Fraction Multiplication Top-It		8.6		■	■								
Fraction/Percent Concentration	9.3	5.8			■							■	
Fraction Spin		8.5			■								
Fraction Top-It	7.10	*	4.2	■	■								
Fraction/Whole Number Multiplication Top-It		8.7		■	■								
Geometry 5 Questions	1.4							■					
Getting to One			9.10			■							
Greedy			7.3						■				
Grid Search	6.5										■	■	■
Hidden Treasure		9.1	3.10								■		
Hidden Treasure (Advanced)		9.3	5.4								■		
High-Number Toss	2.4	2.4	2.6				■						
High-Number Toss—Decimal Version		7.8					■						
Landmark Shark			1.4						■				
Mixed Number Spin		8.3			■								
Multiplication Bull's-Eye		2.7			■	■						■	
Multiplication Top-It	3.3	1.3		■	■								
Multiplication Wrestling	5.2	2.8	9.1		■								
Musical Name-Collection Boxes	7.7				■								
Name That Number	2.2	1.9	1.3		■							■	
Name That Polygon	1.5							■					
Number Top-It (7-digit numbers)	2.4	2.10					■						
Number Top-It (2-place decimals)	4.2						■						
Number Top-It (3-place decimals)	4.6	*					■						
Pocket-Billiards Game	10.2							■					
Polygon Capture		3.7	5.9					■					

Number indicates first exposure at grade level. *Additional games available in *Student Reference Book*

Game	Grade 4 Lesson	Grade 5 Lesson	Grade 6 Lesson	Basic Facts	Operations	Calculator	Numeration	Geometry	Data	Algebra	Reference Frames	Mental Arithmetic	Strategy
Robot	6.6	3.4						▓			▓		
Scientific Notation Toss		7.4	2.8				▓						
Solution Search			6.12							▓			
Spoon Scramble		12.6	4.12				▓					▓	
Spreadsheet Scramble			3.7		▓					▓			
Subtraction Target Practice	2.9	2.3		▓	▓								
Subtraction Top-It	2.6			▓	▓								
3-D Shape Sort		11.2	9.12					▓					
Top-It Games				▓	▓								
Top-It Games with Positive and Negative Numbers		7.7	6.4	▓	▓					▓			
Touch and Match It Quadrangles	1.3							▓					
What's My Weight?	11.1										▓		

Number indicates first exposure at grade level. *Additional games available in *Student Reference Book*

Tables of Measure

Metric System

Units of Length

1 kilometer (km)	=	1,000 meters (m)
1 meter	=	10 decimeters (dm)
	=	100 centimeters (cm)
	=	1,000 millimeters (mm)
1 decimeter	=	10 centimeters
1 centimeter	=	10 millimeters

Units of Area

1 square meter (m²)	=	100 square decimeters (dm²)
	=	10,000 square centimeters (cm²)
1 square decimeter	=	100 square centimeters
1 are (a)	=	100 square meters
1 hectare (ha)	=	100 ares
1 square kilometer (km²)	=	100 hectares

Units of Volume

1 cubic meter (m³)	=	1,000 cubic decimeters (dm³)
	=	1,000,000 cubic centimeters (cm³)
1 cubic decimeter	=	1,000 cubic centimeters

Units of Capacity

1 kiloliter (kL)	=	1,000 liters (L)
1 liter	=	1,000 milliliters (mL)

Units of Mass (Weight)

1 metric ton (t)	=	1,000 kilograms (kg)
1 kilogram	=	1,000 grams (g)
1 gram	=	1,000 milligrams (mg)

U.S. Customary System

Units of Length

1 mile (mi)	=	1,760 yards (yd)
	=	5,280 feet (ft)
1 yard	=	3 feet
	=	36 inches (in.)
1 foot	=	12 inches

Units of Area

1 square yard (yd²)	=	9 square feet (ft²)
	=	1,296 square inches (in.²)
1 square foot	=	144 square inches
1 acre	=	43,560 square feet
1 square mile (mi²)	=	640 acres

Units of Volume

1 cubic yard (yd³)	=	27 cubic feet (ft³)
1 cubic foot	=	1,728 cubic inches (in.³)

Units of Capacity

1 gallon (gal)	=	4 quarts (qt)
1 quart	=	2 pints (pt)
1 pint	=	2 cups (c)
1 cup	=	8 fluid ounces (fl oz)
1 fluid ounce	=	2 tablespoons (tbs)
1 tablespoon	=	3 teaspoons (tsp)

Units of Weight

1 ton (T)	=	2,000 pounds (lb)
1 pound	=	16 ounces (oz)

System Equivalents

1 inch is about 2.5 cm (2.54)

1 kilometer is about 0.6 mile (0.621)

1 mile is about 1.6 kilometers (1.609)

1 meter is about 39 inches (39.37)

1 liter is about 1.1 quarts (1.057)

1 ounce is about 28 grams (28.350)

1 kilogram is about 2.2 pounds (2.205)

1 hectare is about 2.5 acres (2.47)

Units of Time

1 century	=	100 years
1 decade	=	10 years
1 year (yr)	=	12 months
	=	52 weeks (plus one or two days)
	=	365 days (366 days in a leap year)
1 month (mo)	=	28, 29, 30, or 31 days
1 week (wk)	=	7 days
1 day (d)	=	24 hours
1 hour (hr)	=	60 minutes
1 minute (min)	=	60 seconds (sec)

Index

A

Absolute zero, 221
Abstraction, 161, 215, 289
Abstract numbers, 90
Abundant number, 64
Acre, 205
Acute angle, 165
Acute triangles, 166
Addend, 108, 249
Addition, 65, 87–90, 212, 260
  algorithms for, 107–109
  column, 107
  of decimals, 113–114
  distributive property of
    multiplication over, 272
  modified repeated, 117
  opposite-change rule for, 107–108
  partial-sums, 108–109
  repeated, 99
  symbols for, 266
  teaching with diagrams, 88–89
  whole-number, 109
Additive inverses, 75
Advance organizer questions, 20
Ahmes, 171
Algebra, 102
  expressions in, 269
  language of, 15
  patterns and, 254–255
  variables in, 274–275
Algorithms, 100–141
  addition, 107–109
  alternative, 105–106
  for calculators, 133–139, 245–246
  computational, 101–103
  for decimals, 106–126
  defined, 100–101

division, 120–126
Egyptian, 117–118
factor tree, 63
for fractions, 126–133
geometric, 101
invention of, 104–105
modified standard U.S., 117
multiplication, 114
origin of term, 102
paper-and-pencil, 87
subtraction, 103, 110–114
for whole numbers, 106–126
Alloy, 213
Altitude
  of cone, 175
  of cylinder, 175
  of prism, 174
Amicable numbers, 64
Analog clocks, 224
Analytic comprehension, 17–19
Analytic geometry, 177, 179
Angles, 164–165
  acute, 165
  complementary, 182
  corresponding, 181
  measurement of, 211
  negative, 48
  obtuse, 165
  opposite, 182
  positive, 48
  reflex, 48, 165
  relationships among, 182–183
  right, 13, 48, 165, 211
  straight, 165, 211
  supplementary, 182
Apex, 174
Archimedes, 171

Arcs, 48
Area, 92, 205–207
  formulas for, 206–207
  in geography, 148, 216–217
  linking, to volume, 210
Area model, 206
Arithmetic
  mental, 247–250
  symbols in, 265–268
Arithmetic operations, 86–99,
    220–221, 244
  operations with positive and
    negative numbers, 97–99
  powers and exponents, 94–97
  situation diagrams in, 87–94
  tools for, 49–51
  variables in properties of, 276–277
Arm span, 197, 198
Arrays, 60, 91–92
Assessment, 3–5, 21, 52
Assize of Weights and Measures, 198
Atomic clocks, 224–225
Attached meaning, 16
Average, 152, 241
Axiomatic method, 192
Axis, 185, 230

B

Babylonian calendar, 225
Balance, 49
Balance scale, 202–203, 210
Ballpark estimates, 47, 202, 239, 289
Bar, 72
Bar graphs, 146–147
Base, 94
  of cone, 175
  of cylinder, 175

index

index